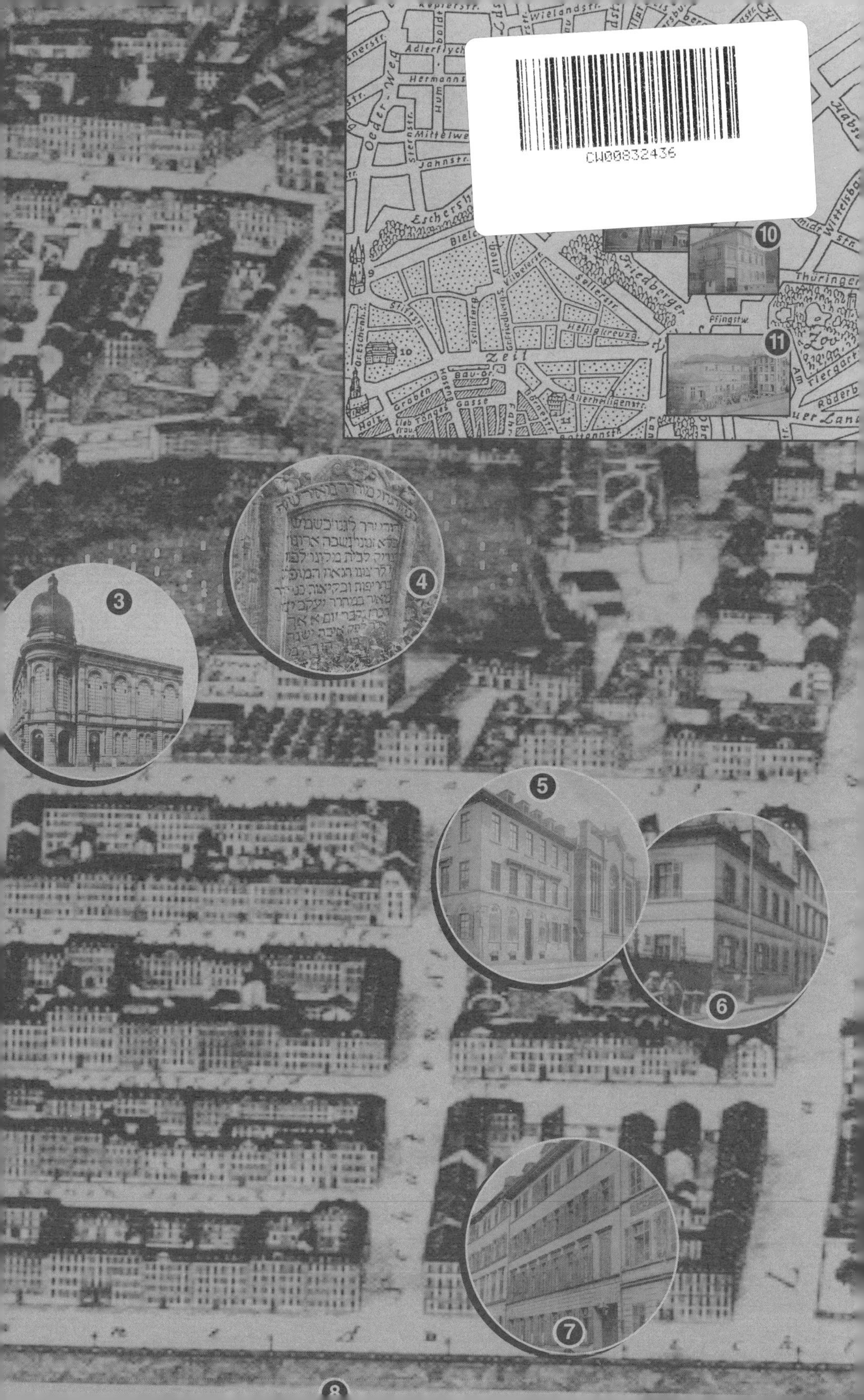

Wielandstr.
Oeder-Weg
Sternstr.
Jahnstr.
Friedberger
Sellerstr.
Heiligkreuzg.
Zeil
Stiftstr.
Graben
Gasse
Allerheiligenstr.
Pfingstw.
Thüringer
Zoo
10
11
3
4
5
6
7
CW00832436

היסטוריה

ArtScroll History Series®

Rabbi Nosson Scherman / Rabbi Meir Zlotowitz
General Editors

Rabbi Samson

by

Rabbi Eliyahu Meir Klugman

Published by

Mesorah Publications, ltd

Raphael Hirsch

Architect of Torah Judaism for the Modern World

FIRST EDITION
First Impression . . . February, 1996
SECOND EDITION
First Impression . . . February, 1996

Published and Distributed by
MESORAH PUBLICATIONS, Ltd.
4401 Second Avenue
Brooklyn, New York 11232

Distributed in Europe by
J. LEHMANN HEBREW BOOKSELLERS
20 Cambridge Terrace
Gateshead, Tyne and Wear
England NE8 1RP

Distributed in Israel by
SIFRIATI / A. GITLER—BOOKS
4 Bilu Street
P.O.B. 14075
Tel Aviv 61140

Distributed in Australia & New Zealand by
GOLDS BOOK & GIFT CO.
36 William Street
Balaclava 3183, Vic., Australia

Distributed in South Africa by
KOLLEL BOOKSHOP
22 Muller Street
Yeoville 2198, Johannesburg, South Africa

ARTSCROLL HISTORY SERIES®
RABBI SAMSON RAPHAEL HIRSCH

ISBN
0-89906-632-1 (hard cover)
0-89906-633-X (paperback)

Typography by Compuscribe at ArtScroll Studios, Ltd.

Printed in the United States of America by Noble Book Press Corp.
Bound by Sefercraft, Quality Bookbinders, Ltd., Brooklyn, N.Y.

This work
is dedicated
with love and appreciation
to
my dear parents

Rabbi Rafael & Mrs. Ruth Klugman שיחי׳

noble scions of Rabbi Samson Raphael Hirsch
whose lives exemplify his ideals

and to
my dear parents-in-law

Reb Lazer & Mrs. Marcia Loewi שיחי׳

a "Shas Yid"
and sterling bearers of
the finest traditions of Eastern European Jewry.

The Author

Table of Contents

AUTHOR'S PREFACE

One does not erect monuments for tzadikim *—*
their words are their memorial
(*Shekalim* 2:5)

Historically, biographies of Torah luminaries have been rare. When their words were studied in the *Beis HaMidrash* and practiced in daily life, they *were* alive and needed no memorial. It was only with the decline of Torah study that biography has become a medium through which to inspire the study of their works and the emulation of their deeds.

Dwelling on the history of one's people and its heroes, Rabbi Hirsch asserted, is a sign of a spiritually infirm present:

> One must examine whether the study of history and of past events is necessary or even useful for men and nations whose present life is completely taken up with vigorous and active devotion to their duty. Only generations in a state of decline feel they must look back to the past in order to be uplifted by the example of long departed heroes. . . . For individuals and nations

> that live as they should, the immediate present will always be their focus; they know what they must do *now*. Their minds and energies are so completely and enthusiastically taken up with their immediate duties that they do not feel the need nor have the time to look back for inspiration. Their search for knowledge will center primarily on one question: "Where does our duty lie and what is our task right now?" Such individuals and nations understand that, for them, the answer to these questions will not be provided by a study of the deeds and fortunes of their ancestors. They know that they can find the answer to their questions only in the Law of G-d that has been handed to their own generation, and that will be handed by G-d Himself to all the generations yet to come, in the same ever-new and direct manner that it was given to the very first generation that witnessed the Revelation with its own eyes (*Collected Writings* VII, p. 440).

If a biography of Rabbi Hirsch is to be justified on his own terms, then it must demonstrate that he belongs not to the past but to the present and that his ideals and the manner in which he put them into practice throughout his long and eventful life still illuminate and instruct today. Any account of his life which does not serve as a guide for living is an epitaph of dubious value, not a living testament.

Our position today in Western society is essentially the same as that of German Jewry in Rabbi Hirsch's time. The answers he provided to the challenge of an open society and the course he charted remain equally cogent today, when the conditions which first gave rise to those challenges characterize much of the Jewish world. Thus, a study of his active and influential life can help us respond to practical issues facing the Jew in today's world.

At the same time, no profile of Rabbi Hirsch can ever take the place of a serious, sustained study of his voluminous works. This book is an attempt to describe how Rabbi Hirsch put the principles enunciated in his writings into practice.

Nineteenth-century European society opened its doors to the Jew, and for the first time since the Karaites, non-observance as an organized movement, complete with leaders, ideology and literature became a reality in Jewish life. Rabbi Hirsch was the first European *Gadol* to set forth a comprehensive Torah response to this institutionalized heresy.

Besides formulating both a theoretical and a practical response to the

Reform movement, he discredited the "Science of Judaism," forerunner of today's Conservative movement, with its recasting of Judaism into a cultural experience. With his *Torah Im Derech Eretz* principle, he ensured Torah's absolute domination of every aspect of life, even in modern conditions. The *Kehillah* he built in Frankfurt became a model for Jewish communal life and was the focal point of Torah Judaism in Germany. The school he founded in Frankfurt remains the prototype for much of today's Orthodox education for girls, and his *Nineteen Letters* and *Horeb* were the inspiration for the founding of *Beis Yaakov* by Sarah Schenirer.

His lucid definition of the meaning of exile and the place of *Eretz Yisrael* in our time remain the approach of the bulk of Torah Jewry to these issues. The organization he created to promote and represent Orthodox Jewry in Germany was the direct forerunner of the Agudath Israel movement. His books and writings exert a powerful influence until this day, with new volumes and editions published yearly. His commentaries on the Torah and *Psalms* continue to exercise a powerful sway over the hearts and minds of our people and to draw estranged brethren back into the fold.

Rabbi Hirsch responded to the dangers of assimilation and non-observance not with anathema and imprecation but rather with a reasoned and convincing presentation of the eternal truths of Judaism. His portrayal of the sublime beauty of a sanctity-filled Jewish life and the uplifting power Judaism grants its adherents remains unparalleled. An account of his life, then, is not arid scholarship, but a vital guidebook for life.

Two years before his passing Rabbi Hirsch explained the statement of *Chazal*: *Do not say of any word that it cannot possibly be heard, for in the end it will be heard* (*Avos* 2:5).

> Even if you should be the only person in your community to hold a given view, do not say that you will never be able to gain a hearing from the other members of the community. As long as the view you represent is truly right and aims only at what is good and true, do not refrain from expressing it. Continue your fight, tirelessly and undaunted, for what is good and right, for years if need be; in the end — provided of course that you have fought for your cause solely for its own sake, without ulterior, selfish motives — you will be heard.

He was.

It is with a sense of complete inadequacy that I express praise and thanksgiving to the Almighty for granting me life and the opportunity to study and teach His Torah.

During the preparation of this book for publication the Torah world suffered the loss of the illustrious bearer of Rabbi Hirsch's traditions, Rabbi Shimon Schwab, *zatzal*, Rav of *K'hal Adath Jeshurun* of Washington Heights, N.Y. The author owes an immense debt of gratitude to the Rav, *zatzal*, for his guidance during the last several years, especially with regard to many aspects of Rabbi Hirsch's legacy. In addition, the Rav contributed, unasked, and by his insistent request, unacknowledged, a significant portion of his life's savings to ensure the publication of *Shemesh Marpeh*, a collection of Rabbi Hirsch's *teshuvos, chiddushim,* and letters.

May the Almighty grant strength and good health to my dear grandmother, Mrs. Etta Guggenheim, תחי', whose life and personality are eloquent testimony to the noble traditions of Ashkenazi Jewry.

Words are inadequate to express my gratitude to my life companion, my wife Rochel, תחי'. As with everything else in our life, without her this book would not have been. May *HaKadosh Boruch Hu* help us raise our dear children, Shoshana, Miriam, Shimshon, Chana Rivka, Moshe, Nechama, Bracha and Tovah שיחי' to walk in the paths illuminated by our forebear Rav Hirsch, *zatzal*, and to dedicate their lives to being מרבה כבוד שמים, the ultimate goal of Creation.

Eliyahu Meir Klugman
Jerusalem, 27 *Teveth*, 5756

ACKNOWLEDGMENTS

Rabbi Meir Zlotowitz and Rabbi Nosson Scherman of Artscroll-Mesorah spared no effort or expense to ensure the publication of this work. May it be another page in the book which details their efforts להגדיל תורה ולהאדירה. Special thanks is due to master craftsman Rabbi Sheah Brander for his painstaking attention to detail.

Professor Mordechai Breuer of Jerusalem, the dean of Orthodox Jewish historians, graciously shared the fruits of close to half a century of research, directed me to countless sources, allowed the use of his yet unpublished manuscript *Am V'eidah,* and served as a bottomless mine of information on all aspects of German Jewish history. In addition, he carefully reviewed the entire manuscript and made numerous suggestions. Without his help this book could not have been written.

My dear friend Reb Yonason Rosenblum of Jerusalem, one of the finest writers in the Torah world, employed his considerable talents in masterfully editing this book and ensuring its readability. In a true labor of love, he lavished much time and great effort to ensure that this work would be a credit to its subject.

I would also like to express my thanks to:
The administration of Yeshiva Neveh Zion where I have had the *zechus* of teaching Torah for close to a decade; Pinchas Asher Rohr for his excellent translation of the original Hebrew biography of Rabbi Hirsch in *Shemesh Marpeh,* which served as the framework for this greatly expanded and extensively revised work; Mr. Jacob Breuer of Jerusalem for consistent support and encouragement; Mr. Yisrael Israel of London-Jerusalem, a bibliophile of note, for invaluable assistance, including the loan of rare books; Machon Moreshet Ashkenaz of Bnei Brak, and its leading spirit, Rabbi Binyamin Hamburger, renowned expert on Minhag Ashkenaz, for assistance in several areas, including the acquisition of rare photographs; Mrs. Karin Paritzky, Mrs. Simcha Breuer and Mrs. Denise Erlanger of Jerusalem for expert translation assistance; Rabbi Eliyahu Berney of Monsey; Reb Avraham Biderman of Artscroll-Mesorah for dedicated and cheerful assistance in the sometimes trying production stages; Mr. Oskar Lehmann of New York for the loan of rare copies of the *Israelit;* and the Jewish National and University Library in Jerusalem for the use of rare books and photographs.

Rabbi Samson Raphael Hirsch

Part One
CONTEXT

Chapter One
HERITAGE

IN 1680, MENACHEM MENDEL SPIRO (D. 1716) MOVED FROM Frankfurt to Hamburg, where he took the name Frankfurter after his birthplace.[a] One hundred and seventy years later, Mendel Spiro's descendant, Hamburg-born Rabbi Samson Raphael Hirsch, then Chief Rabbi of 50,000 Moravian Jews, came to Frankfurt to serve as rabbi of a congregation of barely 100 families. His return to Frankfurt would change the face of Western Jewry forever.

Forebears

MENDEL SPIRO'S SON RABBI SHLOMO SPIRO-FRANKFURTER (D. 1729) served as a *dayan* in Hamburg's neighboring city of Altona, an important Jewish community at the time.[1] Among Rabbi Shlomo's great-grandchildren were two brothers, the sons of his grandson R' Tzvi Hirsch Frankfurter-Spiro. The younger brother, Rabbi

a. Menachem Spiro was a disciple of Rabbi Aharon Shmuel Koidenover of Frankfurt, author of *Tiferes Shmuel* and *Birchas HaZevach*.

Yehudah Leib Frankfurter-Spiro, authored *HaRechasim LeBik'ah*, a commentary on the Torah.[2] The older brother, Menachem Mendel (1742-1823), was named after his great-great-grandfather and was known as Reb Mendel Frankfurter.

Reb Mendel Frankfurter

Mendel Frankfurter studied as a young man in the yeshiva of Rabbi Yonasan Eibeschitz,[b] then rabbi of the tri-partite community of Altona, Hamburg and Wandsbeck.[c] Reb Mendel taught Talmud in Stuttgart and Berlin, but refused all compensation for teaching Torah, a practice his grandson was to follow. In Berlin he also published a new edition of *Toras HaBayis HaKotzer* of the *Rashba.*[3]

In 1805, at the age of 63, Reb Mendel, in conjunction with two others, established the famous "Talmud Torah" of Hamburg, which continued in existence for 130 years, until the Holocaust. The Talmud Torah's goal was to enable Jewish youth, aged 12 to 17, to continue their education and it was originally intended for students from poor families who could not afford to hire private teachers, as the wealthier ones could. In addition to the burden of directing and funding the school, Reb Mendel also took responsibility for the material needs of his students. The school's stated aim was to train rabbis and educators. Besides the usual Torah subjects, the school also emphasized good character traits, *Derech Eretz* and the minimum requirements for making a living so that if the graduates chose to enter business they would have the rudimentary knowledge needed to do so.

In 1812, with the partition of the three *kehillos*, Reb Mendel was appointed *Rosh Beis Din* (Chief Judge of the Rabbinical Court) of Altona, where his

---

b. To portray Rabbi Yonasan Eibeschitz's single-minded devotion to learning, Reb Mendel used to tell of the time when late one night Reb Yonasan posed a difficult question on *Tosafos*. He had to leave the room for a few moments and asked his disciples to check whether the commentators were also troubled by this difficulty. The boys quickly found the answer, and proceeded to sit around chatting. For close to three hours Reb Yonasan did not return, and the students wondered where he was. They sent Mendel Frankfurter to check, and to his great surprise he found Rabbi Yonasan standing in the darkness outside under a tree, totally blanketed with snow. Mendel discreetly tugged at his master's coat and his teacher shook himself out of his reverie with a start. "Yes! I found an answer to the question," said Reb Yonasan.[2*]

c. The three communities were referred to in Hebrew by the acronym — אה"ו — אלטונא, המבורג, וונדסבק.

Tombstones of Reb Mendel Frankfurter and his wife

great-grandfather Rabbi Shlomo Frankfurter had served as a *dayan*. In that capacity, too, he refused to accept financial compensation.

In an ethical will written in 1815, he urged his descendants to adhere to the path of Torah and cautioned them against "modernizers who attempt to divert the hearts of youth away from that which is good and upright towards those who stray after foolish theories that can, Heaven forbid, remove the fear of Hashem from your hearts . . . Avoid the books of the errant and wicked," he wrote, even though they may be written in Hebrew and attractively presented.[4]

Reb Mendel also enjoined his children not to talk during prayer, to study Torah every day before breakfast, and to spend at least half an hour a day studying *mussar* (ethics) or *Pirkei Avos* and its commentaries. He exhorted his male descendants to honor their wives and educate their children in the fear of Heaven, and he requested his female descendants to be scrupulous about covering their hair after marriage. He urged them to be faithful and honest in their business dealings and never to deceive anyone, "for the truth endures forever."[5]

In 1777, a son was born to Reb Mendel, whom he named Raphael Aryeh (d. 1857). Raphael — who changed his family name to Hirsch after his grandfather R' Zvi Hirsch Frankfurter — was a man of pure spirit, pleasant manner and scrupulous honesty.[6] Rabbi Hirsch said of his father that *Tanach* was like a second soul to him and that he was gifted with a most sensitive perception and clear insight into its beauty and truths.[7]

In 1807, Raphael married Gella Hertz (1786-1860), the daughter of Samson Hertz of Hamburg. Raphael Hirsch had a textile business and later made his living as a lottery agent and currency exchanger.[8] Gella Hirsch was active in communal welfare projects, and in 1815 she established an organization to raise funds for distribution to needy mothers who had just given birth. By 1840, the organization had 400 members.

Raphael and Gella Hirsch

On 24 *Sivan*, 5568 (June 20, 1808), the first child of Raphael and Gella was born in Hamburg. His parents named him Shamshon.[d] Shamshon later followed a custom of the period and joined his father's name Raphael to his own. Thus he signed his name: Samson Raphael Hirsch.

Samson Hirsch had a close relationship with his parents whom he described as "the guardians of his childhood, the guides of his youth, and the companions of his mature years."[9] Rabbi Mendel Frankfurter had a profound influence on his grandson and on one occasion presented him with a copy of the *Zohar* as a gift.[10]

The times in which Samson Raphael Hirsch was born were marked by massive upheavals in the established order that had prevailed in Europe for over a thousand years. To understand the stormy world into which he entered and his unique contribution to that world, some knowledge of the rich history of the Jews of Ashkenaz is needed.

Ashkenaz

RABBI HIRSCH WAS HEIR TO THE RICH LEGACY OF ASHKENAZI JEWRY. At the time of his birth, a millennium of Jewish life in Ashkenaz — a millennium which had produced some of the greatest Jewish scholars and most righteous men, men whose greatness of character is indelibly stamped into the consciousness of the

d. In Germany, children were given two names at birth, the *Shem Kodesh* and the *Shem Chol.* The former was given at the *bris milah,* while the latter, usually a Judeo-German translation of the *Shem Kodesh* or a Yiddish name associated with the Hebrew name, was given at a special ceremony called *Chol-Kreish* (*Chol*-secular, *Kreish*-screech or yelling). *Chol-Kreish* took place beside the infant's crib on the first Shabbos the mother went to *shul* after the birth and was attended by the children of the community. The Hebrew name was used for being called up to the Torah and similar occasions, while the *Shem-Chol* was used in day-to-day life. Thus Rabbi Hirsch was known as Samson, Rabbi Yitzchok Dov Bamberger as Seligmann Bär and Rabbi Shlomo Breuer as Salomon.[8*]

Tombstone of Raphael Hirsch

Jewish people — was slowly coming to an end.

Although the Ashkenaz mentioned in the Torah and in the Prophets refers to places in Asia,[11] the region known today as Germany has been called Ashkenaz for over a thousand years.[12] The traditions of the Jews in that area, particularly the Rhineland, where the early Ashkenazi Jews lived for centuries, form the foundation of Ashkenazi law and custom today. The *Rosh*, Rabbeinu Asher ben Yechiel (1250-1327) of Germany, writes that the Torah has been the legacy of the sages of Ashkenaz since the destruction of the Second Temple. And the *Chasam Sofer* quotes approvingly Rabbi Yaakov Emden's (1698-1776) opinion that "one may surely follow the Ashkenazi tradition, for they have lived uninterruptedly in Germany[13] since the days of the destruction of the Temple."[14] The laws and customs of most Jews in the Western Hemisphere, as codified by the *Rema* in his glosses to the *Shulchan Aruch*, are known as *Minhag Ashkenaz*. The major formulators of *Minhag Ashkenaz* were *Rashi*,[15] the *Baalei HaTosafos*,[16] and the *Maharil* (1356-1427).[17]

A Millennium of Persecution

ONE OF THE GREAT LEGACIES OF ASHKENAZI JEWRY WAS A TENAcious adherence to a Torah way of life in the face of constant persecution, expulsion and slaughter. During the Crusades, thousands of Ashkenazi Jews were butchered. Over the centuries, Germany's Jews constituted a distinct social and legal caste. Only Christians were considered full-fledged citizens. Any rights or privileges possessed by Jews were by virtue of special edicts and legislation, and the Jews were entirely dependent on the whims of the local ruler for their safety.

The division of the German Empire into numerous principalities was, on the whole, a good thing for the Jews: When they were expelled from one principality they could usually find refuge in another. But this fact only highlights their complete dependence on local despots.

Typical of the attitude towards Jews was the Golden Bull of 1356 in which the right was granted to the Electoral Princes of the Empire "to keep Jews, in addition to exploiting mines of precious and base metals."[18] Traveling between the dozens of principalities, Jews often were required to pay special tolls. At many borders, there were two crossing points, one for "people" and the other for cattle and Jews.

In the First Crusade, in the year ד' תתנ"ו (1096), a frenzied mob of Christian rabble, which had set out from France to "liberate" Jerusalem from Moslem hands, passed through Germany. En route they vented their fury on the hapless Jews. From 8 *Iyar* until mid-*Tammuz* of that year, the Jews in the Rhine River region and in Bohemia were brutally murdered or forcibly baptized by roving bands of marauders. The first communities to be attacked were those in Speyer, Worms and Mainz, many of whose members willingly allowed themselves and their families to be slaughtered *al kiddush Hashem* (to sanctify the Divine name) rather than convert to Christianity.

Much of Ashkenazi Jewry was murdered or exiled as a result of the First Crusade, and the *kiddush Hashem* of that epoch is movingly portrayed in the *Av HaRachamim* prayer composed in memoriam of the First Crusade and recited on Shabbos morning. The tragedy is also commemorated in specially composed *kinnus* (elegies) for *Tishah b'Av.* Though Jews were better prepared for the Second Crusade 50 years later (1146), many still lost their lives and many others were forced to abandon their homes.[19]

The first blood libel took place in Germany in 1235, in the town of Fulda. Such false accusations were to cost thousands of Jewish lives over the next centuries. The Catholic Church played an active role in fostering hatred of Jews. In 1241, a *Judenschlacht* (Jew slaughter) took place in Frankfurt am Main, in which the entire Jewish community was massacred by the frenzied Christian mob after the community attempted to prevent one of their members from converting to Christianity. Already in the early 13th century, the Jews were ordered by the Church to wear a badge distinguishing them as Jews, and, in 1259, a synod of the Mainz archdiocese fixed its color as yellow, the same color adopted by the Nazis almost 700 years later. The similarity was not coincidental.

The Jew-baiter Rindfleisch organized a mob in the last years of the 13th century which destroyed no less than 140 Jewish communities, including Nuremberg, Würzburg and Rothenburg. Here, too, Jews demonstrated an amazing capacity for self-sacrifice *al kiddush Hashem.* From 1336 to 1337, peasant mobs annihilated 110 communities from

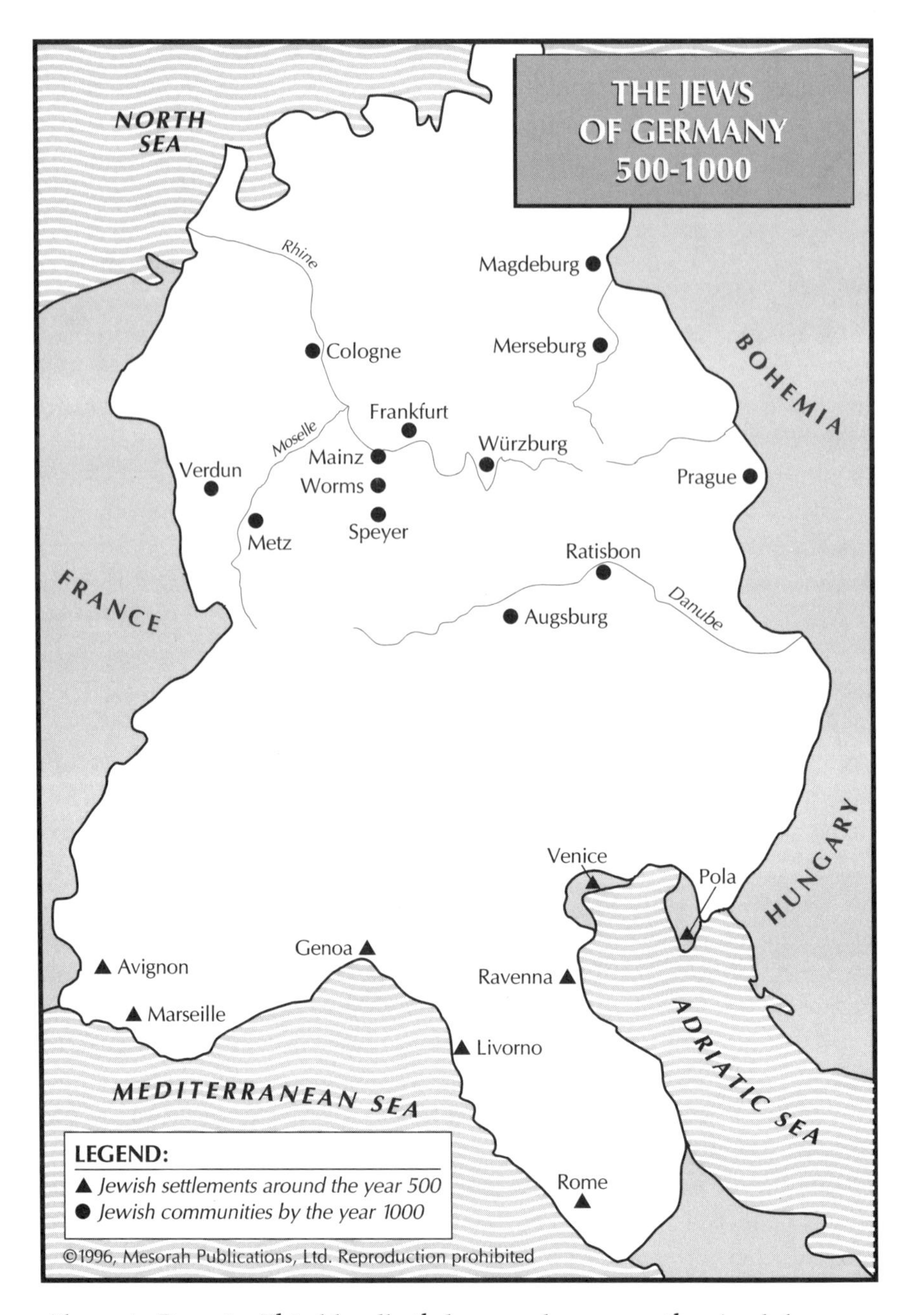

Alsace to Bavaria. This bloodbath became known as the *Armleder* massacres after the leather arm bands worn by the mobs. The Black Death plague from 1348 to 1350 led to pogroms in which 300 Jewish communities in Germany were destroyed. No wonder, then, that the theme of living and dying *al kiddush Hashem* is discussed at length in the responsa of the *Chachmei Ashkenaz.*

The 15th century was marked by numerous blood libels and expulsions. In 1648, the great-grandchildren of the Jews who had found asylum in Poland returned to Germany, driven out by Chmielnicki's hordes.

Mainz typifies the history of Jewish life in Germany.[20] Already during the Roman era Jews arrived in Mainz, and there is concrete evidence of Jews living there in 906. Among the distinguished scholars who graced Mainz with their presence were Rabbeinu Gershom ben Yehudah (ca. 960-1028), known as the *Meor HaGolah* (the Light of the Diaspora), Rabbeinu Yaakov ben Yakar, and the *Maharil.* During the First Crusade, the Jewish quarter of Mainz was destroyed and over 1,000 Jews were massacred. Mainz was not spared during the Second Crusade either. Over the centuries, the Jews of Mainz suffered persecution, blood libels, expulsions of various duration, the Black Death and almost constant harassment on the part of the authorities. In the 15th century alone, the Jews were expelled from Mainz four times.

Despite all these afflictions German Jews did not swerve from their adherence to authentic Judaism, a result of the inner fortitude and spiritual serenity which enabled them to withstand adversity. The Crusades, during which thousands of Jews lost their lives, are hardly mentioned in the writings of the *Baalei HaTosafos.* The persistence of German Jewry in adhering to the religion of their fathers in spite of hatred, scorn and constant massacre — in spite of the ease with which they could have avoided it through conversion to the faith of the Christian aggressor — is lasting testimony to the power that Judaism grants its adherents to overcome physical misery through spiritual serenity.[21] German Jews, Dr. Moshe Auerbach wrote, excelled in their refusal to allow the brutality they suffered, the mass expulsions which were their constant lot, and the slaughters which were a fact of life to adversely affect their spiritual state:

> The continued existence of the Jewish people in Christian Europe of that time . . . where they were hated and scorned, slaughtered in their thousands, and in spite of all this, remained constant in their adherence to the faith of their fathers, is one of the enduring miracles of the history of the world. As a result of their suffering, there was, sometimes, some lessening of the spiritual creativity of Ashkenazi Jewry, but their spiritual and moral greatness never diminished, and this phenomena is without comparison any-

where else especially as regards its duration over hundreds of years. This strength of faith in G-d is the secret of the continuity of Ashkenazi Jewry.[22]

The heart-wrenching *tefillos* that German Jews composed in response to those persecutions remain classic expressions of the yearning for G-d and the faith of the Jew in *galus*.

The Door Opens

THOUGH POGROMS WERE LARGELY A THING OF THE PAST BY THE END of the 18th century, the German Jew remained a second-class citizen. The courts discriminated against him, bureaucrats demeaned him, he was limited in the occupation he could choose, how he was allowed to practice his religion, and even if he was permitted to marry. Each German state still retained its "Jew Law," limiting the rights of its Jewish inhabitants.

But with the spread of the ideals of equality in the wake of the French Revolution, life was about to change radically for German Jewry. What the gentile had failed to accomplish by persecution, he was able to attain through kindness.[23] As the doors of non-Jewish society swung open for the Jew, the survivors of a millennium of humiliation and slaughter eagerly seized upon the opportunities offered. What began as a trickle away from traditional Judaism soon became a stampede. Only a few were able to stand in the midst of the flood and through the power of persuasion alone turn back the tide. Of these, the most effective was Rabbi Samson Raphael Hirsch.

Chapter Two

THE WINDS OF CHANGE

VISIONS OF EMANCIPATION GAINED INCREASING CURrency throughout the 18th century and peaked with the French Revolution of 1789. Emancipation held out the hope of political and social liberation for long disenfranchised classes of society. The well-known slogan of the French Revolution, *liberté, egalité et fraternité* (liberty, equality and brotherhood), proclaimed the ideal that all human beings are created equal and that fraternity should naturally prevail among nations and among all citizens within each country, without regard to race, creed or national origin. One of the consequences of the French Revolution was that France, as well as other countries, began to grant Jews, at least in principle, the same civil rights as those enjoyed by other citizens.

The French Revolution

The new ideology also announced the end of economic and social barriers based on class, race and religion. Previously, Jews were restricted to peddling and money-lending; now, suddenly, all areas of economic pursuit and professional endeavor were opened to them. Housing restrictions were relaxed, and the social and economic status of the Jews of Western Europe improved considerably.

The spirit of the revolution soon breached the walls of the ghetto and spread quickly within its confines. While offering Jews expanded economic and social opportunities, emancipation simultaneously subverted long-established patterns of Jewish life. Previously Jews had lived in ghettos, isolated by both external pressure and by their own free will, their existence governed in minute detail by the Talmud and the *Shulchan Aruch*. Once they were admitted into the political, social and cultural life of the outside world, many Jews assumed that the traditional Jewish lifestyle would inhibit their integration into gentile society, and in particular their participation in economic and professional life.

Observance of the Sabbath and *kashruth* suffered especially. The dazzling lights of science and the arts, the diversions of theater and social life, and the liberation of thought and imagination from prior restraints enticed significant portions of Jewry. The separation from the unique Jewish way of life, whose religious hue had granted it unsurpassed power, rocked the Jewish soul to its core and shook its centuries-old balance. The slogan, "Let Israel be a nation like all others," became a guiding principle for many.

In the ghetto, being a Jew was a given. Although, theoretically, one could convert to Christianity, the social pressures militating against this were so strong it was hardly an option. With the tumbling of the walls of the ghetto, suddenly, being Jewish and the way one practiced Judaism became an open question.[1] Judaism was now relegated, for the first time, to only one sphere of life.[2]

For a not inconsiderable number, especially among the wealthy and educated, apostasy and even conversion to Christianity became viable options. The factors motivating such a drastic step were several, but chief among them was almost always the desire to hasten acceptance in gentile society. Although sometimes this motive was baldly admitted, more often it was accompanied by a veneer of philosophical rationalizations about having lost respect for Judaism and seeing the "truth" of Christian values.

The Enlightenment

THE ENLIGHTENMENT PUT MAN AT THE CENTER OF THE UNIVERSE and appointed human reason the ultimate arbiter of truth. Religion was replaced by belief in the powers of reason and science.[3] Enlightenment thinkers viewed all men as innately good and decent, and deemphasized differences based on nationality, ethnic origin, or religion. A corollary of this optimistic view of man's inherent goodness was extreme confidence in the power of education to ennoble all men and thus to remove any barriers dividing them. Beginning with Jean Jacques Rousseau, the state, representing the "general will," was viewed as the natural instrument for providing the desired education, and the use of the power of the state to intervene in the private affairs of the unenlightened and to educate them, even against their will, was deemed legitimate. Most of the leaders of the movement to "enlighten" the masses were involved in various endeavors for educational reform. Their goals were the shaping of the character of man with an emphasis on reason, progress, equality and tolerance.[4]

In Germany, the phenomenon of Jewish *Haskalah* ("Enlightenment") first appeared in Berlin in the last quarter of the 18th century. Jews had lived in Berlin since the 13th century, under conditions not unlike those which prevailed in the rest of Germany. Even during those periods in which they were permitted to live in Berlin, there were usually severe limitations on the number of Jews granted residence permits, the sections of the city where Jews could reside, and on the trades and businesses in which they could engage.[5] In short, the Jews of Berlin were second-class citizens or worse.

Moses Mendelssohn

MOSES MENDELSSOHN (1729-1786) OF BERLIN WAS ONE OF THE FIRST Jews fully conversant with European culture. An observant Jew, he numbered among his friends and admirers many of Germany's leading intellectual figures. More importantly for our story, he wished to spread "enlightenment" among his people. To that end he published a German translation of the Torah with a Hebrew commentary, the *Biur*, the appearance of which was fraught with controversy.[a]

---

a. The *Noda B'Yehudah*, Rabbi Yechezkel Landau of Prague, explained his oppposition in a letter: "For the translator . . . [used] an extremely difficult German that presupposes expertise in its grammar . . . [and] the teacher will have to spend most of the time in explaining German grammar. . . . It induces the young to spend their time reading gentile books in order to become sufficiently familiar with refined German, to be able to understand this translation. Our Torah is thereby reduced to the role of a maidservant to the German tongue. . . . The intention of the translator may have been good, as I have said before. We have to assume this, since we must judge every man in the scale of merit, especially one who is famous as a scholar. Yet we cannot rest satisfied with the intention that prompted him, if the result of his action is so devastating."

Although Mendelssohn wrote in his introduction that he had undertaken the translation for the sake of his children, and that it was only on the persistent request of their teacher who wrote the commentary to *Bereishis* that he acquiesced to publish it, the truth was, as he admitted in a letter to his friend August Hennings, and as Rabbi Yechezkel Landau had suspected, that he

Moses Mendelssohn

Mendelssohn deviated from traditional Jewish thought in many ways, and it is not difficult to discern the impact of his deviations on his disciples, or on those who viewed themselves as such, from whose ranks would come many of the early leaders of Reform. Most of his own offspring were eventually baptized. Mendelssohn believed that reason is the sole medium through which man can acquire knowledge fulfillment, and that all men are endowed with an innate knowledge of what is good and true. Thus the revelation at Sinai conveyed to the Jewish people no understanding denied to other peoples. At most, G-d gave the Jewish people Divine legislation, not revealed religion. The basic tenets of Judaism, in Mendelssohn's view, are shared by all religions. The Reformer Solomon Ludwig Steinheim (1789-1866) captured this neatly in his memorable formulation: "Mendelssohn," he said, "was a heathen in his brain and a Jew in his body."[6] Judaism, Mendelssohn argued, legislates only actions and does not require conformity in matters of doctrine. He also rejected the traditional view of free will, and argued that every action is determined by some prior cause. Thus Divine punishments are understood as designed only to purge the effect of sins, not as retribution for wrongful acts.

More importantly, Mendelssohn was the first Orthodox Jewish thinker to submit Judaism to judgment according to the ideals of the Age of Reason. Despite his personal *mitzvah* observance, the untenability of that observance with his ideas is demonstrated by the lives of his disciples and descendants.[7] In Isaac Breuer's assessment:

> Mendelssohn did not in any way question European culture and its vision. He accepted that culture as it was, and had we not known that he was a Jew, we would not have been able to discern his Judaism in any of his philosophic writings. . . . With his translation of the Torah into polished German, he wanted to introduce his people gradually to European culture. And then what? On that question Mendelssohn was silent.[8]

---

intended it as "the first step toward culture from which my nation is, alas, kept at such a distance that one might almost despair of the possibility of improvement."

The opposition was clearly not because of the German translation *per se*, as the *Noda B'Yehudah* himself granted an approbation to just such a work in 1785.[5*]

Mendelssohn was instrumental in undermining Judaism by his profound identification of German Jewry with German culture and language.[9] Mendelssohn was the first Jew to participate, as a full-fledged member, in modern European culture. He was, as one writer put aptly, "a reformer of Jewish life but not of Judaism."[10] He embraced the German Enlightenment wholeheartedly, and his ideas led his followers to be among the pioneers and founders of Reform Judaism and enabled others to skip the charade and embrace Christianity without undue difficulty.

Mendelssohn gave European culture and the Jewish tradition equal status. European culture had for him independent validity apart from the truths of Torah, and did not have to be judged in light of those truths. In one of his few direct comments on Mendelssohn, Rabbi Hirsch stressed the tension in Mendelssohn caused by his allegiance to both Judaism and Enlightenment ideals: [He believed] that "it was possible to be an observant Jew *and yet* to shine, highly respected, as a German Plato. This *and yet*," Rabbi Hirsch wrote, "was decisive. His followers contented themselves with eagerly furthering the study of *Tanach* along philosophical and aesthetic lines . . . . adding and expanding the study of the humanities. The proper study of Judaism, through *Tanach* and Talmud, was neglected. Even the zealous study of *Tanach* could not lead to an understanding of Judaism, for it was studied not as a source of instruction, conveying values, but as a poetic composition, to feed the imagination."[11]

> [Mendelssohn] dwelled in the tents of Shem [a metaphor for adherence to traditional Judaism] out of national loyalty, but was attached to the beauty of Japheth [son of Noah and ancestor of the Greeks, used here as a metaphor for Hellenistic aestheticism]. He dwelled in the tents of Shem, *and yet* was attached to the beauty of Japheth. He was attached to the beauty of Japheth, *and yet* dwelled in the tents of Shem.[12]

The *and yet* implied that the role of Plato could be valid too, even when at variance with the realities of Judaism. Mendelssohn's followers went further. For them, the Torah was reduced to a poetic treasury of thought and philosophy without binding force. As a result of Mendelssohn's influence, Berlin became the center of the *Haskalah* Movement. Initially, the *maskilim* ("enlightened ones") attempted to rid themselves of any restraints that might inhibit their absorption into gentile society, without denying their Judaism. Enlightenment and education were measured by the degree of disregard for Jewish tradition. Moses Hess captured the mood of the time in an anecdote about a Jew who came to Mendelssohn and proudly boasted of his son's philosophical abilities. When the philosopher asked of what the son's abilities consisted, the happy man replied, "Why, my son has not put on his *tefillin* for months."[13]

Next, the newly enlightened set out to blur all distinctions and remove any barrier that separated Jews from the rest of society. The literature of the Berlin *Haskalah,* which rejected rabbinic tradition and authority, threatened the entire system of traditional Jewry — its values, structure, and institutions.[14] It is understandable, then, that the leaders of traditional authentic Jewry, the rabbis, and indeed most Orthodox Jews, came to view every manifestation of the *Haskalah* with deep suspicion. Every German word that found its way into the *Judengasse* (Jews' street in the ghetto) was viewed as an enemy incursion.

Rabbi Yechiel Yaakov Weinberg captured the strains placed on traditional Jewish life by the new winds:

> The ghetto stood for hundreds of years and produced men of great stature, righteous people, who devoted their energies to Torah study and *mitzvah* observance, men whose entire joy and pleasure in life was to rejoice in the Almighty. They attained lofty spiritual levels and merited a degree of Divine inspiration that raised them high above the bitter darkness of the exile. Such people's words and deeds were suffused with the sanctity of the Torah, and its presence permeated their lives.
>
> Nonetheless, within the ghetto's walls there lived also masses of people who were not privileged to taste the Torah's pleasures and to experience its inspiration. These people thirsted for life, and their inability to attain it made them depressed. They knew only difficulty, and the lives of a significant portion of them were twisted by an ascetic melancholy.
>
> Finally the day came, new winds began to blow and the walls of the ghetto fell before them. Rays of hope, of light and liberty, the prospects of life and creativity, wealth and social position, wafted into the darkest corners of the ghetto, to human beings who had been so long deprived of any place in society. The innate thirst for a healthy and complete life which is so natural to every Jew, a thirst repressed for so many centuries, was reawakened amid sound and fury.
>
> These radical developments brought the Jewish people to a state of crisis. One-dimensional life-denying religiosity simply collapsed, totally unable to restrain its children who strayed from

its framework, rejecting the indignities of oppression, who strove to break free from their constraints.

Confusion reigned in the Jewish community. On the one side stood the elders, preservers of tradition, who defended with all their might the accepted religious way, which was predicated on a rejection of the pleasures and accomplishments of the material world. On the other side were those drunk and dizzy with their new freedom, who lashed out mercilessly at everything that was precious and holy in the traditional order of Jewish life.[15]

The "salons" of Berlin served as a meeting place for Jew and gentile, a bridge which frequently led all the way to the baptismal font. The conversion certificate became the diploma attesting to its holder's enlightened status. Baptism by Jews became epidemic in Berlin until 1810, when the government passed a law which forbade baptism of Jews by Christian pastors without the sanction of the local police. It is ironic that even after the Jews were granted civil rights, the gentile still did not want to have anything to do with him to the point of not allowing him to convert. Of the 3,610 Jews living in Berlin in 1819, over one third converted to Christianity in the course of four years.[16]

Reform

WITHOUT A THOROUGH UNDERSTANDING OF THE EVOLUTION OF the Reform Movement in the years prior to Rabbi Hirsch's birth and during his formative years, no assessment of his accomplishments is possible. An understanding of that development is also important because the forces which gave rise to the Reform Movement are still operative today: Jews no longer live in the ghetto and, at least in Western countries, they live and work in close proximity to their non-Jewish neighbors.

The growing numbers who cast off the yoke of Torah for the alluring life of society felt an urgent need to fashion for themselves an ideology to justify their actions and give a sense of meaning to their lives. Not content with merely living non-observant lives, they sought to reform Judaism itself, and to achieve their goals were even willing to employ the power of the government.

What divided Orthodoxy and Reform was the very concept of Judaism. Judaism was never "religion" in the usual sense of the word, but rather an all-encompassing system of belief and practice governing every aspect of the lives of its adherents. Reformers confronted the question: What defines Judaism if no aspect of Jewish belief or practice is inviolate?

What is the supposedly unchanging, yet ever unfolding, idea that constitutes Judaism? The Reform response amounted to little more than monotheism, with some Kantian ethical imperative blended in. Nothing else was permanent in the Reform view.[17]

Rabbi Hirsch captured the animating spirit of Reform many years later in one of his most brilliant polemical pieces, "Religion Allied to Progress." Penned in response to a vicious pamphlet authored in 1854 by Ludwig Stein, rabbi of the Reform-dominated Jewish Community of Frankfurt, Rabbi Hirsch describes how the Reform

> distilled the ancient world-ranging spirit of the Torah into one aromatic drop of perfume so fragrant, that in the most elegant party dress they could carry it round with them in their waistcoat pockets without being ashamed. They carved out of the ponderous old Tablets of the Law ornamental figures so tiny, that people gladly found room for them on smart dressing tables in drawing rooms and ballrooms.
>
> [Reform proclaimed to each Jew:] "Be what you are, enjoy what you fancy, aspire to what you will, whatever you may be you are always religious, whatever you may do — all is religion; continue to progress for the more you progress, the further you move from the ancient way, and the more you cast off old Jewish customs the more religious and acceptable to G-d will you be; the more you outshine the ancient fire of Horeb with the brilliance of your own enlightenment, the more you crucify the ancient law by your criticism the happier you will be; for it was for crucifixion and in order to be crucified by its own children that it descended from heaven, and the more a man slaps his old mother in the face the more is she delighted to have given birth to sons with such powerful hands."[18]

In later years, the Reformers Geiger and Holdheim preferred to be known as Germans of the Mosaic faith. The Sadducees and the Karaites had denied the validity of only the Oral Torah; Reform rejected the binding authority of the Written Torah as well. The fundamental internal issue of the Jewish people from the inception of the Reform Movement until the present day has revolved around the question of the acceptance or, Heaven forbid, the rejection of, the Divine nature of the Torah as it was given at Sinai.

Increasing opportunities for Jews in the non-Jewish world were the main, but not only force encouraging the growth of Reform. Sabbateanism and the resultant splits in the Jewish world played its part, as did the weakening of rabbinic authority in the second half of the 18th century engendered by the bitter dispute between Rabbi Yonasan Eibeschitz and Rabbi Yaakov Emden.[19]

The need of German princes for ready sources of capital, following the Thirty Years War (1618-1648), led them to employ capable Jews in various commercial and financial roles. The court Jew, which virtually no Central European ruler was without in the 17th and 18th centuries, helped finance and obtain money for the royal coffers, supplied the army, helped out in diplomatic difficulties and supplied the ruler with luxury items.[20] A class of "court Jews" developed, who traveled in gentile society and were willing to trade some or all of their *mitzvah* observance for entrance to the salons and dinner tables of the wealthy and influential. These Jews had no ideology, but were rather torn between two incompatible worlds.

First and foremost among these was probably the family of Daniel Itzig of Berlin, who became, in 1791, the first Jews to be granted civil rights in Germany. Although Itzig himself was religious,[b] his assimilation into court life made a shambles of the religious observance of his family. As such, he served as an early example of the potential dangers to Jewish observance in civic equality.

Reformers felt that the more Judaism could be approximated to Christianity, the easier would be their integration into gentile society. In this belief, they were explicitly encouraged by Christian philosophers. Immanuel Kant, the greatest of them, made it clear that Jews and Christians could become brothers only if the Jews would "purify their religious ideas," and cast aside their "outdated ritual." Thus, casting aside traditional observance was seen as a precondition for social acceptance and civic equality.[21] In the effort to mimic Christian concepts of religiosity, it became the vogue to ask whether a *mitzvah* provided "spiritual fulfillment" and if the "service" was "uplifting." The object of religious "ceremonies" became "edification."[22]

Another event which must not be discounted for its effect on internal Jewish life was the convocation by Napoleon, in 1806, of a Jewish Assembly of Notables. Napoleon's purpose in convening the Assembly was to secure Jewish support for his political goals, and the diminution of the Jewish people as a distinct national and ethnic group in the lands he controlled. Napoleon presented the Assembly of Notables with a set of twelve questions, which dealt with the vocational life of Jews, their

b. The *Pri Megadim*, Rabbi Joseph Teomim, authored most of his works while living as an endowed scholar in a study house in Berlin funded entirely by Daniel Itzig.[20*]

patriotism, the functioning of rabbis and judges, and divorce and intermarriage. One of the questions, for instance, was whether, according to Jewish Law, a Jew may marry a non-Jew. The Assembly of Notables answered evasively. Their responses were carefully designed to prove the Jews' fealty to the new order and to lay to rest Napoleon's doubts over the Jew's loyalty.

Never one to lose a political opportunity, Napoleon decided to attempt to extend these resolutions to apply to Jewry as a whole. To that end, the same year he convened a "Sanhedrin" which consisted of 71 rabbis, drawn from all the "synagogues of Europe," among them the distinguished Rabbi Dovid Sinzheim of Strasbourg and Rabbi Zalman Trier of Frankfurt. The convocation of the "Sanhedrin" in Paris for one month was accompanied with much pomp and circumstance. Special uniforms were even provided for the rabbis.

The "Sanhedrin" set a precedent for modern "rabbinic" conferences to rule on issues of Jewish law, and was cited in later years as a precedent for the most radical departures from *halachah.* In an attempt to mollify Napoleon, the "Sanhedrin" "decided," in response to the question of intermarriage, that from a civil standpoint mixed marriages were valid, while carefully camouflaging the impermissibility of such unions in Jewish Law. Less than four decades later, the Reformers used this "decision" to permit intermarriage, and declared that there was no prohibition on the intermarriage of adherents of monotheistic religions, if the state permits the parents to raise the children according to the Jewish religion.

Reformers were ready to abandon every ritual they saw as irrational or as standing in the way of emancipation. The early reforms were confined to the liturgy and to the synagogue service. Yet the external changes merely reflected a profound internal shift in how one viewed the essence of Judaism. The concerted effort, for instance, to delete any mention of the Messiah and the rebuilding of the *Beis HaMikdash* showed that the reforms were not concerned solely with outward forms but rather struck at the essence of Judaism.[23]

One of the pioneers in the area of synagogue reform was Israel Jacobson (1768-1828). Born to religious parents in Halberstadt, he was attracted at a young age to Mendelssohn's writings and the *Haskalah.* Jacobson was not an original thinker, and did not even possess a secular education, but he was wealthy and had boundless energy. In 1808, he convened a gathering of influential Jews in Kassel for the purpose of introducing religious reforms. His aim was to create a synod in Germany similar to the "Sanhedrin" convened by Napoleon in Paris. Jacobson also established the first temple in which portions of the services were conducted in German and whose services were modeled after the German Protestant Church. The second of these temples was inaugurated in Seesen in 1810, in a ceremony replete with the ringing of bells as in church, and the singing of hymns in German accompanied by organ music. The *bimah* was moved from the center to the front, an organ was installed and the services were conducted by Jacobson dressed in the robes of a Protestant clergyman.

Israel Jacobson

As head of the Consistory — the government-appointed commission charged with the regulation of Jewish religious life in the Kingdom of Westphalia, a short-lived conglomerate of German states created by Napoleon and ruled over by Napoleon's brother Jerome — Jacobson initiated a number of changes. He altered the marriage ceremony, abolished "klapping" Haman on Purim, and permitted the consumption of *kitniyos* (legumes) on Pesach. Sadly, these changes were met with barely a whimper, except for the response of Rabbi Zavel Eiger.[24]

In 1814, Jacobson moved to Berlin and instituted services with an organ and German hymns chanted by a choir in which non-Jews also participated.[25] The first boy to be "confirmed" in this temple was Jacobson's son Naphtali, who later became Dr. Hermann Jacobson, one of the leading lights of Berlin's Catholic community. Indeed, the majority of Jacobson's ten children converted to Christianity.[26]

The leaders of Jewry fought determinedly against the various Reformers. Yet they did not succeed. While they did their utmost to stem breaches in the tradition, they were unable to suppress the rebellion, and for the most part were left watching helplessly as the things they held most holy were swallowed up in the turbulent and fast-moving waters of Reform.

Jewry, and its rabbis[a] were some of the Jewish people's greatest Torah luminaries.[2]

On December 10, 1810, Hamburg was annexed by France. The tripartite *Kehillah* was divided in 1812, at the order of the French authorities who controlled the city. On February 24, 1813, the citizens of Hamburg rose up against the French occupiers and on May 5, 1814, the French were thrown out of Hamburg never to return. As in other parts of Germany, the conquest of Hamburg by French forces and their subsequent departure caused a massive upheaval in the social order. This was equally true of the city's Jewish inhabitants: The presence of the French authorities, bearers of the Enlightenment and revolutionary values, led to many centuries-old traditions being abandoned and previously unchallenged assumptions being questioned.[3] Even after the French were expelled, the revolutionary vision of liberty, equality and fraternity remained part of the city's intellectual fabric.

The Temple

AT THE END OF 1817, WHEN SAMSON HIRSCH WAS NINE YEARS OLD, the face of German Jewry changed forever. A substantial group of Jews in Hamburg joined together to offer an alternative public expression of Judaism. On December 12, 1817, Reformers in Hamburg established the "New Israelite Temple Association in Hamburg," and less than a year later, on October 18, 1818 (18 *Tishrei*, 5579), they erected a house of prayer which they named *Temple*. The *Temple* was the first Jewish house of worship in Germany to use an organ on the Sabbath and a mixed choir in the services. At the dedication festivities, the assembled were treated to a rendition by a choir of young girls.

The Temple Association also published a new prayerbook for Sabbath and holidays, in which many prayers were in German, and various sections added and deleted at will. The prayerbook omitted *Birchas HaShachar, Birchas HaTorah, Ashrei, P'sukei deZimrah,* mutilated *Birchos Krias Shma,* did away with the silent *Shemoneh Esrei, Maftir* and *Haftarah* and changed the Torah readings to a triennial cycle. All mention of the

a. The *Chacham Zvi,* Rabbi Zvi Hirsch Ashkenazi (1660-1718), served as rabbi from 1707 to 1710, before becoming Chief Rabbi of Amsterdam; Rabbi Yechezkel Katzenellenbogen (1667-1749), author of *Sefer Knesses Yechezkel* (1733), served from 1714 to 1749; Rabbi Yonasan Eibeschitz (1690-1764), author of many works, including *Urim VeTumim* and *Kreisi U'Pleisi,* served from 1750 to 1764; and Rabbi Raphael HaKohen (1722-1804), author of *Toras Yekusiel,* a commentary on *Shulchan Aruch Yoreh Deah* (1772) and *VeShav HaKohein* — a collection of halachic responsa — was rabbi from 1776, at a time when Hamburg was connected to the other two communities of Altona and Wandsbeck. The latter was known as Rabbi Raphael Hamburger. He was one of the leading public opponents of Mendelssohn, and was subject to severe attack for forcefully criticizing Mendelssohn.

Hamburg Reform Temple

future redemption of the Jewish people, the *Beis HaMikdash* and *Mashiach* was expunged, presumably in order to prove their sincere patriotism. The *Temple* was, of course, closed during the week. Within three years, membership stood at approximately 100 families, which still constituted less than 10 percent of Hamburg Jewry.[4]

The significance of the actions of the Hamburg group was that for the first time the reforms were advanced by a unified group from "below." The reforms of Israel Jacobson, by contrast, were essentially those of a single wealthy individual, albeit with a following. Almost 60 years later, Rabbi Hirsch wrote that with the erection of the *Temple* in Hamburg, "the cornerstone was laid for all liturgical reform that was subsequently made in synagogue worship."[5]

The reaction of the Hamburg rabbinate to the establishment of the *Temple* and its prayerbook was swift and uncompromising. On 26 *Tishrei*, the rabbinate, led by the *Rosh Beis Din*, Rabbi Baruch Ozer,[6] issued a prohibition against praying in the *Temple* or using its prayerbook. The notice was hung in all the *shuls* and *klausen* in Hamburg. Rabbi Baruch Ozer also wrote to the leading Torah scholars of Europe and to Sephardic rabbis of the Ottoman Empire, requesting a halachic response to the following three questions: 1) May the *Nusach HaTefillah* be changed? 2) May the prayers be recited in a foreign language (German)? 3) May a synagogue have an organ, even if it is played on the Sabbath by a non-Jew?

Rabbi Baruch Ozer

The responses of 18 of the leading rabbis of the time, including Rabbi Moshe Sofer of Pressburg,[7] Rabbi Akiva Eiger of Posen, Rabbi Yaakov Lorberbaum of Lissa,[8] and Rabbi Mordechai Banet of Nikolsburg, were published in a special booklet, *Eileh Divrei HaBris* (Altona, 1819). The work was prefaced by the blanket prohibition of the local rabbinate on the use of the Reform prayerbook, praying in any language other than Hebrew, and the use of an organ on the Sabbath to accompany the services. In the foreword to *Eileh Divrei HaBris*, the Hamburg rabbinate explained that for some time, there had been individuals who had denigrated the Sages of the Mishnah and Talmud, and after a while, this attitude led to serious transgressions. They had felt it necessary to request the halachic responsa of leading rabbis because the Reformers, basing themselves on a fictitious account of a ruling of the rabbi of Livorno permitting the use of an organ, had informed the Hamburg authorities that their practices were sanctioned by Jewish Law and prevailed upon the authorities to forbid Rabbi Baruch Ozer from issuing his proclamation.[b]

Less than one year after the establishment of the *Temple*, on August 2, 1819, the anti-Jewish Hep! Hep! riots broke out in Germany. Beginning in Würzburg, they quickly spread throughout Germany, including Hamburg (September 1), Frankfurt, Leipzig, Dresden and Darmstadt. Thus, the attempt to draw closer to the gentile was met with swift rejection. Reform and "Enlightenment" circles attempted to

---

b. It is interesting to note that the three questions the distinguished group of Torah luminaries was asked to address by the Hamburg rabbinate were the very issues Rabbi Hirsch responded to 36 years later in his reply to Rabbi Yaakov Koppel Bamberger of Worms. [See *Shemesh Marpeh* (New York, 1992), pp. 2-8.] The fact that even three and a half decades later the same three issues were important indicates that the main thrust of Reform, at least in the prayer service, was reflected in these three areas.

Wolf Heidenheim

play down the riots and to suppress details, in the words of the *Haskalah*-oriented periodical *Shulamith*, "so that this knowledge not weaken our co-religionists' love for our Christian fellow citizens." The response of the non-observant to the Hep! Hep! riots was not to reconsider their eager rush into the arms of Christian society, but rather the establishment of the *Verein für Kultur und Wissenschaft des Judentums* (Society for the Culture and Science of Judaism), yet another attempt to deepen their ties with Christian neighbors.

At this early stage in the Reform Movement, the lines between Reform and Orthodoxy were still not so clearly drawn, and many did not fully comprehend the deep and unbridgeable chasm which separated the two groups. Many Reformers began their careers with Orthodox leanings, and as such were often given the benefit of the doubt, when in fact they had long since crossed over into the other camp. An understanding of this reality makes it easier to grasp many otherwise incomprehensible occurrences. To take one illuminating example: Wolf Heidenheim (1757-1832) — whose scholarship and accuracy in establishing the proper *Nusach HaTefillah* and commentary on the *Piyutim* were effusively praised by the *Chasam Sofer*,[9] and whose works were graced with the approbation of Rabbi Pinchas Horovitz of Frankfurt — published in 1831 a *siddur* with an introduction on the essence of prayer by none other than Michael Creizenach, one of the leaders of the Reform Movement, who had taught since 1825 in the Reform *Philanthropin* School in Frankfurt. Three out of four of Creizenach's children converted to Christianity.[10]

It was only by the fourth and fifth decades of the 19th century that the differences between Orthodoxy and Reform became clear to all. The Reform "rabbinical conferences," especially in Braunschweig,[11] caused both sides to realize that the gap was unbridgeable.[12]

At the outset, Reform contended that their liturgical changes did not violate the *halachah*. Thus, the rabbinic response included in *Eileh Divrei HaBris* contained halachic epistles which demonstrated that the new prayer service was a flagrant violation of the *halachah*. But the Reformers did not really care, and the arguments fell on deaf ears.[13]

One of the identifying characteristics of Reform Judaism was that the reforms came first and then the *post hoc* justifications. The adherents of synagogue reform in Hamburg and Berlin in the second decade of the century acted primarily for social and personal reasons — chiefly the fear that traditional Judaism would hamper social integration and political equality.[14] Only a generation later did they adapt a philosophy and ideology to conform to their practices. In formulating that philosophy, the ends — harmonizing Judaism with modernity — determined the means.[15]

At the time of the establishment of the *Temple* and the publication of its prayerbook, the Hirsch home was the venue of meetings and strategy sessions called to combat the threat posed to Torah Judaism by the *Temple.* Young Samson was deeply affected by the gatherings in his parents' home, and in his later years recalled that it was this struggle which first gave him the impetus to pursue his calling in life.[16]

Despite the efforts of the Orthodox community, it must be admitted that the responses to the establishment of the Hamburg *Temple* were of little effect. While the traditionalists cried, sighed, scoffed and threatened, the Reformers just laughed and continued to gain adherents. There was no one on the Orthodox side in Hamburg able to present the tenets of authentic Judaism in a way that would convince anyone but the already committed. There was no one with the courage and the breadth of knowledge to fight the Reformers on their own terms and on their own turf. It was then that the *Kehillah* decided to hire someone who could.[17]

Chacham Isaac Bernays

IN 1821, WHEN YOUNG SAMSON REACHED BAR-MITZVAH AGE, RABBI Isaac Bernays (1792-1849) was appointed Rabbi of Hamburg,[18] then the largest Jewish community in Germany.[19] On October 30, 1821, he took up his position.

Born in Mainz, Isaac Bernays was a child prodigy, who knew at the age of seven the entire Tractate *Bava Kamma* by heart. In recognition of that feat he received the title *chaver* from the local rabbi, Rabbi Noach Chaim Zvi Berlin.[20] In his youth, he studied under Rabbi Eizik Metz, who later served as a *dayan* in Hamburg and taught in the Hamburg "Talmud Torah."[21] Bernays also studied in the yeshiva of Rabbi Avraham Bing of Würzburg, from whom he received *semichah.* Rabbi Bing appointed him *dayan* in Würzburg at a very young age.[22]

In the University of Würzburg, he became friendly with his fellow student Rabbi Yaakov Ettlinger, with whom he studied *Yoreh Deah* and *Moreh*

Nevuchim, and with whom he maintained a lifelong friendship.[c,23]

Chacham Isaac Bernays

After university studies in Munich, Rabbi Bernays returned to Mainz where he served as a private teacher until he was appointed Rabbi of Hamburg. In a concession to the more Reform-minded members of the Hamburg Community Board, his letter of appointment stipulated that he was not permitted to publicly admonish any individuals or groups in the community in connection with any religious acts which they might commit, nor withhold from such people any benefits of the congregation.[d] "Never," said the Chacham when he assumed the post, "has a rabbi been so dependent in office on a board, as I shall be."[24] As time went on, however, it was the board who hastened to do his bidding, such was the power of his personality.[25]

Upon assuming the Hamburg rabbinate, Rabbi Bernays took for himself the title "Chacham,"[26] as Sephardic rabbis were called, instead of the title "Rabbi," probably as a protest over the use of the title by Reformers, who observed no *mitzvos* and yet called themselves "Rabbi."[e]

Although only 30 years of age, Rabbi Bernays was already an exceptional scholar, noted for his perceptiveness, exceptional memory and honesty. The Chacham possessed a wide-ranging knowledge of many subjects and a pleasant personality.[27] Supremely humble, he spurned personal honor and profit,[28] and devoted himself totally to the study of Torah. His integrity was legendary. At the dedication ceremonies of the synagogue of the Hamburg Jewish hospital, which had been donated by the

---

c. Neither Rabbi Bernays nor Rabbi Ettlinger ever received a university degree.

d. When Rabbi Akiva Eiger was appointed Rabbi of Posen, he was permitted to maintain, at community expense, no more than six disciples who were not natives of Posen, and he, too, was prohibited from criticizing the religious conduct of any member of the community, either privately or from the pulpit.[24*]

e. Rabbi Bernays' use of the title "Chacham" has always been something of a puzzle. Yet knowledge of the demographics of Hamburg Jewry makes his choice easier to comprehend. Hamburg possessed a large and influential community of Sephardic Jews, known in Hamburg as the *Portugesim*, who had fled the Iberian peninsula to Holland and from there to Hamburg. The Sephardim had their own community and rabbinate until as late as 1910, when they conferred the title of "Chacham" on the Ashkenazi Chief Rabbi A. Spitzer. In this context the choice of the title "Chacham" was not as strange as it might otherwise seem.

powerful and affluent Hamburg Jewish banker Solomon Heine, one of the richest men in Europe,[29] the Chacham addressed the assembled guests without mentioning the name, nor even hinting at the identity, of the wealthy and influential benefactor. The public was astounded. But the Chacham was unyielding. "I was designated to take part in ceremonies for the honor of Heaven," he replied, "not in functions whose purpose is to flatter human beings."[30]

Solomon Heine

The noted grammarian Wolf Heidenheim once enumerated the dimensions of the Chacham's greatness. "The entire Talmud, *halachah* and *Midrash* was to him an open book. As a philosopher he was greater than the worldly ones, as a philologist he was supreme, as a grammarian he reminded me of Ibn Ezra. In halachic matters it was as if the Rambam was talking, in esoteric wisdom, like Saadiah Gaon."[31] Rabbi Hirsch's uncle described Rabbi Bernays as:

> a wise, understanding and humble person, whose kindness and love showed on his face, who was able to touch the hearts of his listeners with his gracious speech and with the wisdom of the Torah . . .
>
> He stood on the *bimah* on Shabbos with volumes of the Talmud, *halachah*, and *Midrash* open before him (he was also familiar with all areas of *Kabbalah*), standing with closed eyes. A powerful speaker, his words penetrated to the inner recesses of the hearts of those who understood him, though the masses did not comprehend his holy and righteous ways. . . . He spent all his money on the needs of the poor, and kept for himself just enough to meet the minimum needs of his family.[32]

He was more sage and righteous man than organizer or politician, but it was his very selflessness and lack of any artifice that was the cause of his great success.

Rabbi Bernays played an important role in shaping the character of Orthodox Judaism in 19th-century Germany. His student Rabbi Hirsch once told a friend, "He was the greatest shining light of Jewish thought of

The Elbstrasse synagogue in Hamburg where Samson Hirsch prayed as a youth, as it appeared at the time

his time, and were he alive today, the same would still be true."[33]

On the day of the Chacham's arrival in Hamburg, Reb Mendel Frankfurter showed him a difficult passage in the *Rambam*, which none of the local *rabbonim* had been able to explain. The Chacham resolved the difficulty on the spot.[34] The older *talmidei chachamim* of Hamburg initially treated him with suspicion, apprehensive that with his academic training and philosophical knowledge he would introduce reforms, but when they saw the enthusiasm with which he learned *Gemara*, they too became his supporters.[35]

One reason that the elders of the Hamburg community chose Chacham Bernays as their leader was that he possessed a secular education. They hoped that he would be able to understand the young people of the community and save them from the enticements of the Reformers.[36] He fought the Reformers every step of the way, even appropriating some of their methods and thus stealing their thunder. He introduced and perfected the *predigt* or sermon, one of the main selling points of the Reform service.

He was not a writer; he concentrated on quiet and persistent education, and his circle of students and admirers grew steadily. The Chacham knew how to communicate his deep conviction of the truth of Judaism with intelligence and profundity. He was a hard worker and a pedagogue of rare talent, with powerful emotions.[37] In the late 1830s, he began a weekly *shiur* in

Exterior of the Elbstrasse synagogue in Hamburg where Chacham Bernays and the Hirsch family prayed

Kuzari to a large and enthusiastic audience. As a result of the *shiur's* popularity, all available copies of the work were sold out. It was reprinted in 1838 by Rabbi Hirsch's younger brother Hirsch (Harry) and another young student. The Reformers, in a desperate attempt to limit the Chacham's influence, entered a complaint in 1839 with the local authorities, alleging that the *Kuzari* is anti-Christian and requested the police to put a stop to his *shiur*. Only after a personal appearance by the Chacham was the matter settled.[38]

As Rabbi, he was officially in charge of the Hamburg "Talmud Torah," on behalf of which he expended much time and effort. The Talmud Torah flourished during his tenure and he exercised a powerful influence on the youth of his *Kehillah*.[39] The Chacham also educated a generation of *baalei batim*, who considered Torah study an integral part of their lives. There were many small synagogues or *klausen* in Hamburg, and these were frequented by this solid core of learned *baalei batim* whose days were spent at work and whose evenings were dedicated to Torah study. For decades after his death, the Chacham's teachings were still passed down from father to son in Hamburg.[40]

Perhaps the Chacham's greatest success was that the Hamburg *Kehillah* structure itself stayed Orthodox. This infuriated the Reformers and their sympathizers, who threatened to leave the *Kehillah en masse*. As a result of this threat, the "Hamburg Arrangement" was formulated, a communal framework unlike any other in Germany. Under the "Arrangement," all religious matters were taken out of the hands of the community board and given over to two separate organizations, the *Synagogenverein* for the Orthodox and the *Tempelverein* for the Reform. The rabbi of the Orthodox *Synagogenverein* was always the official Chief Rabbi of Hamburg, and the school and all charitable and humanitarian institutions remained in Orthodox hands. Consequently one of the unique aspects to *Kehillah* life in Hamburg was the fact that there was a minimum of open warfare between the Orthodox and Reform, and all remained members of the Jewish community.[41]

That is not to say that relations were always peaceful. In 1841, the *Temple* asked the government to allocate it more land for expansion purposes. The government passed the request on to the *Kehillah* for an opinion. The Chacham, in his reply to the government, sharply denounced the Reform and their Temple and recommended rejecting the request for more land. The Reformers reacted with unrestrained fury.[42] The battle between the Chacham and the Reformers became even more pitched late that year, with the publication of the second edition of the *Gebetbuch für alle Israeliten*, the prayerbook of the Reform Temple in Hamburg. Chacham Bernays reiterated the prohibition which had been published 23 years earlier by the Hamburg Rabbinate, had the *issur* hung in all the *shuls* in the city, and presented the Hamburg Senate with a request to forbid its dissemination, on the grounds that only he, as Chief Rabbi, had the authority to publish what was purported to be a prayerbook, under the rubric "*Teffiloth Israel*."

The Reformers were outraged and raised a hue and cry. Zachariah Frankel came to the Reformers' defense, publishing a long article[43] in which he criticized the Chacham. Frankel declared that Bernays had erred greatly and had committed a great sin by opposing the prayerbook. The government, at the insistence of the Reformers, ordered that the prohibition notices be removed. Rabbi Bernays circumvented this by issuing an אזהרה, a cautionary notice, that one could not fulfill the obligation of *tefillas chovah* (mandatory prayer) with the use of the prayerbook. In the public uproar that followed, Rabbi Yaakov Ettlinger, Chief Rabbi of neighboring Altona, came to the defense of his friend and colleague, and as a result was himself subject to attack.[44]

Hamburg appreciated Chacham Bernays immensely, as evidenced by the elaborate festivities on the 25th anniversary of his appointment.[45] When he passed away suddenly on 9 *Iyar* 5609 (May 1, 1849) at the age of 55, the shock and grief at his passing were overwhelming.[46] He was eulogized at his funeral and later also in a memorial ceremony in the synagogue by his study partner from yeshiva days, Rabbi Yaakov Ettlinger.[47]

In 1810, Rabbi Mendel Frankfurter brought Rabbi Nosson Nota Ellingen (d. 1827) to Hamburg to open a yeshiva for the more promising youngsters. Among his later disciples was young Samson Hirsch.[48] He also studied in the school of J.A. Isler, a *talmid chacham*, who taught some of the secular subjects as well.[49] At the age of 14, his parents, anticipating that he would enter business, apprenticed him to a merchant in Hamburg, in which position he remained for one year.

In 1824, at the age of 16, Samson Hirsch decided on the rabbinate as his life's vocation,[50] and began to study with the Chacham and attend *shiurim* in the latter's home.[51] Rabbi Hirsch once told his son-in-law Rabbi Salomon Breuer, "Besides his lectures, I learned from Chacham Bernays one *blatt Gemara* and it sufficed."[52] On April 16, 1826, Samson entered a *gymnasium* (the equivalent of today's high school) as a student of theology, where he studied for two years until April, 1828.[53] At the same time he continued studying under Rabbi Bernays, from whom he would later receive *semichah*.[54]

In 1830, Rabbi Bernays, in a letter of recommendation to the Grand Duke of Oldenburg, described his student as one who "dedicated himself with great diligence to the study of Jewish theology, after he acquired a general education at an early age. He participated in the lectures of the undersigned in Talmud and all the classic religious literature over a long period of time. He excelled in his conduct, in his abilities and in his excellent spiritual qualities, and in his diligence and his assiduity in an outstanding manner to such a degree that one can only see in him as an excellent candidate for the rabbinate."[55]

In the summer of 1828, Samson Hirsch set out for Mannheim to study in the yeshiva of Rabbi Yaakov Ettlinger, the first step toward becoming the leader of Torah Jewry in Western Europe.

Chapter Four
MANNHEIM

Self-Portrait

By the time Rabbi Hirsch arrived at the yeshiva in Mannheim in *Tammuz* 5588 (July 1828) at the age of 20, there had already crystallized in his mind the essence of the world view to which he remained committed for the rest of his life. The following letter, written on August 10 of that year, gives us a glimpse into the sensitivity and idealism of the young man who was destined to have such a profound effect on German Jewry.[a]

> So it always goes with me when my inner soul is too full. Then it does not spill over the sides as is common in other people — no, inside there can be stormy, turbulent waves — but on the outside, with pressures and counterpressures — only silence. I am like a clock whose inner components interact with each other constantly

a. The following is a free rendition, in the interest of conveying the unique flavor of the original.

but whose hands are missing, so that on the outside it appears completely still. Superficial people hold a feather to the nose and proclaim it lifeless, but those whose comprehension is deeper sense from the ticking that there is indeed life inside. A wise man knows to attach the missing hands to the face, so that he can read the time. . . .

We were on our way from Darmstadt, riding along the magnificent *Bergstrasse* with its striking scenery. On the right evergreen forests stretched endlessly, and on the left rose a chain of hills, glistening like a string of pearls. All the way to the peaks, vineyards had been planted, and the frail vegetation, totally dependent on human care, climbed up trellises erected for them. Pale young grapes were already peeking out from under green leaves, like a proud young mother showing off her wailing first-born. . . . Mother nature spread out a festive green carpet round about; the rain of the last few days brought it all into the open — burgeoning plants and seeds, poking their heads out into the light.

The landscape was full of mirth, and my soul light and joyful along with it. Suddenly, however, my mood plunged and I groaned inside, saying to myself, "Look at this! Nature is never lazy. Every plant and bush springs to fulfill the task its Creator has set for it. Only man enjoys the prerogative of neglecting his obligations. He is the only one who can disappoint the Divine stamp imprinted in him.[1]

"And what will be of you, Samson? How will you make yourself worthy of the lofty goal to which you aspire in your new path in life? You, who on your native soil neglected more than one of your obligations, and who have now been taken from that soil and are on your own, exposed to every passing wind. How can you hope to remain faithful to your heritage and not be deflected from the narrow path of truth? Where will you find a trellis to support *your* frail stalk when the storms come?"

Inwardly I grew increasingly depressed, and sat listlessly lost in my thoughts as we passed through the magnificent surroundings. The heat and the monotonous clanking of the wagon wheels had lulled my fellow passengers to sleep, and I too, lost in my ruminations, sank into a semi-daydream in which everything seemed very far away.

Then I felt as if someone was tapping me on the shoulder. I turned around involuntarily and there — never have I seen anyone of such splendid appearance and at the same time so filled with friendliness as the person who stood before me. I felt shy looking at his tall, resolute stature and serious, heroic forehead. Still, his friendly blue eyes and the smile that spread precisely from the edges of his mouth inspired in me both awe and trust. Already, the white of age and wisdom graced his face, but his head was not bent over by the burden of his years. The more I gazed on him, the more my depression dissipated.

"What were you depressed about?" he asked in a soft warm voice, his manner filled with compassion. When I told him the reason for my somberness, he exclaimed, "For the sake of the Almighty! I would never have thought that someone from your family, and especially you, my dear Samson, would fall prey to despair at such a moment. Many of your forebears have cast a light than can guide you on your way also, and whose support will be yours too. Look around you in your generation, and select a model for yourself, the person who is most faithful to his heritage."

I sighed and said, "Is their lot better than mine? And how will I recognize them and choose among them?"

"Come, let us see," said the old man, and together we floated to the peak of a hill. "Do you see how they live here?" he continued. "Everyone has his support. You see the old ones resting there; they seem to be sleeping, with their walking-sticks quietly in front of them. Theirs is a good sturdy support, one you can put your weight on, that can guide you. But it's sitting there unused, covered with hundreds of years of dust, and you can barely recognize it.

"Now look over there at those light-headed youngsters dancing about so giddily. Each of them also has a stick, but theirs are just thin rods, mere playthings. When they left their homes, these old men gave each of them one of these sturdy canes, but the arrogant youngsters scorned the sticks so that they could dash away with fast free steps. They thought the old men's sticks were just useless heavy encumbrances. 'Come, let's get rid of all that useless dust and weight,' they said, trying to prance lightly and joyfully. Look at their sticks now; they might be pretty, but what use are they to them? When they came to the first obstacle and tried to lean on their sticks, the flimsy things broke in their hands, and they stumbled and fell, those frivolous people.

"Do you see?" he continued. "They are the majority. However, look closely and you will see a third group, who stride boldly with their sticks. Their radiant faces reflect the joy in their hearts and they face their exalted task with calm confidence. They fear no harm. When they were first given their sticks, they set about removing the layers of dust with great care. Now they have uncovered an old luster that they can take pride in, and they have sticks that give them real support in life.

"And you? Do you understand what this stick is, my Samson? Have you made your choice?"

"My choice is firm," I replied. "But I don't really know the nature of this stick." I blushed.

"Then you may examine it for yourself," he said, handing me one of the sticks. When I grasped it, my heart pounding fiercely, it unfolded in my hand and became a *Sefer Torah*.

"Take it," he said, "and it will guide you throughout your life. In the midst of life itself, the Torah will reveal its power to you. And if you ever know someone who desires to take the same step you are taking, you can offer him this support also."[2]

Yeshivas in Germany

WHEN SAMSON HIRSCH ARRIVED IN MANNHEIM, THE YESHIVA THERE was one of the few in Germany.[3] Until the end of the 18th century there were yeshivas in almost every city in which Jews dwelled, including Prague, Fürth, Frankfurt am Main, Mainz, Worms, Mannheim, Karlsruhe, Berlin, Breslau, Frankfurt on Oder, Halberstadt and in many smaller cities and towns. Lasting damage to the German yeshivas was inflicted by the aftershocks of the French Revolution and the initial period of emancipation. The inroads of Reform contributed further to the precipitous decline in the number of young men interested in learning Torah. David Friedlaender, a close disciple of Mendelssohn and leading proponent of Reform, predicted in 1799, in a letter to his friend Meir Eiger, that in 20 years there would not be even one yeshiva left in Germany. He was not far off the mark.[4]

One of the few outstanding rabbis of the "old school," who was still active in Germany in the third decade of the 19th century, was Frankfurt-born Rabbi Avraham Bing (1752-1841). Rabbi Bing studied under Rabbi Nosson Adler and Rabbi Pinchas Horovitz, together with the *Chasam Sofer* who was 12 years his junior, and with whom he maintained a lifelong friendship. Rabbi Bing was appointed *Klausrabbiner* of Offenbach in 1769 when he was but 17 years old, and after nine years he returned to

Frankfurt where he served as *dayan* and as an instructor in the yeshiva. In 1796, he was appointed District Rabbi of Würzburg. There he stayed, until he retired in 1839 due to the infirmities of old age.

Rabbi Bing had over 100 communities under his jurisdiction, and the yeshiva which he headed in Würzburg was one of the most prominent centers of Torah learning in Germany. Most of the major rabbinical leaders of Germany of the next generation were his disciples, including: Rabbi Isaac Bernays, Rabbi Yaakov Ettlinger, Rabbi Nosson Adler, Chief Rabbi of Hanover and England, and Rabbi Yitzchak Dov Bamberger, who succeeded him as District Rabbi of Würzburg. Rabbi Abraham Rice of Baltimore, one of the first rabbis in the United States who could make any claim to Torah scholarship, was also a pupil of his.

Most of the many manuscripts he left behind at his passing were lost with the passage of time, and only *Zechor LeAvraham* — glosses on *Shulchan Aruch, Orach Chaim* — was published.[5]

Rabbi Yaakov Ettlinger

RABBI YAAKOV ETTLINGER, THE GREATEST HALACHIC AND TALMUDIC authority in Germany in the middle of the 19th century, was born on 29 *Adar* I, 5558 (1798), in Karlsruhe, the capital of the Grand Duchy of Baden in southwest Germany, to Rabbi Aaron Ettlinger, the local *klausrabbiner*.[6] In his youth he studied with the local rabbi, Rabbi Asher Wallerstein (1754-1837), son of the *Shaagas Aryeh*, Rabbi Aryeh Loeb of Metz. Rabbi Ettlinger attributed to Rabbi Wallerstein the most powerful influence on his way of learning. At the age of 18, he went to Würzburg where he studied in the yeshiva of Rabbi Avraham Bing, from whom he received ordination.[b]

Rabbi Ettlinger also studied philosophy at the University of Würzburg. Together with Rabbi Bernays, he was one of the first of several generations of strictly Orthodox rabbis in Germany who possessed university training.[7] He left Würzburg abruptly as a result of the Hep! Hep! riots of 1819, and went to learn under Rabbi Wolf Hamburg of Fürth. Later he returned to Würzburg.

In 1825, Rabbi Ettlinger was appointed *Klausrabbiner* of Mannheim, a city in his home state of Baden with a Jewish population of approximately 1,500.[8] Two years later, he was also appointed District Rabbi of

b. Through his teachers, Rabbi Hirsch was connected to Frankfurt long before he served there as rabbi. Both Chacham Bernays and Rabbi Ettlinger were disciples of Rabbi Bing, a Frankfurt native and disciple of two great Frankfurt masters, Rabbi Pinchas Horovitz and Rabbi Nosson Adler. Thus, the halachic exposition which the young Rabbi of Oldenburg sent at the age of 22 to Rabbi Bing, the elder statesman of German *rabbonim*, was in reality a letter to his teacher's teacher.[6*]

Ladenburg. During his tenure in Mannheim he headed a flourishing yeshiva — one of the last in Germany — with over 70 *talmidim* from all parts of the country. He was, in the words of his biographer, "possessed of great personal charm and warmth, keen social consciousness and a strong sense of communal responsibility." He was also a talented orator.[9]

Rabbi Yaakov Ettlinger

Rabbi Ettlinger served in Mannheim until 1836, when, upon the death of the incumbent Rabbi Akiva Wertheimer, he was appointed Chief Rabbi of Altona, a community of 2,500 members.[10] As Chief Rabbi of Altona, Rabbi Ettlinger's responsibilities also included the rabbinate of nearby Wandsbeck and the principalities of Schlesweig and Holstein. The rabbinical court in Altona over which he presided was the last of its kind in Western Europe to enjoy official government recognition, and its decisions in monetary matters had the binding power of a civil court and were enforced by the police until 1863. Rabbi Yaakov Ettlinger served as Rabbi of Altona until his death in 1871.

The community of Altona was unusual in that none of the *minhagim* and practices of the *Kehillah* were changed under pressure of the Reformers, and the Jewish community remained loyal to traditional Judaism, even though there were quite a few members who were personally non-observant. This was due, no doubt, to the power of the Rav's personality. Rabbi Shlomo Eiger, son of Rabbi Akiva Eiger of Posen, relates that he was greatly impressed by the spirit of the *davening* in the *shul* in Altona — "word for word, and at a much slower pace than all the *shuls* in Poland."[11]

When Reb Yokev, as he was affectionately known throughout Germany, moved from Mannheim to Altona, the yeshiva he headed moved with him. One of his first students in Altona was Rabbi Ezriel Hildesheimer. Thus, the two foremost leaders of Torah Judaism in 19th-century Germany, Rabbi Hirsch and Rabbi Hildesheimer, were his disciples. Among the other distinguished alumni of Rabbi Ettlinger's yeshiva were Rabbi Zvi Binyamin Auerbach, Rabbi of Darmstadt and Halberstadt and author of *Nachal Eshkol*, and Rabbi Gershon Josaphat, Rabbi Hirsch's

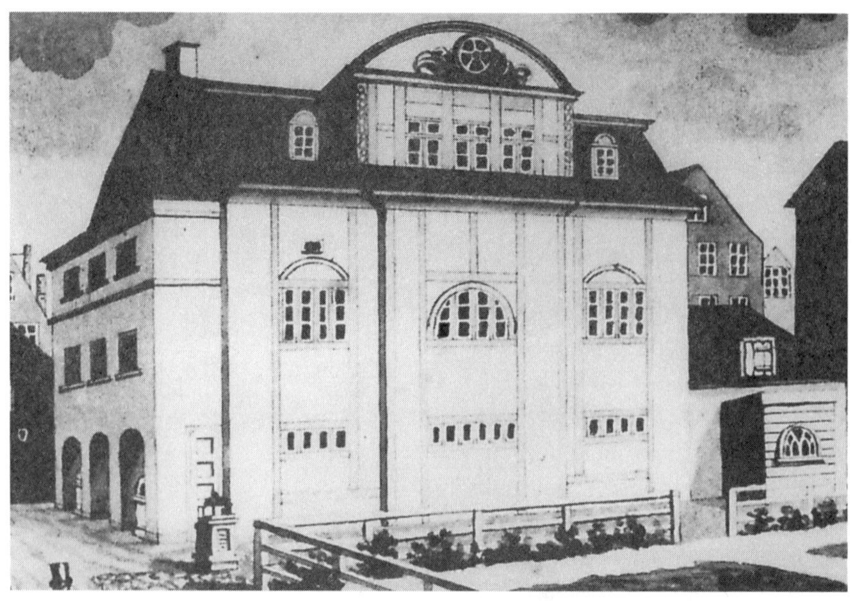

Great Synagogue of Altona where Rabbi Yaakov Ettlinger prayed

roommate and *chavrusa* in yeshiva, who became *Dayan* and *Klausrabbiner* in Halberstadt. During Rabbi Ettlinger's first 20 years in Altona, the yeshiva was a vigorous institution; it subsequently dissolved for reasons which are unclear.

Rabbi Ettlinger's work, *Aruch LaNer,* on various tractates of the Talmud is a standard text in the yeshiva world. He began to write the *Aruch LaNer* on *Sanhedrin* (Warsaw, 1874), when he was only 23 years old. Though he largely completed the work by the age of 26, he did not publish it in his youth, and continued to add to it and amend it during his lifetime. The *Aruch LaNer* on *Yevamos* (Altona, 1850), one of the most important works on that difficult tractate, was written before he was 30, but published only 20 years later. His *Bikkurei Yaakov* (Altona, 1836), perhaps the most significant work of the last three centuries on the laws of *Lulav* and *Succah,* was written while he was still in his early 30s.[12] So although Rabbi Ettlinger was only 30 years old when Rabbi Hirsch studied under him in Mannheim, he was already a world-class Talmudic authority.[13] In addition to his erudition in Talmud and *halachah,* Reb Yokev Ettlinger was unusually proficient in *Kabbalah.*

In 1845, Rabbi Ettlinger commenced the publication of the first of two journals, a weekly in German called *Der Treue Zionswächter,* which dealt with public affairs and served in the forefront of the battle against the Reform. The following year he began publishing a biweekly in Hebrew called *Shomer Zion HaNe'eman*, which was basically a rabbinic journal, with Talmudic research, responsa and belle lettres in Hebrew. The former continued publication, with a brief cessation, until 1854; the latter, until 1856.[14]

Rabbi Yaakov Ettlinger

Reb Yokev Ettlinger was, without question, the foremost Talmudic scholar of his time in Germany, and he was regarded as such during his lifetime. He passed away in Altona on 25 *Kislev*, 5632 (December 7, 1871).

Rabbi Hirsch studied in Mannheim for a year and a quarter,[15] and received *semichah* from Rabbi Ettlinger.[16] In Mannheim, Hirsch's contemporaries were impressed by his wisdom, humility, his ability to make do with little and the profundity of his ideas.[17] Even after he left the yeshiva, he maintained contact with his *rebbe* and referred halachic questions to him.[18]

Bonn

ON OCTOBER 26, 1829, RABBI HIRSCH ENTERED THE UNIVERSITY OF Bonn where he remained for a little more than half a year.[19] Like his teachers, Rabbi Bernays and Rabbi Ettlinger, he never received any degree. Those who called him Dr. Hirsch did so in error.[c]

Less than two months after entering the university, he established a speaking society for the Jewish students, which met every *Motzaei Shabbos* and in which the members could hone their rhetorical abilities. Rabbi Hirsch's first public address, as a 21-year-old student, already evinces some of the hallmarks for which he was renowned in his later years, including his readiness to stand alone in the face of abuse and

c. Rabbi Hirsch once related that when he came to Oldenburg a government official addressed him as Dr. Hirsch. He replied that he had no doctorate, and each time the official called him Doctor, Rabbi Hirsch again reminded that he was not a doctor. The official asked in amazement, "You're really not a doctor?"

"Truly not, your excellency."

"Well then, I am blessed that I have to do with someone who doesn't have this degree. These days it's so rare to find someone who isn't a doctor. You can imagine my previous discomfort and the pleasant surprise now."[19*]

ridicule in the service of authentic Judaism.[20]

In Bonn he did not neglect his Torah study. Abraham Geiger, later one of the leading lights of Reform, recorded that the two studied Tractate *Zevachim* together in Bonn. He added, "I learned to recognize and respect his exceptional powers of expression, his penetrating intelligence, and his quick and clear grasp of things. . . . I esteemed his generous character, his strictly ethical behavior, and I loved the goodness of his heart."[d,21]

In March 1830, less than six months after he entered university, Rabbi Hirsch was recommended for the post of Chief Rabbi of the Grand Duchy of Oldenburg. He was only 21.

d. The religious differences which would divide them were already apparent, Geiger wrote. Not long after he left Bonn, Geiger became one of the most radical leaders of the Reform Movement.

Part Three

THE RABBINATE

Chapter Five
OLDENBURG

GERMANY, IN THE FIRST HALF OF THE 19TH CENTURY, was comprised of a number of independent duchies and principalities each with its own duke or governor, and joined together in very loose confederation. One such principality, located in Lower Saxony in northern Germany, was the Grand Duchy of Oldenburg, named after its capital city. In addition to the town of Oldenburg itself, there were nine or ten other communities, totaling about 700 Jews, under the jurisdiction of the *Landrabbiner*. Although Jews had lived in Oldenburg since the early 14th century, the local Jewish community was very small. By the third decade of the 19th century, there were only 15 Jewish families in the town of Oldenburg itself. Rabbi Adler, the immediate predecessor of Rabbi Hirsch, was forced to impose fines in order to assure the presence of a *minyan* in *shul*.[1]

In 1827, the government of Oldenburg organized Jewish communal affairs, made German names and language compulsory, and created the position of Chief Rabbi whose appointment was contingent on the

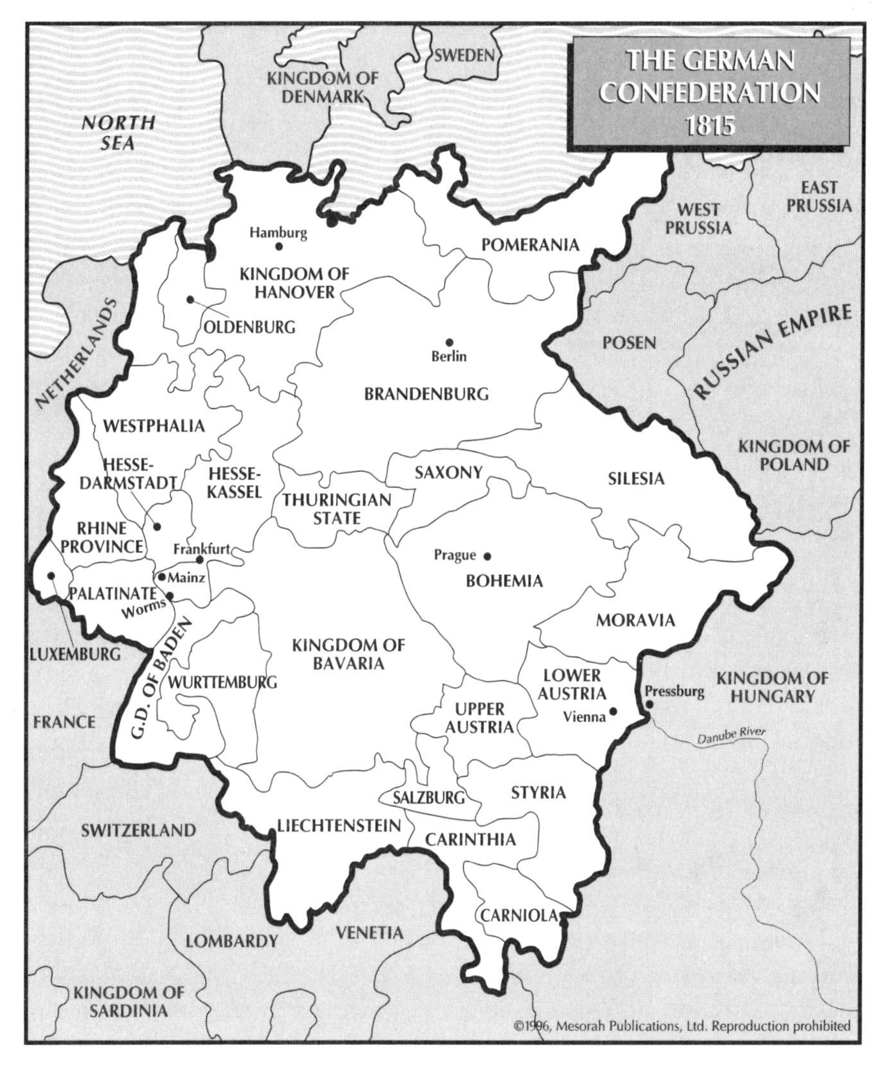

approval of the Grand Duke. The first to fill this position was Rabbi Nathan Adler (1803-1890). A great-nephew of Rabbi Nosson Adler of Frankfurt, principal teacher of the *Chasam Sofer*, Rabbi Adler served as Chief Rabbi from 1829 to 1830.[a]

When Rabbi Adler was selected for the position of Chief Rabbi of the neighboring state of Hanover in 1830, he wrote to the Duke of

a. From 1830 to 1844, Rabbi Adler served as Chief Rabbi of the Kingdom of Hanover. From 1844 until his death, Rabbi Adler served as Chief Rabbi of Great Britain. He authored *Nesinah LeGeir* (Vilna, 1875), a commentary on *Targum Onkelos*. (In an 1878 letter to his son-in-law Michael Levy of London, Rabbi Hirsch requested him to ask Rabbi Adler if he knew of an explanation why *Onkelos* always translates זרע as בר זרעיה.)

Artist's rendering of Rabbi Hirsch in Oldenburg

Oldenburg recommending that young Rabbi Samson Hirsch be appointed his successor.[2] The government of Oldenburg also consulted with and received a warm testimonial from the well-known Orthodox Jewish financier Baron Amschel Rothschild of Frankfurt,[b] who had become acquainted with Rabbi Hirsch when the latter visited him in 1828, on his journey from Hamburg to Mannheim.[3]

On July 8, Rabbi Hirsch went to Oldenburg to be interviewed for the position by Rabbi Adler and by a representative of the Grand Duke. According to a transcript which has recently been published, the interview was a very thorough examination of the young man's views on the fundamentals of Judaism, Revelation at Sinai, *Tanach*, and the commandment of "walking in His ways."[4]

Rabbi Hirsch arrived in Oldenburg on 26 *Elul*, 5590 (September 14, 1830), and was officially installed on 4 *Tishrei*, 5591 (September 21), at the age of 22.[5]

Rural Jewish Life

THE JEWISH POPULATION OF THE GRAND DUCHY OF OLDENBURG, like that of many similar principalities, was made up primarily of those living in small villages. The village Jews of Germany were, for the most part, extremely scrupulous in their performance of *mitzvos* and *minhagim*, without seeking leniencies or compromises. On Shabbos and festivals, the villages took on a special atmosphere of holiness, and public fast days were observed with great earnestness as days for self-examination and repentance. Straightforward and unpretentious by nature, the villagers revered Torah scholars. Rarely did the Reform Movement make much of an impression on them.[6]

---

b. The House of Rothschild made it a policy to back the candidacies of Orthodox nominees for the rabbinate in places where there was a danger of Reform influence.[2*]

A letter written by Rabbi Hirsch in 1838, during his tenure in Oldenburg, offers valuable insights into Jewish village life in that period:

> Concerning religious life in our area, in which you have expressed an interest, there is little exceptional about it, and what is exceptional is not the sort of thing to make one happy. I am referring in particular to the appalling dispersal in which the Jews of northern Germany live. Throughout the region of the Elbe and Moser Rivers, Jews live in scattered tiny villages, most of them with no more than five or ten Jewish homes, and some with as few as two families. Except for the large cities like Hamburg and Altona, there is no community of more than 20 families. . . .
>
> On the other hand, this situation has its positive, and even uplifting, aspects. In spite of the miserable dispersion, the spark of Jewishness is fresh and flourishing in every one of our brethren's homes. Judaism has a particular tenacity in alien conditions, and thus our compatriots preserve their uniqueness, and, in spite of their worries over livelihood, sacrifice themselves to provide a Jewish atmosphere and education for their children and grandchildren. Everything required for a life of Torah, both for adults and children, is available here. When we see this amazing sight we feel only humility before the Divine Presence that dwells within Israel. It gladdens us to reflect that even in such a bitter exile we are still worthy of the title, "the Holy People."[7]

As a result of the small number of congregants, Rabbi Hirsch's rabbinic duties in Oldenburg were relatively light, and he was largely free to throw himself into his studies day and night. He began every day at four with a two-hour *seder* in *Gemara* and *Shulchan Aruch*. Most of his day and a good part of the night were spent learning, and, perhaps, as a result, he suffered attacks of extreme fatigue during which he was so weak that he could not even take anything in his hands.[8] According to Heinrich Graetz, who lived in his home for three years, Rabbi Hirsch was "incapable of anything except learning from his large tomes of the *poskim*."[c,9]

In the course of his 11 years in Oldenburg, Rabbi Hirsch acquired a broad mastery of the Talmud, *Shulchan Aruch, Midrash,* and *Zohar,* as well

c. Elsewhere Graetz wrote: "ואין איש אתו אשר ידבר על אודות לבבו ועל אודות התורה אשר יהגה בה יומם ולילה כלמדן פולני בלי דעת את צאת ואת מבוא העם! — He has no one with him to whom he can speak his innermost thoughts and regarding the Torah in which he toils day and night like a Polish *lamdan* without knowing the ways of the people." Although his diary was in German, Graetz had the curious habit of writing in Hebrew whenever he thought the subject was sensitive.[9*]

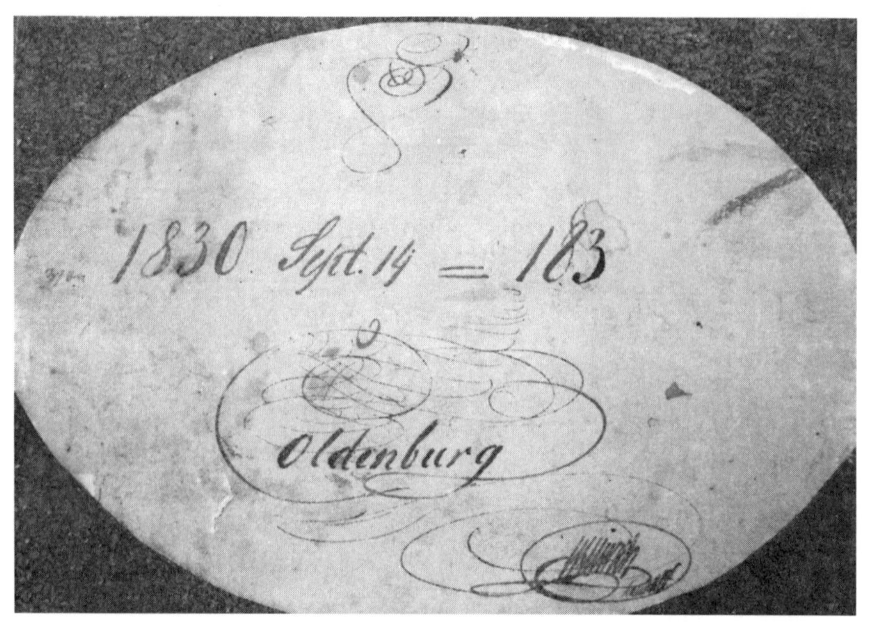

Cover page of Rabbi Hirsch's journal, when he was Landrabbiner in Oldenburg

as a phenomenal command of *Tanach*, as is evident from the notebooks he compiled during this period. Already in his first year in Oldenburg, he carried on a halachic correspondence with Rabbi Avraham Bing, the venerable dean of the German rabbinate, requesting him to induce a husband to either reunite with his wife or to grant her a *get*.[10]

One of the areas in which Rabbi Hirsch expended great effort was in developing schools in the outlying communities and teaching in the local school. In order to furnish instructional materials, he translated entire chapters of the *Mishnah* into German and copied them in adequate quantities for the use of teachers in the outlying communities. All of this he did himself, by hand.[11] Rabbi Hirsch was forced to continually beg the government to help strengthen the Jewish schools and institutions — requests which were often denied. He made periodic visits to all the Oldenburg communities and prepared detailed reports about their institutions, especially the schools. Some of the schools had as few as five children, and his reports frequently discussed each child in detail.[12]

The Oldenburg Jewish community was very poor. Almost from the beginning, Rabbi Hirsch had difficulty obtaining his salary, which was funded by a special Jew Tax, or *Schutzgeld* (protection money). The *Schutzgeld* was also the sole source of funding for various communal institutions. The Oldenburg authorities did not give Rabbi Hirsch their

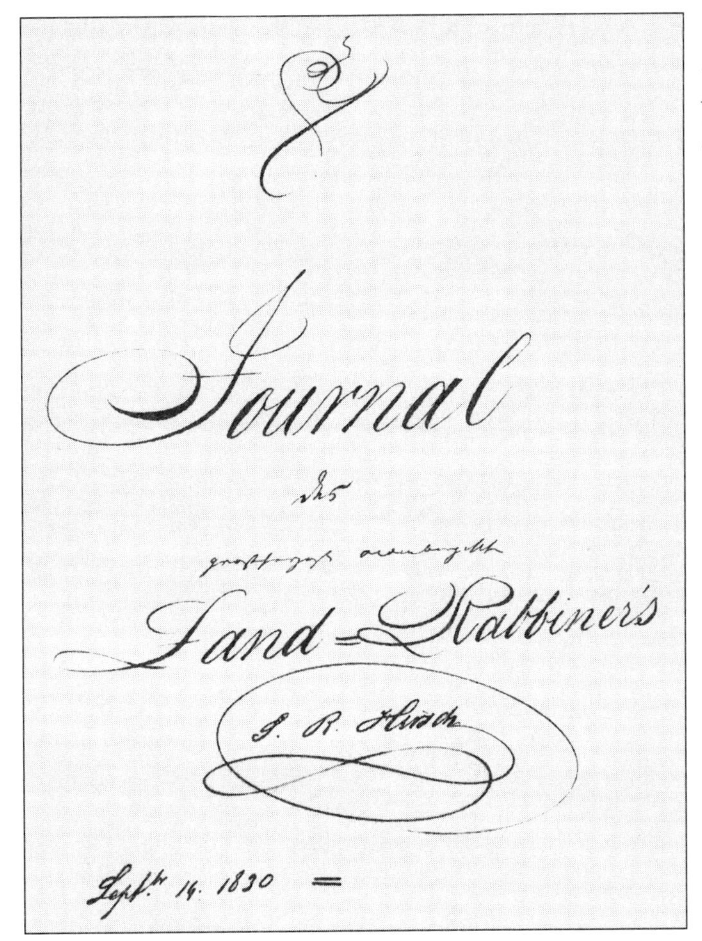

Journal

des

Land-Rabbiners

S. R. Hirsch

Septbr. 14. 1830 =

Title page of Rabbi Hirsch's journal as Landrabbiner of Oldenburg

full backing, never raised his salary in spite of his growing family, and added nothing to the funds of the Jew Tax.

As a consequence he lived in poverty and found it very difficult to support his large family.[d] When he wrote to the government that, as a public servant, they should ensure that his salary was paid regularly, they responded brusquely that as far as they were concerned they could do without the whole institution of *Landrabbiner*, and that he was free to leave should he so desire. The officials added that their goal of bringing Jews closer to Christians and diverting them from their peculiar manners would be better fulfilled without a *Landrabbiner*, especially if he was, like

d. Rabbi Adler had been spared similar difficulty and embarrassment during his tenure because the treasurer of the community was a wealthy congregant, who made up any shortfall in the rabbi's salary from his own pocket. That fine gentleman passed away prior to Rabbi Hirsch's arrival.

the present incumbent, a strong adherent of his faith. They added that he was free to write to the Grand Duke himself. In response to the Duke's questions, which were prompted by Rabbi Hirsch's letter to him, the government replied with a not inconsiderable degree of hostility. In 1834, Rabbi Hirsch experienced further financial difficulties due to the parsimoniousness of the officers of the *Kehillah*, but by that time the government's attitude had improved somewhat.[13]

Marriage

ON OCTOBER 5, 1831, RABBI HIRSCH MARRIED HANNAH JÜDEL (B. March 1805), the only daughter of Marcus (Mordechai) Jüdel, a banker in Braunschweig, Germany. His father-in-law was an honest and straightforward man, scrupulous in the performance of *mitzvos*, and noted for his kindness and generosity to people from all walks of life. Hannah (Johanna) Jüdel inherited many of her father's qualities, and by the age of 15 her exemplary personality had already earned her the nickname, "the Rebbetzin." As her future husband was later to say, in those days such a title was hardly a compliment.

Nonetheless, the name was not inappropriate, for she was a modest and retiring woman who throughout her long marriage never grew discouraged even in the darkest of times. Her husband said of her, "She was convinced that in the end the truth would emerge victorious in its war with falsehood, and so she accompanied me for over 50 years, wherever our path led, and bore everything together with me. All the stones that were cast at me, all the filth that was actually slung or threatened, all that she bore also." He recalled that in the early years of his public life she would greet him when he returned home as follows, "Have the newspapers been attacking you again? Good! I'll enjoy reading your rejoinder." Rabbi Hirsch once described his family life in the following terms:

> If a man cannot bring into his home the same spirit that he propounds in the outside world, then his work is worthless. If he does not conduct his home life with the same dedication to truth, fear of Heaven, and belief for which he fights and pours out his heart-blood outside the home, then his efforts are in vain. He would be better setting down his torch if he cannot open his home to the world and say, "Here, look and see if there is any contradiction with what I preach in the world." And if it was the case that our home reflected this same earnestness, it was her doing.[14]

While in Oldenburg, Rabbi Hirsch wrote to Rabbi Akiva Eiger of Posen, and the latter apparently proposed him for a rabbinical position.

The community accepted Rabbi Eiger's suggestion, but for some reason nothing ever came of the offer.[15] In 1838, Rabbi Hirsch was offered the rabbinical chair of Amsterdam, but nothing came of that either.[16]

Reform Ascendant

WHILE THE YOUNG CHIEF RABBI OF OLDENBURG SAT IMMERSED IN Torah study, around him the Reform Movement continued to wreak its devastation. The efforts of the Orthodox leadership to stem the tide were largely in vain. In the rapidly changing times, there was an enormous gap between the older and younger generation, and the chasm was so deep that the older rabbis simply had no idea how to reach the hearts and minds of the younger generation.[17] The older rabbis recognized from the outset the dangers of modern trends and ideologies, yet their attempts to warn their younger compatriots fell on increasingly hostile and scornful ears. Dr. Isaac Breuer summed up the situation:

> Over the years, most of that generation was lost. . . . [The Reformers] found a powerful ally in the government, whose concern was to further the cause of social emancipation. . . . In all the large cities of Germany they succeeded in having the *mikvaos* filled in, the schools and *yeshivas* closed, and the production of kosher food shut down. . . . Men who lacked only a few drops of water to make them complete Christians were appointed as leaders of the "communities." . . . Those who remained Orthodox were seen as living in darkness, and it was considered a great *mitzvah* to "enlighten" them.[18]

The Reformers acted in high-handed fashion in many communities, often using the authorities and even the police to enforce their version of Judaism, often in defiance of an Orthodox majority. They considered rabbinic Judaism to be a sickness which must be cured, even against the express wishes of the "patient" if necessary. Writing 20 years later, Rabbi Hirsch described their attitude:

> These "progressives" declared that they considered it their mission to save their ignorant, foolish communities and to make them happy, enlightened, cultured and civilized, even against their will. They persuaded the authorities that the state should therefore appoint them as guardians of those poor, old weak-minded communities, with their unfortunate senile habits and attitudes.

> And so we have lived to see rabbis and boards of trustees, armed with government edicts, with help from the police and with the authority to deprive their fellow Jews of the right to work, who manipulated synagogues, worship and all the sacred institutions of the Jewish community like so many different puppets delivered into their hands. . . . We have lived to see how, in the face of this despotism, the time-honored prayers and the ancient hopes expressed in them were silenced, how new liturgies were introduced, synagogues were closed, and Torah scrolls were carried off. We have lived to see how the Torah-true members of the community had to take refuge in cellars, in the woods and even abroad in order to be able to worship in accordance with Torah law. We have lived to see how, in the face of this despotism, the traditional schools and their time-honored modes of teaching were silenced, how schoolchildren were forced to flee to attics and barns with their Torah textbooks, weeping as they watched their Torah teachers being driven out of the city. We have seen how this despotism pursued the Torah into the houses of worship and convinced the police to forbid Jews to gather on the Sabbath for readings from the lessons of the Prophets. We have seen how the manipulators of these despotic powers pushed for the repeal of concessions made by the government to help Jewish businessmen observe the Sabbath. We have seen how they. . . enforced the registration of non-Jews as Jews in the records of the Jewish community.[19]

Enlightened society, the Reformers felt, must ensure freedom of conscience to all beliefs, with the exception of "ancient superstitions" which deserved, in their view, no such tolerance. The contradiction between their demands for acceptance of their views on the part of Jew and non-Jews alike and their vehement denunciation of Orthodox Judaism was clear. "Liberal Judaism," writes Professor Mordechai Breuer, "was always liberal only to its friends."[20] Rabbi Hirsch put it in his inimitable fashion:

> How is it that people who have that educated character which . . . enables the most diverse persons to meet each other without objection and discord . . . are totally blind towards the most common rules of behavior when this social obligation is to be practiced towards ancient Judaism and its adherents?

If in their presence the Catholic kisses the image of his saint, the Armenian counts his prayer beads, the Turk turns towards the Kaaba, and even if the Huron worships the fetish, they will respectfully and tactfully remain silent to what seems to them incomprehensible, even repugnant. They will accord respectful tolerance and will be wary not to hurt the religious feelings of any person by derision and scorn of his religious and sacred objects. More, they will even overdo that consideration by joining in at the practice of what is strange and meaningless to them, only to avoid giving offense and to dispel the slightest appearance of a denigration.

But let one of their old Jewish brothers acknowledge the eternal, world redeeming Word of the One and Only God, let him in their presence kiss the *mezuzah,* let him in their presence consecrate head and hand and heart with the *tefillin* straps, let him in their presence turn towards Jerusalem in prayer, let him in their presence fulfill any of their, as well as his, duties of their ancestral religion, then our "modern" Jewish brothers will purposely show their non-involvement. They will take pride in . . . no longer practicing and knowing the sacred customs of their fathers, and in 99 out of 100 cases it will not end without a jeering insult.

Tolerance will be expected everywhere. They will practice tolerance towards every man of every color and faith; they will also demand tolerance in their own circle towards their desertion from the ancestral Judaism. Woe to the elderly Jew who permits himself more than a quiet sigh! . . . They praise themselves as the first born son of the "era of tolerance," yet they still blindly, fanatically practice the meanest, most insensitive intolerance towards their own brothers who conscientiously and faithfully continue to acknowledge and practice as duty, and to revere as a high and holy treasure, what their fathers recognized and practiced and what inspired their fathers in life and death.[21]

A telling example of the means employed by the Reformers was their conduct in Fürth in 1830. The yeshiva of Rabbi Wolf Hamburg (1770-1850) in Fürth was then one of the few remaining in Germany. Like Rabbi Bing in Würzburg, Rabbi Hamburg counted among his students many of the future rabbinic leaders of Germany, including Rabbi Yaakov Ettlinger, Rabbi S.B. Bamberger and Rabbi Avraham Sutro.[22]

In 1830, the Reformers gained control of the community and had Rabbi Hamburg removed from all his posts (he was also *chazzan* and *mohel*), except for his position as head of the *klaus*, to which he had legal rights as a descendant of one of the founders. That same year his yeshiva was closed at the instigation of the Reformers, who had the police forcibly expel his 100 students from Fürth. Rabbi Hamburg, too, was ultimately driven from the city. His torment can be felt in the anguished appeal he penned in 1830:

> Every day we must mourn afresh the lowly state of our people. How insolently have they laid waste what is holy, the brazen ones that destroy and corrupt everything. They wanted to drive me out of the *Beis HaMedrash* and expel the students, those beloved and sincere souls who study the Torah and commandments of the Almighty, until not one remained. Finally only two students were left and these they attacked until one was in great danger, at death's very door, and I had no one left to copy letters concerning legal decisions. . . . Not since the day the *Beis HaMikdash* was destroyed has such wickedness and such vituperation been perpetrated among us.[23]

Abraham Geiger

NO ONE BETTER TYPIFIES SOME OF THE MAJOR INTELLECTUAL TRENDS within the Reform Movement of Rabbi Hirsch's day than his erstwhile friend and fellow student in Bonn, Abraham Geiger (1810-1874). Geiger was one the "Founding Fathers" of the Reform Movement as we know it today, and in his time was considered the first among his peers. His declared intent was to rid Jewish life of all "obsolete, temporary forms."[24] A brief account of the man and his views can serve as a paradigm of the Reform Movement as a whole, and will help us to gain an understanding of the forces in Jewish life with which Rabbi Hirsch had to contend.

Born in Frankfurt to an old established family, Geiger's maternal grandfather was Rabbi Lazer Wallau, a close disciple of Rabbi Nosson Adler of Frankfurt and later a *dayan* on the Frankfurt *Beis Din*.[25] His principal teacher was his older brother Solomon Geiger (d. 1875), a Torah scholar of no mean standing and author of "*Divrei Kehillos*" on *minhag Frankfurt* (Frankfurt, 1863). As a young man, Geiger studied in Bonn University. His views had not yet changed completely, and although there were already the stirrings of his later impiety, he became friendly with the young Samson Hirsch and was the co-founder with Hirsch of the speaking society. Geiger wrote in his diary that after Hirsch's first speech they had a long debate, "which did not bring us closer since it touched also on religious matters."[26]

Abraham Geiger

Geiger began his reforms already in 1832 when he became rabbi in Wiesbaden, Germany. In 1837, he was chosen to serve as assistant rabbi in Breslau, where his appointment and further activity was a source of acrimony for years. Geiger was one of the initiators of the *Jüdisch-Theologisches Seminar* of Breslau, which nevertheless refused to hire him because he was too radical. In 1863, he was appointed rabbi of the Reform community in Frankfurt, and from 1870 until his death he was rabbi in Berlin.

In a March 18, 1845 letter to Leopold Zunz, Geiger described *bris milah* as a "barbaric act of bloodletting." Elsewhere he wrote: "The Talmud must go; the Bible, that collection of mostly so beautiful and exalted — perhaps the most exalted of *human* books — as a Divine work must also go."[27]

He declared his opposition to prayer in Hebrew, since the worshipers could not understand what they were saying. In a prayerbook he published in 1854, he omitted any mention of the return to Zion, and although he retained some of the Hebrew, he changed the translation to suit his fancy; for example, rendering *mechayeh hameisim* as "the source of eternal life."[28] His attitude toward the Holy Land was consistent with his disbelief in any future redemption: "Jerusalem is for us an entirely indifferent city. It is nothing more than a veritable ruin — a decayed knight's castle."

Geiger was a firm believer in emancipation, albeit only for "enlightened" Jews. He harbored such a deep hatred for "Talmud Jews" that he seriously suggested that Jews who still abided by its dictates and accepted its authority were not worthy of emancipation.[29] In a letter of November 21, 1837, he wrote that schism would not be such a great misfortune for the Jewish people,[30] and in 1842, he advocated splitting the Jewish communities into two, as the only way to advance the cause of Reform Judaism. The same call was put forth by other Reform leaders at different times. Thus, the later clamoring of Reform leaders for Jewish unity as a reason for opposing secession from Reform-dominated communal structures was more than a little hypocritical.[31] A radical assimilationist, Geiger opposed Jewish solidarity, to the point of even opposing intervention to help the Jews of Damascus during the 1840 blood libel.[32]

As one community after another fell into the hands of the Reformers, the younger generation abandoned the traditions of their fathers *en masse.* Rabbi Ezriel Hildesheimer wrote that in the 1830s and 1840s "at least nine-tenths of the youth belonged . . . to the deprecators of religion, . . . to religious traitors, or, at best, to the indifferent. They were ashamed to display their descent or their Jewish faith. . . ."[33] No one stepped forward to stem the tide until, at the age of 28, Rabbi Hirsch authored a small book that was destined to change the face of Germany Jewry.

Chapter Six

THE NINETEEN LETTERS

IN 1836, THE STILL UNKNOWN 27-YEAR-OLD RABBI OF Oldenburg published a slender volume that electrified the German Jewish world unlike any other book of that era.[a] The enduring influence of *Neunzehn Briefe über Judenthum* (*Nineteen Letters about Judaism*) has seldom been matched before or since. It quickly became the definitive work in Germany on the essence of Judaism, and thousands of young Jews in Western Europe drew guidance and inspiration from it.[1] Rabbi Zalman Spitzer, rabbi in Vienna and son-in-law of the *Chasam Sofer*, writing 50 years after the first appearance of *The Nineteen Letters*, captured well the force with which the work hit its

a. Since his name could have neither added nor detracted from the force of his arguments, Rabbi Hirsch originally published *The Nineteen Letters* anonymously under the pen-name "Ben Uziel." "The truth," he wrote, "will make itself known, no matter who says it." Some were convinced that only Chacham Bernays could have written such a book, but before long it became common knowledge that the author was his student, the young *Landrabbiner* of Oldenburg.

readers: "Anybody who reads *The Nineteen Letters* will find that until now he did not know Judaism as he knows it now, and literally becomes like a new being. . . ."[2]

With *The Nineteen Letters,* Rabbi Hirsch virtually created a new genre of works explaining Judaism in a language other than Hebrew. It was the first work explicitly addressed to the intellectual and spiritual confusion of young Jews who found themselves poised before the rapidly opening doors of gentile society. Though originally written in German, its influence has not been confined to that language, and it has found a ready audience for over 150 years among Jews looking for guidance in the conditions of the modern world. The three Hebrew translations[3] and four English translations to date (the first in 1842)[4] attest to the work's enduring popularity.

The potency of *The Nineteen Letters* was recognized immediately not only by the Orthodox public and those wavering on the borderline, but by the leaders of Reform as well. It marked the beginning of a public counter-offensive against the ascendant Reform Movement. The old German Orthodoxy had until then shown itself helpless before the Reform onslaught — its leaders unable to do battle with their educated opponents, for whom they were no match in sophistication. The significance of *The Nineteen Letters,* written in an elegant High German, was that it signaled to the Reformers that they would no longer have the playing field to themselves in the battle for the minds of Jewish youth intoxicated by Enlightenment and Emancipation.[b] Reform circles were quick to recognize the threat to their growing hegemony posed by Rabbi Hirsch's elegant defense of traditional Judaism, and the liberal Jewish press was filled with a string of articles attacking the work and its author.[c,5]

The Nineteen Letters is written in the form of an exchange of letters between two young men. The first letter is from Binyamin, an idealistic young Jew impressed by the rapid progress in the arts and sciences, to his boyhood friend Naphtali, a young rabbi. The next 18 letters are

b. The founding of the monthly journal *Der Treue Zionswächter* in 1846 by Rabbi Yaakov Ettlinger was another manifestation of resurgent confidence among the Orthodox.[4*]

c. The initial response of the leader of radical Reform and Rabbi Hirsch's erstwhile friend from the University of Bonn, Abraham Geiger, was surprisingly moderate: "And so we would like to extend our hand in friendship . . . to shake the hand of that noble-spirited man, . . . respected and admired, that lofty and powerful personality, who burns with deeply held convictions, that friend who from the moment we gazed into his heart won our respect and friendship, which will never stir from our heart." A subsequent review in Geiger's own journal, however, was filled with a number of personal attacks. Geiger had continued to write to Rabbi Hirsch for several years after their student days together, though Geiger's letters already reflect the unbridgeable chasm.[5*]

Naphtali's response to the challenge presented by Binyamin's first letter. Rabbi Hirsch forcefully presented the doubts of Binyamin's generation:

> To what sort of happiness does Judaism lead its loyal followers? From time immemorial, misery and slavery have been their lot; they have been misunderstood or despised by the other nations; and while the rest of mankind has ascended to the summit of culture, attaining prosperity and fortune, the adherents of Judaism have always remained poor in everything which makes human beings great and noble and which beautifies and dignifies existence.
>
> The Torah law itself forbids every enjoyment; it is a hindrance to all the pleasures of life. Moreover, for two thousand years we have been tossed around by others, like a plaything, a bouncing ball; and we are, even at this time, banished from all the paths of happiness. . . .
>
> Every one of us is doomed by his very birth to form an additional link in this chain of misery. The Torah is chiefly at fault in all this. By its very laws that ensure our isolation in life, it arouses, at the very least, suspicion and hostile distrust. . . .
>
> And what is [the Talmud's] effect upon one's heart and life? The heart becomes exclusively absorbed in anxious scruples about insignificant trifles. Nothing is taught except to fear G-d. Everything, down to the smallest, pettiest details of life, is referred directly to G-d. Life becomes a continuous monastic service, nothing but prayers and ceremonies. . . .
>
> Where is there a single word concerning our duties toward the active, busy life around us? Why, it is quite impossible to keep these laws, intended for an entirely different age. . . .[6]

Naphtali began his response by asking Binyamin to consider a yardstick other than subjectively defined happiness and self-perfection to determine the purpose for which man was created. He invited Binyamin to read the Torah as a guide to "what we are and what we should be during our earthly existence." "Let us place ourselves within Judaism," he urged Binyamin, "and ask ourselves: What kind of people are they who accept this book as the G-d-given basis and way of life?" The intent of the whole system, he wrote his friend, was to provide instruction on living, and only when Binyamin understood that instruction on its own terms would he be in a position to cast stones upon it.[7]

Rabbi Hirsch set out to demonstrate that the Torah provides answers to the questions of a rational and skeptical age.[d] In the process, he addressed a wide range of questions posed by Jewish history and practice: the meaning of human life, the Exodus from Egypt, the formation of the Jewish people in the desert, Jewish history in exile and in redemption, the relationship between Jews and gentiles, classification of *mitzvos*,[e] Emancipation and Reform.

Naphtali rejected out of hand the claim that Judaism was not suited for modern times and had no guidance to provide to the "active, busy" life all around. The very purpose of the Jew, he stressed, was to demonstrate at all times and in all places the Torah's ability to completely dominate the surrounding reality. Though the term *Torah Im Derech Eretz* does not appear in *The Nineteen Letters*, the concept, as developed by Rabbi Hirsch in his later writings, is at the heart of the book's argument. Thus in Letter Seventeen, he characterizes the Jew's task as "the realization of the eternal ideal within the setting of our particular age and through the use of the specific circumstances that it provides."[8]

A Sense of Mission

REMARKABLY, GIVEN THE OVERWHELMING SUCCESS OF *THE NINETEEN Letters*, Rabbi Hirsch had not initially intended to write such a work. He did not view himself as a particularly gifted writer. As Naphtali writes in Letter Nineteen, "My strength does not lie in writing. All my life I have engaged in

d. Some authors, most recent among them Noah Rosenbloom in *Tradition in an Age of Reform* (Jewish Publication Society: Philadelphia, 1976), have attempted to find the sources for the ideas in *The Nineteen Letters* in the works of German thinkers. The honest student of Rabbi Hirsch's works, with a working knowledge of Jewish thought, will find, without great effort, that their origins are all to be found in Torah sources, and are normative Jewish thought, expressed with eloquence and in a modern writing style in a language other than Hebrew. The issue of the influence of German philosophers on Rabbi Hirsch's thought, which has been bandied about in one form or another for the last century, has been disposed of conclusively by Rabbi Joseph Elias in his new, annotated edition of *The Nineteen Letters* (Feldheim Publishers: Monsey, 1995).

e. One of the aspects of *The Nineteen Letters*, about which Rabbi Hirsch's critics both from the right and from the left have made much ado, is its criticism of the *Moreh Nevuchim* of the *Rambam*. Rabbi Joseph Elias, in his new edition of *The Nineteen Letters*, has taken the wind out of the sails of most of these critics by demonstrating convincingly that Rabbi Hirsch was merely reflecting the views of the *Chasid Yaavetz* in his work *Ohr HaChaim*, a book which Rabbi Hirsch was particularly influenced by and which he quotes at length in his *Erste Mitteilungen* (1838). In particular, Rabbi Hirsch was bothered by the fact that many misused the Rambam's view that the ultimate perfection of the individual was to be found in contemplation of the truths of the Torah and in the "acquisition — as far as is possible for man — of the knowledge of G-d, of His providence and of the manner in which he guides His creatures." The danger in such an emphasis was the abandonment of *mitzvos* as the essential fabric of the life of a Jew. In his generation, when the gradual recasting of the essence of Judaism had transformed *mitzvah* observance into optional "ceremonies," the dangers of such an approach were self-evident.[7*]

thinking more than in speaking, and in speaking more than in writing." Only an irresistible sense of mission led him to take up his pen in the cause. "[Although I find it difficult to write,] if I succeed in awakening one of the sleeping here and there, that would suffice for me, and even if I would receive heaps of criticism I wouldn't mind."[9] In Letter Nineteen, Naphtali describes the sense of urgency that led him to respond to Binyamin's initial challenge:

> I see a child enveloped in flames. The bystanders are afraid; they do nothing, or else they are only trying to save the building. I see the child. I rush in. Should I first ask my neighbor whether he, too, sees the child? Should I worry whether, in my haste, I am jostling someone, or perhaps hindering the salvage of the building by running in? Perhaps I am causing a draft, fanning the fire? "But," you might ask, "if it should be too late? If the building were to collapse on top of the child in a roaring conflagration before you reached it?" Were I to be buried under it, I would at least have done my duty![10]

Once he had decided upon his course, however, he was perfectly prepared to stand alone, if need be, in his defense of traditional Judaism:

> Even if thousands will forsake the cause of life and light, if thousands will turn their back on the destiny and name of Yisrael — whose way they abandoned long ago — the cause of truth is not concerned with the number of its adherents. Even if only one remains — one single Jew holding the book of life in his hand, Yisrael's teachings in his heart and Yisrael's radiance in his spirit — that one Jew suffices, and the cause of Yisrael will not be lost.[11]

Baseless insults and denunciation, threats and scorn did not faze him, he wrote to his friend Gershon Josaphat. Once he had decided on the necessity of such a work, only the fear that his decision to enter the fray might cause more damage than good to his cause could have dissuaded him from writing.[12] The title page to *The Nineteen Letters* summed up his attitude succinctly: "It is revealed and known before You, that I have not acted for my own honor, nor for that of my family, but only for *Your Honor,* so that disagreement not increase in Israel."

Nothwithstanding his sense of mission, Rabbi Hirsch felt very much alone in Oldenburg. To Gershon Josaphat he wrote of his desire to find one impartial friend, knowledgeable in Judaism and the times, who was

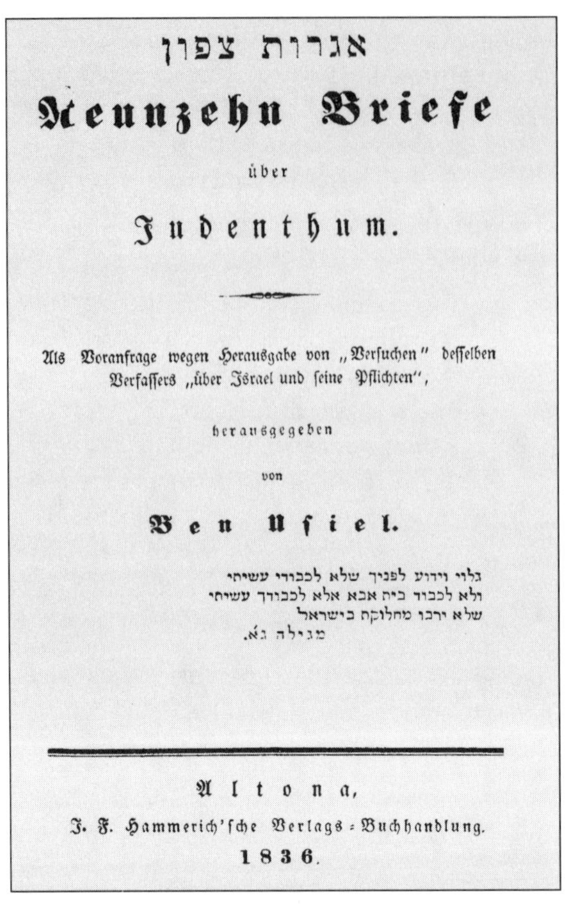

אגרות צפון

Neunzehn Briefe

über

Judenthum.

Als Voranfrage wegen Herausgabe von „Versuchen" desselben Verfassers „über Israel und seine Pflichten",

herausgegeben

von

Ben Usiel.

גלוי וידוע לפניך שלא לכבודי עשיתי
ולא לכבוד בית אבא אלא לכבודך עשיתי
שלא ירבו מחלוקת בישראל
מגילה ג׳ א׳.

Altona,

J. F. Hammerich'sche Verlags-Buchhandlung.

1836.

Title page, The Nineteen Letters

willing to disregard egos and concentrate only on the issues, but, he concluded, "I live in a wilderness."[13] To a relative he confided:

> You complain that you are alone in life but look at me: I am even more alone — totally alone with my books. Everyone has to stay in the place where G-d put him and, like a reliable watchman, make the best of his abilities, however few or many his friends may be. The most important things, in any case, are accomplished, not by man but by G-d, Who causes the sun to rise sooner or later. We, whose hearts have been awakened and whose eyes have been opened, must wait for the sun even in the midst of the moonless and starless night, for the dawn will surely come.[14]

When he wrote of loneliness to his father and expressed the need for a *chavrusa,* the latter replied with a pun on the *Mishnah* (*Avos* 1:6), קנה לך

חבר, *Acquire a friend for yourself.* "Let a pen (קנה) be your friend," his father wrote.[15] And he did. Rarely have private need and public necessity been so in consonance with each other.

Even when the decision to start writing had been taken, *The Nineteen Letters* was far from his thoughts. Initially he sought a publisher for *Horeb: Essays concerning Israel's Duties in Its Dispersion,* which was almost complete by 1835. But in 1835 no Jewish publisher felt there would be a market for a book urging allegiance to traditional Judaism. Rabbi Hirsch was forced to turn to a non-Jewish publisher in Altona, who, being unfamiliar with Jewish books, suggested that the author write a smaller work incorporating his ideas, a prospectus of sorts, in order to test whether there was sufficient public interest.[16] In response, Rabbi Hirsch wrote *The Nineteen Letters.* Thus *The Nineteen Letters,* still considered the most captivating of his works, was written at the suggestion of a gentile.

Even the decision to write in literary German — a decision that had so much to do with Rabbi Hirsch's impact on his generation — was not a foregone conclusion. The decision to abandon the Judeo-German idiom traditionally employed for religious works was not easily taken. Rabbi Hirsch had originally intended to write in that language using Hebrew characters. His father also felt strongly that the proper milieu for a discussion of Judaism was Judeo-German rather than polished High German. Eventually, however, Rabbi Hirsch convinced his father that he could only reach the present generation in contemporary language and style. A work in Judeo-German, he wrote the latter, would be automatically ignored by half of those for whom it was intended, and for the other half it would lose half its impact because of their unfamiliarity with, and distaste for, the language. He added that he felt it imperative to hold those who defamed traditional Judaism to the light of truth in their own language.[17]

As a prospectus, *The Nineteen Letters* was successful on two counts. The huge popular success of the work created an eager market for *Horeb,* which was published the following year. In addition, the short first work proved to be a remarkably complete adumbration of all Rabbi Hirsch's subsequent writings, which are marked by a high degree of cohesion and consistency. It is as if it was all clear in his youth — in one flash of insight. At the age of 27 he had already worked out a system of thought, which over the next 50 years he elaborated upon in greater detail.[18] When *The Nineteen Letters* was republished half a century after its original publication, Rabbi Hirsch made few changes in content; almost all his revisions were stylistic in nature, dictated by linguistic developments in the German language.[19]

An Enduring Influence

FEW WORKS HAVE PROVEN OF SUCH LASTING IMPACT AS *THE Nineteen Letters.* More than a century after its publication, Reb Shraga Feivel Mendlowitz, the first great Torah educator in America, told his students, "I cannot understand how it is possible for an American yeshiva student to be Jewish without *The Nineteen Letters.*"[20] Until the destruction of German Jewry, the work was found in virtually every Orthodox home in Germany, and many German Jews committed long sections to memory.

In 1873, Rabbi Yisrael Salanter met Rabbi Hirsch in Berlin. In the course of the conversation, Reb Yisrael expressed his opinion that the only way to bring the younger generation in Russia back to traditional Judaism was through books written in the Russian language. He bemoaned the fact that those who had remained observant Jews could not write literary Russian, while most of those who had received a general education and knew how to write a polished Russian had already abandoned their traditions. As a result there were almost no qualified writers available. Rabbi Hirsch suggested translating German works aimed at a similar audience. Under the circumstances, he said, it would even be justified to have a non-Jewish translator.

This suggestion pleased Rabbi Salanter enormously, and he asked Rabbi Hirsch to suggest appropriate works. The latter mentioned the writings of Rabbi Salomon Plessner, but Rabbi Naftali Herz Ehrmann, who was present, suggested that the writings of Rabbi Hirsch, in particular *The Nineteen Letters*, would be better suited for this purpose.

On the way back to his quarters, Reb Yisrael asked Rabbi Ehrmann to obtain a copy of *The Nineteen Letters* that very evening and to read it to him so that he could form his own impression of it. The two men read together deep into the night, but, inasmuch as Reb Yisrael was just learning to read German at that time, it took them several weeks to finish the entire work. When they had done so, Reb Yisrael opined that the book should be translated not only into Russian but into Hebrew as well.[21] Later he would remark: "Where is there a *Gan Eden* big enough for Rabbi Hirsch!"[22]

Although Rabbi Salanter did not realize his plan to publish *The Nineteen Letters* in Russia, the work ultimately revolutionized Torah education in Eastern Europe in another way. On *Shabbos Chanukah* of 1915 a young Polish refugee in Vienna went to the *Stumpergasse* synagogue. There she heard the *drashah* of Rabbi Moshe David Flesch (1879-1944), a student of

Rabbi Hirsch's son-in-law and successor, Rabbi Salomon Breuer. Rabbi Flesch often quoted Rabbi Hirsch, and that Shabbos was no exception. The young refugee was electrified by Rabbi Flesch's words, and through him she was introduced to *The Nineteen Letters* and *Horeb.* The young woman was Sarah Schenirer, and she often said in later years that it was these two works that inspired her to found the Bais Yaakov movement.[f]

Horeb

HOREB, THE OTHER CLASSIC WORK THAT RABBI HIRSCH PENNED IN Oldenburg, was published in 1837.[g] Similar in some ways to *Sefer HaChinuch, Horeb* provides a broad description of the commandments, both the duties of the heart and those governing the body. It sets forth a complete system of *taamei hamitzvos,* the lessons to be learned from each *mitzvah,* along with a basic outline of the various laws pertaining to each *mitzvah.*

Each of its 118 chapters begins with verses from the Torah relevant to the *mitzvah* under discussion, followed by a general introduction to the laws pertaining to that *mitzvah* culled from the *Shulchan Aruch* and its expositors. On the basis of the details of each law, Rabbi Hirsch described the lessons to be learned from its performance and the sentiments that it should evoke. No *mitzvah,* Rabbi Hirsch asserted in his introduction, can be conceived apart from the composite laws governing its observance, and thus there can be no incongruity between the explanation given for each *mitzvah* (*taamei hamitzvah*) and any of the fine details of its observance.

At the same time, he emphasized that it is not the rationale of a *mitzvah* that obligates a Jew to observe it but rather the fact that it is the Divine command:

> Even if every Divine precept were a complete riddle to us presenting a thousand unsolved and insoluble problems, the obligatory character of the commandments would not be in the slight-

f. Rabbi Hirsch's thought came as a revelation, Sarah Schenirer often told her students. From the moment she was first exposed to it, she felt an obligation to pass his legacy on to the young girls of her native country. In the first Bais Yaakov Seminary in Cracow, hundreds of mimeographed copies of selections from Rabbi Hirsch's works were passed from hand to hand, and no other books in the school library were so sought after as were his commentaries on the Torah, *Psalms,* the *Siddur,* and his *Collected Writings.* From the first class she taught in the Cracow seminary until the last month of her life, Sarah Schenirer continued to teach *The Nineteen Letters.* Her co-workers in the founding of the Bais Yaakov movement insist that the movement would have been unthinkable without Rabbi Hirsch's writings, especially his *Commentary on the Torah,* which was the basis of the lessons on that subject taught by Sarah Schenirer and her staff.[22*]

g. *Horeb* was originally intended to be the second part of a two-volume work, entitled *Moriah and Horeb.* The first part was to be an exposition of the basics of Jewish thought. It is unclear why Rabbi Hirsch never wrote *Moriah.*[23*]

Title page, Moriah and Horeb

מוריה וחורב,

Versuche

über Jissroél, und über Jissroéls Pflichten in der Zerstreuung,

zunächst

für Jissroéls denkende Jünglinge und Jungfrauen,

von

Samson Raphael Hirsch,

Großherz. Oldenb. Land-Rabbiner.

Zweyter Theil, חורב, über die Pflichten.

Wenn auch Verstoßene man dich nennet,
Denkmal bleibt's — Forscher fehlt ihm nur.
ירמי' 30, 17.

Altona,

bey Johann Friedrich Hammerich.

1837.

est degree impaired. There is, in the final analysis, but one answer why we should do this or refrain from doing that: Because it is the will of G-d, and it is our duty to be the servant of G-d with all our powers and resources and with every breath of our life. This answer is not only adequate; it is essentially the only one possible, and it would remain true even if we were able to penetrate into the reason for every commandment, or if G-d Himself had disclosed to us the reasons for His commandments.[23]

Horeb successfully advanced the view that the laws of the Torah and the obligation to observe them in their entirety constitute the essence of

חורב,

Versuche

über Jissroéls Pflichten

in der Zerstreuung,

zunächst

für Jissroéls denkende Jünglinge und Jungfrauen,

von

Samson Raphael Hirsch,

Großherzoglich Oldenburgischem Land-Rabbiner.

Wenn auch Verstoßene man dich nennet,
Denkmal bleibt's — Forscher fehlt ihm nur.
ירמי' 30, 17.

Altona,
bey Johann Friedrich Hammerich.
1837.

Title Page, Horeb

Judaism, a concept which was under constant attack in Germany throughout the 19th century.[24]

Rabbi Hirsch initially undertook to write *Horeb* as part of his responsibility of educating the Jewish youth under his jurisdiction. As he wrote his cousin Z.H. May, "I am in charge of a few hundred young souls; I have to provide teachers for them, of whom I have to ask that they introduce our youth into Judaism. But I cannot ask that of the teachers, because they themselves do not know what Judaism really means, and one cannot even blame them for their ignorance. Moreover, there is no textbook available which I can give them for guidance. It was these circumstances which pressed the pen into my hand and made me write these essays."[25]

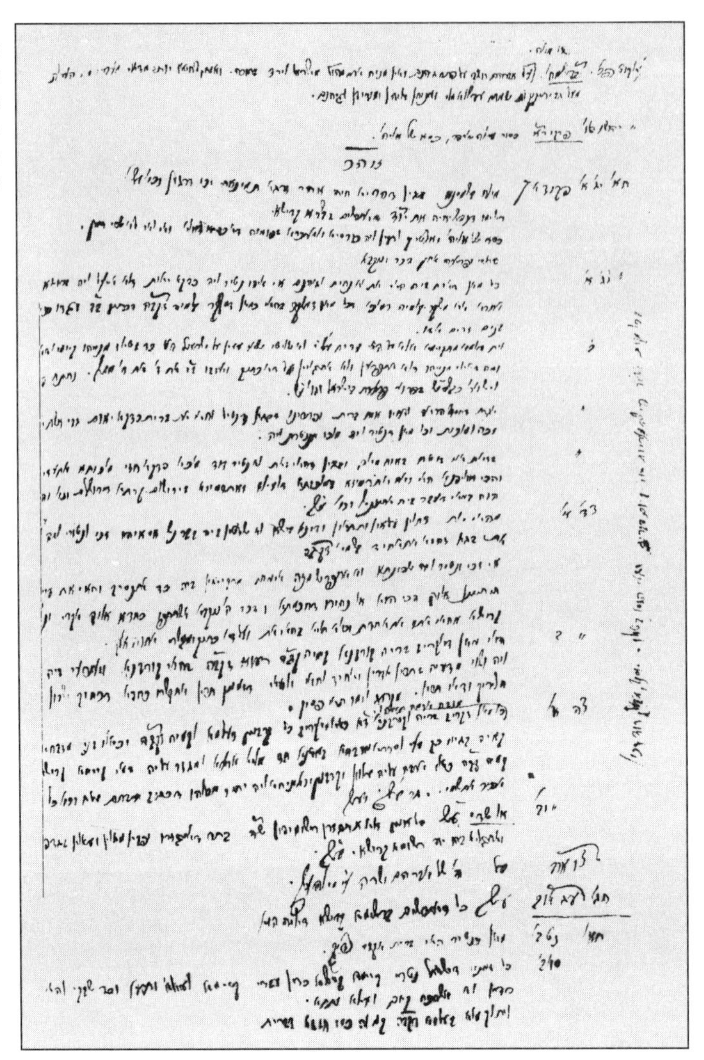

Copious citations from Zohar in Rabbi Hirsch's notebook — preparation for Horeb

The workbook from which he prepared *Horeb* reveals that for each *mitzvah* he meticulously copied dozens, and at times hundreds, of sources from the Babylonian and Palestinian Talmuds, as well as *Tosefta, Midrash, Zohar,* and *Shulchan Aruch.*[26] Based on these, he developed a highly original approach to understanding the rationale for and the lessons to be learned from G-d's commandments.

Rabbi Hirsch anticipated that his writings would draw fierce attacks from the Reformers. In the same letter to his cousin Z.H. May, he wrote:

> I am prepared for rebuke, bitter rebuke, and even abuse. I am not expecting approval or fame — although I never attack real

or imaginary persons. In fact, I do not attack at all, only compile, develop, point a way and seek truth; where I think I have found it, I try to bring it home to my readers. Generally, I only try to think aloud and ahead, and I should feel rewarded if people did not disdain to follow my thoughts. But there are people who consider it an impertinence that in 1835 one is still exhorted to think about certain matters. Such people will reproach me bitterly, because they are being disturbed in their calm. However, these people do not belong to the trend of thought of our century; they are out of date and relics of the last decades of the previous century. In the last 50 years it has been clearly noticeable that trends of thought only enter Jewish circles when they have already become obsolete elsewhere. . . . I shall perhaps be blamed from all sides. But just because of that I must not and will not be silent. If I knew of even one person more capable than myself of pleading the true cause of Israel, my incapable and inexperienced pen would have rested for a long time yet. . . .

I do not ask for the prize of battle. I shall be happy to be merely the herald who utters the battle cry. But I am not afraid of the battle, even if I have to fight it on my own. You regret that I have no reputation. Nevertheless, I shall publish the book under my name, but only because in the view of many people a cause for which one does not even stake one's name cannot have much value.

I am glad, however, that I am without fame and reputation; for it is not a matter of arguing with the backing of shining authority, but simply a matter of presenting the truth, which will fight for itself; if anything I say finds praise and recognition, let the cause gain by it; if anything arouses indignation, I am prepared to accept the blame myself. In this way there is less danger of harming the cause I would like to serve; it was indeed this fear which made me hesitate until now.[27]

The anticipated attacks were not long in coming. B.H. Fassel published an entire book entitled *Chorav Betzayon* (Leipzig, 1839) attacking *Horeb*, Abraham Geiger lashed out at *Horeb's* author in his journal,[28] and the liberal Jewish press launched a campaign against *Horeb* which continued for a long time. Rabbi Hirsch replied to his attackers in a special publication called *Postscripta* (Altona, 1840).

Horeb, like *The Nineteen Letters*, was required reading for Orthodox

Jews in Germany for over a century.[h] Rabbi Hirsch wrote in his introduction that it was not his intention to decide questions of practical *halachah;* yet, generations of German Jews looked to *Horeb* for practical guidance in *mitzvah* performance. Rabbi Meir Eisenstadt (*Imrei Eish*) of Ungvar, a leading disciple of the *Chasam Sofer,* remarked that *Horeb* contained the finest exposition of the underlying ideas of the laws of Shabbos.[29]

Naphtulei Naphtali

IN *THE NINETEEN LETTERS* AND *HOREB,* RABBI HIRSCH SPENT LITTLE time directly responding to the arguments of the Reform Movement. He preferred to focus instead on a positive presentation of the Torah world view and on an exposition of the *mitzvos.*[i] He did not directly enter the battle against the Reform until the publication of *Naphtulei Naphtali* or *Die Erste Mitteilungen aus Naphtali's Briefwechsel* (First Report of Naphtali's Correspondence) in 1838, when he was 30 years old.

In *Erste Mitteilungen,* he refuted the theories of the Reform Movement. He demonstrated how the Reformers either deliberately falsified or misunderstood the sources in *Tanach* and the Talmud on which they attempted to base their arguments. The book concluded with a gloomy description of the situation of Judaism in Germany, in which young rabbis, some even incapable of reading Hebrew properly, are trained without any understanding of the spirit of *Tanach* and are taught to learn the Talmud by rote without any true interest or appreciation. For this reason, he wrote, the young flock to the universities in search of substitutes for Judaism. There they find "a mixture of classical Heathenism, Historical Criticism and Dogmatic Philosophy, of New Testament introductions to the Old Testament, and of Christian Church doctrine," from which they conceive a dislike of that Judaism which they have never really understood.[30] The work criticized and poked fun at Creizenach and Geiger, especially of the latter's characterization of observant Jews as being "doglike" in their obedience.[31] It caused a considerable stir in liberal Jewish circles, and for a full year, articles attacking it appeared in Ludwig Philippson's *Allgemeine Zeitung des Judentums.*

Six years later, when Rabbi Hirsch had already assumed his post in Emden, the *Zweite Mitteilungen aus einem Briefwechsel über die Neueste Jüdische Literatur* (Second Report of Naphtali's Correspondence About the

h. It is interesting to note that the directions Rabbi Hirsch included in *Horeb* for the preparation of a calendar extended only until 5700 (1940), the last year in which the Jewish community in Germany existed.

i. Only the 17th and 18th letters discuss Reform directly.

Newest Jewish Literature), was published in Altona as a sequel to the *Erste Mitteilungen*. The second volume was devoted primarily to rebutting the claims of Samuel Holdheim (1806-1880), one of the leaders of the extremist wing of the Reform Movement. Holdheim moved the Sabbath to Sunday, rewrote the prayer service into German, deleting any mention of *Mashiach* and the redemption, and proclaimed that there was no bar to mixed marriages from a Jewish perspective.[32] In 1844, he publicly defended the right of children who were not circumcised to be considered as Jews, and in 1848, he went a step further and said that one who does *not* circumcise his son is a more complete Jew.[33] He argued that the Bible was but a human reflection of Divine illumination and the commandments were but a "crutch." True religion, he said, consisted of sentiment, belief and moral commitments. According to Holdheim, after the destruction of the *Beis HaMikdash* all rabbinic ordinances ceased to be binding. In the *Zweite Mitteilungen,* Rabbi Hirsch rebutted his arguments. The title page of that work contained a saying of the Sages which Rabbi Hirsch used frequently in his speeches and writings: קושטא קאי, שיקרא לא קאי — *Truth endures; falsehood does not.*[34]

Response to Anti-Semites

ALSO DURING HIS TENURE IN OLDENBURG, RABBI HIRSCH DISTINguished himself as a defender of Judaism against the vituperations of an anti-Semitic Protestant. In 1841, an anonymous pamphlet appeared in Oldenburg attacking the Bible in particularly vicious and anti-Semitic fashion. Rabbi Hirsch's prompt reply was published anonymously under the name *Jüdische Anmerkungen zu den Bemerkungen eines Protestanten,* etc. (Jewish Comments to the Remarks of a Protestant etc., by a Jew). He decisively disproved the claims of the pamphlet and demonstrated the ignorance of its author. The time has come, he wrote, for Christianity to stop building itself up by attempting to destroy Judaism.[35] Toward the end of his life, Rabbi Hirsch related to his son-in-law Rabbi Salomon Breuer that of all his many literary efforts this was the one he had most enjoyed writing.[36]

The work made a powerful impression, especially on the non-Jewish population of Oldenburg. When word got out that Rabbi Hirsch was the author, numerous Christians personally thanked him for his defense of the Bible, including the Adjutant General of the Grand Duke of Oldenburg, who came to express his master's appreciation for the *Landrabbiner's* work. The Grand Duke also granted him an audience to express his thanks in person.[37] Rebbetzin Hirsch once related that it was on a Friday that the news that her husband was indeed the author became public. The press of visitors in their house was so great that she was finally forced to insist, politely but firmly, that they leave so that she could light Shabbos candles.[38]

The years in Oldenburg were, on the whole, good ones. There Rabbi Hirsch was able to study and write virtually without interruption, and there, too, five of his ten children were born. With the publication of *The Nineteen Letters* and *Horeb,* however, he found himself thrust to the front rank of Orthodox rabbis in Germany. He needed a broader field for his activities,[39] and when the position of Chief Rabbi of East Friesland became vacant, his name was put forward as a candidate.[j]

Invitation to Emden

EAST FRIESLAND WAS ONE OF THE PROVINCES IN THE KINGDOM OF Hanover, one of the independent states in northern Germany. While the district capital was Aurich, the rabbinate was based in the city of Emden, and included nine other communities, to which the district of Osnabrück was added in 1844.[40] The election campaign for Chief Rabbi was a bitter one. The Orthodox party, fearing that Rabbi Hirsch was too modern, preferred Dr. Gabriel Lippman from Memelsdorf.[41] Rabbi Hirsch's opponents fought long and hard to prevent his election, and when on April 30, 1841 he won the vote, the losers painted the entire house of the leader of the winning faction with tar, from top to bottom.[42]

On October 22, 1841 (7 *Cheshvan,* 5602), Rabbi Hirsch was officially installed as Chief Rabbi. A measure of the residual bitterness from the election campaign is evident from the fact that the government, fearing demonstrations by Rabbi Hirsch's opponents, provided 50 armed guards to protect him. In his installation speech, he declared, "My enemies will soon become my friends," and indeed his fiercest opponents soon realized that the *yiras shomayim* of their rabbi was unsurpassed.[43]

j. The previous Chief Rabbi was Rabbi Abraham Loewenstam who served from 1810 until his passing in 1839.

Chapter Seven
EMDEN

SET YOUR MIND AND YOUR HEART TO ALL THE NEEDS OF your followers; be a brother and friend to them in all their affairs; and do whatever is in your power to add to their well-being and peace with G-d and man. Do not tell yourself that this is beneath your honor, for your true glory, your true honor is the diligence with which you serve the public. Strengthen yourself to spurn personal profit in all its forms so that you can treat great and small alike with equal fairness and attend to the public's needs for the sake of Heaven alone; then you will be beloved in Heaven as on earth, and the hearts of your flock will dote on you, and they will hang willingly on the nuances of your every word, for they will have faith that your every word and every deed is directed to their well-being.[1]

Tireless Activity

RABBI HIRSCH'S DESCRIPTION OF THE RESPONSIBILITIES OF A RABBI sums up his work in Emden. Immediately after his induction, he quickly began to exert his influence in all spheres of Jewish activity in the Kingdom of Hanover. It was in Emden that his organizational genius, which was to serve

Rabbi Hirsch's shul in Emden

German Jewry well for the next half century, first came to the fore. The residents of the region, who had by and large stayed faithful to authentic Judaism,[2] lived in abject poverty and Rabbi Hirsch worked assiduously to serve them.[3] His rabbinic journal of those years is filled with correspondence to the communities under his direction and reports to the government. From these emerge a picture of prodigious activity. There was hardly an area of Jewish life in which he was not active, and his enduring achievements in the face of formidable obstacles were remarkable.[4]

He instituted detailed regulations for community life that still remained in effect 70 years after he left. One of his more interesting directives was a ban on shouting and carrying on in communal meetings. The need for such a rule speaks volumes about life in Emden and its satellite communities.

Rabbi Hirsch established a free loan fund in Emden, one of the first of its kind in Germany. He personally went from home to home soliciting donations until the fund had accumulated considerable capital. The fund provided loans to the needy families of Emden and the surrounding area. For each *thaler* loaned, a payment of one *groschen* was due every week, so that the debt would be repaid within two years. So eager were his congregants not to betray his trust in them that not once did the fund have to write off a bad loan.[a,5]

a. It was still in operation over 70 years after its inception.

In Emden, he established a reputation as a peacemaker, and even after his passing nearly a half century later, his impartiality in resolving disputes was still remembered. In cases of discord, he made unscheduled appearances at meetings of community organizations, and with his engaging manner usually managed to restore harmony among conflicting factions. Nonetheless, he was capable of acting fearlessly and without favoritism when decisive measures were required. Once he ordered that a particular synagogue be closed for a period of time because its officers were unable to control the disruptive arguments that broke out regularly during the services.[6]

Rabbi Hirsch was active in the fight for the emancipation of the Jews of Osnabrück and Emden, which was granted in 1842. In addition, he succeeded in winning government support for the acceptance of Sabbath observers into the professional guilds.[7]

In stark contrast to Oldenburg where he could devote himself almost completely to his studies, Rabbi Hirsch was overburdened to the point of exhaustion with the manifold responsibilities of his position. "I am overwhelmed with work from morning until evening and, more often than not, I do not put my pen down until after midnight. I am a beast of burden bearing the load of the quarrels and affairs of the holy flock whose shepherd I am," he wrote his friend Rabbi Hirsch Lehren in Amsterdam.[8] His heavy workload may explain why during his six years in Emden his prolific pen was almost entirely silent, except for the second volume of *Naphtulei Naphtali*.

Yet, despite the heavy workload, he found his work in Emden fulfilling. The communities under his jurisdiction were composed almost entirely of devout people, who willingly accepted his guidance, and this was a decisive factor in his decision to turn down several offers to serve as rabbi in other communities, including Mainz and Hessen. When he did seek the vacant position of Chief Rabbi of England, his letter referred to the "remarkable happiness and public confidence" he enjoyed in Emden.[9]

A glimpse of Rabbi Hirsch's standing among the older generation of German rabbis can be gleaned from an affair in 1844, which involved a *kohen* who attempted to marry a *chalutzah*. Dr. Gabriel Lippman, the losing candidate for the position of Chief Rabbi of East Friesland, sent letters to various rabbinic leaders in Germany, accusing Rabbi Hirsch of having acted improperly. Rabbi Wolf Hamburg of Fürth, one of the senior rabbis of Germany, came to Rabbi Hirsch's defense with a biting reply to Lippmann: "I am absolutely astounded. Everything you wrote is untrue, and you lied in saying that Rabbi Hirsch, who has remained upright as a banner for the people [*Isaiah* 11:10], has raised this matter again."[b] The letter continued with blistering criticism of Lippman.[10]

Rabbi Hirsch's influence was not limited to the Jewish community; his advice and counsel were sought by many Christians as well, and when it became known that he had been offered the position of Chief Rabbi of Moravia, a delegation representing the Christian merchants of the city pleaded with him not to leave them.[11]

A Jew once noticed a portrait of Rabbi Hirsch hanging in the office of a prominent non-Jewish industrialist in nearby Norden, and asked how a picture of a Jewish rabbi came to be in such an unlikely place. His host told him that his father had once been involved in a lawsuit against a Jewish businessman and that the court had ordered the Jew to take an oath, which, according to law, was to be administered by Rabbi Hirsch as Chief Rabbi. Rabbi Hirsch arranged to spend the Shabbos preceding the oath ceremony in Norden, and delivered an address in the synagogue in which he stressed the seriousness of taking an oath, and that it is always better to avoid swearing, even if the failure to do so would result in substantial personal loss. Unbeknownst to him, the gentile litigant happened to be present, and Rabbi Hirsch's words made such an impression on him that after Shabbos he approached Rabbi Hirsch and told him that he would forgo his right to insist on an oath, even though he might thereby forfeit the lawsuit. Later that evening, the Jewish litigant also came to see Rabbi Hirsch, and told him that after hearing his address he had decided not to take an oath under any circumstances, even if it were to cause him a substantial loss of money.[12]

Schools

IN 1843, RABBI HIRSCH FOUNDED A SCHOOL FOR BOYS IN EMDEN. IN his address at the cornerstone-laying ceremony, he cited the words of the prophet Zachariah (4:6), which he often employed in connection with new undertakings: *Not by might, nor by power; but by My spirit, says the G-d of hosts.*[13] He reorganized the Jewish schools in the communities under his jurisdiction and bettered the position of the teachers by establishing the rule that teachers receive their salary from the school and not, as had been the practice, from the parents. He introduced continuing education under school auspices to enable those who left school to continue to benefit from organized *shiurim*. His efforts were not in vain, and the school he founded in Emden was still in existence after the turn of the century.[14]

---

b. תמה תמה אקרא, כל דבריך שכתבת אינם אמת, ושקר ענית ואמרת במה שכתבת שהרב ר' שמשון הירש אשר עומד תמיד לנס עמים, העיר מחדש על ענין זה, וזה שקר מוחלט. . .

The Rebbetzin founded a school for girls, which was still functioning at the time of her passing 40 years later. She herself recruited the students, who would otherwise have likely lost their connection with Judaism, and went tirelessly from door to door to raise money for the school's operations.[15]

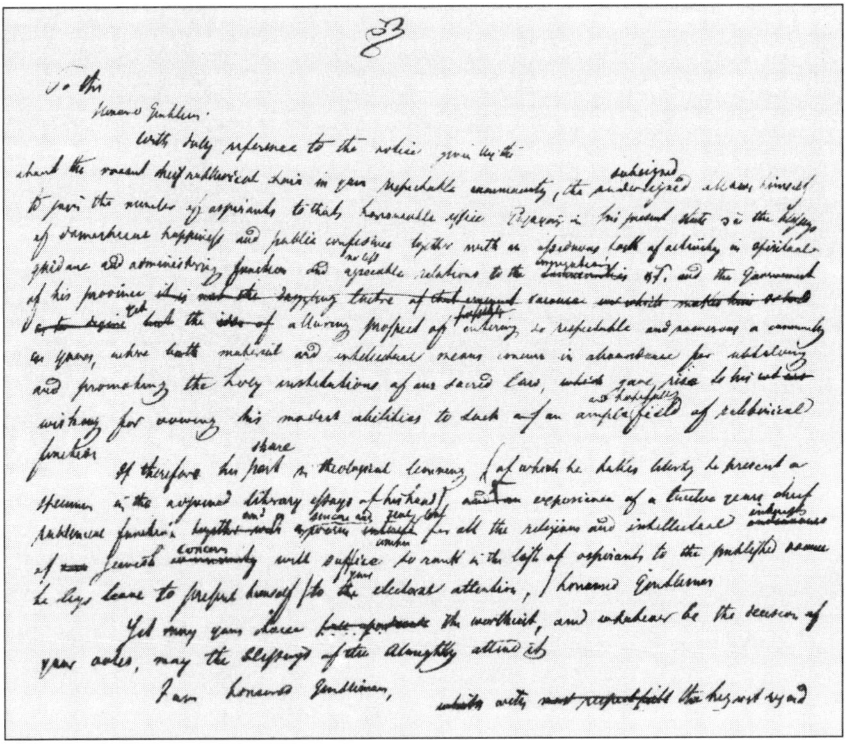

Rabbi Hirsch's draft letter in English to the "Committee Appointed for the Selection of Candidates for the Office of Chief Rabbi" of England

Chief Rabbinate of England

A LITTLE KNOWN EPISODE IN RABBI HIRSCH'S LIFE CONCERNS HIS candidacy for the Chief Rabbinate of England. In 1842, Rabbi Solomon Hirschel, Chief Rabbi of Britain — a position which at the time consisted of little more than a few London synagogues — passed away.[c] Candidates for the position were required to be able to preach in English. Rabbi Hirsch's friends and his *rebbe,* Rabbi Yaakov Ettlinger, encouraged him to apply for the post. Only under pressure from his friends did he consent to write Rabbi Hirsch Lehren in Amsterdam for a

c. The United Synagogue, embracing almost all of synagogue life in England, was a creation of Rabbi Nathan Adler who was elected to the post.

Rabbi Hirsch's biographical data in official report of the "Committee Appointed for the Selection of Candidates for the Office of Chief Rabbi"

מהו'רר שמשון בן כ'ה רפאל ארי' הירש א'בד דק'ק עמדען

REV. SAMPSON RAPHAEL HIRSCH,

סמיכה (*Ordained*) by Rabbi Isaac Bernays, Spiritual Director of the Congregation of Hambro', dated 1st September, 1830.

BORN, 20th JUNE, 1808.

PROVINCIAL RABBI OF OLDENBURG, FROM 1830 TO 1831; AT PRESENT PROVINCIAL RABBI OF THE PROVINCE OF OST FRIESLAND, FROM 1841.

TESTIMONIALS.

1. Letter from Messrs. M. Warburg and Co., Hamburgh, dated 13th December, 1842, to Messrs. De Rothschild, London, testifying to his high moral character, and literary and scientific attainments.

2. Certificate of Rabbi Isaac Bernays, dated Hamburg, July, 1830, stating that Rabbi Hirsch had attended his Lectures on the Talmud, and on Jewish Theology.

3. Further Testimonials from Rabbi Bernays, dated 1st September, 1830, as to the distinguished ability of Rabbi Hirsch (being the ordination of Rabbi Hirsch).

4. Government Testimonial, dated Oldenburgh, March 17th, 1843, signed Matsenbecher, stating that Rabbi Hirsch had been provincial Rabbi of that dukedom, from 1830 to 1841, till called to a larger sphere of action; that his conduct had secured the approbation of the government, and speaking highly of his moral conduct and knowledge.

5. Letter from Mr. Solomon Heine, dated Hamburgh, 13th December, 1842, to Baron De Rothschild, London, stating that he had made inquiries of the Chief Rabbi of Altona, and Rabbi Bernays of Hamburgh, and that he had been assured of the religious character and high attainments of Rabbi Hirsch.

6. Certificate of having attended with diligence Lectures on Natural Philosophy. (Dr. Munchen, *dated 24th March*, 1830.)

7. Certificate of having attended Lectures at the University of Bonn, on Philology and History, and of Rabbi Hirsch's scientific knowledge and moral character. (M. A. Brandis, *Deacon of the Philosophical Faculty, dated 28th March*, 1830.

8. Certificate of attending Lectures on Juvenal. (Dr. Heinrich, *Ordinary Professor, dated 28th March*, 1830.)

9. Ditto on the Philosophical Systems and Logic.

10. Ditto on History. (Niebuhr, *Bonn, dated 28th March*, 1830).

11. Ditto on the Theological branches of Science, at the Gymnasium of Hamburgh, (J. E. Kealer, *Rector, 26th March*, 1828).

12. Testimonial, dated 13th July, 1844, Royal Hanoverian Landdrostic, eulogising Rabbi Hirsch as Provincial Rabbi for the last two years of the province of Ost Friesland.

13. Testimonial from Rabbi Moses Tobias Southam, Chief Rabbi of Hanau, dated 12th Tishri, 5590, to Rabbi Hirsch's ability and character.

14. Testimonial of the Chief Rabbi of Altona, dated 5590, highly eulogising Rabbi Hirsch's character and theological attainments.

Letter of application, wherein Rabbi Hirsch states that from his earliest youth he has cultivated English Literature; see letters dated 26th May, 1844, which are written in the English Language.

Has published several works, (among others) "Chorab" (Digest of Jewish Law), and Critical letters on Judaism.

Rabbi Sampson Raphael Hirsch is the son of Raphael Mendel Hirsch, descendant of Rabbi Mendel Frankfort.

recommendation. Rabbi Lehren not only sent the requested recommendation with alacrity, he also importuned Rabbi Hirsch to write to London himself and to send the election committee copies of his literary works. Rabbi Hirsch did write a letter in English, but he steadfastly refused to send his books on the grounds that basic Jewish modesty did not permit him to do so.[16] Initially there were 13 candidates for the post,

REPORT

OF THE

COMMITTEE APPOINTED FOR THE SELECTION OF CANDIDATES

FOR THE OFFICE OF

CHIEF RABBI.

The Committee report, that, at their first Meeting, held on the 31st of March last, they determined that all applications which might be made for the vacant appointment of Chief Rabbi, together with testimonials, be forwarded to their Chairman, S. H. Ellis, Esq., on or before the 15th day of Ab, corresponding with the 31st July last.

At the same Meeting, the Committee determined upon certain arrangements, for the purpose of declaring the vacancy and giving publicity throughout the continent to the declaration of such vacancy, and also the regulations to be observed by those who might be desirous of becoming Candidates.

The period limited to receive applications having expired on the 31st ult., the Committee again met on Monday Evening the 5th inst., for the purpose of selecting Candidates.

The Committee deem it a duty to express their obligation to Dr. Benisch, their Secretary for foreign correspondence, who has most efficiently performed his arduous duties, in collating and translating the many and voluminous documents forwarded by, and on behalf of, the several reverend applicants.

The applicants were thirteen in number, of these, nine not having complied in various particulars with the published requisitions, were deemed disqualified for election.

The names of the four selected Candidates are as follows:—

מהו"רר נתן בן מהו"רר מרדכי אדלר הכהן אב"ד דק"ק הנובר
Rev. Dr. Nathan Marcus Adler, Chief Rabbi of Hanover.

מהו"רר צבי בנימן בן מהו"רר אברהם אויערבאך אב"ד דק"ק דארמשטאדט
Rev. Dr. Benjamin Auerbach, Chief Rabbi of Darmstadt.

מהו"רר צבי בן כ"ה שמעון הירשפעלד אב"ד דק"ק וואלשטיין
Rev. Dr. Hirsch Hirschfeld, Chief Rabbi of Wollstein.

מהו"רר שמשון בן כ"ה רפאל ארי' הירש אב"ד דק"ק עמדען
Rev. Samson Raphael Hirsch, Chief Rabbi of Emden.

The testimonials and other documents belonging to the several reverend gentlemen who have been selected, have been carefully, and it is believed impartially, epitomised; these epitomes or abstracts form an Appendix which is annexed to this Report.

The Committee have determined upon a series of regulations, to be observed by the several uniting Congregations, in the election of the Chief Rabbi, which are as follow:—

1st.—That the abstracts forming the Appendix to this Report be printed and transmitted to every Elector; and that the original documents remain for the inspection of the electors at the Vestry Chamber of the Great Synagogue, for one month, at the least, prior to the election.

2nd.—That the election take place on Sunday, the 13th October next, א' דר"ח חשון תר"ה.

3rd.—That the day of Election be the same in all the uniting Congregations.

4th.—That no proxies be allowed, and that every elector vote by ballot.

5th.—That the election returns for the several uniting Congregations, be signed by the Warden President, or presiding officer, and also by the Secretary; and that such returns respectively be transmitted under seal by post to S. H. Ellis, Esq., President of the Great Synagogue, at the Synagogue Chambers, not later than the day next following the election.

6th.—That this Committee shall meet on Wednesday the 16th October, to declare the result of the Ballot, and all returns not received by that day shall be void.

7th.—That every ballot not taking place on the day appointed, shall be void.

In conclusion, the Committee feel pleasure in observing, that so highly satisfactory are the testimonials of the selected Candidates, and so high a reputation do these reverend gentlemen respectively enjoy, for religion, morality, and learning, that on whomsoever the election may fall there can be no doubt as to the competency of the successful applicant adequately to fulfil his sacred and important functions.

S. H. ELLIS, Chairman.

August 5th, 5604.

but the list was subsequently whittled down to four, with Rabbi Hirsch as one of the remaining contenders. At one time in the deliberations Rabbi Hirsch was even agreed upon as a compromise candidate.

Also presenting his candidacy was Rabbi Nathan Adler of Hanover, Rabbi Hirsch's predecessor in Oldenburg and great-nephew of Rabbi Dovid Tevele Schiff, who had served as Chief Rabbi of the Great

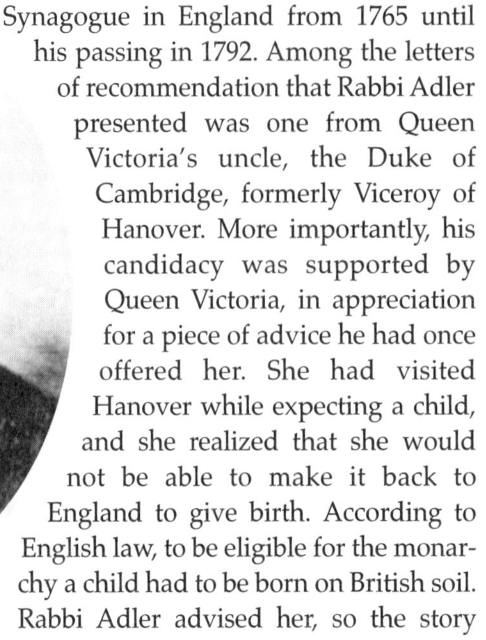
Rabbi Nathan Adler

Synagogue in England from 1765 until his passing in 1792. Among the letters of recommendation that Rabbi Adler presented was one from Queen Victoria's uncle, the Duke of Cambridge, formerly Viceroy of Hanover. More importantly, his candidacy was supported by Queen Victoria, in appreciation for a piece of advice he had once offered her. She had visited Hanover while expecting a child, and she realized that she would not be able to make it back to England to give birth. According to English law, to be eligible for the monarchy a child had to be born on British soil. Rabbi Adler advised her, so the story goes, to give birth aboard a ship flying the British flag, which would be considered British soil. The Queen followed this advice. With the Queen's endorsement Rabbi Adler's candidacy became a virtual certainty.[d,17]

The Braunschweig Conference

THE EFFORTS TO REFORM JUDAISM IN THE FIRST FOUR DECADES OF the 19th century constituted something less than a uniform movement. The initial changes were primarily liturgical and relating to the synagogue service, using the Protestant Church as a model. They varied greatly from place to place, with each rabbi doing what he thought necessary or felt the traffic would bear. Although most of the Reformers were personally non-observant, they did not yet have the audacity to launch a broadside attack on the essence of Judaism. For that reason, the originators of Reform in Berlin claimed that their reforms were halachically acceptable. They commissioned Aaron Chorin and Eliezer Liebermann to write a responsum and a book called *Or Nogah* and *Nogah Zedek* respectively.[18] For that reason also, the responsa of the leading sages of Europe in reaction to the Hamburg

d. Due to Rabbi Adler's leadership, the Reform Movement never really made any headway in England and was never recognized there as an authentic version of Judaism. Rabbi Adler's successor was his son, Rabbi Dr. Naphtali (Hermann) Adler; Rabbi Anselm Stern, Chief Rabbi of Hamburg, was a son-in-law.

Temple and the new Reform prayer book were primarily halachic in nature.[19]

The Enlightenment and the rise of scientific thinking placed many fundamentals of religion under attack in the Christian world at the time and these trends were soon felt in the Jewish world as well. First the Talmud was attacked as outdated and no longer binding. Next the debunkers, led by Abraham Geiger, set upon the Written Torah itself, which they described as no more than a Divinely inspired human creation, subject to human criticism and the observance of which is optional.

At the same time, profound knowledge of the Talmud had sunk to a low state among German Jews, and there was hardly a yeshiva of any significant size still functioning anywhere in Germany. Greatness in Torah, which is the *sine qua non* of authentic Jewish life, was quickly disappearing, and the Torah was a closed book to a large segment of the Jewish people. Even where Jews were still observant, their observance tended to be more rote than informed by any understanding of what they were doing. By the 1840s, there had arisen a generation of German Jews so Germanized and Europeanized that many of them remained Jews in name only.[20] With the migration of the village Jews to the big cities, the disintegration of authentic Jewish life accelerated. The influence of the Orthodox rabbis was for the most part limited to their communities. Rabbi Hirsch was the first to break that mold and attempt a countrywide rejuvenation of Torah-true Judaism, with the publication of his *Nineteen Letters* and *Horeb*.

Although most larger communities still included observant members in the 1830s and '40s, they were in no position to successfully challenge the growing domination of community life by the Reformers. For their part, the Reform rabbis were careful, in most cases, not to go too far too fast. They instituted their reforms slowly so as to ultimately reform completely. So even as Reform became widespread, it lacked a single clear position and the reforms varied widely from community to community.[21]

One of the first to call for a rabbinical conference to institutionalize and create uniformity in Reform ranks was Ludwig Philippson (1811-1889), the founder and editor, until his death in 1889, of the *Allgemeine Zeitung des Judentums* (1837-1922), the most influential advocate of Reform in Germany during the 19th century. Newspapers and periodical literature wielded great influence in 19th-century Germany, and the *Allgemeine Zeitung des Judentums* was a powerful tool on behalf of Reform. Its masthead, which described it as "the non-denominational organ for all Jewish matters," was viewed by the Orthodox as just one more piece of deception practiced by the Reform. In truth, though, Philippson did see himself as non-denominational. His Judaism just did not include observant Jews. As he put it: "It is self-understood that we cannot see the superstitious Hasidic beliefs . . . as movements connected to Judaism."[22]

Philippson was one of the initiators and prime movers in the three major Reform "rabbinical conferences" of the 19th century: Braunschweig, 1844; Frankfurt, 1845; and Breslau, 1846. Part of the impetus for these conferences was that the struggle for emancipation had suffered some reversals in the 1840s. One of the aims of the conferees was to reformulate Judaism in a way that would leave it so bland and devoid of any national character that it would prove acceptable to the German intelligentsia and to the public at large, and the authorities would grant Jews the civil liberties they so deeply craved.[23]

These three conferences introduced new and radical reforms and institutionalized already existing aberrations. The conferences focused primarily on what was being excised from normative Judaism. Their final declarations rejected the authority of the Talmud, eliminated prayers for the return of the sacrifices and expressions of hope for redemption from the liturgy, instituted a three-year cycle of *Krias HaTorah*, permitted the playing of an organ in the synagogue on the Sabbath, even by a Jew, and finally, discarded the laws of *kashruth*.

The first conference, attended by a group of 20 or so Reform rabbis and laymen, including Abraham Geiger and Samuel Holdheim, opened on June 22, 1844 in Braunschweig, Germany. The eight-day conference was filled with the most brazen attacks on almost everything sacred in Jewish life. The final resolutions declared that the commandments of the Torah are not obligatory. Whereas the Paris "Sanhedrin" had declared in 1807, in response to Napoleon's pressure, that marriage between a Jew and a non-Jew was permissible from a civil standpoint, and carefully avoided mentioning the Jewish prohibition on intermarriage, the Braunschweig Conference went further and declared that if both partners were adherents of monotheistic religions, intermarriage was permitted, if the children were raised as Jews.

The Jewish world in Europe was in an uproar. Rabbi Yaakov Ettlinger initiated a public denunciation signed by 77 of the leading rabbis of Europe, representing, as they termed themselves, "*Shlomei Emunai Yisrael*." Their denunciation stressed that the majority of German rabbis were with them.[24] In addition, Rabbi Hirsch Lehren of

Amsterdam organized another public response by several of the leading rabbis of the time. A collection of these letters was published in 1845 under the title *Toras HaKana'us,* and included a lengthy Hebrew epistle from Rabbi Hirsch.[25]

In his lengthy response condemning the conference, Rabbi Hirsch stressed that religious persecution in the past, as in the times of the Maccabees, was usually preceded by Jewish "reforms." Without the subversion of Judaism on the part of Jews, he wrote, our enemies would never have attempted to forbid religious observance. The work and the decisions of the conference, he declared, were nothing more than the work of ignorant people, who, by flouting the Written and Oral Torah had effectively removed themselves from Jewry. They could only be termed, on the basis of their own words, members of a religion other than Judaism. He decried the artificial distinction they made between commandments which they thought to be ethical to which they assigned importance, and the others which they were willing to abolish. In any event, he concluded, their willingness to allow intermarriage with a non-Jew, providing the partner was a member of a monotheistic religion, was an indication that all that had remained of their Judaism was the belief in one G-d.

Traditionally, continued Rabbi Hirsch, when there arose spiritual dangers to the Jewish people the entire nation closed ranks to remedy the situation. One who remains silent in the face of such sacrilege admits with his silence to their blasphemy. Thus, it was incumbent on every Jew to do what he could to lend a hand to cure the ills of the Jewish people. This, he asserted, could be accomplished only by strengthening the three pillars of Jewish public endeavor: *Torah, Avodah* and *Gemiluth Chasadim.* The first would entail the declararation by word and deed, and the education of our children, toward the veneration for, the study of and adherence to every word of *Chazal.* It would mean also the establishment of schools which would inculcate their students with Torah and *Derech Eretz;* through the teaching of both there is hope to cure the ills of Jewry. The *Avodah,* the sanctity and earnestness of prayer in *shul,* must be addressed as well.

Rabbi Hirsch concluded by warning the participants of the Conference that the result of their actions would be the splitting of the Jewish People into two parts, and "in grief we will part man from his brother."[26]

The importance of the Braunschweig Conference lay in its institutionalization of what had hitherto been done only by individual "rabbis" on the local level. The Conference also electrified European Orthodoxy, which responded to it with a vengeance. Their reaction served only to clarify the Orthodox position, and to draw the lines clearly between Orthodoxy and Reform. The Orthodox response to the Conference did little in terms of turning back the tide, less in terms of convincing the Reformers of the disastrous consequences of their thought and deed, and nothing at all in terms of a dialogue, which, in truth, had never been possible.

In the Frankfurt conference of 1845, the Reformers "permitted" civil servants to work on the Sabbath. To get around the Biblical prohibition of work on Shabbos, they determined that work for the State was nothing less than a positive *mitzvah,* since the State was an early stage in the new world order of the messianic era and hence part of G-d's master plan. Work on behalf of the State, even if only in a clerical capacity, was thus elevated to a positive commandment which was *"docheh"* (set aside) the Sabbath.[27]

The Breslau Conference of 1846 continued the trend by canceling the second day of Yom Tov and Rosh Hashanah. If the first day of Yom Tov were to fall on the Sabbath, the conferees instituted *shofar* blowing and *lulav* taking even on the Sabbath. Samuel Holdheim tried to pass a motion to move the Sabbath to Sunday, as the only way to reconcile the conflicting demands of religion with those of civilian life. He even cited *Pesach Sheni,* which was instituted for those who were impure or too far away to reach Jerusalem by Pesach, as a Biblical precedent for the proposition that holy days can be moved for convenience sake. A suggestion was also raised to abolish *kriah al hameis* as not befitting modern times.[28]

As time went on, Rabbi Hirsch's fame and reputation spread and at the age of 40, he was already considered the leader of the German rabbinate in its struggle against Reform. One of the leading Jewish newspapers in Germany described him in the following terms: "In both seriousness and determination, without paying heed to public acclaim, he goes on his way as an honored public leader in Israel. We know of no other rabbi in Germany who even approaches his stature."[29]

His election as Chief Rabbi of Moravia in 1847 with its 50,000 Jews[30] in 52 communities, the largest such rabbinate in Europe, reflected his evergrowing stature. The election committee cited as reasons for their choice: his renown as a Torah scholar, the quality of his writings "which reveal his exceptional knowledge of all aspects of the Jewish faith," and his 16 years of rabbinical experience "during which he has led his followers peacefully, honestly, and wisely."[31] Upon receiving the news of his election, the communities then under his leadership entreated him to stay and offered various inducements, including a raise in salary that he sorely needed to support his large family. He refused the proffered raise, however, on the grounds that it was offered by communities whose members were so poverty stricken that it would have imposed hardship on them.[32]

Rabbi Hirsch's farewell *drashah* in Emden was packed with listeners including many non-Jews, such was the esteem in which he was held. It was an emotional event and both speaker and audience wept unashamedly.[33]

Chapter Eight

NIKOLSBURG

ON WEDNESDAY, 9 TAMMUZ, 5607 (1847), RABBI HIRSCH set out from Emden on his way to Nikolsburg. All of the Moravian communities through which he passed accorded him an honored and enthusiastic welcome. Upon his arrival in Nikolsburg, he was greeted by an assemblage of all the Jews in the city, from the elder *talmidei chachamim* to young schoolchildren carrying flags emblazoned with the blessing: "Who has apportioned of His knowledge to those who fear Him." His first Shabbos in Nikolsburg he delivered an address in the *Altschul,* and the festivities surrounding his inauguration continued for a full week, culminating in an official ceremony which took place on Wednesday, 16 *Tammuz* (June 30).[1]

Moravia

THE HAPSBURG EMPIRE WAS A VAST CONGLOMERATION OF COUNTRIES and peoples, each with its own language and system of law, culture and customs, and the position of the Jews varied from country to country. Moravia (Mähren), in what is today the Czech Republic, was part of Austria and located in the northern part of the empire.

Altschul, Nikolsburg

Jews began living in Moravia almost from the beginning of the millennium. The *Rashba* (d. 1310) mentions Austerlitz and Triesch, two Moravian communities, in his responsa. Moravia absorbed refugees fleeing from the massacres of Chmielnicki in 1648, among them the *Schach* who became Rabbi of Holleschau, Moravia. The seat of the Moravian Chief Rabbinate was Nikolsburg (its Czech name is Mikulov; Nikolsburg is German), where Jews first settled in the 14th century.[2] There were 3,670 Jews living in Nikolsburg when Rabbi Hirsch arrived.[3]

Jewish communal life in Moravia was highly organized and the Chief Rabbi was invested by the government with extensive powers, as reflected in the name by which he was popularly known: the "*Rosh Medinah*" (head of state). Public Torah study was organized and advanced: Each locality was required to hire a rabbi in charge of Torah instruction, to maintain schools and to provide for the needs of a number of yeshiva students in proportion to the size of its population. Those communities too small to maintain their own yeshivas were required to contribute an appropriate sum toward the operation of the nearest existing yeshiva.

Presiding over the entire system stood the Chief Rabbi, who also served as head of the Yeshiva of Nikolsburg. He had the responsibility of

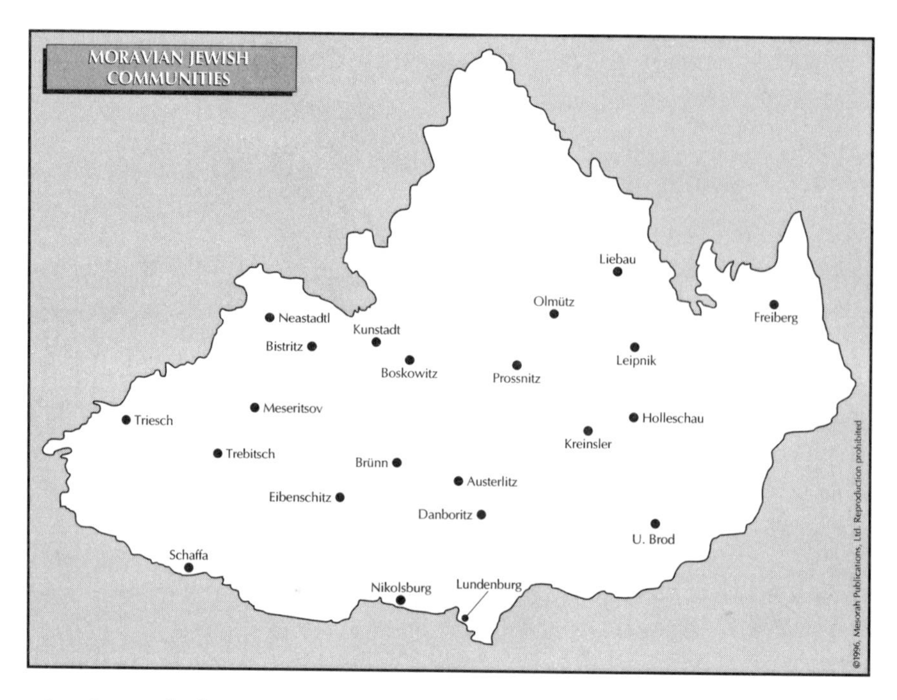

deciding which tractates would be learned each term in the Moravian yeshivas and ensuring the printing and distribution of an adequate quantity of *Gemaras* for this purpose. He was also charged with the testing and certification of candidates for rabbinical positions in the province.[4]

In addition to the schools for youth, three additional types of institutions of higher learning functioned: yeshivas, study circles and *batei midrashim.* Yeshivas were intended for older students studying full-time. The study circles were made up of merchants who met for fixed hours each day, with various members taking turns as lecturers. The *batei midrashim* (public study halls) were kept lit through the night and heated in the winter. They were open 24 hours a day to anyone who wanted to learn, free of charge. All of this was made possible by the financial support of the communities, in which great importance was placed on Torah study.[5]

The Rabbinate

NEARLY ALL THE CHIEF RABBIS OF NIKOLSBURG WERE SIMULTANEOUSLY Chief Rabbi of Moravia and thus Nikolsburg served as the center of Jewish life in Moravia. Among Rabbi Hirsch's predecessors were some of the greatest scholars of their times, including: Rabbi Yehudah Loew (the *Maharal* of Prague), who assumed the position in 1553 and served two decades; Rabbi Yomtov Lippman Heller, author of *Tosefos Yomtov* on the *Mishnah*, who was appointed in 1625; Rabbi Menachem Mendel Krochmal, author of Responsa *Tzemach Tzedek* who served as chief rabbi from 1648, and Rabbi Gershon Ashkenazi, author of *Avodas HaGershuni*. In 1773, Rabbi Shmuel Shmelka Horovitz, famous Chassidic leader, was appointed Chief Rabbi of Nikolsburg, and two years later Chief Rabbi of Moravia.

Rabbi Nachum Trevitsch

Rabbi Mordechai Banet (1753-1829) was appointed Chief Rabbi in 1790 and continued in that position until his passing. Rabbi Banet was one of the foremost opponents of the Hamburg *Temple*, and together with the *Chasam Sofer*, waged a strong battle against Aharon Chorin, Rabbi of Arad, who wrote a book purporting to give a halachic basis to the *Temple* and its prayer book.[6]

Rabbi Nachum Trevitsch (1779-1842)[7] succeeded Rabbi Banet. Although the *Landesrabbiner* traditionally enjoyed the prerogative to appoint rabbis for the various communities, it was a sign of the times in Moravia that the government stripped Rabbi Trevitsch of this right in 1833 because he refused to appoint rabbis with Reform leanings, and also, it seems, because he refused to permit German language sermons in the synagogue. He was in constant conflict with the forces of "liberal" Judaism and lost quite a few of those battles, with the government deciding in favor of the moderns.

In 1842, Rabbi Trevitsch passed away. Two years later his position was first offered to Rabbi Hirsch, but the appointment was not finalized until 1847.[8]

Old School vs. Modernity

MORAVIA AT THAT TIME WAS WRACKED BY A FIERCE STRUGGLE between the Orthodox on the one side and the modernizers on the other. Upon Rabbi Hirsch's arrival, there were more than a few who did not know exactly what to make of the new Chief Rabbi in this regard. One must remember that Rabbi Hirsch came to Nikolsburg only 16 years after the passing of Rabbi Mordechai Banet, a figure held in awe and reverence,

Judengasse, Nikolsburg

who was a legend of piety and holiness in his own lifetime. The women of Nikolsburg, it is told, would bribe his attendant to give them the rabbi's clothing, so they would have the merit of mending it. In contrast to his esteemed predecessor, Rabbi Hirsch dressed in modern garb, took walks with his wife in the street, did not begin his tenure with the traditional *drashah*, and gave a more *peshat*-oriented *shiur*, without audience participation and without the traditional *niggun*. At first, the older generation did not know what to make of him, and the *rabbonim* of the old school received him with not a little ambivalence. But, as in Emden, as they came to know him their attitude changed.

Indications of tension between the moderns and the old school were already evident at Rabbi Hirsch's inauguration. Chosen to deliver the main address at the inauguration was Isaac Noah Mannheimer (1793-1865), preacher of the *Kultusgemeinde* in Vienna. Early in his career, he was considered one of the champions of moderate reform of synagogue liturgy, but as he got older he slowly backed away from his earlier enthusiasm for change.[a]

Isaac Noah Mannheimer

The following is the contemporary account of the inauguration ceremony by Rabbi Shalom Kutna, a student in the Nikolsburg yeshiva.[9] His account demonstrates the extent to which Rabbi Hirsch went out of his way from the very outset of his tenure as Chief Rabbi to allay the fears of the old-school rabbis, and their warm response to his gesture:

> Rabbi Hirsch mounted the steps leading up to the *Aron HaKodesh* and began his remarks with the verse (*I Chronicles* 29:12), *Wealth and honor come from You, and You rule everything.* He continued, "True honor comes only from Hashem, and to whom does the King of the World wish to give honor and respect more than to *talmidei chachamim,* who learn Torah and keep its *mitzvos* and go in His ways."
>
> In passionate tones he described how he was but dust under the feet of these Torah scholars and he promised the assembled rabbis that he would defer to them and stand by them at all times. In tears he said, "What am I, who am I, to sit in the place where such a distinguished succession of great men have sat before me?"
>
> Conspicuously absent from his remarks was the slightest mention of Mannheimer, whom normal protocol would have required that he thank. Mannheimer bore his humiliation in silence.[10]
>
> After Rabbi Hirsch's remarks, Rabbi Naphtali Banet of Schaffa, eldest of the *rabbonim* present and son of Rabbi Mordechai Banet, a predecessor as Chief Rabbi, ascended the podium and gave effusive thanks for the heartfelt words they had just heard. Addressing Rabbi Hirsch, he promised on his own behalf and on

a. In 1817, Mannheimer was appointed head teacher of "religion" in Copenhagen, and given the job of preparing the students for "confirmation." The confirmation was held to the accompaniment of organ music. In addition, he conducted services for Reform Jews. Mannheimer was appointed "preacher" in Vienna in 1824. Over the years, he gradually edged away from Reform, keeping organ music out of the services, not deleting the prayer for *Mashiach* and the redemption, and insisting that the prayers be recited in Hebrew only. The *siddurim* with German translation that he published in 1840 and 1851 hewed to the traditional *Nusach HaTefillah* in every way, with no deletions or changes of any kind.[8*]

Altschul of Nikolsburg where Rabbi Hirsch davened and where the inauguration ceremony took place

behalf of the members of the elder generation of *rabbonim* present to assist him whenever he would request it. He apologized on their behalf for having assumed that their Chief Rabbi would turn out to be like many other German rabbis who did not fully sympathize with the older generation. Now they realized their mistake, he said, and in their name he asked forgiveness. It made a stirring sight: Rabbi Hirsch weeping because they had suspected him and the *rabbonim* weeping over their mistrust of him.[11]

The difficulties of the new Chief Rabbi are nicely captured by the following incident. Traditionally, *Kol Nidrei* in Nikolsburg was recited after

Neuschul in Nikolsburg

the rabbi's *drashah*. As a result, the congregation recited *Kol Nidrei* after sunset, a practice contrary to the *halachah*. To rectify the matter Rabbi Hirsch directed that *Kol Nidrei* be recited first. On *Yom Kippur* night, one rich old man began to yell: "Only new things! The old way was good enough for our old *rabbonim*. Why is it not good enough for him? All year we're not Jews, and now on Yom Kippur we're also not Jews!" Rabbi Hirsch left the *shul* and did not return that evening. The gentleman was fined 100 gulden and not permitted to enter the *Altschul* for a full year, an unusually harsh punishment for one who sat on the *Mizrach*.[12]

The following exchange is a striking example of the state of mind that prevailed among Moravian youth during the time Rabbi Hirsch served as Chief Rabbi, and gives eloquent expression to one dimension of the difficulties he faced there.[13]

Lundenburg, 7 Adar II, 5608
Most honored and revered Chief Rabbi:

The occasion for my writing is the letter I received from you in which you reproached me over the unfounded charge that has been brought against me, alleging that I, a Jewish baker, do my work on our holy Sabbath.

It is true that work is done in my bakery on the Sabbath, but it is also true that this work is done, in my humble opinion, in a manner that is permitted by our Sages, for I have a non-Jewish baker to perform all the tasks. This is permitted in several ways: It can be done by means of either a partnership, rental, or sale. In order to satisfy all the opinions, I have been careful to employ all of these extremist means.

Your excellency, Chief Rabbi! I am filled with joy at the privilege I have of speaking to you from my heart and sharing with you what is being said by all our youth, or at least the youth here. No words can describe my disillusionment at the rebuke I received, and it amazes me that you believe rumors that insinuate that a Jew in Israel has intentionally desecrated the holy Sabbath. I was particularly astounded that I should come under the suspicion of the Chief Rabbi, the hope of our youth. It was on the initiative of the youth that we arranged a royal welcoming ceremony upon your arrival, for we felt that a new era was beginning; we thought that as Chief Rabbi, your honor, a wise and learned philosopher, would vigorously employ the power of your high office to fulfill the mission with which he was charged, namely to take the dirty, lowly and despised Jew, with whom we and the Christian populace are equally disgusted, and to make of him a "man."

But instead of this, you argue that the civil authorities should be called upon to forbid me from baking on the Sabbath! In a place whose Jewish community is so small that I am forced to make a living from gentiles, must I tell my Christian customers that I have nothing for them today because it is the Sabbath? Will they accept this answer? Will they buy bread from me all week and on the Sabbath go to the gentile bakery? Will they not curse the Jew and his religion and his entire existence, instead of saying, as our teacher Moses wanted them to say, "Only such a wise and understanding nation as this . . ."? For the sake of observing the Sabbath properly, shall I be forced to abandon the occupation that is my pride and joy and to become a peddler from Sunday to Friday afternoon, wandering from village to village with a sack on my back, a disgrace to myself and my people?

Do you truly believe that it is possible to observe the Sabbath today as it was a hundred years ago, when the cost of living now has grown tenfold and incomes shrunk twentyfold? And if it has indeed been decreed upon us that you will persist in your views, then I say there is no escape for us and we are all lost.

I must restrain myself from writing further, for the mere thought of this matter causes me heartache, as it would cause any honest and thinking person. I am also mindful to the Sages' dictum, "A word is worth one coin, silence two."

I assure you that whatever I have written expresses my opinion and that of all our youth.

Rabbi Hirsch's Reply

In your recent letter you found it proper to present to me the essence of your beliefs, which, you inform me, is also the conviction of the youth of your city. And by transmitting your program of requests and aspirations, you hope that I will be the one to bring your plans to realization.

The determination as to whether and to what extent you fulfill your obligations with regard to the laws of the Sabbath, I must leave in the hands of your local rabbi, who is the final authority in this matter, and it is to him that you must address all your halachic questions.

However, concerning that which is relevant to the foundations of faith which determine your standards of behavior, I feel bound to make a few friendly remarks.

It is true that I believe firmly that the Sabbath will continue to be supremely holy, not just as it was a hundred years ago, as you pointed out, but as it will remain even a thousand years from now. The command to keep the Sabbath will be holy to our children and to our children's children forever and ever, just as it was to our parents and to our parents' parents. Never has anyone dared tamper with it.

I do not believe the Torah's commandments to be made of wax such that anyone at any time can come along and remodel them to suit his fancy and convenience. For me, the Torah's commandments are the words of the holy Living G-d, given to us by our eternal Father, to guide our lives on this earth and sanctify them to Him above. The Torah does not derive its complexion from the times, but rather the times must derive their complexion from the Torah, and in this Torah I am aware of no distinctions: The same G-d Who forbids false oaths also commands honoring parents and sanctifying the Sabbath, and this command is no less holy than any other commandment, since it has its origin in G-d Himself, and we are therefore required to dedicate ourselves fully to every commandment, and to revere its holiness.

My views on this matter have been acquired both orally and through the writings I have studied, and I have fought battles for their sake and have gladly accepted the ridicule of those scoffers who speak in the name of the misguided "spirit of the times." Therefore, I do not understand what is my misdeed, that you and all the youth whose views you share have spread such nonsense about me, based on entirely different expectations. If you have erred about me then I am, indeed, very sorry; however, I must continue to teach that which I am able to justify to G-d and to my conscience.

I recognize only one goal in the world, a goal than which there is nothing greater, and which we are capable of achieving. Would that our youth — especially our youth! — could dedicate itself to strive for this goal with all its vigor and enthusiasm!

This goal can be described in only a few words: to be a complete Jew in both spirit and heart, in word and deed, to sanctify life under any and all circumstances, to devote oneself to studying G-d's word with all its depth and beauty, to grasp happily and passionately all its sublime meaning and to implant it in one's self both by speaking of it and by performing it, to take one's soul in one's hand and to bring heaven down to the earth, to make ourselves into a "kingdom of priests and a holy nation."

You can see, my good sir, that this is the goal to which our eyes must be lifted, the goal which must light up our path like an eternal fiery pillar that casts its light upon the Jew whether in tattered rags or in modern dress. This is the goal — that of firm and fast goodness — to which our youth, and the youth of which you speak, should aspire.

Alas, as long as our youth, and you with them, gaze down with scorn from their imagined heights on the ragged Jews, the Jews attired in the garments of the previous "unenlightened" generation, and think of them as dirty, lowly, and despised, and therefore think that this Rabbi was sent to them, as you express it, to make Jews into "men" rather than to make what you call "men" into Jews, then your youth cannot begin to grasp this goal of which we have been speaking.

Can you not see how debased this youth really is, how blind are the very ones who hold themselves so lofty, how small they are compared to the ancestors for whom they show such scorn? Their ancestors were not ashamed to live as Jews in the face of a hostile world, and they had the courage to hold their necks stiff against the axe and the gallows, the blows and the sputum, without yielding a hair's-breadth in their observance of the teachings of their G-d. It is only the craven grandchild who can ask, in all seriousness, "Must I tell my Christian customers that I have nothing for them today because it is the Sabbath? Will they buy bread from me all week and on the Sabbath go to the gentile bakery? Will they not curse the Jew and his religion?" and so on.

Yes, you may certainly tell them that today is your Sabbath, and with this simple answer you can give testimony that "it is an eternal sign between Me and the Children of Israel," and that some things are more important that livelihood and sustenance — you can give testimony that Jews are only too happy to make any sacrifice for the sake of their faith in their G-d.

Be aware that you are mistaken about the Christian, the true Christian, just as you are mistaken about the truly loyal Jew, and may the good Lord open your eyes!

Rabbi Yehudah Aszod

The relationship between Rabbi Hirsch and the rabbis of the old school in Moravia and neighboring Hungary has been the subject of a good deal of attention by historians. Much has been written about the supposed tension and distrust between them and Rabbi Hirsch, which purportedly led, in the end, to his acceptance of the offer in Frankfurt. The available evidence suggests that this tension has been exaggerated, although already in his day there were rumors of some friction. Soon after the announcement of Rabbi Hirsch's decision to leave, Rabbi Meir Eisenstadt of Ungvar wrote to Rabbi Yehudah Aszod (1794-1866) of Semnitz that he heard that Rabbi Hirsch was leaving Nikolsburg "because some Moravian rabbis are disrespectful to him."[14] In any event, it is unclear from Rabbi Eisenstadt's letter who these rabbis were and what was the source of the friction.

Upon his arrival in Nikolsburg, Rabbi Hirsch received a letter from Rabbi Yehudah Aszod , one of the leading Hungarian rabbis of the old school, and an important halachic decisor.[15] Rabbi Aszod, a disciple of Rabbi Mordechai Banet, and a frequent correspondent of the *Chasam Sofer*, wrote in warm and respectful tones offering his cooperation and assistance in any area which Rabbi Hirsch deemed necessary.[16] Several years later the two men carried on a correspondence regarding permission to remarry for an *agunah* whose husband had reportedly been killed in battle. Rabbi Aszod fully supported Rabbi Hirsch's decision granting the woman permission to remarry.[17]

In 1851, Rabbi Aszod was told in a private conversation that Rabbi Hirsch had severely criticized the Hungarian rabbinate for being lax in various religious matters. He responded immediately, and respectfully requested that Rabbi Hirsch specify what needed correction and offered, if the latter deemed it necessary, to travel to Nikolsburg to consult on possible solutions.[b] Rabbi Hirsch replied that the report of his criticism was a fabrication, and that he would never speak in such fashion about the Jews of other countries, and would certainly not assault the honor of the Torah and its sages. It pained him, Rabbi Hirsch wrote, that Rabbi Aszod lent credence to anything the man said. What he had said was that if it were true that in many Hungarian towns kosher meat was sold without supervision in non-kosher butcher shops, he could not understand how the great Hungarian rabbis could allow this. Rabbi Hirsch took great pains to stress that he would never criticize the Hungarian Jews or their spiritual leaders. Rabbi Aszod later wrote to Rabbi Meir Eisenstadt describing his excellent relationship with Rabbi Hirsch.[18] According to the correspondent of the *Allgemeine Zeitung des Judentums*, Rabbi Aszod requested Rabbi Hirsch as Chief Rabbi of Moravia not to grant ordination to any native of Hungary on the suspicion that the rabbinical candidate would preach in German, and Rabbi Hirsch agreed.[19]

Rabbi Shlomo Kvetch (1798-1856), a disciple of Rabbi Mordechai Banet and from 1833 Rabbi of Leipnik, Moravia — a rabbi of the "old school," who had been one of the contenders for the post of Moravian Chief Rabbi — was initially a strong antagonist to Rabbi Hirsch. The two carried on, however, an extensive correspondence regarding two brothers, both of whom refused to grant *chalitzah* to the wife of their deceased brother. Nowhere in this lengthy and detailed halachic correspondence is there even the slightest hint of any tension between the two. To the contrary, the correspondence is filled with mutual expressions of respect and great esteem.[20] And it was Rabbi Kvetch himself, supposedly Rabbi Hirsch's leading antagonist, who led the delegation comprised of rabbis and leaders of all the Moravian communities that entreated Rabbi Hirsch not to leave Moravia for Frankfurt.

Halachah

IN ADDITION TO STANDING AT THE HEAD OF THE LARGE YESHIVA IN Nikolsburg, Rabbi Hirsch was active in responding to halachic queries from the rabbis of the Moravian communities. He also headed the local Nikolsburg *Beis Din*. Serving as *dayanim* were Rabbi Yoseph Knopfmacher (1815-1909), a pupil of Rabbi Mordechai Banet, Rabbi Zvi Hirsch Trenschin, and the elderly Rabbi Moshe Pashkus (died 1854),[21] who had served as a *dayan* on the *Beis Din*

b. The expression he employed, that he would be willing to come במקלי ובמעותי (with my staff and moneybelt), is one which the Talmud uses to denote great subservience.

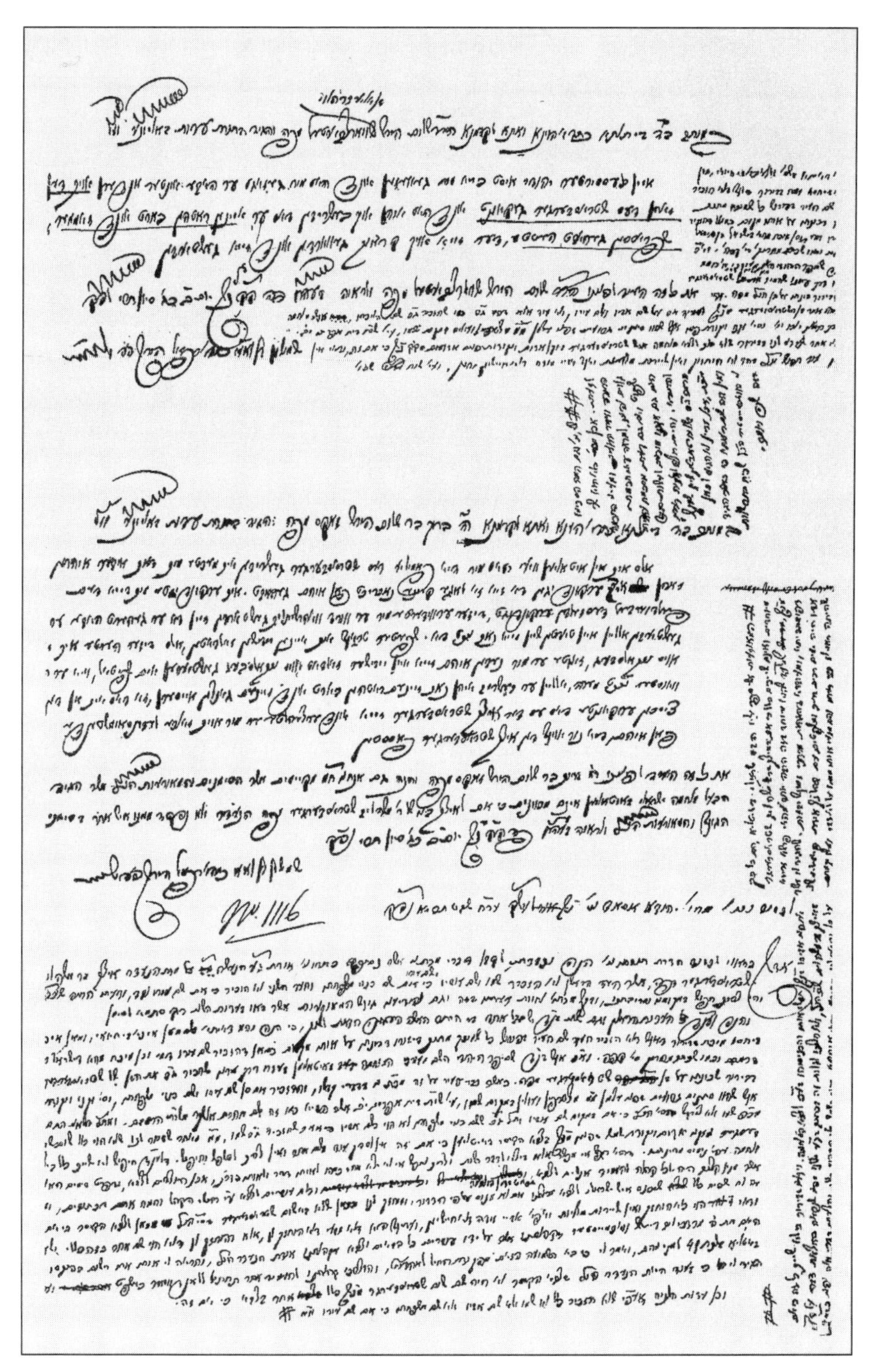

Decision of Rabbi Hirsch, in his own hand, as Chief of Nikolsburg Beis Din and accompanying responsa to Rabbi Aszod

Rabbi Yoseph Knopfmacher, dayan in Nikolsburg

since 1804, four years before Rabbi Hirsch's birth. Several responsa of Rabbi Hirsch bear his signature as well.

As Chief Rabbi, Rabbi Hirsch was called upon to rule on questions referred to him by the rabbis of Moravia and elsewhere. The dates on responsa that survive from that period suggest that during the four years he served in Nikolsburg he must have responded in writing to hundreds of halachic queries. Through these responsa and personal contact, the rabbis of Moravia and of neighboring Hungary came to greatly respect his scholarship and integrity.

We also have the assessment of the *K'sav Sofer,* Rabbi Avrohom Shmuel Binyamin Sofer, Rabbi of Pressburg and leader of Hungarian Jewry. The *K'sav Sofer* first met Rabbi Hirsch in Vienna, not long after the latter assumed his post in Nikolsburg. On the first Shabbos after his return to Pressburg, a large crowd came to his home for *Shalosh Seudos* in order to hear his observations about the new Chief Rabbi. Their curiosity was understandable, since, as followers of the *Chasam Sofer*, the *K'sav Sofer's* father, they harbored deep suspicions of anyone versed in secular studies, which they considered a potent danger to the Jewish people. The *K'sav Sofer* described his meeting with Rabbi Hirsch in the following terms:

> We spoke at length on Torah subjects with the new "*Rosh Medinah*" and whatever topic we discussed, his reply showed that he had *Shas* and *poskim* on his fingertips. We, the *rabbonim* of Hungary, have to consider ourselves very fortunate that he holds us to be his superiors as scholars, for if he were only aware of the extent of his own scholarship, we would have no rest from him.[22]

Rabbi Hirsch was also remembered in Nikolsburg for the stirring addresses he delivered in the main synagogue, or the *Altschul*, as it was called. People would flock to hear his *drashas* from all 12 synagogues in Nikolsburg, and when Yom Tov fell right before or after Shabbos, he would sometimes deliver a three-part *drashah,* one section on each day.[23]

AS CHIEF RABBI, RABBI HIRSCH ATTEMPTED TO IMPLEMENT CERTAIN urgent changes in Jewish public affairs and to subsume the dozens of Moravian Jewish communities into one unified framework. These steps met with opposition from both the more modern and the more traditional elements in the Jewish community, neither of which understood what he was trying to do. He sent a detailed list of regulations to every synagogue in Moravia, directed toward increasing the sanctity of the synagogue.

Communal Improvements

In Moravia, he introduced the ancient German custom of performing marriage ceremonies in the synagogue itself, and, in addition, had the rabbi address the newlyweds under the *chuppah,* a practice which he continued in Frankfurt.[24] He did not, however, permit women to enter the main synagogue on such occasions, with the exception of the bride and the two mothers. It happened once in Nikolsburg that, in the middle of his address under the *chuppah,* a group of women entered the men's section of the *shul.* He interrupted his speech and insisted that they leave immediately.[25]

The revolution of 1848, and the extension of civil rights to Moravian Jews,[c] brought in its wake an easing of government supervision of the Jewish community and an attendant weakening of communal control. One of the immediate consequences of the general weakening of the community structure was mayhem in the supervision of *shechitah,* with the proliferation of unauthorized *shochtim.* Rabbi Hirsch required *shochtim* to be licensed by the local rabbi, and to be employees of the community in order to ensure proper supervision.[26]

In 1848, the Austerlitz community wrote to Rabbi Hirsch that they had elected a rabbi, but that the losing candidate had gone to the authorities and alleged that the rabbi-elect was unfit for the post. As a result, the government refused to accept the elected candidate. The Austerlitz community asked Rabbi Hirsch to examine their rabbi-elect and certify his qualifications for the post. After doing so, Rabbi Hirsch replied that despite the candidate's suitability in many respects, his halachic knowledge was unsatisfactory and he was unable to grant him the certification. He suggested that the community provide him time to learn and make up those areas in which he was deficient, and then accept him as their rabbi. At the same time, he wrote a blistering letter to the father of the other candidate, who apparently had asked Rabbi Hirsch to intervene on behalf of his son, excoriating him for his attempts to have Rabbi Hirsch tip the scales in the

---

c. See Chapter 23 for an account of Rabbi Hirsch's extensive activity on behalf of emancipation for Moravian Jewry in 1848-49.

favor of his son. He expressed his utter disbelief that anyone who considered himself even somewhat of a *ben Torah* could act so deviously.[27]

Rabbi Hirsch canceled the traditional trial sermon which had heretofore been an important factor in the choice of rabbis. He felt that the ability to deliver a sermon was largely irrelevant to the main task of a rabbi and that the entire spectacle was demeaning.[28]

He also attempted to establish a *beis medrash* to train rabbis and teachers in accordance with his principles. Nothing came of this plan, however, and like many of his other proposals for the reorganization and improvement of communal life,[d] this too fell on deaf ears.

Invitation to Frankfurt

GIVEN HIS LACK OF SUCCESS IN IMPLEMENTING HIS PROPOSAL FOR communal improvements, it is not altogether surprising that when Rabbi Hirsch was invited to head the newly formed congregation in Frankfurt am Main in *Adar* II, 5611 (March 1851), less than four years after his arrival in Nikolsburg, he responded immediately in the affirmative.

The proposal came from his old friend Rabbi Gershon Josaphat (1808-1883), with whom he had studied and roomed in his yeshiva days in Mannheim.[e] In his letter describing conditions in Frankfurt, Rabbi Josaphat praised the sincerity and dedication of the founders of the new congregation, who were eager to undertake the ambitious task of restoring Torah to its former glory, amidst the ruins of Jewish life in Frankfurt. Rabbi Hirsch, he wrote, with his energetic and sincere personality, would find in Frankfurt a fertile field in which to pursue his aspirations to spread the light of Torah in his native Germany. "It is true," Rabbi Josaphat argued, "that you presently hold a most important rabbinic post and stand at the pinnacle of the world; nonetheless, because you are a native of Germany, my acquaintance with you leads me to think that this post will be more suited and more agreeable to you than your present one. The people here are upright and peaceloving and I can assure you that they will respect you greatly and, more importantly, that you will be able to accomplish here a great deal. The material and the means exist

d. See also Chapter 23.

e. Born in Kassel, where his father Rabbi Shmuel Josaphat was *dayan*, Rabbi Josaphat entered the yeshiva in Mannheim at 18. He was appointed *dayan* and head of the Behrend Lehman *klaus* in Halberstadt in 1835 and stayed there for the rest of his life. Considered one of the great *talmidei chachamim* of Germany, he was a pedagogue *par excellence*, whose chief joy in life was to learn with his students. Among his disciples were Rabbi Meir Lehmann, Rabbi Hirsch Plato, Rabbi Hirsch's son-in-law and Rabbi Ezriel Hildesheimer, whom he subsequently sent to learn under his own teacher, Rabbi Yaakov Ettlinger in Altona.[28*]

Rabbi Hirsch's home in Nikolsburg (1992)

here in ample measure, and all that is required is someone who can combine them together. My beloved Samson, you are that someone."

Rabbi Hirsch's reply was not long in coming. On April 10, 1851 (8 *Nissan*), he wrote to Rabbi Josaphat, informing him of his acceptance and thanking the Almighty that he would be reunited with his old friend once again.[29] On May 4 (2 *Iyar*), he wrote to the Moravian government informing them of his decision to leave and requested the authorities not to delay in appointing a successor.

The reaction of the Jews of Nikolsburg and Moravia was one of shock. They refused to believe that he intended to resign from the largest rabbinate in the Austro-Hungarian empire to serve in a congregation of barely 100 members.[f,30] The heads of Moravian Jewry quickly circulated a letter to all the Moravian communities to send representatives to Nikolsburg to entreat Rabbi Hirsch to stay. The delegations first met in Brünn to plan their moves, but their inability to fathom the reasons for his wanting to leave made it hard to do so.[31]

Hirsch Kolisch

On May 13 (11 *Iyar*), a delegation composed of 49 rabbis and the leaders of all Moravian communities came to Nikolsburg to entreat him to reconsider his decision. They insisted that his efforts to improve communal life in Moravia were not in vain, and that the government was ready to remove all obstacles. Among the conditions they agreed to was the establishment of a rabbinical seminary. They also put under his control all the schools in Moravia, and began to raise the necessary funds to bring all his proposals to fruition. The Moravian *kehillas* also agreed to separate the Nikolsburg rabbinate from that of Moravia as he had requested, and move the Chief Rabbinate to Olmütz, seat of the Moravian government. The president of the Nikolsburg Jewish Community, Hirsch Kolisch, offered to provide a dowry of 10,000 gulden for each of Rabbi Hirsch's then eight children.[32]

With the acquiescence by the representatives of the different communities and their *rabbonim* to Rabbi Hirsch's proposed changes and organizational plans, including his plan for a rabbinical seminary, Rabbi Hirsch agreed to request the congregation in Frankfurt to release him from his commitment. Without their consent, however, he told the delegation, he

f. The Frankfurt offer was not the first he considered. Some months before, he was approached by a member of the search committee of the Hamburg Jewish community who asked him to consider the rabbinical chair of his home town left vacant by the death of Rabbi Isaac Bernays in 1849. He was told that in Hamburg he would find יראה (fear of Heaven), but no Torah. There were some negotiations but nothing came of them.[30*]

would not consider going back on his word: "I gave my word to Frankfurt." Moreover, he was not convinced that these agreements would be of lasting duration, and he called on the Moravian communal leaders not to allow these decisions to evaporate.[33]

On May 19, 1851, Rabbi Hirsch wrote to Frankfurt, requesting that the fledgling congregation release him from his pledge. "My word to you is holy," he wrote, "but I gave them time, and they will ask you to release me from my pledge in the name of more than 50,000 souls." The decision, he continued, lay in the hands of the Jews of Frankfurt. Hirsch Kolisch, the head of the Nikolsburg Jewish community, traveled to Frankfurt to ask the congregation to release Rabbi Hirsch from his promise. They refused. To release Rabbi Hirsch, they asserted, would be tantamount to suicide for their holy cause, and this they had no intention of doing.[34]

Rabbi Hirsch, it seems, was not entirely convinced of the strength and determination of the Moravian communities to see the changes through. In a letter to his son Mendel, on 2 *Sivan* (June 2, 1851), he wondered if "this comes simply from their first stunned dismay, and if so will it eventually give way to the strains of prosaic reality?" The congregation of Frankfurt, he reported, had replied "that they were totally incapable of making such a sacrifice [to release him from his promise]. My coming to them is a question of life and death as far as everything that is holy to them is concerned, and therefore they gave me their unequivocal response that they will under no circumstances release me from my pledge, and indeed, that it would be forbidden for them to do so. . . . I now await the decision [of the committee of Moravian communities] with a serene mind, confident that Heaven will guide us in the proper course."[35]

The steadfast refusal of Frankfurt to release him made his decision final.[g] Thus Rabbi Hirsch left his position as Chief Rabbi of 50,000 Jews in favor of a tiny congregation with scarcely 100 members. How had the once glorious Jewish community of Frankfurt fallen to such a low state? To answer this question, let us take a look back at its history over the previous 50 years, a half-century that will serve as a microcosm of the upheavals within German Jewry in the first half of the 19th century.

g. On July 11, he officially tendered his resignation, and on July 31 he sent a farewell circular to all the 51 Moravian communities, explaining that he was not able to fulfill many of what he felt were his duties, especially communal and school improvements. On August 12, he left Nikolsburg with his family, and was accompanied by a delegation to the next town.[35*]

Chapter Nine
FRANKFURT

FRANKFURT WAS ONE OF THE OLDEST JEWISH COMMUNITIES in Germany, with a Jewish presence as early as the second half of the 11th century.[1] Torah scholars from all over Germany flocked to Frankfurt over the centuries, and its residents were justifiably proud of their rich heritage.[2]

An Illustrious Past

Like most other German Jews, those of Frankfurt experienced repeated persecution. In 1241, several hundred members of the community were killed as punishment for their refusal to undergo mass conversion,[a] and in 1349, there was a second general slaughter, this time without the option of conversion.[3] For the next several hundred years, Frankfurt's Jews suffered persecution of every sort, including death at the hands of the mob.

a. One of the *piyutim* recited in German Jewish communities on *Tishah B'Av* was composed as a memorial to that mass murder.

The old shul in Frankfurt, erected 1711

The Jews of Frankfurt were fiercely proud and zealously protective of their traditions, and changes in the services were not undertaken lightly.[b] Entire books detail the intricate customs known as *Minhag Frankfurt*, which were practiced for hundreds of years.[4]

The growth of the community was stunted by the ghetto walls, a prohibitive levying of "special" taxes, laws of residence which kept the number of families fixed, and a limit on the number of marriages permitted per year. In spite of all this, Frankfurt was always one of the leading Jewish communities, not only of Germany but of all Europe. Beginning in 1462, the Jews of Frankfurt were confined to a ghetto, or *Judengasse* (Jews Street), surrounded by walls and gates. Although the ghetto walls were built for the sole purpose of keeping Jews in, they also had the positive effect of keeping non-Jewish influences out. But even if the lives of Frankfurt's Jews were thus severely confined in a physical sense, they flourished spiritually. As the *Chasam Sofer* (1762-1839) once described his native city, "אחת היא לאומתה אין בכל העולם דוגמתה — She is unique to her people, in the whole world there exists not her equal."[5]

b. An interesting illustration of the power of tradition in Frankfurt is the way the community reacted to the recital of *Kabbalas Shabbos*, which, since the 16th century, has become part of the Friday night service. In Frankfurt, acceptance of *Kabbalas Shabbos* was the subject of major controversy, and for centuries it was not a component of the Friday night *davening*.

Judengasse in Frankfurt

Without question, Frankfurt in its prime was the crown jewel of German Jewry.

IN KEEPING WITH ITS PREEMINENT STATUS, THE RABBIS WHO SERVED Frankfurt were at the front rank of Torah luminaries throughout the ages.

The Rabbinate

Rabbi Shimon Hadarshan, compiler of *Yalkut Shimoni* lived in Frankfurt, as did Rabbi Alexander Zuslin Hakohen author of the *Sefer Agudah* (Cracow, 1571). Rabbi Isaiah Horowitz, universally known as the *Sh'loh Hakodosh,* after his classic work *Sh'nei Luchos Habris,* was appointed rabbi there in 1606. Other rabbinic luminaries of Frankfurt included Rabbi Meir ben Yaakov

Interior of the synagogue (erected 1711) as it appeared in the Chasam Sofer's youth

Hakohen Schiff (b. 1605; d. 1641), a native son and author of *Maharam Schiff* on the Talmud,[c] and Rabbi Aharon Shmuel Koidenover, author of *Tiferes Shmuel* on the Talmud (Frankfurt, 1696), who served on the Frankfurt rabbinate from 1667. In the 18th century, Rabbi Yehoshua Falk (1680-1756), better known by the name of his classic work *P'nei Yehoshua*, served as rabbi from 1741 until his passing.

Rabbi Pinchas Halevi Horovitz (1730-1805) — author of two classic works on the Talmud, *Haflaah* and *Hamakneh*, and *Panim Yafos* on *Chumash* — was appointed Rabbi of Frankfurt in 1771. During his tenure (1771-1805) Frankfurt produced numerous Torah scholars, most prominent among them Rabbi Moshe Sofer (known as the *Chasam Sofer*),[d] many of whom were called to serve as rabbis of other communities. Yet the winds of enlightenment and moderate reform began to penetrate the Frankfurt *Judengasse* toward the end of Rabbi Horovitz's life. An indication of his diminishing influence can be seen from the fact that despite his public

c. The *Maharam Schiff* did not serve on the Frankfurt rabbinate.

d. The *Chasam Sofer* was himself a grandson of Rabbi Shmuel Schotten, author of *Kos Hayeshuos* on the Talmud and a member of the Frankfurt rabbinate.

denunciation of Mendelssohn's *Biur* in 1783 there were still 49 subscribers in Frankfurt. While the Frankfurt yeshiva still had 60 students in 1793, this number was dwindling rapidly. With Rabbi Horovitz's passing in 1805, the golden age of Frankfurt Jewry, which had lasted for seven centuries, came to a close.[6]

The Chasam Sofer

So even mighty Frankfurt was assailed by the Berlin "Enlightenment" and the changes in Jewish life set in motion by the French Revolution. As in many other cities, when the walls of the ghetto came down, the long-standing foundations of its Jewish community crumbled along with them. Frankfurt's glorious traditions which had remained rock steady for centuries were unable to withstand the onslaught of Enlightenment and Reform.

Abolition of the Ghetto

THE FRANKFURT GHETTO SUSTAINED HEAVY DAMAGE DURING THE French revolutionary wars, and in 1796 the *Judengasse* was almost completely destroyed by fire in the wake of the French bombardment. As a result, Jews were permitted to live outside the ghetto until such time as it could be rebuilt. It never was.

Napoleon made Frankfurt the capital of a newly formed state and a member of the Confederation of the Rhine, and appointed Prince Primate Karl von Dalberg as regent. This appointment, though short lived, was to have disastrous results for Frankfurt Jewry. In 1808, the year of Rabbi Hirsch's birth, the regent packed the governing council of the Jewish community with those sympathetic to the Reform cause. He granted this group the power to appoint to the council new members of their own choice, without the necessity of holding elections. That change ultimately allowed the Reformers to gain control of all aspects of Jewish community life and to dismantle the established communal structures that had been built up through the centuries.[7]

In 1811, Jews were granted "equal rights," at least on paper, in return for the payment of the outrageous sum of 440,000 florins. To be sure,

Remains of the Frankfurt ghetto (circa 1865). Reform Temple is at far left on site of the old shul.

those rights did not remain unchallenged for long, and over the next decades the status of Frankfurt Jews and the restrictions on their activities changed frequently, often in tandem with shifts in the political climate and status of the city. As a result of the termination of French control of Central Europe with their defeat at the Battle of Leipzig in 1813, Prince Dalberg lost his position and the rights of Jews were again restricted. Only in 1864 were the last limitations on the civil rights of the Jews repealed. Frankfurt was a "free city," an independent city-state equal to the other German states, until 1866 when it was annexed by Prussia.[8]

Reform Tyranny

ALREADY IN 1805, "ENLIGHTENED" FRANKFURT JEWS, WITH THE cooperation of the government, established the Reform-oriented *Philanthropin* school, over the determined, but futile, opposition of the rabbinate. The *Philanthropin,* with its decidedly assimilationist leanings, became a powerful influence on behalf of radical Reform throughout Germany. Under the control of the Reform-dominated Community Board, funds and endowments which were originally set aside for the specific purpose of Torah study were diverted to support the school, which made no secret of its goal of the eradication of Torah study. In 1811, the *Philanthropin* instituted a Sunday morning "devotional hour," which consisted of German hymns

Temple in Kompostellhof, Frankfurt, where Reform services were held until the construction of the new Temple in 1864

accompanied by an organ and a sermon, with no prayers in Hebrew. Only after three years, in 1814, was it moved to Saturday.[9]

Upon the death of Rabbi Zvi Hirsch Horovitz, son of Rabbi Pinchas Horovitz, in 1817, Rabbi Salomon Trier (1758-1847) was appointed Rabbi of Frankfurt. Son of Rabbi Abraham Trier, *dayan*, *Rosh Yeshiva* and *Klausrabbiner* in Frankfurt until his passing in 1794, Rabbi Trier was appointed to the Frankfurt rabbinate upon his father's demise, and in 1807 was a delegate to the Paris "Sanhedrin" convened by Napoleon. During his three decades as rabbi, he was increasingly ignored by the Community Board.

Already in 1812, the government reorganized the Community Board and set new regulations governing its activity and authority. Over the years, most of the board members and community officials were strong adherents of Enlightenment and Reform. As such, the Board launched a systematic campaign to eradicate the study of Torah, and endeavored to bring about the complete atrophy of all religious institutions.[e] Not content with merely banning religious studies from the *Philanthropin*, the only officially sanctioned Jewish school in the city, the Community Board refused to tolerate them anywhere in the city. Thus, from 1818 to 1838, at

e. In 1854, three years after his arrival in Frankfurt, Rabbi Hirsch wrote a comprehensive account of the changes in community life that had occurred during the previous 30 years, on which some of the history recounted in this chapter is based.[9*]

the Board's initiative the Frankfurt authorities made it illegal to operate a *Talmud Torah,* and young people who wished to study Torah were forced to do so in hiding. All teachers of religious subjects were banished from the city, and anyone who attempted to teach Torah in spite of this edict was subject to a civil fine of 50 florins. The intention of the Board was to compel all parents to send their children to the *Philanthropin,* and to a great measure they succeeded. In no other Jewish community in Germany did the proponents of assimilation work so diligently, and for that matter so successfully, to achieve their aims.

Dr. Michael Creizenach, one of the leading educators of the Philanthropin

In 1837, a group of about 200 Jews who had remained faithful to tradition sought permission to renovate, at their own expense, the two abandoned and dilapidated synagogues. (Reform services were held in the *Philanthropin* building.) Their request was denied. Similarly, permission to renovate the old *mikveh* was refused, and women who wished to perform ritual immersion were forced to use facilities in the nearby towns of Bockenheim or Offenbach. Eventually the Community Board ordered the old *mikveh* to be sealed up completely.

Traditionally, the community had provided kosher meals to patients in the city's hospitals, but this practice was also stopped. When Rabbi Trier forbade work on the renovation of the Jewish hospital on the Sabbath, the Community Board overruled him and ordered that the work proceed, especially on Shabbos, in spite of the objections of the hospital's administration. One of the directors of the hospital volunteered to cover the added cost of the cessation of work on Shabbos out of his own pocket, but this offer was also refused.

In 1838, the Community Board declared, in an official report to the Senate of Frankfurt, that the value of *Tanach* was doubtful,[10] and the Board also decided that any Jew who still put on *tefillin* was ineligible to serve as a Board member.[11]

That same year, over the vehement protest of Rabbi Trier, the Board canceled the right of the *Chevra Kadisha,* which served on a purely voluntary basis, to perform the *taharah* (purification) and burial. Instead, this duty was assigned to paid, uniformed undertakers.[12] "Functions which until that time had been acts of pure religiosity and selfless humanity," Rabbi Hirsch later observed, "were turned over to paid hirelings, because the latter would more willingly dress in black funerary uniforms. After all, the outer trappings, the 'uniform,' was more important than any warm heart, throbbing with piety and devotion."[13]

It was illegal for young people or adults to study Torah together in groups, even in private homes. For a number of generations, there had existed in Frankfurt a group called the *Tzitzis Society*, which met in members' homes on Shabbos morning after services to study *Tanach* and the weekly Torah portion. This study group, which attracted close to 100 participants, was also outlawed, and the police commissioner, acting at the behest of the Board, ordered them to discontinue their sessions. In 1842, the teaching of *Tanach* in the traditional fashion was made illegal. That all this was done at the instigation of the Community Board was confirmed by the police authorities at the time.[14]

Emanuel Schwarzschild (1825-1896), later head of the Orthodox *kehillah,* described the situation in his youth:

> [At the age of 15,] I was *the only one of my age group* who still put on *tefillin.* The others were all either younger or older. If anyone still lived a religious life, he was regarded as one who clings to inherited superstitions and to ancient prejudices. Old people might be excused but younger ones were looked upon as either fools or hypocrites. It had to be experienced to be believed — the weight of contempt expressed in the look of scorn that greeted an avowal of adherence to religious observance.[15]

Schwarzschild reported that in the Frankfurt of the 1840s, regular daily prayer services were held in just two locations, and even there the required quorum of 10 men was not always present. Once, when he was invited to a Reform home and refused to eat the meat, his hosts promised not to tell his parents that he had partaken of their food. When he replied that it was not his parents who prevented him from eating forbidden foods, but rather his own awareness of the transgressions involved, "they considered [him], to put it mildly, insane, hypocritical, and stupid."[16]

Professor Jacob Katz has uncovered an interesting fact, which goes some way in explaining the success of the extreme Reform elements in their relentless crushing of any Orthodox tendencies in the Frankfurt Jewish community. Most of the members of the Community Board and the leading figures in the *Philanthropin* were members of the Morgenröthe Freemason Lodge of Frankfurt. A large worldwide secret society, freemasonry teaches the brotherhood of man and seeks to promote harmonious relations between all men regardless of their faith. Freemasonry subscribes to the belief that all people are children of one G-d, that all persons are related to each other and that the best way to worship G-d is to help people. Those universalistic moral principles were congruent with watered-down Reform Judaism.

From the second decade of the 19th century almost no one was elected to the Frankfurt Jewish Community Board who was not a member of the Lodge, and from 1817 to 1832 all Board members, without exception, were Masons. As Masons, they were determined to, and succeeded in, shaping the community along the lines of their view of enlightenment, liberal humanism and hence Reform. Although the principles of Freemasonry did not in and of themselves demand the destruction of traditional Judaism, yet Freemasonry's Deist principles, and its stress on humanism and ethical behavior — in tandem with its Masonic symbols and ceremonies — could, and did, serve as an alternative to traditional Judaism.[17]

Thus, the Community Board in those decades was not a random group of members, but a cohesive unit, sharing common goals as Masons.[f] The affiliation of the leaders of the Jewish community with freemasonry was unique to Frankfurt, and explains, in Katz's view, why, 2,800 out of 3,000 Jewish families, or 95 percent of the Jewish population, were Reform in 1842, as compared, for instance, to Bohemia, where adherents of Reform constituted half of the Jewish population, and Hamburg, where they constituted only a third.

Thus, Rabbi Hirsch's charge that the destruction of authentic Judaism with such success in Frankfurt was the result of the single-minded efforts of the Community Board is a historical fact.[18] Even the Reform rabbi of Frankfurt, Leopold Stein complained, in a pamphlet explaining his resignation in 1861, of the tyranny and the total lack of tolerance of the Board.[19]

Reform Judaism, of course, was hardly a phenomenon unique to Frankfurt. But as one observer put it, there was a difference. Whereas elsewhere the Reformers were, by and large, *mumarim le'tayavon* (sinners for pleasure), in Frankfurt they were *mumarim le'hach'is* (premeditated sinners).[20]

For all the Reformers' successes in uprooting *mitzvah* observance in Frankfurt, they remained constantly fearful that the Orthodox would

f. One non-Jewish Masonic leader of Frankfurt even praised the Jewish members of the Lodge for their intention to bring Judaism closer to Christianity by founding schools and houses of worship that were religiously neutral.[17*]

somehow manage to recover lost ground. Thus, in the late 1840s, when the traditional elements requested the Community Board to bring in an Orthodox rabbi possessing a secular education to serve the needs of the Orthodox segment of the community, the Board vehemently refused. "If you want to bring in a Polish *rav* from the Ukraine with a long white beard, certainly. But someone with a secular education, under no circumstances," they replied.[21]

Reformfreunde — Circumcision

IN 1843, THE *VEREIN DER REFORMFREUNDE* (SOCIETY OF THE FRIENDS of Reform) was organized in Frankfurt and headed by Theodore Creizenach.[22] The program of the *Reformfreunde* was threefold. It posited that: 1) Judaism is capable of unlimited development; 2) The Talmud is not authoritative — neither in dogma nor as regards *mitzvah* observance; 3) Jews do not await the coming of the Messiah, and they view the country in which they are living as their fatherland. Motivated by the desire to win acceptance into German society, the *Reformfreunde* began a campaign to convince its members not to circumcise their children. Not that it helped. The newspapers of the time reported that a Jewish banker named Floisheim had refrained from circumcising his son in the hope of being admitted to the local "Casino" club, which had until then excluded Jews. A Christian banker reacted contemptuously: "*Wir wollen keine Juden, keine beschnittene und keine unbeschnittene* — We want no Jews, not cut ones and not uncut ones."[23]

In response to the Board's decision to include in the community's official Jewish population register even those who were not circumcised, 85-year-old Rabbi Zalman Trier organized the publication of a collection of expert opinions entitled *Rabbinische Gutachten über die Beschneidung*, the purpose of which was to establish that circumcision was required by Jewish law and that uncircumcised Jews cannot be considered part of the community.[24] The first letter in the collection was that of Rabbi Hirsch, at the time Chief Rabbi of Emden.[25] Even some of the Reformers felt that the attempt to abandon circumcision was going a bit too far, and the abolition of circumcision never really gained acceptance.[26]

The Rothschild family offered, in 1843, to build and furnish a new synagogue at their own expense, as a gift to the Jewish community of Frankfurt. An agreement was concluded with the Community Board stipulating, *inter alia*, that a new rabbi be hired to assist the elderly Rabbi Trier. The latter was to interview all candidates for this position, and to approve of the choice of his assistant. Without Rabbi Trier's knowledge, the community council appointed to the post, on December 9, 1843, one Leopold Stein (1810-1882),[27] a staunch Reformer and a public advocate of the use of an organ in the synagogue. This willful violation of the terms agreed upon with the Rothschilds caused them to withdraw their offer.

Dr. Leopold Stein

The appointment of Stein was a deep affront to the elderly Rabbi Trier, whose faculties were unimpaired in spite of his 87 years. With no other choice, he resigned in 1844 and refused the offer of a pension. He passed away not long afterwards.[28] As his successor, the board appointed the same Leopold Stein, who proceeded to "decide" that students were permitted to write on Shabbos in school[29] and to declare that rabbinic enactments had no binding force on Jews. Not long after his appointment, Stein replaced *Lecha Dodi* with German lyrics.[30] Such was the heir to the rabbinical seat that had been occupied by such giants as the *Shelah*, the *Pnei Yehoshua*, and the *Haflaah*.

With Rabbi Trier's resignation, the path was open for the introduction of the Reform prayerbook and organ into the synagogue, whereupon the Orthodox, who still comprised most of the regular worshipers — the Reformers came only on special occasions — promptly left in protest.

In 1844, the municipal authorities passed an ordinance which required all banks, even those owned by Jews, to process checks on the Sabbath. The religious Jewish bankers, and there were several, organized a petition to the local government to release them from this obligation, and at the same time turned to Stein to support their request and to write a Jewish legal opinion supporting their appeal. Stein agreed, but the Community Board insisted on deleting from his letter any mention of a necessity to respect the religious conscience of Jews who did not wish to desecrate the Sabbath. The ordinance was enacted, but the Rothschilds ignored it just the same.[31]

That was the situation in Frankfurt in the late 1840s, a mere four decades after the passing of the *Haflaah*. From having been the most illustrious *Kehillah* in Germany, the community had rapidly degenerated to one where almost no level of Jewish observance was tolerated. Matters had reached a breaking point.

Chapter Ten

KEHILLATH JESCHURUN

Turning Point

BY THE MIDDLE OF THE CENTURY, THE REMAINING Orthodox Jews in Frankfurt had long since reached the point of desperation. The Community Board, with the support of the government, had so successfully usurped the traditional communal structures that the Orthodox had virtually no freedom of action. Their only hope was to establish an independent organization within the community, an arrangement at that time unheard of in Germany. Finally an incident occurred that was the straw that broke the camel's back.

When the *dayan* of the community, Rabbi Yaakov Posen, passed away at the end of March 1849, his family asked the Rabbi of Darmstadt, Rabbi Zvi Binyamin Auerbach, to deliver a eulogy at the graveside. The Community Board refused permission, and the visitor was forced to address the funeral procession in the street outside the cemetery. In view of the Board's behavior, he began, appropriately enough, with the words of the prophet Jeremiah describing the decline of Jerusalem: "איכה היתה לזונה קריה נאמנה — How has the reputable city become a harlot." The observant were incensed at the refusal of the Board to permit a decent Jewish burial. Salomon Posen, son of the deceased *dayan*, decided that the time had finally come for the remaining Orthodox Jews in Frankfurt to found an independent religious organization. And they did.[1]

Rabbi Zvi Binyamin Auerbach

In 1849, a group of 18 committed Jews in Frankfurt held a meeting. Eleven of them, including Emanuel Schwarzschild and Moshe Mainz, signed a petition to the Senate (city council) of Frankfurt stating that as a result of their religious beliefs, and in light of the consistent refusal of the local community to respect those beliefs, they had "seceded" from the community and established an independent religious community. The Senate responded positively, but noted that, according to the Frankfurt constitution, secession from the community was against the law. Thus it could only approve the establishment of an independent religious association, but not the establishment of a community. Within a short time, the membership of the new organization, the *Israelitische Religionsgesellschaft* (Jewish Religious Society), or *IRG*, had swelled to around 80, among them Baron Amschel Rothschild.

For the purpose of conducting prayer services, the *IRG* rented rooms in the community center, which also included an infirmary and various other communal institutions. By 1850, the membership of the *IRG* had grown to around 100. The members already had plans to build a synagogue and a sizable pledge from the Rothschild family to cover all, or most, of the cost. They had not yet decided what to do as regards the use of the communal cemetery.[2]

While permission was no longer necessary for the existence of the organization, the appointment of a rabbi required special approval from the Senate. The chairman of the Senate committee, whose authorization was needed, strongly opposed this step, at the instigation of the Reformers. Providence, however, arranged it that on the day a decision was to be taken, the chairman was called away to another city and the

Rabbi and Rebbetzin Hirsch ca. 1851

committee, chaired by his deputy, granted the request.[3]

In September of 1850, the board of directors of the new organization invited Rabbi Jechiel Michael Sachs (1808-1864) of Berlin to serve as their rabbi. Rabbi Sachs — who served as Rabbi in Prague from 1836-1844, and was Rabbi of Berlin from 1844-1860 — accepted the position of Rabbi of the *IRG*, but after a few months he returned to Berlin, apparently because of the dissatisfaction of his wife with life in Frankfurt. The fact that the *IRG* was willing to accept Sachs — who was a good deal more accommodating than Rabbi Hirsch — as their rabbi is an indication that the members of the *IRG* were still unsure of their way.[a]

In 1851, at a meeting attended by 44 members of the *IRG*, it was decided to invite the Chief Rabbi of Moravia, Rabbi Hirsch, to serve as rabbi of this congregation, which consisted of barely 100 members and did not even possess its own synagogue building. The boldness of this request reveals the depth of their spiritual aspirations, and their understanding of the demands of the situation. The negotiations between Rabbi Hirsch and the *IRG* proceeded with exceptional dispatch, for he imposed virtually no conditions on his acceptance of the position.[4]

In his letter of resignation to the Minister of Religious Affairs of

a. In 1850, the job was also offered to the 31-year-old Rabbi Ezriel Hildesheimer, who turned it down. It is not unreasonable to assume that the one behind the offer, as in the case of Rabbi Hirsch, was Rabbi Gershon Josaphat, who was Rabbi Hildesheimer's teacher in Halberstadt.[3*]

Map of Jewish section of Frankfurt, 1830

Moravia, Rabbi Hirsch wrote that he had received an "appeal from Frankfurt to go to the aid of a tiny group, whose very founding is, in my view, given the goals I have had all my life, the most promising development that has occurred in Jewry within the last several decades. For now, for the first time, a Jewish community has been formed, which is openly and proudly dedicated to a most holy principle, in an area which had been successfully conquered by the forces of confusion. What can I do! This holy cause is the very one to which I have consecrated my life."[5] His words were prophetic. On September 17, 1851 (20 *Elul*), he took up his post.

A New Beginning

IN HIS FIRST ADDRESS TO HIS CONGREGATION, RABBI HIRSCH explained, as he often did at the outset of new undertakings, that success was not to be measured by numbers of people, but rather by the intensity with which they dedicated themselves to their holy purpose: *Not by might, and not by power, but by My spirit, says the Lord of the Hosts.*[6]

During the first year in Frankfurt, his congregation continued to hold prayer services in the rooms they had rented in the communal building

Rabbi Hirsch's residence in Frankfurt Schöne Aussicht, 5

(the *Kippe-stub*), controlled by the Community Board. Matters came to a head rather quickly. Not long after "Mr." (as the Reformers referred to him)[7] Hirsch's arrival, the *chazan* wished to wait for the new rabbi to finish the silent *Shemoneh Esrei* prayer before beginning the reader's repetition, a gesture of respect practiced in synagogues all over the world. The director of the building, an employee of the Community Board, ordered him not to wait, since he did not acknowledge Rabbi Hirsch's position. The members of the *IRG* decided that they had had enough, and proceeded to rent an apartment with large rooms for use as a synagogue.

At the time of Rabbi Hirsch's arrival in Frankfurt, there was no kosher butcher and it was necessary to journey to Darmstadt to purchase kosher meat. Nor was the *mikveh* functional since the Reformers had had it filled in, and the women were forced to go out of town. The members of the fledgling congregation wanted to begin building a synagogue immediately, but Rabbi Hirsch insisted that their first priority was a *mikveh*,[b] and then a school. Only after the construction of these was assured did he consent to build a synagogue.

Rabbi Hirsch's first years in Frankfurt were a flurry of activity. On

b. Not long after his arrival in Frankfurt, Rabbi Hirsch convened a meeting of the married women to discuss the importance of family purity and other matters relating to the *mikveh*. At the close of the meeting he asked for a volunteer to serve as the secretary of the group so that he could call meetings and publicize information through her without having to contact each person individually. A young bride offered to serve as the secretary and organizer. Rabbi Hirsch took her to the next room, which served as the temporary quarters of the *shul*, directed her to the *Aron Hakodesh*, and told her, "I hereby promise you that because of your willingness to serve in this capacity, you will have a long life, without worries of health or livelihood." This woman met the Lubavitcher Rebbe some time around World War I, and she appeared to be no more than half her 80-plus years. She told the Rebbe that she had never been ill in her long life, nor had she ever had any financial worries.[7*]

Artist's rendering of the synagogue on the Schützenstrasse, 1853

February 2, 1852, his last two children — twins, Sophie and Jenny — were born. On September 9, 1852 (17 *Tishrei*, 5613), exactly a year after his arrival, the fledgling *kehillah* held a cornerstone-laying ceremony for their new *shul* and *mikveh*, located on the Schützenstrasse in Frankfurt. The cost of the building was 100,000 florins, of which the Rothschild family contributed 70 percent. Although they had offered to pay for the entire building, the members of the *IRG* insisted that at least 30 percent come from the membership.[8] On Sept. 29, 1853 (26 *Elul*, 5613), the synagogue was completed. The dedication ceremony of the synagogue was attended by both mayors, most of the members of the Frankfurt Senate, Catholic and Protestant representatives, and many other dignitaries.[9] As a result of the magnificent *shul* building, the Reformers also felt pressed to erect a synagogue building, but were unable to raise the necessary funds.

Rabbi Hirsch and family at wedding of Sara Hirsch-Guggenheimer

At the beginning of July 1852, Rabbi Hirsch proposed the establishment of a school to the *IRG* board, and on October 18, 1852 he formally submitted a request to the Senate of Frankfurt for the establishment of a school. On April 1, 1853 the school opened its doors.

The new congregation, composed primarily of younger people,[10] began accepting a steady stream of new members, not a few of whom moved to Frankfurt from rural areas to join Rabbi Hirsch's congregation. They were captivated by Rabbi Hirsch's addresses and the *shiurim* he gave several times a week in his home.[11] In addition, he taught a two-hour *shiur* in *Gemara* for youth every day until the school was established.

The IRG

RABBI HIRSCH CREATED AND BUILT FROM SCRATCH ALL THE INSTITUTIONS that constitute a Jewish community. As time went on, the *IRG* came to be the most respected Orthodox community in Germany. The community was seen by its members as one large family, with a warmth and unity that extended support and a strong sense of belonging to even its weakest members.[12] Members of the *IRG* regarded themselves, not without some justification, as a model congregation for all of Western Europe, although to be sure, this elitism existed in Frankfurt already in ghetto times. For most, being a part of the *IRG* meant an obligation to be truthful and upright.[13] Here is how Rabbi Yechiel Yaakov Weinberg described the *Kehillah*:

The children of the Kehillah after services in the Schützenstrasse synagogue

Rabbi Hirsch was not only a visionary thinker and speaker, he also possessed the ability to carry his visions through to realization. He devoted the best of his spiritual energy and poetic soul to building the outstanding community of Frankfurt, especially its educational institutions. This community was magnificent in all regards; no other congregation in Europe was so well organized and so orderly as this one. From the beginning, it was founded on principles of true democracy; the right to vote, and to serve as officers, was granted equally to all members, with no distinction between the wealthy, who were required to pay high membership fees, and the poor, of whom only a minimal contribution was expected. Even the well-known *tzaddik* and philanthropist, Baron Willy Rothschild, had no greater rights than any other member. Anyone could be elected as president, if he was suitable by virtue of his religious and ethical accomplishments.

The community had educational facilities for men and women, young and old, as well as associations to promote charity, self-help, care of the sick, provision for the needs of the departed and comfort for the mourners. This whole structure was organized to perfection and served as a shining model for the other Jewish communities of Germany, and later America, of how to

> preserve the holy tradition of Torah in the context of contemporary social conditions.[14]

Rabbi Ezriel Hildesheimer wrote that the members of the *IRG* held Rabbi Hirsch in a degree of esteem that had no equal anywhere.[15] They prided themselves on their rabbi and their community. All this required enormous efforts by Rabbi Hirsch to resolve the inevitable internal conflicts that arose in the course of the community's development. He often returned home exhausted after committee meetings in which he was forced to fight for majority support for his point of view.[16]

Membership

THE REGULATIONS OF THE IRG, ADOPTED FORMALLY IN 1874, INcluded clearly worded provisions as to who was entitled to membership in the community, and who was allowed to serve on the board. Among those excluded from the community was anyone who was uncircumcised or who had not circumcised his sons, anyone married to a gentile, one whose marriage was forbidden by *halachah,* or whose marriage ceremony had not been conducted in a halachically acceptable manner. Violation of any of these provisions was also grounds for automatic termination of membership. One who kept his business open on Shabbos or who admitted to eating non-kosher food was ineligible to serve on the board of the congregation, or in any other official position in the community.[17] These regulations were adopted by all the other independent *kehillas* in Germany.

The membership of the congregation grew rapidly. From the original 44 families in 1849, it comprised 200 members (heads of family) in 1865, and 325 families, or a total of around 1,800 people by 1874. The latter number was approximately one-sixth of the total Jewish population of Frankfurt. The synagogue contained 1000 seats, and nearly 500 boys and girls studied in the schools. There was no connection at all between the *IRG* and the Reform community, except for a common cemetery and several community charity organizations, such as the Jewish hospital. In 1899, a decade after the passing of Rabbi Hirsch, membership of the *IRG* numbered nearly 1000 families.[18]

Among the founders of *IRG* was Amschel Meir Rothschild, one of five brothers of that famous family and one of the wealthiest men in Germany at the time. Having no children of his own, he adopted two nephews, Meyer Karl and Wilhelm Karl (Shimon Wolf). Meyer Karl was not religious, but Willy, as he was known, became a legend among the

Jews of Europe for his deep piety and philanthropy. He gave lavishly to charity and the needy, as well as to religious organizations and undertakings. Stories of his devout nature were the stuff of legend for Jews all over the world. In particular, Willy enjoyed a close relationship with Rabbi Hirsch, as well as with his son-in-law and successor, Rabbi Shlomo Zalman Breuer.

Baron Wilhelm Karl Rothschild in his youth

However, the Rothschilds were not the only wealthy Orthodox Jews to distinguish themselves in Frankfurt, or the rest of Germany. Orthodox German Jewish businessmen maintained special ledgers for *maaser* (tithe) disbursements, and every large business concern had a partner or other official with responsibility for charity and other forms of public aid. It was common for wealthy men to serve as *mohalim* (performers of circumcision) and heads of the *Chevra Kadisha* (burial society). The story has yet to be told of the wealthy Orthodox Jews of Germany and of their acts of generosity and public service. These wealthy and devout people were perceived as the best proof that it was possible to be a successful, and even wealthy, businessman while remaining a pious and devout Jew.[19]

If there was a deficit at the end of the year in the budget of the *IRG*, it was considered a particular honor for one of the wealthy members of the community to make it up out of his pocket.[20] One wealthy member of the community made it a practice to carry home his *Arba Minim* with him from the synagogue on the first days of *Succoth*. Even though he could certainly have afforded a second set to leave at home for his family to use, Rabbi Hirsch advised him that in those times, when the "enlightened" elements of Jewry scorned the performance of *mitzvos*, it would be a *Kiddush Hashem* if someone of his status made a public display of his religious commitment in one of the most affluent neighborhoods in the city.[21]

But, if the *IRG* began to slowly reverse the tide in Frankfurt, in the rest of Germany the picture was far from sanguine. Rabbi Hirsch described Germany in the 1850s as a place where:

> there are entire provinces . . . where the Jewish youth barely knows how to read Hebrew; where the Jewish schools teach everything except Jewish knowledge and Jewish life; where the Jewish teachers themselves are strangers, indeed hostile, to Jewish knowledge and Jewish life; where the youth . . . is being kept in complete ignorance of its vocation and responsibilities; where the youth, in fact, is taught in principle to misinterpret and despise its Jewish vocation and obligations; where the rabbis have been officially forbidden to use their influence to supervise and guide even that pitifully atrophied remnant of religious instruction which is still being given; where, un-Jewish teachers and Christian inspectors have been left in complete charge."[22]

In 1866, Rabbi Ezriel Hildesheimer calculated that of the 495,000 Jews in Germany, only about five percent, or 25,000, could be termed strictly Orthodox. That is not to say that the rest were adherents of Reform; a great number were somewhere in the middle. In 1880, it was estimated that approximately 100,000 German Jews, or about 20 percent of German Jewry, still insisted on kosher meat, the lowest possible level of observance. In all, it was a sad picture.[23]

Part Four

TORAH NATION

Chapter Eleven

COMMUNITY

ISRAEL IS A NATION AND BECAME A NATION ONLY through and for the Torah; it possessed land and statehood only as instruments for translating the Torah into living reality. This is why Israel was a people even before it possessed land and statehood; this too is why Israel survived as a people even after its land was destroyed and its statehood lost, and this is why it will survive as a nation as long as it does not lose its only inheritance, the sole foundation for its survival and significance.[1]

A Nation in Microcosm

EVERY JEWISH COMMUNITY, IN RABBI HIRSCH'S VIEW, IS A MICROCOSM of the people as a whole, and just as Torah is the sole unifying force of the Jewish people, so must it also be the bond which unites each community.[a] If Israel as a nation is centered around Torah, or, in Rabbi Saadiah Gaon's

a. To avoid confusion, in the following chapters we will refer to the Reform community of Frankfurt as the "Community," and to the congregation of Rabbi Hirsch as the "*Kehillah*" or the *IRG* (its official name was the *Israelitische Religionsgesellschaft,* or Israelite Religious Society).

formulation, "Israel is a nation only through the Torah," then the community must also be centered around the Torah. Wherever Jews live together, they are obligated to organize for the purpose of upholding the Torah, and each individual — wherever he lives — is required to consecrate his strength and his property to fulfilling this public responsibility.[2]

> Every Jewish community represents Israel within a limited geographical territory, and within this limited territory each Jewish community must discharge all the great tasks that have been set for Israel as a whole. For this purpose, but for this purpose only, the Jewish community is vested with its authority over the individual.[3]
>
> . . . Israel is like a tree whose vital strength is replicated independently in each of its branches, twigs, leaves and root fibers. This tree may be felled, its trunk may be split and its branches chopped off; its broken parts may be scattered far and wide. But even the tiniest of these scattered remnants, if given the proper soil, is capable of striking new roots. . . . [T]he tiny remnant can reproduce the whole tree. . . . Such is the strength of Israel in exile. . . .[4]

Not only is each individual required to take an active role in the community, which serves as the local representative of the nation as a whole, but only by being part of a community can the individual fulfill his role as a Jew and find his true meaning and purpose in life. A Jew comes into this world for the purpose of translating the ideals of the group into living reality:

> It is true that even where Jewish communal life has ceased to exist, Jewish individuals are still capable of accomplishing their mission as Jews. Even a Jew living in complete isolation can continue to be a Jew; he can do this even without a synagogue and without a rabbi. At the seashore, on lonely moors and in remote mountain areas, the traveler may come upon isolated Jewish families who, in many instances, have preserved the vital warmth of Judaism over generations. It is in this blessed perseverance that Judaism has proven its wonderful Divine strength. This is the purpose for which G-d has endowed Judaism with the rich treasure of His *mitzvoth*, . . . which uplift the humblest, enrich the poorest, unite even the most isolated with G-d. *Mitzvoth* transform his hovel into a temple, his table into an altar, his bread into

an offering, turning every aspect of his life into a hallowed life of priesthood, a life which, if necessary, he is able to carry on even when he has no contacts with his brethren or with "priests."

Nevertheless, it is only in and through communal life that Judaism can attain the highest level of perfection. It is within the Jewish community as a collective unit that the Almighty wishes to be hallowed, ונקדשתי בתוך בני ישראל, and every Jewish child learns, in his very first profession of faith, that he has received the Torah from קהילת יעקב, the community of Jacob.[5]

Thus, the primary function of a Jewish community is not merely as a social and organizational framework for a group of Jews, but rather to enable Jews to fulfill their purpose in life. The community exists for the sake of the Torah, not vice versa.

At the same time, Rabbi Hirsch felt there was no halachic imperative for *kehillas* to join together in a countrywide framework. In a lengthy correspondence with one Hungarian rabbi, Rabbi Hirsch wrote that while it might sometimes be desirable for all Torah-true forces to join together to declare their allegiance to Torah-true Judaism and to fight together, it was not a halachic requirement. He refused, however, to allow his correspondent to publish his opinion on the grounds that since he did not live in Hungary he was perhaps not aware of all the practical ramifications of his view.[6]

Community Laws in Germany

THE LEGAL STATUS OF THE JEWISH COMMUNITY IN THE 19TH CENtury differed widely depending on the part of the world. The separation of church and state in the United States, for instance, causes all religious communities to be viewed as merely aggregates of autonomous individuals cooperating with each other to satisfy their own religious needs, without intervention, regulation or enforcement, on the part of the Federal government or local authorities. France made the Jewish community into a consistory — a state-recognized religious structure. Russia dissolved the *Kahal* and appointed in their stead members of government-created communal organizations. In central Europe, the Jewish community was recognized as a corporate body, with the right of taxation, subject to government regulation and intervention.[7]

The principle that all Jews automatically became members of the single local Jewish community at birth was gradually accepted into law in most of the German states towards the middle of the 19th century. At maturity, one was obligated to pay membership fees; the only way to avoid membership was to convert to Christianity. Until the 1840s, in many German states circumcision was a condition of membership in the Jewish community, but gradually the states ceased to insist upon it.[8]

With only one Jewish community permitted in each city, and therefore no option of seceding and forming an independent community, all power was effectively in the hands of the majority of the Community Board. In Frankfurt, where the Community Board had no need to resort to elections, the community came to be controlled by a small group of self-appointed individuals.

Prussian law as of 1847 granted the boards of the Jewish communities total control over all religious and communal matters. As a consequence, laymen usurped positions of real power in religious matters, which had heretofore been the province of the rabbis. Since the law stipulated no religious credentials for membership on the community boards, it became a not uncommon occurrence for those who attended synagogue barely twice a year to have a decisive role in determining religious issues for the community. The very law, which so greatly increased the power of the board members, commensurately weakened the authority of the rabbinate, by according it almost no official role in the community structure. Rabbis were effectively relegated to the role of clerks. The attitude to the rabbinate on the part of the board members usually reflected this reality.[9]

During the period in which Rabbi Hirsch came of age, the Reform Movement increasingly began to gain control of community structures in Germany. Orthodox Jews who lived in towns dominated by the Reformers were forced to contribute, in effect, to the ruin of traditional Judaism by paying dues to the local Jewish community. Such was the situation in Frankfurt where the community had fallen under the absolute control of the Reformers. Although the members of the *IRG* had received permission in 1849 to organize as a religious association, they were, nonetheless, required to pay membership dues to the Reform-dominated community. The recognition they won in 1849 gave them the right to *exist* as a private religious organization, but nothing more; legally they were still members of the community. This insufferable situation continued for many years, during which no alternative status was available to Orthodox Jews. However, because the law gave no choice but to pay the community tax, such payments were not considered in the eyes of the Orthodox as an admission of the validity of Reform Judaism.[10]

IN 1863, RABBI HIRSCH PUBLISHED AN ARTICLE IN *JESCHURUN* IN THE form of "The Legal Case of the Jewish Cobbler" against the government.

The Protest of the Jewish Cobbler

The cobbler objected to being compelled to pay membership fees to a Reform-dominated community that represented everything that he, the shoemaker, opposed and that wantonly demolished all that was holy to him. He stressed that the sum involved was one he could easily afford and was not in itself the issue; his objection was purely a matter of principle. He described in detail how the Community Board had desecrated all the institutions of the community — the synagogue, the religious school, the *mikveh,* ritual slaughter, and so on. Prayer services were conducted according to the Reform liturgy to the accompaniment of an organ on Shabbos and festivals, and the Hebrew language was forbidden within the synagogue. In short, the objective of the Reformers was obviously to dismantle as much of traditional Judaism as they could.

The "cobbler" pointed out that although the gap between the beliefs of Orthodox and Reform Judaism was far wider than that between Catholicism and any of the Protestant sects,[11] the government granted recognition to the latter groups as independent denominations but did not recognize the disparity between Orthodox and Reform Judaism. The distinction between Orthodox and Reform was clear: Does one accept the Written and Oral Torah that has been passed on for millennia or not? There was no legal or moral justification for forcing him to contribute to an organization whose basic principles and objectives he not only opposed, but which his religion required him to combat with all his might. Any contribution he made to such a community was a transgression against his religion.

He pointed out that in the early stages of Christianity, the only distinction between the new faith and Judaism, of which Christianity was an offshoot, was the question of whether or not one accepted the obligations of the Torah. It seemed, then, that anyone who shed the obligations of the Torah stands "not just with one foot but with both feet, inside Christianity."[12]

Rabbi Hirsch explained at length that by any standard of human conscience, justice or reason, as well as from the standpoint of Judaism's basic tenets, there was no justification for requiring a Jew to affiliate with and pay membership fees to a community controlled by Reformers.

He ridiculed the argument that every Jew is required to "share the yoke of his fellow" and "not to separate himself from the community"

(*Pirkei Avos*, 6:6 and 2:5). Those who reject the authority of the Oral Law have no right to use it in support of their position. And one who rejects the binding power of any part of the Law, however minor, has, in effect, asserted that it carries no authority over him. When a member of a Reform community board denies the validity of the *Shulchan Aruch,* he has *ipso facto* removed the basis of his own position as community officer, for the entire source of the power of the community and its officers lies in the Oral Torah. Moreover, the strictures against separating oneself from the community apply only within the framework of Torah observance, and not, Heaven forbid, to separating oneself from activities whose purpose is to contravene the Torah. Far from being a case of an individual separating himself from the community, this was rather a case of a community that separated itself from the Torah.[13]

The Obligation to Secede

SINCE THE JEWISH COMMUNITY IS A MICROCOSM OF THE TORAH Nation, a Jewish communal structure that fails to acknowledge the complete authority of the Torah has no status as a legitimate Jewish community. Nor does a community that is willing to tolerate an Orthodox subgroup within its framework thereby become any more acceptable in halachic terms. A hybrid community proclaims by its very existence that it does not consider truth to be of supreme importance.

Rabbi Hirsch concluded that it is forbidden for a Jew to affiliate himself with such a community of his own free will, and that he is *obligated* to secede from it once the law allows him to do so. This requirement is not just another *mitzvah.* It is a reflection of the recognition that the observance of the Torah's commandments is the sole *raison d'etre* of the Jewish people. One who fails to utilize a legal right to secede thereby proclaims his rejection of the belief that Israel's sole purpose is to observe the Torah.[14] The principle that *Yisrael, af al pi shechata, Yisrael hu* — a Jew remains a Jew even if he sins — is irrelevant:

> . . . It is true that even those Jewish sons who have most openly deserted their calling and their irrevocable Jewish duty remain Jews nevertheless, just as, according to the basic principles of Judaism, even a baptized Jew remains a Jew. But a Jew can never form one religious community with baptized Jews, or regard as his own a community or communal institutions established and administered by and for baptized Jews. By the same token he cannot accept as his own a religious community or religious insti-

tutions that have been established and are managed by and for Reformers. The Orthodox and Reform do not belong together in spirit before G-d, and a tax penny paid under legal duress into a common treasury does not make a Jewish community.[15]

Rabbi Hirsch considered the above principles so self-evident that he did not see a need to give halachic justification for his position on the subject.[16] Later, as we shall see, he was forced to do so because of opposition to secession that arose from within his own community.

Kehillah Membership

THE CONVICTION THAT A COMMUNITY HAS LEGITIMACY ONLY IF IT is rooted in commitment to Torah implies that its status in the eyes of the Torah is altogether unaffected by any official recognition it may or may not receive from the governing authorities. Thus, the constitution of the *IRG*, adopted in 1874, before it was granted community status by the government, stated clearly: "The *Kehillath Jeschurun* constitutes the original Jewish community of Frankfurt am Main, it perpetuates the goals and functions of the ancient community and remains faithful to its principles and ideals, and is heir to its religious rights."

A corollary of this view was the fact that every Jew in Frankfurt had the right to belong to the *Kehillah*, except those who were not circumcised, or who failed to circumcise their children, or whose marriages were contrary to *halachah*. Every member had the right to be elected to the governing bodies of the *Kehillah*, with the exception of those who publicly desecrated the Sabbath and festivals, those who ate non-kosher food in public, and those who "openly disavowed the principles of traditional Judaism."[17] The other secessionist communities in Germany adopted these provisions in their constitutions also.[18] In a responsum to Babenhausen and in a similar reply to Karlsruhe, Rabbi Hirsch explained that one who desecrates the Sabbath may not serve as an officer of the *Kehillah*, citing, among other sources, the ruling of the *Ramah* (*Choshen Mishpat* 37:22), that the selection of community officers is subject to the same criteria as those required for the selection of a *dayan*, and the law (*Choshen Mishpat* 34:2 and 7:9) that one who is halachically unfit to serve as a witness is also ineligible to serve as a *dayan*.[19]

In 1843, in a response to Rabbi Zalman Trier of Frankfurt, printed by the latter in a book of rabbinical opinions as to how the community should treat those who refuse to circumcise their sons, Rabbi Hirsch wrote that by their declaration that they will not circumcise their children they have publicly declared their acceptance of heretical views and have completely removed themselves from the Jewish community, and cannot and will not continue as members. The time has come, he wrote, to publicly declare that it is impossible to be both Jewish and un-Jewish at the same time. True, a Jew who has sinned is still a Jew, he continued, and even one who has converted to Christianity will remain with all the obligations of a Jew until the end of time, but as far as the community is concerned he has joined the group of deniers and heretics who can have no part in it.[20]

In 1847, he advised Rabbi S.Y. Rapoport of Prague to exclude from the population register of the Jewish community anyone who was not circumcised and to resist government pressure in this matter.[b] In addition, he wrote, matters had come to the point where the only means available to the community to enforce any type of adherence to Jewish law was its jurisdiction over the Jewish population registry. Relinquishing that right to outside meddling would only lead to an even more rapid deterioration of Jewish life, and a total breakdown of even the minimum requirement of circumcision. As to the concern that such actions would further alienate people from Judaism, he wrote that those who did not circumcise their children would in any case not raise them with any allegiance to authentic Judaism and a Torah way of life. Only three generations ago, he wrote, only one who observed all the *mitzvos* was considered a Jew. Matters had deteriorated to the point where Torah observance was seen as some kind of optional piety. Without forceful insistence, even the last *mitzvah* that was still being observed by most, that of *bris milah,* would go the way of all the other commandments.[21]

A Consistent Approach

IT IS WORTH EMPHASIZING THAT RABBI HIRSCH FORMULATED HIS position on the question of secession not in the 1870s, when the legal possibility finally arose. It found its first expression in a public letter he penned in 1845, while still rabbi in Emden, in response to the "decisions" taken by the Rabbinical Conference in Braunschweig. "Know full well," he wrote, "that in the event your views were to be realized, the House of Israel would be split in two, we would be disgraced before our enemies and suffer the loss of our heritage. For if those who accept your authority were to heed your urgings to rebel against the Talmud and to permit forbidden foods and the performance of illegal marriages, our

b. See Chapter 12 for a discussion of Rabbi Hirsch's views on government intervention in general.

unity could have no future and in sorrow we would have to part from each other."[22]

In 1858, in response to a halachic inquiry, Rabbi Hirsch wrote to Rabbi Yaakov Koppel Bamberger of Worms:

> No observant Jew may participate in prayer services that incorporate any one of these changes.[c] By doing so he would be making a public denial of principles for the sake of which he is required to sacrifice his life. He would have no choice but to declare his dissociation from this group, which, by introducing these innovations in the prayer service, rejects the very foundations of a Judaism that remains faithful to the Torah and its commandments.[23]

In 1867, he wrote that secession would be "the best means to preserve the true and pure spirit of Judaism in the community [of Hamburg],"[24] and in an 1872 letter to Rabbi Aaron David Deutsch of Hungary, Rabbi Hirsch declared, regarding the situation of Judaism in Vienna: "If the outrages perpetrated in Vienna are not sufficient to arouse the ire and anger of those Jews there who still hold fast to Hashem's covenant, and do not drive them to withdraw from that wicked congregation, then there is no cure for their weakness and no hope of arousing them from their stupor . . . They will not stir until an idol is actually erected in Hashem's sanctuary, Heaven forbid."[25]

Secession in Hungary

IN THE LATE 1860S RABBI HIRSCH WAS HEAVILY INVOLVED IN THE efforts of the Hungarian Orthodox rabbinate to keep the communal frameworks in Hungary loyal to traditional Judaism. He published, anonymously, a long memorandum in *Jeschurun* in 1868 describing the rights of the Orthodox in terms that would be understood by Hungarian parliamentarians. The article was subsequently translated into Hungarian and given wide circulation.[26]

The Congress of Hungarian Jewry, which took place in the early part of 1869 in Pest, was the scene of intense acrimony between the Orthodox and the "Neologues," the Hungarian permutation of Reform. Leo Hollander, one of the leaders of the Reform party, in a speech to the Congress, placed the blame for Orthodox resoluteness, or, in his view,

c. The reference is to changes in the prayer service, prayers in German and the use of the organ in the synagogue.[22*]

intransigence, squarely at Rabbi Hirsch's feet. The latter, he declared, had urged his Hungarian Orthodox counterparts not to compromise. "Are our traditional rabbis," he asked, "not learned and wise enough to chart their course under their own steam that they feel compelled to copy them from Bismarck's states?" In response to the insult, even the "moderate" Orthodox left the hall in protest.[27]

At the close of the Congress, which ended in discord and lack of agreement, an anonymous article appeared in a Hungarian Jewish newspaper, the author of which, historian Jacob Katz is convinced, was none other than Rabbi Hirsch. It argued that the failure of the Congress to reach a *modus vivendi* between Orthodox and Reform was a good thing because no accommodation was possible. Even organizational unity was a hoax, since the leadership positions would be open to anyone, and one who is non-observant is halachically prohibited from serving in any public position in Jewish institutional frameworks. The conclusion from all this, wrote the author, was that it was imperative to grant religious autonomy to each *kehillah*.[28]

After the fiasco of the Congress, Rabbi Joseph Guggenheimer prepared at the behest of his father-in-law, Rabbi Hirsch, a memorandum for the Austrian Emperor, which set out the Orthodox proposals for the organization of the Hungarian Jewish communities. The memorandum, which bears the fingerprints of Rabbi Hirsch's style and thought, was presented to the Emperor after being signed by representatives of the Hungarian Jewish communities.[29]

The Hungarian struggle was but a dress rehearsal for that in Germany. The battle for secession in Germany in the 1870s was far more complicated than it had been in Hungary. Whereas the imperative of separation from heresy was a given in Hungary, where the *Chasam Sofer* and his disciples were the leading spirit in the Orthodox world, in Germany, as we shall see, the implementation in theory and practice was considerably more complex.

Chapter Twelve
THE BATTLE FOR SECESSION

RELATIONS BETWEEN THE ORTHODOX AND REFORM communities in Germany deteriorated rapidly towards the middle of the 19th century. The increasingly acerbic relations were partly a reaction to the establishment of the radical Reform Associations (*Reformfreunde*) and the three Reform "Rabbinical Conferences" held in the 1840s — Braunschweig, 1845; Frankfurt, 1846; and Breslau, 1847.

The readiness of the Orthodox to stand firm in the face of growing Reform domination of communal structures may have been inspired, at least in part, by the wave of popular revolution which spread over cen-

The account of the events related in this chapter relies heavily on that of Professor Mordechai Breuer in *Am V'eidah*. We are deeply indebted to him for his gracious permission to use this unpublished manuscript.

tral Europe in 1848. As the Orthodox applied the ideals of individual liberty and democracy to their situation, they were increasingly unwilling to tolerate a Reform-dominated communal structure, invested with the power of the state, which rode roughshod over their rights. Having at first been ambivalent about Emancipation, the Orthodox now used it to salvage something from the situation it had brought into being. In any event, the shifting political trends in Germany left their mark on the various factions within the Jewish world.

In December 1848, the German parliament — a legislative body of the German states located in Frankfurt, possessing limited powers — formulated a constitution intended to be binding on all German states. Its bill of rights stipulated, *inter alia*, that every citizen has the right to freely choose his religion and that such choice would have no positive or negative consequences on his rights and privileges as a citizen. Although the constitution was never adopted by the German states, its ideals concerning civic rights made an impact.[1] At the same time, the governments of various German states continued to follow Jewish affairs with close interest, and intervened, at times heavy-handedly, in internal Jewish matters.

A variety of different arrangements to accommodate both Orthodox and Reform were tried in various German cities. In 1856, as a result of the untenable situation caused by the long-running feud between the Orthodox and the Reform in Breslau, the *Einheitsgemeinde* (unified community) was born. It allowed two separate religious groups to exist within one communal framework, with the religious affairs of each being controlled by their respective *Kultuskommision* (religious commission), which was outside the purview of the community board.[2]

Then there was the independent *kehillah*, in which the Orthodox established their own independent full-service *kehillah*, while still paying, under compulsion of law, taxes to the Reform-dominated community. These *kehillas* were generally not recognized by the government as public bodies, and were treated as nothing more than private religious associations. The flagship of these was Frankfurt, which was the largest, wealthiest and most influential, and whose rabbi was the leader and inspiration behind the entire movement. In the eyes of the Reformers, the thriving Frankfurt *Kehillah* was simply an abomination.

As a result of Frankfurt's success there came into existence other independent *kehillas*, some of whom even adopted the formal name of the Frankfurt *Kehillah, der Israelitische Religionsgesellschaft*. Such *kehillas* were established in Mainz (1854), Offenbach (1869), Wiesbaden (1870, Rabbi Eliezer Lipmann Kahn), Darmstadt (1871, Rabbi Lemel Marx), Bingen

(1872), Karlsruhe (1874, Rabbi Herz Ehrmann), Giessen, Kassel, Cologne (Rabbi Hirsch's son-in-law, Rabbi Hirsch Plato), Strasbourg and Stettin (Szczecin).[3] Some of these were short lived.

Government Intervention

THE REFORMERS HAD NO SCRUPLES ABOUT USING THE AUTHORITIES and the legal system as a weapon in their crusade to eradicate authentic Judaism. In the town of Moisling near Lübeck, for example, they sought in civil court to force the community rabbi to resign his post, charging that his lack of fluency in German and his unwillingness to assent to their proposed liturgical changes rendered him unfit to serve as rabbi. In Bernberg, the Reform rabbi requested the government to ban the separate Orthodox congregation.[4] In Rabbi Hirsch's opinion, the steady decrease of Jewish autonomy in their own internal affairs was caused by Reform pressure on the authorities to involve themselves in internal Jewish matters,[5] and he bitterly criticized this phenomenon.

> Congregations. . . . dominated by Reformist efforts are well advised to refrain from turning to civil authorities for assistance in coercing a religious minority into joining a quasi-secular body, which is fanatically opposed to its most sacred values. . . . Freedom of conscience is supposedly the greatest spiritual achievement of our age. Is there a more crass violation of the lofty concept of personal freedom than when someone is forced against his will to join a religious body that abuses every value he holds dear? . . . In many ways the modern Reform Movement seems to take its cue from the methods of the Spanish Inquisition, which trampled gleefully on every human right imaginable. A government that supports the Reform congregations in such coercion of the local Orthodox segment must be aware that its practice reduces the state to the demeaning role of a Torquemada, causing suffering of a similar, albeit spiritual, nature.[6]

It is worth mentioning, however, that the Orthodox were not exactly guiltless in this matter. They, too, utilized the government to accomplish their aims, albeit with less frequency than the Reform.

A theme that emerges time after time in Rabbi Hirsch's writings, even before the battle over secession, is that government intervention in religious or personal affairs is never justified or sanctioned. The government has no knowledge or understanding of Judaism and its practices. And just as government interference *against* the observance of Torah and *mitzvos* was unthinkable, so interference *on their behalf* was also untenable. "What business does the government have getting involved in the prayer service, *Pitum Haktores, Aizehu Mekoman* or the custom of beating *aravos* on *Hoshana Rabbah*?" he asked.[7] His efforts on behalf of the secession law were in a very real sense an attempt to remove the government from its involvement in Jewish affairs.

In an 1847 reply to Rabbi S.Y. Rapoport of Prague, he advised the latter to make it clear to the government that the Jewish community would not list anyone in the population register who was not circumcised, even at the risk of causing the authorities to deprive the community of its prerogative in this area. The government, he wrote, had no right whatsoever and should be prevented at all costs from interfering in internal Jewish affairs. If, as it claims, it cannot enforce adherence to Judaism, and is thus willing to accept as Jews even those who are not circumcised, by the same token, it can not force any representative of the Jewish community to do anything it views as opposed to Jewish religion. Any weakening of this position would only invite further intervention in internal Jewish affairs.[8]

Rabbi Hirsch was asked in 1850 by the rabbi of Uhersky Brod (Ungarisch Brod) in Moravia how to respond to a government official who insisted that the students of the local Jewish school sit in class with bared heads. Rabbi Hirsch replied forcefully that the official was out of line in ignoring the local rabbi's directive in religious matters — matters in which the official had no knowledge, competence or jurisdiction. Wearing a head-covering is an ancient Jewish custom, he wrote, and no government official has the right to tamper with it.[9]

In 1855, a German rabbi refused to perform the wedding ceremony for a woman who had not immersed in a *mikveh* and enlisted the government's help in his dispute. Rabbi Hirsch sharply criticized the invocation of governmental assistance, which, in the long run could only result in diminished religious autonomy. In 1858, a father in a Bohemian city refused to circumcise his son, and the *Kehillah* revoked the man's membership in the *Kehillah*. While supportive of that decision, Rabbi Hirsch condemned the rabbi's request for government support for his stand.[10]

Political Developments

IN 1871, THE NEWLY UNITED GERMAN EMPIRE ADOPTED A CONSTITUTION guaranteeing the right of free religious practice for all citizens. A year later, the *IRG* sent a petition drafted by Rabbi Hirsch to the Prussian Minister of the Interior, which requested an end to compulsory membership in the Jewish community structure. The Prussian Chancellor

Bismarck was at that time engaged in efforts to weaken the power of the Catholic Church, which had hitherto functioned as a virtual state within a state in much of Germany. He envisioned the newly united Germany as a liberal and progressive state, adhering to modern notions of freedom of conscience and religion, and he could not tolerate the autocratic power of the Church, which took its marching orders from the Pope in Rome.[a] To weaken the Church, Bismarck brought about the passage of a law granting every Catholic the right to secede from his local diocese and every Catholic denomination the prerogative to organize freely its own faith community.

In October 1872, as the law was being prepared in the parliament, German Orthodoxy, led by Rabbi Hirsch, approached government officials and members of the Prussian legislature (*Landtag*) with a request to amend the "Jew Laws" as well. Until then, those laws had required all Jews to affiliate with the local community, whether or not they were in sympathy with its policies or leadership. Rabbi Hirsch advocated the Orthodox position before the Prussian government in Berlin, and over the next four years, according to one account, he visited the Prussian capital

a. The clash between the Church and State was referred to at the time as the *Kulturkampf*, an appellation that is still used to describe the clash between church and state.

no less than 27 times until the Law of Secession was finally passed.

The government officials with whom Rabbi Hirsch met during his visit to Berlin in October 1872 explained to him that at the present time the law would not include Jewish communities, as sufficient preparation for such a law had not yet been made. Contrary to their pessimistic forecasts, however, the question of secession from the Jewish community arose in the parliament already in early 1873. Members of the parliamentary committee in which the law of secession for Catholics was discussed were unanimous in their view that similar considerations of freedom of conscience should apply to Jews no less than to Christians. But the law, as formulated in March 1873, only provided that Jews could secede for reasons of conscience from their local community. Although doing so no longer required him to register as a Christian, he still forfeited his identification as a Jew in the eyes of the State. The law as it was formulated accomplished nothing for Orthodox Jewry, for it was untenable for even the most vehement opponent of Reform to take a step which meant seceding officially from Judaism.

One of the leading members of the Prussian *Landtag* at the time was a liberal Jew named Eduard Lasker (1829-1884), a distinguished jurist and a gifted writer and speaker. Born to a religious family in the Posen region, he founded the National Liberal Party in Prussia in 1867. With the establishment of the German Empire in 1871, Lasker joined the Reichstag and assisted Bismarck in passing the legislation limiting the power of the Catholic Church and in making Prussia the dominant leader of the Empire. Lasker believed that the best solution to the age-old problem of anti-Semitism was for Jews to abandon their traditional segregation and establish a place for themselves in non-Jewish society.

Eduard Lasker

Thus it is ironic that Lasker, a thoroughly assimilated Jew — who numbered among his closest friends many of the pillars of Reform Judaism of the time, including the headmaster of the Reform *Philanthropin* of Frankfurt — should have been the most powerful ally of the Orthodox in realizing their goal of secession from Reform-led communities. Lasker was no admirer of Orthodox Judaism, but nonetheless sided with it as a minority persecuted by the Reform majority. As such it had his support, no matter that the cause of Orthodoxy was anathema to all he stood for and detested by most of his friends and colleagues. Not to be discounted in comprehending his activism in this matter is the enormous respect in which he held the leader of the Orthodox camp, Rabbi Hirsch.

Legislative Progress

WHEN THE LAW OF SECESSION FOR CATHOLICS WAS SENT TO SUB-committee for consideration, Lasker asked Rabbi Hirsch to draft a memorandum explaining why the legislature should grant Jews rights similar to those enjoyed by Christians. In an essay entitled "Memorandum on Government-Enforced Membership," Rabbi Hirsch presented the case in favor of granting the right of secession to Jews in terms that would be understandable to non-Jews. His arguments were phrased in the currency of freedom of conscience and human justice. The differences between traditional Judaism and Reform, he asserted, were no less than those between Protestants and Catholics, and it was therefore wrong to coerce Orthodox Jews to remain in a religious structure against which their conscience rebelled. The claim that permitting secession would inevitably weaken religious institutions did not outweigh the inviolable principles of freedom of conscience and natural justice. In any case, he wrote, a religious denomination which could not survive without coercion by the State has lost its right to exist.[11]

The memorandum was presented to government ministers, including the Office of the Chancellor, and was distributed also to members of Parliament before the debate on the law on March 19. The protocol of the parliamentary session records that several legislators even quoted from it during the debate on the floor.[12]

March 1873 found Rabbi Hirsch in Berlin in connection with the parliamentary debates on the Law of Secession.[b] While there he paid many visits to government officials, and also prepared a memorandum which demonstrated that Reform and Orthodox Judaism are further apart in

b. In Berlin at the same time was Rabbi Yisrael Salanter who, according to the report of his attendant Rabbi Herz Ehrmann, was studying chemistry in order to qualify for the profession of inkmaker and thereby become eligible for a German passport. Upon learning that Rabbi Hirsch was in Berlin, Reb Yisrael expressed a great desire to meet the man whom he viewed as "the regenerator of German Judaism," and to consult with him concerning his own plans for the rejuvenation of Russian Jewry. Though Rabbi Hirsch had no time to spare, he nevertheless said that for Reb Yisrael he would be available at any time. Rabbi Herz Ehrmann, who brought Rabbi

their basic beliefs than Protestantism and Catholicism.

On March 19, Parliament held a full-fledged debate on the question of secession for Jews. Eduard Lasker, in a lengthy and well-organized speech, discussed all the aspects and ramifications of extending the law to cover Judaism as well, and declared that Jews have the same right of freedom of conscience as do Christians. "The litmus test of true religious feeling is a voluntary commitment," he told the parliament. If a particular Jewish community were to disintegrate as a result of the law, all the better; the individual adherents of Judaism would find a way to satisfy their religious requirements. After Lasker's speech, the Minister of Religious Affairs declared that the only reason the law was not formulated to extend to Jews as well was because that aspect had not been adequately prepared. He promised to draft such a law, and the house passed a resolution committing the government to prepare a law that would grant similar rights to Jews. The Law of Secession for Christians was finally passed on May 14, 1873.[13]

In the beginning of 1874, it became public knowledge that Lasker had undertaken to work for passage of a Law of Secession for Jews. The Reformers, through their "Association of German Jewish Communities" *(Deutsch-Jüdischer Gemeindebund)* — who had long since recognized the danger to their dominant position in Jewish communal life posed by such a law — initiated a campaign of petitions, newspaper articles, and political pressure against the proposed law. The *DJG* submitted opinions from, among others, the *Hochschule* Seminary (Reform) in Berlin and Frankel's Seminary in Breslau, stating that the religious differences between Orthodoxy and Reform were not deep enough to allow for sectarian separatism within the Jewish fold.[14] Rabbi Hirsch, in turn, launched a counter-attack, pointing out that the Reformers' obstinate attempt to wield communal coercion was itself clear testimony to the wavering allegiance of their followers. A religion that required government coercion to survive was not worthy of being called a religion.

Salanter to visit Rabbi Hirsch, described the impression the sight of these two Torah luminaries together made on him:

> I had the privilege of. . . . accompanying Rabbi Yisrael Salanter on his visit to Rabbi Hirsch. I will never forget the meeting between those two humble yet powerful personalities. I never again saw the awesome power of Torah to purify man, as during that moment when these two men shook hands.
>
> Each. . . . described the situation of Jews and Judaism in his country, and reflected on strategies for strengthening the continually deteriorating pillars of Judaism. Rabbi Hirsch related the reason for his visit to Berlin, saying, "אנן בדידן ואינהו בדידהו — Let us be for ourselves and them be for themselves." Reb Yisrael answered with an emphatic nod of his head and said with full force, "Amen, may Hashem so will it!" Then these two giants spoke about the loftiest topics.[12*]

As Professor Mordechai Breuer has pointed out, it is ironic that the Reform Jews who had agitated so long and hard for emancipation and were at the forefront of the battle for progress, culture and enlightenment in Jewish society, as well as being vigorous supporters of Bismarck's liberalism and secularization of the state, resisted the government's efforts to extend freedom of choice to the Jewish communal structure. Freedom and liberalism were fine for the Reformers — only so long as they did not encroach upon their domination of the Jewish communal apparatus. Rabbi Hirsch put it in his inimitable style: "You speak so glibly about freedom of conscience, and yet you yourselves are guilty of the most wicked coercion. You speak so glibly about tolerance, and yet you yourselves are intolerant to the point of fanaticism."[15]

In an address before the legislature in May of that year, Lasker answered his Reform critics, declaring, "One man from among the members of the religious association of Frankfurt who has long battled for its independence, a man by the name of 'Dr.' Hirsch, has declared to me that he has different religious principles than the other segment of the Jewish community. This man possesses very unselfish aspirations." At that point, the Reformers unleashed a furious, no-holds-barred attack on the resolution and its author. The *Allgemeine Zeitung des Judentums*, which had previously lionized Lasker, now descended to personal attacks and cast aspersions on his motives in this matter. One of the central points of debate was whether there was truly a difference in religious principles between Orthodox Judaism and Reform. The Breslau school of Frankel and Graetz consistently supported the Reform position and its journal bitterly denounced the Orthodox, with personal attacks on Rabbi Hirsch and even on Lasker.

During the following two years, until the law was finally passed, there ensued a pitched battle between the Orthodox and Reform factions fought in all arenas and employing every means. In April 1876, in the midst of the parliament's consideration of the law, the president of the Reform *Deutsch-Jüdischer Gemeindebund*, a man by the name of Kohner, made a desperate, last-ditch effort to stop its passage. In a memorandum to the chairman of the petitions committee, whose job was to report to the parliament on petitions received, Kohner made slanderous and vituperative charges against Orthodox Judaism and its leaders. "While opponents of the Law of Secession support German ideals and progress, and are concerned with the needs of all Jews, no matter what their religious affiliation," wrote Kohner, "the Orthodox supporters of secession are enemies of progress, un-German, and concerned only with the inter-

Rabbi Marcus Lehmann and family

ests of their own minuscule extremist groups and do not recognize anyone else as being in any way Jews." He proceeded with personal attacks on the three Orthodox leaders who led the fight for secession, Rabbis Hirsch, Hildesheimer and Lehmann. It was another instance where the champions of Jewish "liberalism" asked for tolerance only for their own beliefs, but were unwilling to extend it to those who adhere to Torah Judaism.[16]

"The Law of Redemption"

ON APRIL 10, 1876, THE PRUSSIAN GOVERNMENT PLACED THE LAW OF Secession, or the "Law of Redemption," as it was dubbed by the Orthodox, on the agenda of the Prussian *Landtag*. The proposed legislation allowed any Jew to withdraw from his local community framework without having to forfeit his legal status as a Jew. The act of withdrawal was to be accomplished by declaring one's intention before a local magistrate and specifying that it was motivated by reasons of conscience. Immediately upon making this declaration, one would lose all rights in the community, including the right to be buried in the Jewish cemetery, although one would still be required to pay membership fees until the end of the civil year.

The law was passed by Parliament on May 22, 1876 and confirmed by the Kaiser on July 28 of that year. The final version contained one important change, a new clause allowing those seceding to retain the right to be buried in the Jewish cemetery, unless they had established an alternative burial site for themselves. The law took effect on September 12, 1876 (23 *Elul*, 5636), the day it was published in the official government gazette.

An immediate consequence of the new law was that the Reform-controlled local council in Aachen, under threat of secession by traditionalist members of the community, retreated from its plan to modify the *shofar*-blowing service on Rosh Hashanah.[17]

The Law of Secession had passed and Frankfurt was about to become the scene of one of the most pitched public battles Torah Jewry in Germany had ever known.

Chapter Thirteen
SECESSION IN FRANKFURT

The Lull Before the Storm

NOW THAT THE LAW OVER WHICH SO MANY BATTLES had already been fought was finally a reality, there were no signs of a mass movement to secede. Even in Frankfurt, the "hothouse" of the secessionist movement, a wave of secession did not seem to be in the offing and from the time the law took effect, weeks passed without much indication of any significant interest in secession on the part of the membership of the *IRG.* Perceiving this, the Frankfurt Community Board did not move to offer compromises to the members of the *IRG.*

The lack of movement towards secession was not an indication that the Community Board in Frankfurt had somehow become sympathetic to the observant Jew. To the contrary, the atmosphere was still one of intense antagonism. When requested in 1872 to publicize the misdeeds of the Reformers in Vienna in the Frankfurt press, Rabbi Hirsch replied that the local newspapers had such an aversion for traditional Judaism that they would probably refuse to publish it as news and would accept only a paid advertisement, which would be placed "together with all the butter and cheese advertisements." Even were they to print it as an article, he wrote, they would be sure to drown it out in a torrent of opposing views.[1]

The feeling of the Orthodox toward the Reform was not much different. It included some pity and a great measure of contempt. The Reform synagogues were called *Tiflah* — a play on the word *tefillah* — a term heretofore employed to describe a church.[2] But as the Orthodox had a full range of community institutions in place and the average observant Jew had almost no personal contact with Reform communal institutions, he did not feel pressure to withdraw from a framework with which he in any case had no dealings. Another important reason for the lack of interest was the fact that the *IRG* did not have a cemetery of its own and was dependent on the Reform community for burial space. Members of the older Frankfurt families did not want to lose the right to be buried alongside their parents and ancestors. In addition, the procedure of secession was a disagreeable one, as one was required to appear publicly in court and make a declaration before a magistrate. Four to six weeks after the first court appearance, one was called a second time to reaffirm one's intention before the magistrate. Apart from the publicity this entailed, the declaration exposed the would-be seceder to the many personal and economic pressures the Reformers were only too willing to employ.

While Rabbi Hirsch did not expect the adoption of the law to result in mass secession throughout Germany, he certainly assumed that his own congregation would join him in leaving the Reform community without undue delay. It did not happen. Instead, there arose a conflict within the *IRG* over this issue that lasted from the beginning of September 1876 until after Shavuos of that year, some nine months later. It was to be one of the most bitter struggles German Jewry had known, and split German Orthodoxy into two camps. Rabbi Ezriel Hildesheimer compared it to the bitter dispute that had raged between the followers of Rabbi Yonasan Eibeschitz and Rabbi Yaakov Emden.[3] The scars from the *Austritt* feud lasted for decades, and its repercussions were felt until German Jewry was finally destroyed by the Nazis some 65 years later.

Controversy

DURING THE HIGH HOLY DAYS OF 5737 (SEPTEMBER 1876) THERE WAS a festive atmosphere in Frankfurt as the *IRG* commemorated the 25th anniversary of Rabbi Hirsch's arrival. In an address to the congregation on Simchas Torah, he declared that it was an absolute obligation to secede,[4] and in another public address, he called for the elders of the *IRG* to set an example for the congregation by withdrawing from the Reform community. When he and his sons took the lead by doing so themselves, they were followed by a few members of the leadership, but the great wave of secession in the *IRG* that they expected to follow did not materialize. On Sunday, 27 *Tishrei* (October 15), there was a general membership meeting of the *IRG*, during which the chairman Emanuel Schwarzschild made an impassioned appeal for the members to take the active step of seceding.

Emanuel Schwarzschild

Rabbi Moshe Mainz (1805-1886), a prominent member of one of the oldest and most respected families in Frankfurt, arose to speak in opposition to Schwarzschild's appeal. One of the original 11 who, in 1849, signed the petition to the Frankfurt Senate requesting the right to establish the *Israelitische Religionsgesellschaft*, Mainz was a *talmid chacham* of no small stature, who had occasionally served on the *Beis Din* of Rabbi Trier. He was also the leader of the Frankfurt *Shas Chevra* and conducted a private *minyan* in his home. He argued that if all the Orthodox were to secede, many of the community help organizations and charity funds would be irrevocably relinquished to the Reformers. His main objection, however, centered on the issue of the cemetery, in which the Orthodox would be barred from burying their dead. He therefore proposed that the *IRG* enter into negotiations with the Reform community — a course of action in total opposition to the wishes of Rabbi Hirsch, the halachic authority of the *IRG*. Schwarzschild rejected this proposal out of hand and refused even to submit it to a vote, since Rabbi Hirsch had taken such a strong stand in opposition to it.[5]

In the course of that meeting, approximately 70 members of the congregation signed a document committing themselves to secede, bringing the total number of those who seceded to 80.[6] A decisive majority,

Rabbi Moshe Mainz

however, approximately 75 percent of the membership, decided to wait and see how the negotiations of the *IRG* with the Reform community over the use of the cemetery, the hospital, and other community social welfare institutions were concluded. These negotiations eventually failed, primarily because of interference and compromises offered under the table by the faction within the *IRG* that opposed secession on principle.[7] This group's motives were many and varied, though among them was certainly the fact that their ancestors and parents were buried in the communal cemetery, whose gates would be slammed shut in their faces in the event of their secession. Many were also intimidated by threats of economic retaliation that had been brandished against those who seceded.[8] Jacob Rosenheim, a Frankfurt native, described their feelings and motivations:

> From a psychological perspective, one can understand this unfortunate outcome. The majority saw secession, which was after all a public legal act, as personal and social estrangement from local Jewish society, to which they were bound by thousands of intricate social and functional ties. Some, among them my father, *zatzal,* backed off because of the required declaration in a court of law, and asked themselves if they could honestly make an official declaration with the legal force of an oath, that they wished to withdraw for reasons of religious conscience, when, in fact, their only motive was to obey the ruling of their Rav.
>
> The factor that tipped the scales against withdrawal was the reaction of the small group of old Frankfurt residents led by Rabbi Moshe Mainz, a renowned *talmid chacham,* and his family. This group wanted to use the Law of Secession only as a means of bringing pressure to bear on the Reform community to achieve concessions on various religious matters. In their mind, their association with the historical community (which had, in fact, ceased to exist as such) was stronger than their disgruntlement with the war the Reform community had been waging against

> Judaism for the previous 50 years. This group had no understanding of Rabbi Hirsch's ideals or of his personality; to them he was a "hothead," and in spite of his unimpeachable credentials as a *talmid chacham,* they could not forgive him (is not history full of small-minded people at every turn) if, in the course of his active life, his authoritative manner had offended some of them.[9]

The Community Board soon announced a proposal to establish separate accounts and exempt the Orthodox from contributing to the support of Reform synagogues and schools. They also promised to operate the hospital and the cemetery in a fashion acceptable to Orthodox Jews, and to include Orthodox representatives drawn from those who did not secede on the directorates of those institutions.

Both factions of the *IRG* waited for Rabbi Hirsch's reply with bated breath, and his response was not long in coming. On Shabbos *Parashas Toldos,* the second of *Kislev,* he delivered a passionate address in the synagogue, stating his position in no uncertain terms. Not only was secession permitted by the Torah, he asserted, it was a positive obligation totally unaffected by any concessions the Community Board might offer. An opponent of secession, he related, had asked him to cite a source in the *Shulchan Aruch* for this requirement. The *Shulchan Aruch,* he replied, as a rule, does not state the self-evident, such as the prohibition against conversion to Christianity.[10]

Secession from the Community

SEVERAL DAYS LATER, RABBI HIRSCH PUBLISHED A 20-PAGE PAMphlet entitled "Secession from the Community" (*Austritt aus der Gemeinde*) in which he repeated the central points of his address in *shul,* while omitting the halachic principles. He explained that remaining in the Reform community voluntarily, when the option of withdrawal existed, constituted willful and knowing recognition of Reform as a legitimate branch of Judaism. When membership was compulsory, it did not constitute a personal declaration of professed belief. Now, however, that one had the possibility to withdraw, continued membership in an organization professing Reform Judaism, even if not required to pay membership dues, was an admission of the viability of Reform principles. Orthodoxy and Reform, he asserted, are mutually exclusive. Whereas Orthodoxy affirms the binding character of the Torah and the Talmud, Reform denies these. If one is the truth then the other, perforce, must be a lie. One who belongs to a Reform community implies that denial and mockery of the Law are just as legitimate before G-d as its devout observance. The maintenance of two separate institutions of worship and education within one communal framework was possible only for thoughtless individuals to whom all things religious are no more than meaningless forms and matters of individual taste and for whom sincerity and integrity are unimportant.

To charges that secession subverted the fundamental principle of keeping peace, he replied with his well-known interpretation of the verse (*Zachariah* 8:19), *Love truth and peace* — in that order. Only when truth is adhered to can there be genuine peace. Peace, he always said, is the child of truth, not its progenitor. Furthermore, what was involved here was not separation from heretics as individuals, but rather from institutionalized heresy. The break is not from personal relationships with people but rather from "a belief system upheld, taught and represented by the moral entity that is the Reform community." To those who argued that secession would lead to disintegration of whole communities, he replied that such a claim was, in fact, an argument in favor of secession. For if the Reform communities were able to survive only because of Orthodox participation, how much more so was it incumbent on them to withdraw.

The claim that remaining in one community would help bring the Reformers back from their errant ways was spurious; half a century of Reform and Orthodox in one communal framework had proven the exact opposite — it resulted in the steady advance of Reform. As far as the joint humanitarian endeavors and charitable causes were concerned, these in any case had been based on voluntary cooperation from time immemorial and would remain so. To the claim that concern for one's livelihood was a valid reason to refrain from secession, he replied that if there was actually any reason for concern on this score, then to the contrary, one should rejoice that one had been granted an opportunity, at least once in one's lifetime, to sanctify G-d's name with his actions, "for there can hardly be a greater *Kiddush Hashem* than to forget about economic profit or loss when it comes to performing the solemn duty of one's conscience before G-d. It would be an opportunity to put into practice, publicly and in all sincerity, the commandment to love Hashem 'with all your resources.' "

To the argument that secession might entail forfeiting the right to be buried alongside one's ancestors and put families in the position of having to bury their members in a site that did not comply with *halachah*, his response was unequivocal:

> Even in that extreme case, it would be wrong for me to waver for even a moment in my resolve to secede. As long as I am alive and

> conscious, I am responsible for anything I do or fail to do. Hence, my failure to secede would accompany me into the next world as a personal reproach, an omission for which I would be held personally responsible. On the other hand, I will not be held responsible for what happens to my remains after I have died. As for my family, they would have no other choice but to do what the police force them to do, and just as in the days of compulsory membership and compulsory contributions, they would bear no burden of guilt for what would be done with my dead body.[11]

But Rabbi Hirsch's forceful stand did not sway his congregants. When the Community Board discerned the sustained opposition to secession within the membership of the *IRG*, it hardened its stance commensurately and announced that henceforth they would refuse to allow the secessionists or any members of their families to be buried in the communal cemetery.[a] This threat was counterproductive, as up until then the Orthodox were willing to cooperate with the Reform on a limited basis in the management of the communal help organizations, such as the hospital and the cemetery. The decision to keep the secessionists out of the cemetery only served to strengthen the *IRG* leadership's resolve to establish a separate cemetery and totally sever any ties between the Orthodox and Reform.

In a synagogue address soon afterwards, Rabbi Hirsch said that one of the first questions members of the *Kehillah* would be asked after death would be: "Did you secede?" and he added that, "it would be better to be buried in Sachsenhausen (a local Christian cemetery) under the sign of the cross than to give any support to the views of such people."[12] This address brought some results, and some who had previously opposed secession changed their minds and decided to go ahead with it. It is an interesting sidelight that, from the time the Community Board refused to bury secessionists in its cemetery, until the *Kehillah* opened its own cemetery adjacent to that of the community a few months later, not one of its members died. This was widely seen at the time as a special act of Divine kindness.[13]

On December 22 (6 *Teves*), the Community Board issued "Amendments to the Bylaws of the Israelite Community" granting some measure of autonomy to those Orthodox who were willing to remain within the

a. Although, by law, the Orthodox could have forced the burial by court order since they did not have alternative burial grounds, this was a procedure they were understandably loathe to undertake. It is not difficult to imagine the disgrace to the deceased and the anguish of his family waiting for a court order to allow burial in the Jewish cemetery.

community framework. The major concession was an exemption from payment of that part of the membership fee designated for the operations of the Reform institutions. On January 26, 1877 (12 *Shevat*), Rabbi Hirsch issued a reply in the form of an "Analysis of the Amendment to the Bylaws etc." which was distributed to the membership of the *IRG*. He categorically rejected the Reformers' proposal. The close scrutiny to which he subjected the proposed bylaws led him to conclude that continued membership — even if exempt from paying the fees to support directly the Reform educational and worship facilities — still sanctioned, by one's signature, the denial of principles which are most sacred to the conscience of every Jew. The essence of the proposal, he said, was an attempt to achieve a working coexistence between two denominations in the same structure. Membership in such an organization, he wrote, even if one was exempt from all fees, constituted recognition of the right of Reform to exist.[14]

The Würzburger Rav

AT THIS POINT IT IS IMPERATIVE THAT WE INTRODUCE A MAN WHO was to figure importantly in the battle over *Austritt* in Frankfurt, one of the great Torah luminaries and halachic decisors of 19th-century German Jewry, the Würzburger Rav, Rabbi Yitzchak Dov Halevi (Seligmann Bär) Bamberger (1807-1878).[b]

Born in Wiesenbronn near Kissingen in southern Germany, he spent his youth far from the bustle of urban life. Before he reached the age of 15, he was sent to learn in the yeshiva in Fürth headed by Rabbi Wolf Hamburg, one of the pre-eminent rabbinic authorities in Germany. As he never intended to pursue a career in the rabbinate, but desired only to become a *talmid chacham* like many Jews of previous generations in Lower Franconia, he felt no need to engage in secular studies.

In 1839, 87-year-old Rabbi Avraham Bing, District Rabbi of Würzburg, retired from the rabbinate, and a year later Rabbi Bamberger was elected his successor, at the culmination of an election campaign in which the Reform elements did their best to thwart his candidacy. As he had no academic training, at the time *de rigueur* for any young man wishing to enter the rabbinate in Germany, Rabbi Bamberger acquired a thorough knowledge of Greek, Latin and Modern German, and in short order learned to speak a polished German, in which he now delivered his sermons.

b. Much of the biographical information on Rabbi Bamberger is from Rabbi Binyamin Shlomo Hamburger, "Nesi Haleviim," a biographical introduction to *Kisvei Rabbeinu Yitzchok Dov Halevi* (Bnei Brak, 1992), pp. 497-566.

His first public endeavor after his election was the re-establishment of the yeshiva which had disbanded when Rabbi Bing took ill. The Würzburger Rav was a *masmid* of rare diligence, whose idea of happiness was having an uninterrupted stretch of time in which to learn. He was a warm and caring father to his students, who retained a lifelong affection for their beloved *rebbe*. The fact that Würzburg was also home to a major German university had no small effect on the yeshiva and its students. Rabbi Bamberger did not encourage his students to attend university, and not one of his children, most of whom went on to serve as *rabbonim*, studied in university.[c] When they reached maturity, however, he did ensure that they receive private lessons in secular subjects. He was at best apathetic, if not opposed, to the *Torah Im Derech Eretz* espoused by Rabbi Hirsch, a fact which the latter makes note of in his "Open Letter" to Rabbi Bamberger.[15]

Although Rabbi Bamberger did not embrace the *Torah Im Derech Eretz* of Rabbi Hirsch, and disapproved of the time and effort expended on scientific pursuits championed by Rabbi Hildesheimer, he realized that rabbis and teachers in Germany needed to acquire secular education in order to function properly. In 1864, he established a Teachers Seminary, the *Würzburger Israelitische Lehrerbildungsanstalt*, to train Jewish teachers, of which there was a scarcity in Germany. Over the years, the seminary in Würzburg supplied many small, rural and urban communities with able teachers. On average, there were 30 students per year in the Seminary. By 1889, it had 210 graduates and 15 years later over 400. By the time the school was finally shut down by the Nazis in 1938, it had graduated over 700 students, many of whom had been trained not only for teaching, but also as *mohalim, shochtim* and *chazzanim*.[16]

It is not a coincidence that Rabbi Hirsch established a secondary school in Frankfurt, while Rabbi Bamberger only founded an elementary school in Würzburg. Whereas Rabbi Hirsch favored advanced secular education even for the Jewish businessman, Rabbi Bamberger felt that the state requirements would suffice, and even then was wary of the expansion of secular studies, which, he felt, came at the expense of time spent on *limudei kodesh*.

c. Rabbi Bamberger was unusual among all the German rabbis of his time in that almost all of his children became practicing rabbis serving various German communities. Among them were: Rabbi Shlomo Zalman, rabbi of various communities; Rabbi Simcha, Rabbi of Fischach and Aschaffenburg; Rabbi Moshe Aryeh Leib, Rabbi of Kissingen; Rabbi Seckel, *dayan* in the *IRG* in Frankfurt who passed away in 1885 at the early age of 45; Rabbi Nathan, who succeeded his father as Rabbi of Würzburg; his son-in-law Rabbi Pinchas Seligmann Fromm, Rabbi of Bad Homburg; his son-in-law Rabbi Moses Unna, a teacher in Würzburg; and his son-in-law Rabbi Menachem Adler, Rabbi of Meinbernheim.

Rabbi Bamberger exerted a powerful influence on Jewish life in Germany. He was not only one of its leading halachic decisors, but also the *rebbe* of many important rabbinic figures in Germany, who turned to him for guidance and support in difficult moments. Among them were Dr. Abraham Sulzbach, an influential educator who taught in the *IRG* school in Frankfurt, Rabbi Alexander Adler of Lübeck, Rabbi Anselm Stern of Hamburg, Rabbi David Zvi Hoffman, later head of the *Rabbiner-Seminar* of Berlin, Rabbi Yonah Rosenbaum of Zell, Rabbi Hile Wechsler, and Rabbi Salomon Carlebach of Lübeck.

The Würzburger Rav was a *talmid chacham* of rare erudition. He authored classic works in several areas of practical *halachah*, especially in those whose proper observance had suffered due to ignorance or misunderstanding. They included works on the laws of *S'TaM* (writing *Sifrei Torah, Tefillin* and *Mezuzos)* (*Meleches Shomayim:* Altona, 1853); family purity (*Amirah Lebais Yaakov:* Fürth, 1858); *Shechitah* (*Moreh Lezovchim:* Fürth, 1863); and *Chalitzah* (*Nachalei Dvash:* Frankfurt, 1867), the latter having been written in his youth. His works were widely used in their time, and even today are considered authoritative in their respective disciplines. Hundreds of his responsa were published in the two-volume *Shaalos U'tshuvos Yad Halevi* (Jerusalem, 1965-1987). At his passing he left behind 28 volumes of responsa, Torah novellae and sermons, only a small portion of which has been published posthumously.

Rabbi Bamberger was very active on behalf of the *yishuv* in Eretz Yisrael and was a central figure in raising money for Jews in the Holy Land at a time when most of the funds supporting Jews in Palestine were raised in Germany. Together with Rabbi Ezriel Hildesheimer, he was one of the initiators of the Batei Machseh housing project in the Jewish Quarter of the Old City of Jerusalem, which was built by Baron Willy Rothschild of Frankfurt. In 1873, he signed a public proclamation together with Rabbi Hirsch, urging the public to contribute money for a Jerusalem hospital which would be run according to *halachah*, and invested much time and effort in raising funds to erect the hospital, so that local residents would not be forced to use the "free" services of the missionary hospitals, due to overcrowding at the Jewish hospitals, Bikur Cholim and Rothschild. His efforts in this matter continued until his passing, and it was only 20 years after his death that the project came to fruition, when the funds he raised were used by Dr. Moshe Wallach to establish Shaare Zedek Hospital in Jerusalem.

In 1876, Rabbi Bamberger was at the height of his fame as one of the foremost rabbinic figures in Germany.

ON JANUARY 29, 1877 (TU B'SHVAT, 5637), SEVERAL OPPONENTS OF secession sent a request to Rabbi Bamberger, asking his opinion as to whether, in light of the new concessions on the part of the Reform Board, it was permitted to remain in the Reform community. Three days later, Rabbi Bamberger replied that after studying the proposed "Amendments to the Bylaws," he had not retracted his previously stated opinion that:

Rabbi Bamberger's Position

> it is the obligation of an Orthodox Jew to secede from a Reform community, as your esteemed rabbi, Rav Hirsch, has already made clear in his analysis of the additional ordinances. . . . It is categorically forbidden for Orthodox Jews to participate in any manner in the operation and maintenance of a hospital run by a Reform community. The reason for this is clear when one considers the observance of the Sabbath and dietary laws. The conscientious observance of these commandments is only possible when the administration of such institutions is placed into the hands of men of recognized Orthodoxy, and for obvious reasons Reformers cannot be considered reliable. Nor can the mere selection of a member of the *Religionsgesellschaft* to the hospital committee effect a change or serve as a guarantee that these commandments will be duly observed. I would state, in addition, that the members of the executive committee of a community must be as scrupulously observant as those of a rabbinical court. . . . Hence an irreligious board must not be recognized by Orthodox Jewry and no believing Jew may become a member of it. Since, according to the law of July 26, 1876, the right to secede from such a community has been granted, those who fail to take advantage of it would actually be guilty of a breach of the above-mentioned religious ordinances.[17]

Basing his decision on the *Shulchan Aruch*, Rabbi Bamberger expressed his opinion that the Community Board was not worthy of recognition and that no believing Jew could remain a member in the community. At the conclusion of his response, the Würzburger Rav wrote that it would be a source of "joy to [my] heart and soul" if his opinion were to sway those who had not yet renounced their membership in the Reform community to do so.[18]

The Würzburger Rav's stance in this matter was not particularly surprising. On a number of occasions over the years he had made known his opinion that were secession to become a viable option, it would be an appropriate course of action in the struggle against Reform. In response to queries

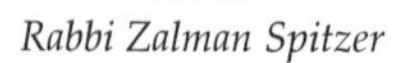

Rabbi Zalman Spitzer

from Bavaria in 1850 and Karlsruhe in 1859, Rabbi Bamberger replied that it was forbidden to elect Sabbath desecrators to community boards, and should such men be chosen, they could not be recognized as board members. In a published responsum in 1869, on the question of community structures in Hungary, he supported withdrawal from Reform-dominated communities. In 1872, the board of the Jewish community in Vienna decided to delete from the prayers in *one* of Vienna's synagogues any mention of the *korbonos* (sacrifices), the Messiah and the redemption. In response Rabbi Zalman Spitzer (1826-1893), heading a large Orthodox group, threatened to resign from the Vienna rabbinate.[d] He asked for, and received, a proclamation signed by 389 European rabbis, including Rabbi Bamberger and many other German rabbis, which declared:

> Any Jew who does not believe in the ultimate coming of a Messiah from the descendants of David, in the reunification of the Jewish people in the Holy Land, and in the restoration of the sacrificial rites as commanded in the Torah is to be considered as having defected from Judaism. Furthermore, the elimination of, or failure to recite, the passages in the prayer book referring to the above-mentioned [Divine] promises implies a defection from Judaism. *Therefore, a Torah-true Jew must not and cannot remain associated in one religious community with persons guilty of such apostasy.* Moreover, according to Jewish doctrine, it is also forbidden to pay taxes to a religious community whose spokesmen have adopted such resolutions that deny the Divine promises and whose institutions are not based on the unshakeable foundations of religious law as codified in the *Shulchan Aruch.*[e,19]

d. Rabbi Spitzer was a disciple of Rabbi Moshe Schick *(Maharam Schick)* of Chust, Rabbi Meir Eisenstadt *(Maharam Ash)*, and Rabbi Avrohom S.B. Sofer *(K'sav Sofer)* of Pressburg. In 1849, he married the daughter of the *Chasam Sofer*, ten years after the passing of the latter. In 1853, he was appointed a rabbi of a *shul* in Vienna, and with the demise of Rabbi Elazar Horowitz in 1868, he was appointed *dayan* of the *Kultusgemeinde* of Vienna. In 1872, he was appointed Rabbi of the secessionist *Adath Israel* of Vienna.

e. As a result of this decision Rabbi Spitzer resigned as rabbi of the *Kultusgemeinde.*[19*]

Indeed, Rabbi Bamberger's own son Rabbi Seckel Bamberger, a Frankfurt resident, had seceded from the *Gemeinde* already on November 2, 1876.

On December 17, 1876 (*Rosh Chodesh Teves*, 5637), only a month and a half before he released his first statement on the Frankfurt issue, Rabbi Bamberger supported secession in Wiesbaden,[f] and on January 8 (23 *Teves*), in response to a request from Wiesbaden for clarification of his earlier opinion, he replied that his intention was to say that affiliation with the Reform community was strictly forbidden.[20]

Outside Interference

AS PREVIOUSLY MENTIONED, ON FEBRUARY 1, RABBI BAMBERGER replied to a group of opponents of secession in Frankfurt that Torah Law required them to secede. This group, however, decided not to follow his ruling and made no move to withdraw. In response, the Community Board, which closely monitored the tension levels in the *IRG* and exploited every opportunity to cause a rift in the *Kehillah*, attempted to strengthen the position of those Orthodox who did not want to secede by establishing its own *shechitah* operation, under the supervision of someone acceptable to the non-secessionist Orthodox.

This move completely altered the rules of engagement. Whereas until then, the Community Board had coerced its Orthodox members to pay community taxes, it provided for none of their religious needs in return. Now, however, it was making an effort to establish institutions under their own control, parallel to those of the *IRG*. By this time, matters in both communities were not far from the boiling point.[21]

And then the unthinkable happened. On March 19th (5 *Nisan*), the Würzburger Rav came to Frankfurt, at the invitation of *proponents* of secession, who hoped he would be able to have some influence on those who opposed withdrawal. Although, in response to the invitation, he had

---

f. The following is the basic text of his reply to the Orthodox Jews of Wiesbaden:

> A traditional Jewish community, i.e. of a Judaism which is true and uncorrupted, can be so considered if it functions with all religious institutions and requirements of the Torah, according to the true and undistorted Jewish laws, as laid down in the Talmud and the *Shulchan Aruch*, and as were always taught by the true and believing rabbis in the same fashion and in the same manner. Primarily included in this are the synagogue and the *tefillos*, the *mikveh*, a religious school and *shechitah*. These are the most basic points, while in general the principle must be abided to, that membership in the community may not be accompanied with a threat to the conscience. A believing Jew should not belong to a community which does not adhere to these principles even if he runs the risk that after his death the Reform community will not permit his burial in the Jewish cemetery under its control and he will be forced to be buried in a non-Jewish cemetery.[20*]

replied that it was possible that after viewing the situation he might decide that secession was not necessary, the proponents of secession insisted that he come anyway. Tensions were running high, with many of the usual manifestations of public controversy in evidence, including vituperative anonymous posters and leaflets, fictitious announcements to the press and a good measure of disinformation.

Upon arriving in Frankfurt, Rabbi Bamberger went directly to meet with a group of anti-secessionists, headed by his good friend Rabbi Moshe Mainz, without the usual courtesy visit to the Rabbi. After presenting a variety of arguments in support of their position, the group explained to their guest that now that the Reform community wanted to establish religious institutions of its own, it would be a blessing to future generations to refrain from seceding. Rabbi Bamberger accepted his hosts' arguments without consulting Rabbi Hirsch as rabbi of the city, and before he left Frankfurt that same evening, his hosts hastened to release an announcement in his name to the *Frankfurter Bourse und Handelszeitung*, a commercial newspaper, stating that under the present conditions "it could no longer be deemed necessary to secede from the Reform community."[22] The following is the text of the notice to the press:

> A short time ago I was asked by several members of the *Religionsgesellschaft* of Frankfurt to go there with the objective of persuading a certain person,[g] who had hitherto refused to do so, to secede. In view of the importance of the matter, I complied with this request. In the course of the discussion, I learned that the Community Board was now prepared to deal fairly with Orthodox members who did not secede; that the institutions which they needed would be established on their behalf out of communal funds and would be entirely under Orthodox guidance and supervision and that, on the other hand, Orthodox members would be exempted from contributing towards the cultural institutions of the Reform Movement. I thereupon replied that provided all the necessary guarantees were given for the carrying out of these concessions, it could no longer be deemed necessary to secede from the Reform community.[23]

Rabbi Bamberger's announcement, released on Tuesday, March 20 (6 *Nisan*), plunged the Orthodox community into turmoil. The immediate

g. The reference is to Rabbi Mainz.

response of the supporters of *Austritt* was to publish in the Thursday, March 22, edition of the *Frankfurter Journal*, the text of Rabbi Bamberger's response to Wiesbaden on December 17, where he advocated secession.

Rabbi Hirsch's own response was not long in coming. Four days after Rabbi Bamberger's statement, he delivered the customary *Shabbos HaGadol drashah* in the synagogue, whose 1,000 seats were filled to capacity. In his address he sharply denounced the stand of the Würzburger Rav, saying that the first *mitzvah* of *Shabbos HaGadol* was that of "withdraw and take for yourselves" (*Shemos* 12:21), which means, as *Rashi* comments, "withdraw your hands from idol worship and cling to *mitzvos*." The obligation to secede applied to every Jew and was not in the slightest connected with any concessions the Reformers might make. The requirement to draw away from Reform was no less binding than the requirement to distance oneself from idol worship. Concerning Rabbi Bamberger's statement, he paraphrased a famous Talmudic epithet, "Surely he must have been sleeping when he said that."[24]

Open Letters

ON TUESDAY, MARCH 27, THE 13TH OF NISAN, THE DAY BEFORE *EREV Pesach*, and a mere six days after Rabbi Bamberger's announcement, Rabbi Hirsch published an open letter to Rabbi Bamberger covering 28 printed pages. That he found the time and the peace of mind during one of the busiest weeks of the year to compose this *teshuvah*, which is one of the most eloquent expositions of the imperative to separate oneself from heresy ever composed, is nothing less than extraordinary. The speed with which Rabbi Hirsch penned his long and detailed letter indicates clearly that the halachic principles requiring secession were clearly organized in his mind from the outset, and that his actions in the matter were the result of a serious study of those issues. It is not unreasonable to assume that had he made his halachic reasoning public before the Würzburger Rav came to town, the latter would have found it infinitely more difficult to interfere in the manner that he did.[25]

His tone was one of severe pain and intense grief. He explained at length why secession was an obligation, and also reproached Rabbi Bamberger for interfering in a matter outside his jurisdiction and permitting that which he, as *mara d'asra*, had forbidden.[h] Several anonymous

h. The part of this letter that involves pure halachic issues appears in translation in *Shemesh Marpeh*, responsa no. 46, pp. 51-57.

pamphlets had been published in response to Rabbi Hirsch's previous statements regarding secession. To these Rabbi Hirsch gave no direct response, except for the following short note, which appeared at the beginning of his Open Letter to the Würzburger Rav:

> Various publications opposing our call for secession . . . have already appeared under the cover of anonymity. Their contents only show that their authors are in no position whatsoever to voice any opinion worthy of note on this question. . . . Any replies written anonymously or signed with a fictitious name will not receive any consideration from me. One who lacks the courage to sign his true name to his views must be aware that what he is saying is meaningless, and that therefore he cannot expect others to take notice of it. Let the anonymous gnats buzz happily in the sunny meadows. I certainly do not want to spoil their pleasure.

Rabbi Hirsch reiterated in his Open Letter that voluntary membership in a religious community of necessity implies espousal of the principles to which that community ascribes. An Orthodox Jew, who remains a member of a Reform community when he has the requisite religious institutions available in his own community, thus remains a member only for the sake of being a member. He has thereby declared that Jews may create, for use by non-observant Jews, Reform institutions that violate religious law. This is true even if he does not make payments to support those institutions. In addition, as a member of that community, all use of its joint assets for Reform purposes are with his approval, direct or indirect.

Rabbi Bamberger's statement, Rabbi Hirsch averred, sets forth in unequivocal terms, that Reform has full legitimacy in the eyes of the Orthodox, as long as it tolerates the existence of Orthodoxy at its side and accords it proper consideration. A community which, as a matter of principle, has stricken from its prayer book every reference to *Mashiach* as a person, to the ingathering of the exiles, to the rebuilding of the *Bais Hamikdosh* and to the *Seder Ha'Avodah*, a system whose school and pulpit teach and preach that the *mitzvoth* are outdated can be classified as nothing other than institutions of *minuth* (heresy) and *apikorsus* (apostasy). And the Torah commands us to keep an even greater distance from *minuth* and *apikorsus*, which are likely to lead a Jew astray, than from idolatry. Thus an Orthodox Jew cannot remain in such a community of *minuth* and *apikorsus*, which are defined as "the violation of Jewish truth and law by Jews as a matter of principle."[26] Doing so violates the commandment to distance oneself from it and constitutes a *chilul Hashem* and a flagrant strengthening of heretics and sinners.

The fact that the Reformers were willing to grant the Orthodox their own *kashruth* organization only made the *chilul Hashem* greater. A house of idol worship does not cease to be one just because it has a *mezuzah* attached to the doorpost. Under what principle does a Reform community cease to be a hotbed of *minuth* just because it sets up "kosher" institutions for its Orthodox members? he asked. In addition, Rabbi Hirsch reminded Rabbi Bamberger that he himself had declared membership in such a community forbidden, as late as February 1, and nothing the Reform Board had done had changed the basis for that *p'sak.*

The new phase of this controversy increased quickly in intensity. It is sufficient to cite the remark of Rabbi Ezriel Hildesheimer, on the 24th of *Iyar* of that year, that the intervention of the Rav of Würzburg was "the work of the Satan that has already succeeded in bringing about a situation similar to the conflict between Rabbi Yonasan [Eibeschutz] and the *gaon* Rabbi Yaakov Emden."[27]

On May 7 (24 *Iyar*), Rabbi Bamberger responded to Rabbi Hirsch's "Open Letter" with an "Open Reply" in which he attempted to defend his decision and his intervention. Rabbi Bamberger began by explaining why, in his view, there was no halachic impediment to him expressing a lenient opinion in a matter which Rabbi Hirsch as *mara de'asra* had forbidden. He declared that the fact that the Reform Community Board was willing to allow an Orthodox group to establish their own services and provide for their religious needs removed them from the category of *minim lehach'is* (premeditated heretics) and put them only in the category of *letayavon* (for pleasure's sake). These, he asserted, were not to be considered heretics. In addition, he wrote, the *min* from which one is required to distance oneself refers to one who has converted to idol worship, "and are no longer Jews."[i]

The *Austritt* affair had by that time taken a serious toll on Rabbi Hirsch's health, and he replied now with great effort.[28] Still, his response was not long in coming. Owing, however, to his weakened state it was written with great effort. Only six days later, on May 13 (*Rosh Chodesh*

---

i. For the full text of Rabbi Bamberger's reply in English translation, see *Collected Writings of Rabbi S.R. Hirsch* VI, pp. 226-253.

Sivan), he issued his 61-page "Open Response," that was more sharply worded and considerably more bitter than the "Open Letter." In his "Response" he quoted a letter he had received from Rabbi Zalman Spitzer asserting that conditions in Vienna, where Rabbi Bamberger had ruled that it was "strictly mandatory" to secede from the Reform Community, were much more agreeable to the Orthodox than those in Frankfurt.[29]

Rabbi Hirsch concluded by citing the famous responsum of the *Chasam Sofer*, written in response to the establishment in 1818 of the Hamburg Temple and the publication of its prayerbook, where the question had been posed whether Torah-true Jews may remain in one religious community with the followers of Reform, if conditions were such that separation were possible:

> If it were within our power to implement a practical decision in respect to this matter, it would be my opinion that there should be a complete separation between them and ourselves so that our children should not intermarry with theirs lest our children become tempted to follow in their footsteps. Our relationship with them as a community should be the same as our relationship with צדוק ובייתוס ענן ושאול (the Sadducees, the Boethusians and the Karaites); they should go their own way and we should go ours. But all this is my opinion in theory only; it cannot be implemented in practice without permission from the State. Without such permission, let my words be inoperative as if they had never been spoken.[30]

"But today," Rabbi Hirsch concluded, "under the Secession Law we do have this needed permission from the State. As a consequence, the decision which the *Chasam Sofer* during his lifetime could pronounce only in theory has now become operative in practice. Therefore, this decision, bearing as it does the full weight of that great rabbinic authority, further tilts the scales in favor of mandatory secession."[j]

But the die had already been cast. A glance at the list of those who seceded shows that there were only two members of the *IRG* who seced-

j. The facts, issues and halachic principles discussed in Rabbi Hirsch's "Open Response," including a lengthy discussion of the halachic dictum of חכם שאסר אין חבירו ראשי להתיר and a long and detailed exposition on the essence and definition of מינות and אפיקורסות, are too broad and too intricate to be summarized briefly. It is available in English translation in the *Collected Writings* VI, pp. 254-317.

ed after March 19. One of them, Ludwig Rapp, was such a devoted follower of Rabbi Hirsch that it is inconceivable that anything but technical reasons had prevented him from acting earlier.

Following publication of the "Open Response," both men laid down their pens in this matter. But, from then on, German Orthodoxy was divided into two factions, the "separatists" or members of the secessionist communities (*Austrittsgemeinde*) and the "non-separatists," who were Orthodox members of an overall Reform community (*Gemeinde-Orthodoxie*). The push for secession was most vigorous in those places where the domination and intolerance of the Reform were strongest.[31]

Deep bitterness remained. Rabbi Hirsch and the leaders of the *IRG* were furious at Rabbi Bamberger's intervention, and when the latter passed away suddenly, in *shul*, on the second day of Succoth, 1878, the *IRG* and its rabbi were not represented at the funeral. It was a powerful gesture of anger. This split remained unhealed until the final destruction of German Jewry by the Nazis.

Rabbi Hildesheimer's Position

IT IS WORTH POINTING OUT THAT RABBI EZRIEL HILDESHEIMER cooperated with Rabbi Hirsch in the efforts to pass the Secession Law. At first discreetly and then openly, he was a firm supporter of Rabbi Hirsch in his disagreement with the Würzburger Rav. Initially, he refrained from printing anything about the controversy in his newspaper, the *Jüdische Presse*, reasoning that the damage that would certainly be sustained by the worthwhile institutions he headed in Berlin and in *Eretz Yisrael* would outweigh the benefit of anything he might write about this volatile subject. "To defend [Rabbi Bamberger]," he wrote, "is out of the question." In a personal letter to an associate, Rabbi Hildesheimer described the non-religious newspapers as "casting stone after stone at Rabbi Hirsch, who has restored to contemporary Orthodox Judaism its former glory."[32]

Rabbi Hildesheimer shared the distress Rabbi Hirsch had expressed in the "Open Letter," and attempted to give him solace and encouragement. In a later letter dated 16 *Tammuz* of that year, written after he received the "Open Response," he said, "I cannot express in words the great pleasure I had in reading your all-encompassing and incontrovertible reasoning. . . . In my opinion, you have brought to the question a conclusion that is inevitable for anyone who recognizes the truth. This service you have done joins your many achievements in presenting the clear truth to the Orthodox community. This latest accomplishment is worthy of all the others and as important as any of them."[33]

Rabbi Ezriel Hildesheimer

After the publication of the open letters, the two Orthodox weeklies in Germany, *Der Israelit* published by Rabbi Marcus Lehmann of Mainz and the *Jüdische Presse* of Berlin, both declared their unequivocal support for Rabbi Hirsch. The *Jüdische Presse* published a series of articles, apparently authored by Rabbi Ezriel Hildesheimer himself, detailing the events in Frankfurt and leaving no doubt as to the author's loyalties.

Chapter Fourteen
AFTERMATH

ONLY 115 MEMBERS, OR ABOUT ONE-THIRD OF THE MEMbership, of the *IRG* seceded.[a] Of those who did not secede, some based themselves on the statement of Rabbi Bamberger, and some were undoubtedly influenced by Baron Willy Rothschild's decision to continue as a dues-paying member of the *Grossgemeinde*. Most of those who did not secede remained nonetheless firmly committed members of the *IRG* and had no connection with the *Grossgemeinde*, save for the payment of dues and official membership. Although unwilling to take the step of secession, they were not denied any rights in the *Kehillah*, not even that of sitting on the Board of Trustees (*Vorstand*).[b] The *Kehillah* itself continued to grow and flourish, and, apart for this one matter, Rabbi Hirsch's stature in his *Kehillah* was in no way diminished.

---

a. The complete list is part of the Sänger Collection and is reprinted here in an appendix.

b. For many years after Rabbi Hirsch's death, even the Chairman of the Board of the *IRG* was also a member of the *Grossgemeinde*.

For Rabbi Hirsch himself, the failure of most of his membership to follow his lead was a personal tragedy. A principle for which he had fought for many years and which formed an integral part of his world view was not accepted by his own community, a *kehillah* which he had built from scratch with his own hands. Although his spirit was not dimmed (a year later he published his commentary on *Devarim*, and several years later commentaries on the Psalms and the *Siddur*), it took a considerable toll on his health and he aged greatly as a result.

An Unhealed Breach

ANY DESCRIPTION WE MIGHT OFFER OF THIS NEVER-TO-BE-REPAIRED rupture in Frankfurt would surely suffer from the deficiencies and inaccuracies of second-hand information. Instead, we will cite the account of one prominent native of Frankfurt whose father did *not* secede,[c] and his description of the atmosphere there in ensuing years. Herewith, then, the account of Jacob Rosenheim:

> It can be imagined how this attack [of Rabbi Bamberger] affected Rabbi Hirsch. Only then, when he saw his whole fundamental principle in danger, did he turn his attention to the halachic aspect of the matter in two immortal and unparalleled works of politico-religious polemics (the "Open Letter" and later "The Open Response"). . . . I must admit that these two compositions, which I read at the age of 18, made an indelible impression on me. Recognizing the inadequacy of my own opinion in this matter, I rejoiced when many years later I found the following statement in a letter from Rabbi Ezriel Hildesheimer to Rabbi Marcus Horovitz: "The ruling of Rabbi Hirsch on the question of secession was presented so marvelously and irrefutably that no *gaon* could have improved on it."
>
> Only a giant like Rabbi Hirsch could have foreseen from the outset the "tragedy to the generations" that the *Gemeinde-Orthodoxen* ("Community Orthodox") caused, with their hybrid "Reform-Orthodox" communities, by granting the Reformers equal status as a legitimate stream within a secular Jewish nation, united only by shared racial identity. At the same time they reduced authentic Judaism to the status of a denomination, a mere sect within the Jewish national collective, "neutral" concerning matters of religion.

c. Jacob Rosenheim himself was only 7 years old at the time of the *Austritt* battle in 1877. In any event, he attended for some time the sermons of Rabbi Horovitz of the *Grossgemeinde*.

Only decades later, when the nationalist movement was born, did it become clear for all to see that the struggle over secession was not at all a local issue. . . .

The incomplete realization of secession affected Rabbi Hirsch for the rest of his life. Indeed, I remember one of his last addresses on *Shabbos Shuva* sometime between 1886 and 1888. In the middle of his remarks, which were filled with lucidly expressed ethical admonishments, he suddenly stopped and with no transition said, "Even so, we must protest incessantly the monstrous outrage that exists in our midst, willful affiliation with a community representing heresy. . . ." At that point he was overcome with emotion and could not continue. It made an awesome sight.

It was only about 10 years following the death of this great teacher that everyone came to see how true is the Sages' saying, "The righteous are greater in death than in life." The new "Community Law" of 1899 allowed every Jewish resident of Frankfurt to leave the Reform community and join the Orthodox community by making a simple written declaration. As a result, at least 80 percent of the members of the *IRG* (whose numbers had grown in the interim to over 1,000) immediately ceased to pay taxes to the *Grossgemeinde*. Now that the mental obstacles to secession were removed, as far as everyone but a handful of dedicated *Gemeinde-Orthodoxen* was concerned, it became simply a matter of choosing between two communal organizations with equal legal status.

Rabbi Hirsch's followers treated Dr. Marcus Horovitz (1844-1910) [the rabbi of the Orthodox branch of the *Grossgemeinde*] as an outcast.[d] The latter had accepted his position against the wishes of one of the leaders of the generation and in opposition to the clearly stated opinion of his own teacher, Rabbi Ezriel Hildesheimer. Rabbi Hirsch himself refused ever to meet with his

---

d. Rabbi Horovitz studied in Rabbi Ezriel Hildesheimer's yeshiva in Eisenstadt. He married the daughter of Rabbi Yaakov Ettlinger in 1872 more than a year after her father's passing. In 1873, he was the only Orthodox rabbi who refused Rabbi Ezriel Hildesheimer's request to sign a petition to the Prussian *Landtag* supporting the right of secession from the Jewish community, and he was also one of the few Orthodox German rabbis not to join the 389 rabbinic signatories who supported Orthodox secession from the Reform-dominated Jewish Community in Vienna in 1872.

Rabbi Horovitz came to the *Grossgemeinde* in Frankfurt from Gnesen over the objections of his *rebbi* Rabbi Ezriel Hildesheimer (see exchange of letters in *Israelit*, Sept. 2, 1932). Yet, after he took the position, Rabbi Hildesheimer kept up the relationship, even to the point of sending him a *shochet* for his synagogue, much to the chagrin of Rabbi Hirsch and his followers.

"competitor" from the *Börneplatz*.[e] His successor Rabbi Salomon Breuer refused to even stay in the same room as Horovitz.[1] Within Rabbi Hirsch's circle there was no inclination to recognize the Orthodox group that formed within the Reform Community structure, the *Gemeinde-Orthodoxen*, as having any legitimacy at all. As far as they were concerned, this group had formed without the benefit of the ruling of any Torah luminary, not even an erroneous ruling. Rather they saw them as a threat to the future existence of the *IRG*, a source of impurity that could never be cleansed. In their eyes, the *Gemeinde-Orthodoxen* were like a *mezuzah* affixed to the door of a temple of idol worship. Relations deteriorated to the point that some people avoided even walking on the sidewalk outside the synagogue on the *Börneplatz*.[2]

Community Structures

AS A RESULT OF ALL THE MANEUVERING DURING THE 19TH CENTURY, the beginning of the 20th century saw several types of Jewish communities in Germany. There were the purely Reform communities; communities where the Orthodox element, although in the minority, took the lead with the sanction of the Reform members and ran the community along traditional lines, and there were the secessionist communities *(Austrittsgemeinde)*, such as in Frankfurt. In many of these, the Reform Community also tolerated an Orthodox component, whose members were known as *Gemeinde-Orthodoxen*. Then there were the *Einheitsgemeinde* (unified communities) where both Orthodox and Reform were part of the same community structure. In a class of their own were the communities of Breslau and Hamburg, where the Orthodox and Reform each had their own respective religious organizations.[3]

Although the arrangement of the Jewish Community of Hamburg reduced friction between the Orthodox and Reform to a minimum, in Rabbi Hirsch's view it was unsatisfactory. In 1864, the Hamburg Senate abolished compulsory membership in the Jewish Community, and thus paved the way for the "Hamburg Arrangement." The Community Board put outside of the range of its responsibility any activity that was a matter of contention. It recognized two separate synagogue associations, one Orthodox and one Reform, each of which had complete autonomy in running its religious affairs. Communal institutions, which included charitable activities, the orphanage, hospital, the Hamburg *Talmud Torah*,

---

e. According to a family tradition, Rabbi Horovitz attempted to visit Rabbi Hirsch upon his arrival in Frankurt to serve in the *Grossgemeinde*. He was not allowed into the house.[1*]

kashruth, Beis Din-related issues and contact with the government remained the province of the Community. These were controlled by a mixed Community Board, but their bylaws stipulated that they were to be conducted in accordance with Jewish tradition. Hamburg's official Chief Rabbi, recognized as such even by the *Tempelverein* (Reform), was the rabbi of the Orthodox Synagogue Organization (*Deutsch-Israelitischer Synagogenverband).*

As a result of this arrangement, the Orthodox and Reform in Hamburg never clashed with such vehemence and ferocity as in Frankfurt, where the Reformers gained control of *all* the formerly Orthodox institutions and made them into bastions of Reform theory and practice.

According to Rabbi Hirsch, however, the Hamburg arrangement was completely unsatisfactory. In his view, a *Kehillah* which did not recognize the Torah as binding could perhaps be considered a community of Jews; it could hardly be considered a Jewish community. Were such a community to grant the Orthodox minority the same religious status as the Reform minority, this would not make this community any more Jewish; to the contrary, by this "equality" it would be merely showing that it has no true interest in the essence of religion. Such an arrangement, Rabbi Hirsch asserted, takes the very central issue of community life and relegates it to subsidiary committees, i.e. it takes what is to be the essence of Jewish communal life and assigns it to the personal choices and predilections of its members.[4]

Conclusions

RABBI BAMBERGER'S RULING REMAINS A SOURCE OF MYSTERY EVEN today. He himself championed the cause of secession in many other instances, as we have seen, and the situation in Frankfurt was far less agreeable to the Orthodox than it was in other cities in which Rabbi Bamberger ruled *in favor of* secession.[f] Over the years there have been various conjectures concerning Rabbi Bamberger's motives, and we will be forgiven for saying that many of these speculations are far-fetched and difficult to accept. Some have claimed that he was only applying principles laid down by Rabbi Yaakov Ettlinger.[5] Proponents of this notion, however, must ignore the fact that Rabbi Ettlinger's monthly journal, *Der Treue Zionswächter,* consistently favored secession for reasons considerably more extreme than those of Rabbi Hirsch. Another point to consider is an address by Rabbi Ettlinger, in which, in no uncertain terms, he encouraged Jews to distance themselves

f. See also the responsum of Rabbi Moshe Schick of Chust to Rabbi Bamberger in *Shaalos u'Tshuvos Maharam Shik, Orach Chaim,* no. 306.

from those who had departed from the path of Torah.[6] Rabbi Hirsch himself made reference to Rabbi Ettlinger in this context. "What a pity," he remarked in 1877 to his son-in-law Rabbi Salomon Breuer, "that Rabbi Ettlinger passed away five years ago. He was the only one whom Rabbi Bamberger respected, and he could have prevented this whole tragedy."[7]

One further misunderstanding deserves clarification. Some have presented this affair as fundamentally a disagreement in principle: Rabbi Hirsch stood for secession and against cooperation with the Reform, while Rabbi Bamberger took the opposing view, against secession and in favor of cooperation with those who reject the path of Torah.[8] The facts, however, do not support this interpretation. As we have shown, Rabbi Bamberger consistently supported secession whenever he was asked to express an opinion, except for the special case of Frankfurt. Even at the height of the controversy, Rabbi Bamberger wrote in his "Open Reply" that he regarded "the Secession Law. . . . as a great blessing for Orthodox Judaism. It has allowed Orthodox Jews the choice of detaching themselves from Reform communities. . . . Such separation has already taken place in a number of communities, for the welfare and honor of those communities."[9] And the Orthodox non-secessionists freely admitted that the rise of Orthodoxy in the *Grossgemeinde* communities was due in no small measure to Rabbi Hirsch and the secessionist *kehillas.*[10]

Further, Rabbi Bamberger's statement exempting Orthodox Jews in Frankfurt from the obligation to secede was subject to certain very stringent conditions, namely that fees paid by Orthodox members would not be used to support Reform activities in any way, that Orthodox members would have neither active nor passive voting rights in elections for the Reform Community Council (neither the right to vote nor to be elected), and that their obligations and responsibilities in the Reform Community would be strictly limited. Another condition was that the Orthodox would establish independently financed institutions and ensure that they would be totally protected from any form of Reform interference. His statement of position contained no reference whatsoever to any form of cooperation with the Reformers, or even to joint membership on any council or committee.

Thus, those in Frankfurt who remained in the Reform Community did so without the support of any rabbinic opinion, since the conditions Rabbi Bamberger attached to his assent were *never* fulfilled. As he wrote in his letter of February 1, 1877, "It is categorically forbidden for Orthodox Jews to participate in any manner in the operation and maintenance of a hospital run by a Reform community. . . . In addition, . . . the members of the executive committee of a community must be as scrupulously observant as those of a rabbinical court. . . ."[11] Later, in 1901, Orthodox members of the *Grossgemeinde* began to participate in elections and to sit on the governing council of the Frankfurt Community, practices that Rabbi Bamberger had explicitly forbidden.[12] Thus the claim that there were two opposing attitudes within traditional Judaism on the issue of cooperation with the non-observant, or even on the question of sitting together with them in one communal framework, has no basis in the facts of this affair.[13]

Despite the fact that the differences between Rabbi Bamberger and Rabbi Hirsch in terms of *Austritt* were not as great as some would like to portray them, it is nevertheless a fact that Rabbi Bamberger's approach to cooperation with non-religious Jewish organizations differed from that of Rabbi Hirsch. A case in point were his ties with the *Alliance Universelle Israelite,* an organization which Rabbi Hirsch shunned (see Chapter 15). Whenever the *Alliance* issued calls to raise funds for Jews in various countries like Morocco, Iran and Turkey, Rabbi Bamberger raised great sums for that purpose. He was in steady contact with the heads of the *Alliance.* Whereas Rabbi Ezriel Hildesheimer initially refrained from joining the *Alliance,* Rabbi Bamberger had no such hesitations, convinced as he was that it was important to exert influence on the *Alliance* from within.[14]

Perhaps the most succinct synopsis of the Würzburger Rav's views was formulated by his grandson, Rabbi Moshe Aryeh Bamberger, Rabbi of the independent *Kehillah* in Mainz:

> Bamberger's opinion has very often been misunderstood and misrepresented by followers as well as by opponents. The following points clearly show his attitude:
>
> — He determined that if certain conditions stipulated by him were fulfilled that there was no religious duty to withdraw.
>
> — He never went back on his earlier decision that if these conditions were not fulfilled it was a religious duty to withdraw.
>
> — He was never against secession, even if these concessions were made.
>
> — His decision never justified Reform or Liberalism in considering themselves as legal within Judaism.[15]

However, Rabbi Bamberger's true views nothwithstanding, German Orthodoxy until the Holocaust was split into two groups: those who cooperated with the Reform and those who did not. This division has remained the reality for Orthodox Jews to this day.

Chapter Fifteen

ASSOCIATION WITH THE NON-OBSERVANT

RABBI HIRSCH'S OPPOSITION TO PARTICIPATION IN AN organizational framework that does not accept the authority of the Torah pertained not only to communal structures. It extended also to Jewish organizations which do not accept the Torah as their guiding principle. Although Rabbi Hirsch's opposition to membership in a Reform-dominated community stemmed *in part* from his conception of the Jewish community as the local representative of the Torah nation, once the Law of Secession was enacted, however, he made no further mention of this principle in any of his public statements or halachic rulings. His recurrent theme was that membership in a Reform community constituted identification with the Reform rejection of the Torah.[1]

This principle applies equally to membership in any kind of organization whose basic goals and premises implicitly reject the Torah, regardless of whether membership fees are levied. If the organization's general or specific goals conflict with the Torah, then the mere fact of membership constitutes identification with the principles of that organization. This is applicable to any organization or institution established for the sake of any Jewish cause or goal that rejects, or even fails to affirm its support for, the foundations of the Jewish faith.[2]

The Alliance Universelle Israelite

RABBI HIRSCH'S UNEQUIVOCAL REJECTION OF COOPERATION WITH the *Alliance Universelle Israelite* (Heb. name: *Kol Yisrael Chaveirim*), the paradigm of the secular Jewish organization, is clear proof of his views in this area. The first modern, international Jewish organization, the *Alliance* was founded in Paris in 1860, with the aim of representing Jews everywhere before the government. It sought to raise Jewish prestige, to combat anti-Semitism, and to work for Jewish emancipation through the education and guidance of "the masses," with an emphasis on the "moral" and "ethical" betterment of Jews and the encouragement of manual labor. It founded educational institutions and agricultural schools in various places, including Morocco and other North African countries, and extended assistance to Jewish refugees.

The officers and directors of the organization were non-observant, and not a few of them were blatantly anti-religious. Its first president was the French-Jewish statesman Adolphe Crémieux (1796-1880), French Minister of Justice after the February revolt of 1848. Crémieux permitted the baptism of his wife and children, as a result of which he was forced to resign from the presidency of the Central Consistory of French Jewry. Nevertheless, he was elected president of the *Alliance* in 1864.

In 1861, not long after the *Alliance's* establishment, Rabbi Hirsch was invited to join. He replied that so long as the *Alliance* strove not only for the external political representation of the Jewish people but also for the dissemination of Jewish culture through the establishment of schools, no one who took Judaism with any degree of seriousness could be associated with it. He later cited the fact that the *Alliance's* president had allowed members of his family to convert to Christianity as an additional reason for refusing all cooperation. Rabbi Hirsch objected further to the presence among the *Alliance's* leaders of men associated with the Breslau Seminary. Such people, he noted, although they might personally observe the traditions to some degree, espoused opinions about the Oral Torah and the

Sages of the Talmud that constituted a dire threat to Judaism as a whole.[a,3]

In an 1864 article in *Jeschurun*, Rabbi Hirsch explained his opposition in detail. If the *Alliance* would limit itself to the protection of Jews everywhere from injustice, he wrote, it would have the sympathy of all Jews. Since, however, it has another, and in its eyes, more important task — i.e., the establishment of schools designed to increase the exposure of Jewish students to European culture — it is forbidden to join them. We can work together, he declared, only if the *Alliance* were involved strictly in the external betterment of the welfare of Jews. But we cannot cooperate on any issue pertaining to internal Jewish matters, which touch upon the essence of Judaism. How, he asked, could there be cooperation when the *Alliance* viewed Orthodox Jewry and the Oral Law as obstacles? "There is no bridge between their principles and ours," he wrote. "They are as dissimilar as yes and no."[4]

The leaders of the *Alliance* persisted in their attempts to convince Orthodox rabbis and lay leaders to join the organization, recognizing the great influence they would wield with observant Jews. And indeed they found important Orthodox allies. Rabbi Zvi Hirsch Kalischer of Thorn and Rabbi Eliyahu Guttmacher of Grätz, founders of the *Chibas Zion* Movement, issued a public call for Orthodox Jews to join the *Alliance* in 1869. They were persuaded to issue this call by the promise of the *Alliance* to support settlement activity in Palestine. One of the Orthodox rabbis who agreed to join was Rabbi Ezriel Hildesheimer, who had previously resisted the organization's invitations of membership. He consented to join in 1872 because he was convinced that he would be able to influence the organization's policies from within and perhaps impede unfavorable decisions, in addition to being able to assist the indigent in time of need. In explaining his decision, Rabbi Hildesheimer expressed the view that Orthodox Jews should not isolate themselves more than necessary.

Rabbi Hirsch was beside himself. He wrote Rabbi Hildesheimer:

> I cannot understand how any straight-thinking Jew can belong to an organization established for Jewish purposes, whose founder and director is completely removed from anything truly Jewish, and whose president returned several years ago to his homeland crowned with laurels from all Jewry, and who saw his first task as the baptism of his children. It pains me to the depths of my heart to see the name of such an honorable personage, such as

---

a. Rabbi Hirsch's dispute with the Breslau Seminary will be discussed in greater detail in Chapters 20-22.

> yourself, in association with the people of the *Alliance* and the Breslau Seminary. Your name only serves to lend respectability to all these objectives, and the uncomprehending masses will surely follow and mistakenly accept all of it.
>
> In the end, the difference between he who serves G-d and he who does not, is fast disappearing. . . . It seems to me, that if ever there was an age which needed clear thinking, the clear demonstration of adherence to Judaism by each individual, that is our poor and debilitated age.[5]

Years later, Rabbi Hirsch's son-in-law Rabbi Salomon Breuer told Jacob Rosenheim: "When the *Alliance* was founded in Paris some decades ago, my father-in-law Rabbi Hirsch strongly opposed the goals of that organization. Not all observers of the scene agreed with him at that time. However, the years that have passed since then, especially the experience of the last few years,[b] have proven that his position was the correct one, and demonstrated how great was his wisdom and foresight."[6]

Rabbi Hirsch's final words on the subject were expressed in a letter to London in 1888, where he wrote: "I have learned from experience that there can be no compromise between observant and non-observant Jews in religious matters. Any compromise only brings renewed trouble all over again."[7]

Distinction Between Heresy and Heretic

RABBI HIRSCH'S OPPOSITION TO PARTICIPATING IN REFORM-controlled communities was not because he forbade contact with the non-observant. Such contact did not in itself constitute implicit support for heresy. Contact with institutionalized heresy, not with the heretic, was the issue.[8] Nevertheless, he counseled against too close association with the non-observant. In his commentary to *Pirkei Avos,* published a decade after the fight over secession, he explicated the *Mishnah* (1:7), *Keep away from an evil neighbor and do not associate with a lawless man:*

> In our daily dealings with others, however, we cannot avoid contact with individuals who have thrown G-d's Law aside. But we neither need nor should enter into close relations with them. "Do not associate with them," do not make common cause with them and particularly — and this is the literal meaning of *hischaber le*

b. This is a reference to the Zionist movement.

> — do not become a member in communities in which *reshaim* dominate. In the end there is a penalty to pay for all these things, for remaining near an evil neighbor as well as for association (*gemeinschaft*) with evil men.[9]

This *Mishnah*, however, did not appear in any of his writings during the battle over secession itself.

As we have seen, the only requirements for membership in the *IRG* were that one be circumcised, have circumcised his children, and be married according to *halachah*. The absence of conditions concerning Shabbos or *kashruth* observance makes clear that there was no restriction on acceptance of non-observant individuals *per se*. The membership of non-religious Jews then, did not invalidate a communal organization. But the presence of non-religious Jews in leadership positions, in which they determined the organization's direction, did.

Rabbi Hirsch also distinguished between those who do not observe the *mitzvos* and those who influence others not to follow the path of Torah. As Rabbi Hirsch wrote: "Hate wickedness but not the wicked man. Only where a wicked man has so identified himself with wickedness that he is to you the very source of wickedness. . . . may you hate, for you hate only the wickedness in him. . . . Worst of all is the seducer who. . . sows the seeds of wickedness in others and brings it to maturity."[10]

Thus the *IRG* could include members who were less than strict on many matters of *halachah* in their private lives; the mere fact of being residents of the city gave them the right to join the local Jewish *kehillah*. This was acceptable because the *Kehillah* was guided entirely by the Written and Oral Torah.

Isaac Breuer has described the essential distinction by which Rabbi Hirsch and his followers were guided:

> Only individuals can be given the benefit of the doubt and judged favorably, and only individuals can have the [halachic] status of "*tinokos shenishbu*," those held captive by gentiles as infants. However when a rebellious organization, which purports to be a Jewish community, attempts to usurp the Jewish communal structure, when heresy incorporates itself and claims equal status as a Jewish body, it can have no place within the ranks of the Torah nation. There is room in the Torah nation even for sinners and rebels, because, as the Sages taught, a Jew who sins is still a Jew. But institutionalized sin and organized heresy have no place in the Torah nation.[11]

While non-observant Jews could be members of the *IRG*, that dispensation extended only to those who could be considered "captive infants" *(tinokos shenishbu)*, and who did not attempt to influence others to follow them.[12] Thus Rabbi Hirsch wrote in 1844 of the *Reformfreunde* group in Frankfurt, which organized with the express aim of abolishing circumcision:

> This group and this father have segregated themselves from Hashem's congregation by their espousal of these blasphemous principles, and by their practices resulting from this blasphemy. Anyone who admits to holding such heretical views and acts on them publicly can no longer be considered a member of the Jewish people. In my humble opinion, the rabbinate of the community in which this was perpetrated has an obligation to announce to its followers in strong and unambiguous terms that because these people have excluded themselves from the community of believers, they have renounced the fundamental principles of Judaism and are no longer to be considered members of the community. The *rabbonim* are required to issue this ruling with full force and to divest the people involved of all rights in communal life.
>
> It is true that a Jew who sins remains a Jew, and therefore, according to *halachah*, when one converts to another religion, he and all his descendants are still obligated to observe all the commandments of the Torah. Nonetheless the Jewish community can no longer consider him as a member, since he has willingly renounced his Jewishness from that point on, and has put himself into the category of apostates and heretics who have no part in the life of the community.[13]

On Rabbi Hirsch's personal contacts with non-observant Jews the evidence is scanty. He had a non-religious brother in Paris named Harry, to whom he sent greetings every year before Rosh Hashanah, and for whose repentance he said a special prayer every day in *Shemoneh Esrei*.[14] On his contact with non-Jews there is not much evidence either. The well-known German philosopher Arthur Schopenhauer lived in the same building as Rabbi Hirsch in Frankfurt, but the two apparently had no contact whatsoever. Nor did he have anything at all to do with his erstwhile friend from Bonn, Abraham Geiger, who served as the rabbi of the Reform congregation in Frankfurt from 1863 to 1870. On the other hand, Rabbi Hirsch did collaborate with Eduard Lasker, a liberal Jew, in order to secure passage of the Law of Secession.

WHENEVER DISCORD ARISES BETWEEN OBSERVANT AND NON-observant Jews, there are always those observant Jews who argue for tolerance on the grounds that close contact will enable them to exert a positive influence on their wayward brothers. To isolate and exclude the non-observant, they claim, will simply result in further deterioration of their religious practices.

Counterproductive Dialogue

Rabbi Hirsch believed that the reverse was true. He felt that experience has usually shown that when the two groups sit together, the invariable result is that the observant suffer a deterioration and drop-off in religious commitment. When the contact is formalized, the weaker elements within the observant camp conclude that the path of the non-observant is equally legitimate.[15]

For this reason, Rabbi Hirsch's teacher Rabbi Yaakov Ettlinger advocated separation as early as 1848 as the only way to deal effectively with the threat of Reform. An article in his weekly journal *Der Treue Zionswächter* called for "complete and absolute segregation" as the only protection against "the unchecked spread of Reform."[16]

Rabbi Hirsch took the view that it was futile to attempt to refute the arguments of the Reformers in face-to-face confrontation:

> What should be said to the members of this fallen generation who, in their apostasy, fancy themselves to be the "progressives," and deride the loyal elders as "backward?" *To them nothing should be said!* The Divine Word teaches in relation to the wondering child, the inquiring boy, and the searching youth: ואמרת לבנך, ואמרת אליו, והגדת לבנך, tell your son, say to him, say to your son. But in relation to the scornful generation it does not say ואמרתם אליהם, but simply ואמרתם, because to *them* you have nothing to say. They expect no instruction from you. They have, indeed, "advanced" so far beyond you that they wish to instruct *you*. They wish to move you, by means of their "refined" mockery, from your stale "narrow" views, which appear to them to be burdensome encumbrances, up to their level, up to the bright, easy unrestraint of their "progressiveness."
>
> What would you have to say to them? They, after all, do not speak in order to receive instruction, but in order to instruct *you*, to reason with *you*. They are not tolerant enough to countenance silently your "different orientation." They do not yet feel so secure about their defection that they do not see in your loyalty a

reproach which bothers them. They still love you too much to be able with a calm eye to see you biased by "foolish prejudice."...

The key to the hearts of this estranged generation rests in the Hands of G-d. Only experience can bring them back, the experience of the hollowness, the nothingness, the bleakness and emptiness of all those delusions into whose arms they have thoughtlessly thrown themselves. One day those hearts will once more be filled with yearning for the happiness of possessing the ancient Truth which was thrown away. One day these words will be put in their mouth: אלכה ואשובה אל אישי הראשון כי טוב לי אז מעתה (*Hosea* 2:9), "I would fain return to G-d, to my ancient loyalty; because I was happier then than now!"

You must wait for such a time. Until then, *you* have *nothing* to say to *them*. You have nothing to say to *them*, even in response to their ridicule.

Altogether silent you may not be. To the extent that G-d's Word does not teach you ואמרתם אליהם, all the more firmly does it require ואמרתם! The less you have to say to *them*, the more resolutely and clearly must you in general express what the Divine precepts are to *you*. All the more firmly and distinctly must you testify to the blessed joyfulness that you find in the fulfillment of the precepts. All the more clearly and unambiguously must you set your conviction against their doubt, your loyalty against their apostasy, your determination against their wavering. You must show the vigor of your life as compared to their degeneracy, and set your joyful earnestness against the vapidity of their easy way and raucous delights....[17]

Without Anger or Invective

RABBI HIRSCH ALWAYS INSISTED THAT THE OPPOSITION TO THE NON-observant, even to the Reform community, be expressed without anger and be free of invective. He preferred to stress the excellence of his own *Kehillah* and not concentrate on the misdeeds of the other. When he counseled Rabbi Zalman Trier of Frankfurt to expel from the community those who refuse to circumcise their children, he added that the expulsion should be made in a strong, unambiguous, yet calm manner, without anger or invective. Not, he wrote, that one could expect this to make these people change. But it must be clear that this expulsion is not intended as punishment or as a means to embarrass them, but only to rescue pure Judaism.[18]

He refused to comply with the request of a leader of the separatist *Kehillah* of Strasbourg, who asked that he declare the *shechitah* of the hybrid congregation non-kosher so that the *shechitah* of the separatist congregation would thereby become economically viable. The situation in Frankfurt, he wrote, was much worse when he arrived, and he could have easily declared the *shechitah* of the community to be non-kosher and those partaking of it to be eating non-kosher food. "But I never did that. Together with the *Kehillah* we established a slaughterhouse and a butcher shop of the highest standards, and then we announced, 'Whoever would like to eat meat with a clear conscience should buy his meat from our *shechitah*.' That was enough then, and now." The fact that the *shechitah* of the independent *Kehillah* in Strasbourg could not exist in competition with that of the mixed community did not suffice to issue a *p'sak din* declaring the other *shechitah* to be non-kosher.

Rabbi Hirsch added the following:

> Leave alone the *kashruth* or lack thereof of the other congregation and totally forget about it. Raise your hands to G-d with serenity and without pique, not taking into account others or scorning them, to live only for the sake of the Divinely sanctified cause. Build your own institutions. . . . In short: Do not pay any attention to the other congregation, but rather do that which will advance the cause in your own *Kehillah,* and G-d will be with you and cause everything done purely for His sake to succeed.[19]

Chapter Sixteen

JEWISH UNITY

THE VIGOROUS CAMPAIGN BY RABBI HIRSCH ON BEHALF of *Austritt* has been interpreted by some as manifesting a focus on narrow partisan concerns, and a disregard for and an insensitivity to the fate of *Klal Yisrael*. Rabbi Hirsch has been accused of having been unconcerned with the Jewish people as a whole and as viewing schism and isolation as an ideal.

Nothing could be further from the truth. Rabbi Hirsch consistently stressed that his battle was with heresy, not with heretics as individuals. *Austritt* cannot be construed as a move to shun the broader Jewish world. Rather it was precisely his concern with the historical mission of the Jewish people that led him to insist on a radical break from anything threatening that mission.[1]

The significance of the Jew is as a bearer or potential bearer of G-d's Word on this world. And Jewish unity is important, even a supreme value, only if it furthers, or at least does not impede, the purpose for which the Jew was placed on this world. Unity for the sake of the transgression of His Will, or as a substitute for authentic observance, is not Jewish unity at all. Peace, harmony and unity are to be obtained first and foremost between man and his Maker. It is only as the Torah nation that the unity of Jews has meaning and significance. Rabbi Hirsch became the principal advocate of Jewish unity as a bulwark against a debasement of the Jewish people's historic mission.

> It is essential . . . that, bound together by their common relationship to G-d, and to His Law, the righteous gather into one united group, lest the desirable elements in the body of G-d's nation be choked off by less desirable growths and, in the resulting indiscriminate hodgepodge, the entire nation would be lost to the fulfillment of G-d's aims and purposes. Therefore the call to Divine judgment is phrased in the words אספו לי . . . אסף denotes a gathering into one spiritual unit, withdrawing from any group or force that holds contrary views. This spiritual unity is "לי." Bondage to G-d, the relationship to Him, and the designation of the character of him who enjoys G-d's favor — all this is included in חסידי, "those who, in complete selflessness, devote themselves to the fulfillment of G-d's will.[2]

The "Orthodox Union"

RABBI HIRSCH WAS THE PRINCIPAL JEWISH THINKER AND LEADER illuminating a path for Torah Jews in a rapidly changing new world, and his last major undertaking was the creation of an organization dedicated to strengthening Jewish life from within and to serving as German Orthodoxy's representative to the outside world. Today the concept of Orthodox Jewish organization is so entrenched that one may assume that it was ever thus. Yet such organization was largely non-existent 100 years ago. Rabbi Hirsch's last contribution to his people's national heritage was to be the *Freie Vereinigung für die Interessen des Orthodoxen Judentums* (The Free Union for the Interest of Orthodox Jewry), the forerunner of the Agudath Israel movement.

Rabbi Hirsch founded the "Orthodox Union" (*Freie Vereinigung*) in September 1885. Its goal was to strengthen Orthodox Judaism in Germany. To that end it took upon itself the task of preserving existing institutions and providing the means necessary to support all aspects of Jewish life. Its objective vis-a-vis the outside world was to combat the Reform Movement and to represent the interests of Orthodox Jewry before the government. In the course of time, these political activities came to occupy an important portion of the Orthodox Union's agenda and it became recognized as the voice of German Orthodoxy, both by

German Jewry and in the eyes of the government.

The Lubliner Rav, Rabbi Meir Schapiro, with Rabbi Salomon Breuer

Rabbi Hirsch stood at the head of the Orthodox Union until his death, whereupon the leadership was assumed by his son Dr. Naftali Hirsch. When the latter died in 1905, Jacob Rosenheim assumed the leadership, a position he used to lay the groundwork for the founding of Agudath Israel.

The Orthodox Union undertook various projects, including finding jobs and providing unemployment compensation for Shabbos observers, setting up kosher eating establishments, producing *tefillin* and *mezuzos* of a high standard of reliability, training competent and pious *shochtim*, and dealing with problems of government intervention in the procedure of circumcision, specifically *metzitzah*. The Union granted financial subsidies to small communities that could not maintain schools, supported ritual slaughter and *mikvaos* and provided stipends to help train rabbis and teachers.[3] The Orthodox Union was active until the Nazi rise to power, and during that time it played a role that far exceeded the sum total of its activities.

Jacob Rosenheim

The Agudath Israel movement was a direct outgrowth of the Orthodox Union.[a] The latter organization provided the model for an international organization of Torah Jews, as well as many of the core of organizers and activists who built the Agudah. It was at the 1908 convention of the Orthodox Union in Frankfurt that the international

---

a. Rabbi Yitzchok Isaac Halevi, author of *Doros Harishonim*, who was living in Bad Homburg near Frankfurt, conceived the idea that the *Freie Vereinigung* should be the nucleus of a world organization — Agudath Israel. "The Orthodox Union," Jacob Rosenheim put it, "was the bud from which first blossomed the Agudath Israel organization and movement."[3*]

organization was first proposed,[b] and the Orthodox Union even paid for the initial expenses of the as yet nascent Agudath Israel.[4]

Pogroms in Russia

BUT RABBI HIRSCH'S CONCERN WAS NOT JUST WITH THE ESTABLISHMENT of Orthodox organizations. His intense efforts on behalf of Russian Jewry during the pogroms of 1882-84 have received too little attention. Those efforts were as discreet as they were extensive, and a full account could fill several chapters.[c]

The condition of Jews in Czarist Russia began to deteriorate markedly in the 1870s.[5] For many years Jewish settlement had been confined to a region known as the "Pale" and only a few "noble" Jews, most prominently the baronial Ginzburg family, were permitted to reside in St. Petersburg, Moscow and the other cities of central Russia. The result of the restrictions on settlement was an almost total lack of interaction between the Jewish "nobility," those with access to government circles, and the masses of Jews in the Pale. That segregation was one of the reasons why the efforts of this Jewish "nobility" to intervene to stem the wave of pogroms were so few and ineffectual.

After the assassination of Czar Alexander II in 1881 and the accession to the throne of his son Alexander III, pogroms and rioting erupted in various parts of Russia especially the Ukraine, with the tacit consent of the upper echelons of the government. The lives of four million Jews in Russia were placed in imminent danger. There was a common pattern to these pogroms throughout the country: As vandals and plunderers assembled, the police and military suddenly disappeared, leaving the rioters free to pillage and burn Jewish homes and businesses and to terrorize the population. Only after personal attacks on Jews reached serious

b. At the 1909 "Bad Homburg Conference," such leaders of Eastern European Jewry as Rabbi Chaim Soloveitchik of Brisk, Rabbi Chaim Ozer Grodzenski of Vilna and the Gerrer Rebbe, joined with the leading German *rabbonim*, headed by Rabbi Salomon Breuer of Frankfurt, to authorize the leadership of the Orthodox Union to serve as a temporary steering committee, until a permanent executive committee could be elected to direct the affairs of the Agudah. During Agudath Israel's formative years, the Frankfurt contingent, all of whom had grown up under the influence of Rabbi Hirsch, were among its primary spokesmen, and his spirit could be tangibly felt in most of those early discussions.[4*]

c. Much of the extensive correspondence conducted by Rabbi Hirsch on behalf of Russian Jewry during that period still exists, and is part of the Sänger Collection, German and Hebrew MS. A few samples, and they are no more than that, were reprinted in Hebrew in *Shemesh Marpeh* (pp. 249-258). They serve to give some conception of Rabbi Hirsch's activities and to reveal the depth of his pain over the persecution of Russian Jewry. They also hold important lessons on how to work on behalf of Jews in exile and, in particular, how to present requests to gentile governments. The thread that runs through these letters, even in his petition to the German Emperor, is the constant awareness that the only meaningful help comes from Hashem and that we can rely on Him alone for salvation.

Rabbi Yitzchak Elchanan Spektor

Dr. Isaac Rülf

proportions did the police and the army enter the picture to arrest a small number of the instigators, most of whom were released a few days later. The remainder were brought to trial and subsequently released, regardless of the verdict. They were even forbidden to return any of the plundered property to its owners. Much of this was organized with the approval of the Russian Minister of the Interior Ignatyev, with the implied assent of the Czar. In order to conceal its involvement, the government circulated rumors that the pogroms were the work of socialist rebels, a transparent lie to anyone familiar with the situation.

Ignatyev further incited the masses against the Jews by establishing local committees to "investigate" Jewish crimes and make recommendations as to how to protect the innocent Russian "sheep" from the predatory Jewish "wolf." His ministry imposed a series of edicts to strictly limit the means by which Jews were allowed to earn their livelihood, and devised a plan to banish Jews from the Asian part of Russia.

In the autumn of 1881, Rabbi Yitzchak Elchanan Spektor (1817-1896), Chief Rabbi of Kovno (at the time, part of Russia), called upon Rabbi Hirsch to aid Russian Jewry in its hour of distress. Considered the preeminent leader of Torah Jewry of his generation, Reb Yitzchak Elchanan, also enlisted the help of Dr. Isaac Rülf (1831-1902) of Memel, a city on the Russo-German border. Dr. Rülf had headed a committee to raise funds to provide for Russian Jews during the famine of 1868, and had led relief efforts following the great fire in Vilkomir, in the Kovno district, in 1876. Rabbi Spektor also turned to Dr. Asher Asher, a well-known writer who served as Secretary of the United Synagogue of England. The latter was the right-hand man of Lord Nathaniel Rothschild, who had direct access to Queen Victoria of England.

Rabbi Spektor requested these men to publicize the details of the pogroms in the international press in order to arouse public opinion against the persecutions, and thereby put pressure on the Russian regime. He also asked them to appeal to royal and ministerial circles in their countries to intercede with the Czar, through both family and diplomatic ties, to stop the attacks against the Jews.

For these efforts to be effective, detailed documentation was required concerning the events in each city and the campaign of government edicts planned against the Jews. Understandably, considerable danger was involved in gathering this information and smuggling it out of Russia. To protect the identity of the authors of these reports, they began and ended only with the phrase "היה עם פיפיות שלוחי עמך בית ישראל — May You be with the mouths of the messengers of Your people the House of Israel," or in abbreviated form: היה עם פיפיות. The individual letters were sent separately by Rabbi Spektor, their contents generally couched in hints and allusions. The entire effort was coordinated by Rabbi Yaakov Lipschitz, the personal secretary of Rabbi Spektor.[6]

Although 74 years old and in frail health, Rabbi Hirsch threw all his energies into the struggle for a period of two years. He carried on extensive correspondence with various public officials and made appeals on the subject to the German Kaiser and to the kings and ministers of other countries.

A fact not often mentioned in connection with this affair is that he received little support in these efforts from rabbinic leaders in other countries. A letter to Rabbi Hirsch from Rabbi Shlomo Zalman Spitzer, rabbi in Vienna and son-in-law of the *Chasam Sofer*, leaves nothing to the imagination:

> The truth is that in this country for several weeks now, nothing has been heard about the plight of our brothers in Russia, and the [efforts to arouse the world's sympathy] have become something of a farce. . . . Much caution is required. As of now I have no good suggestion how to proceed, for the Galician rabbis refuse to raise their voices and the rabbis of Hungary are not in favor of the matter, and what can I do alone. I . . . plan to consult with several people over Purim, including my brother-in-law [Rabbi Shimon Sofer] of Krakow, who is here now.[7]

In a letter to Reb Yitzchak Elchanan in *Shevat* 5642 (1882), Rabbi Hirsch implored the former to give him some direction as to what actions would be beneficial. Rabbi Hirsch was afraid to do something that might be counterproductive, yet unwilling to allow that fear to cause him to do nothing.[8] In a letter to Dr. Rülf several weeks later, Rabbi Hirsch reported, "I've found a way to get to the German Crown Prince, Frederick III [son of Kaiser Wilhelm I and a nephew of the Czar], and I hope we will succeed, although, as always, we cannot assume any friendship for Jews in the German Royal House."[9]

One of the ways to influence the Russian government was by publicizing the pogroms in the press. When Dr. Rülf suggested that Rabbi Hirsch issue a call to all German congregations to set aside a specific day for fasting and public prayer to call attention to the plight of Russian Jewry, Rabbi Hirsch replied mordantly that 90 percent of German Jewish communities would pay no heed to a declaration bearing his name (a reference to his stand on the *Austritt* question). But more importantly, he felt that calling for one central day would not have the desired effect because it would be widely perceived as an orchestrated event, not as a spontaneous outpouring of sympathy for Russian Jews. He suggested, instead, that each community organize its own day of prayer and fasting, on a day of its own choosing. The result would be hundreds of items in the press reporting, over a period of several weeks, yet another instance of public prayer and outcry. The cumulative impact would be much more powerful than a one-time report of public *tefillah* gatherings on a single day.[10]

In Frankfurt, *Erev Rosh Chodesh Adar* 5642 (1882) was set aside as a day of fasting and prayer and a special *tefillah* was added at *Shacharis* and *Minchah* every day until such time as the persecutions ended. Rabbi Hirsch had the prayer and fasting reported in the press.[11] Despite doubts as to the reception a call in his name would have, he issued a circular to the German rabbinate describing the pogroms and calling upon every Jew to do everything in his power to publicize the atrocities in the press:

> [B]ecause the only thing these anti-Semites take into consideration is the good will in foreign countries. I know for a fact, that the demonstrations and especially the public prayers in England have hindered Ignatyev's plans. Therefore, the greatest thing we can do for our brethren is to conduct fasts and public prayer in every place, and maybe the Merciful One will listen to our prayers and transform the anguish of our suffering brothers to joy.[12]

There is an interesting report of the public prayer in Frankfurt on *Erev Rosh Chodesh Adar* on behalf of Russian Jewry, contained in a letter from Rabbi Simcha Zissel Ziv, the "Alter" of Kelm, to his son:

> Yesterday, Rabbi Dovid Dessler brought me some good news, and something about which I have boundless amazement. The Royal Post from Germany reported that on the previous *Erev Rosh Chodesh* several thousand people fasted because of the persecution of our Russian brethren, and prayed with much weeping and donated immense sums to help them. Rabbi Hirsch spoke for over three hours powerful words of inspiration. . . . All of the members of the *Kehillah* fasted, including the nobility, and they spent the entire day in *shul* in tearful prayer just like on *Yom Kippur*. That day there was a great demand for *tefillin* and *tzitzis* and several non-kosher kitchens were closed.

Rabbi Simcha Zissel continued with an analysis of why Frankfurt Jews were able to rouse themselves to such depths of caring to entreat G-d for the well-being of other Jews, whereas [in Lithuania], "we do not have such feelings to fast and pray for Jews in other countries." "Imagine," he wrote, "if they were to call for a fast day on behalf of our brethren in Bulgaria. We would see it as strange and we would surely not shed any tears." The "Alter" explained this "unique excellence" of German Jews with the statement of the Sages, *"kol she'ain bo derech eretz eino min ha-yishuv* — One who is not possessed of *derech eretz* is not part of society." Due to the refined sense of *derech eretz* inculcated into German Jews, he wrote, they possess the ability to empathize with Jews everywhere.[13]

Rabbi Hirsch reported to Rabbi Spektor that he had published an article detailing the extent of the pogroms in the most prestigious Frankfurt newspaper. That article was reprinted in important European newspapers, including *The Herald,* which was published also in the Russian capital, St. Petersburg. He asked Reb Yitzchak Elchanan for more information so that he could again publicize the persecutions in the same manner. Rabbi Hirsch wrote, "Although we cannot boast that we have been successful in all our efforts until now, a doctor will do whatever he can for someone severely ill, even though he knows that his condition is almost hopeless. . . Ultimately, though, real salvation is in any case in the hands of G-d."[14]

Influential German Jews went to the summer home of the German Emperor in Wiesbaden to request an audience, but when they conveyed the purpose of their request, they were refused an appointment. Subsequently, Rabbi Hirsch wrote a personal letter to the German Kaiser. He began with a prayer to the Almighty that he find the proper words to enter the Emperor's heart. He described the pogroms and persecutions and argued that if the Czar wanted to stop them he could. Rabbi Hirsch

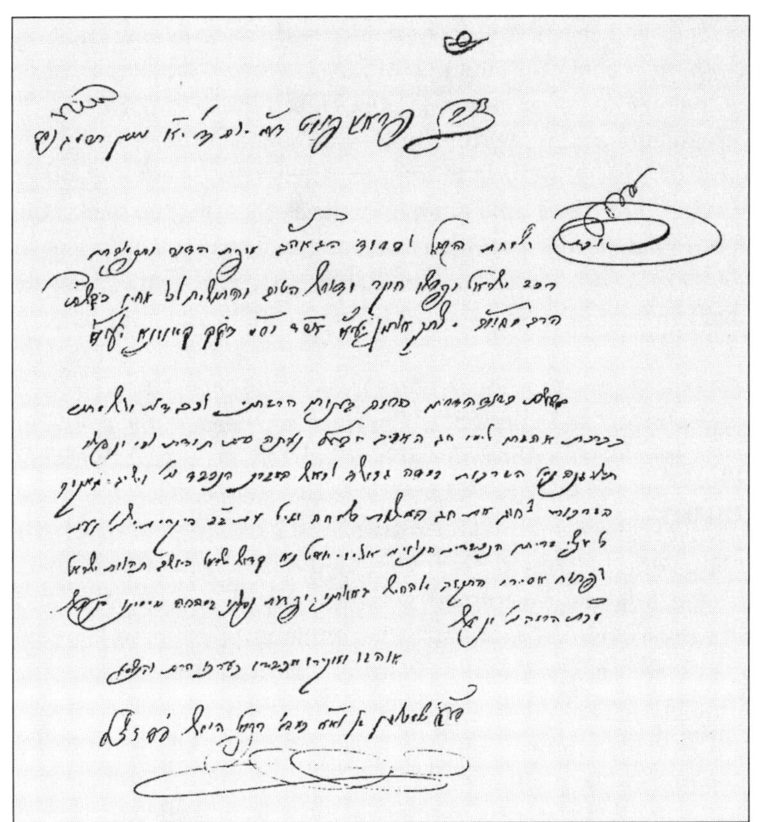

Pesach greeting to Rabbi Spektor in Kovno

then described the great deeds that G-d had done through the agency of the Emperor, and entreated him to demonstrate that his rulership was a reflection of the Divine monarchy, and that he walked in the ways of the merciful G-d in sparing innocent victims from suffering.[15]

Several months later Rabbi Asher Lemel Marx of Darmstadt succeeded in obtaining an audience with the Kaiser, who was sympathetic and promised to do whatever he could. The Kaiser, however, did not hold out much hope. The climate in Germany, too, had changed for the worse, Rabbi Hirsch wrote, and the government ministers and officials were clearly anti-Semitic.[16]

Rabbi Hirsch's letters are suffused with a deep personal anguish at the situation in Russia. Dayan Moshe Avigdor Chaikin of St. Petersburg once visited Rabbi Hirsch when the latter was already very old. Rabbi Hirsch's sons told the visitor that their father was not well and could not receive visitors that day. But when they showed their father the letter of introduction Rabbi Chaikin had brought from Rabbi Yitzchak Elchanan Spektor of

Kovno, he requested that the visitor be admitted immediately. His first concern was to hear about the situation of Russian Jewry. When his visitor told him of the ongoing persecutions, Rabbi Hirsch broke into tears.[17]

As a consequence of the pogroms in Russia, a steady flow of refugees streamed out of Russia, finding temporary shelter in Brody and other places. Since they often had little more than the clothes on their backs, the refugees required material support, as well as assistance in emigrating to America or *Eretz Yisrael.* In this area too Rabbi Hirsch took an active role and was instrumental in raising money for their aid.[18]

A Threat to the Talmud

IN 1884, THE RUSSIAN GOVERNMENT, IN AN EFFORT "TO RESOLVE the Jewish question," established a commission, headed by a Count Pahlen. This official had publicly expressed the opinion that the Talmud was the source of all the Jews' problems and the reason for the contempt in which the nations of the world held them. Such views led Rabbi Spektor and others to fear that the Russian government would order all the yeshivos and *chadarim* in Russia closed and prohibit the printing of the Talmud. At the suggestion of both the Grand Duke of Hessen-Darmstadt, an uncle of the Czar, and Rabbi Yitzchak Elchanan Spektor, Rabbi Hirsch wrote a pamphlet setting forth the Talmud's views on business and social values. Rabbi Hirsch's pamphlet in German entitled "The Talmud and Its Teachings on Social Virtues, Civic Duties, and Commercial Integrity" clarified the Sages' attitudes towards social and business credibility, relations with government, family affairs, and human interaction in general, as reflected in the Talmud. Rabbi Hirsch requested and received a letter of recommendation from the Grand Duke for his pamphlet. He then sent copies of the article accompanied by the letter of recommendation to Count Pahlen and the other members of the commission. The article made an extremely favorable impression on the commission and was instrumental in persuading them to abandon their plans to ban study of the Talmud.[19]

Rabbi Hirsch assisted in various other undertakings in the Jewish world. In 1885, he issued a call to contribute generously to the Kovno *Kollel,* which supported a select group of 100 scholars, in addition to over 100 unmarried students, with the goal of producing great scholars and rabbis. It was headed by Rabbi Yitzchak Elchanan Spektor and by Rabbi Yitzchak Blaser, known as Reb Itzele Peterburger. The latter wrote Rabbi Hirsch that his impassioned appeal to support the *Kollel* was the source of their success in raising funds in Germany.[20]

Part Five

TORAH IM DERECH ERETZ

Chapter Seventeen
THE PRINCIPLE

BAR KAPARA LEARNED: WHAT IS A SMALL PHRASE on *which all dimensions of Torah depend? (Mishlei* 3:5*) "Know Him in all your ways, and He will straighten your paths."* (*Berachos* 63a)

In Israel there is now, and has always been, one national endeavor, and that is Talmud Torah. . . . *This nation is occupied with discoveries and inventions in only one field, and that field is the* Torah! *To preserve and to disseminate the teachings of the* Torah, *to comprehend and to communicate the eternal truths drawn from the* Torah, *to "study and to teach," to draw upon the timeless sources of Torah for a proper assessment of the problems posed by every age, to delve into the precepts of this Torah and into the spirit of its institutions with ever growing clarity and thoroughness, to make every age and every generation increasingly aware of these concepts* — that has been the national endeavor of Judaism for thousands of years.[1]

No concept is so associated with the name Rabbi Samson Raphael Hirsch as *Torah Im Derech Eretz.* Much has been written in exposition of this concept — which encompasses both a complete Torah *Weltanschauung* and a specific educational program — by both proponents and opponents. While this is not the place for an extensive analysis of *Torah Im Derech Eretz,* at the same time, no account of Rabbi Hirsch's life would be complete without a discussion of the general outlines of this concept.[2]

Basic Premises

RABBI HIRSCH'S STARTING POINT WAS THAT THE PRIMARY DWELLING place of the Divine Presence is in this world — עיקר שכינה בתחתונים.[3] Each of the Torah's commands is expressed in terms of this world, for it is this world that man is enjoined to transform into an earthly paradise, in which he experiences the "protective nearness of G-d."[4]

The Torah is the blueprint for Creation, the owner's manual with complete and detailed instructions as to how man can create in this world a dwelling place for the Divine Presence. No aspect of life is outside of the Torah's purview and there is no issue concerning which the Torah is not the final arbiter.[5] As Rabbi Yechiel Yaakov Weinberg aptly put it,[6] the physical and social circumstances in which man finds himself is the matter — the *Derech Eretz* — upon which Torah imposes its form. And this is equally true in every historical epoch. "*Torah Im Derech Eretz,*" wrote Rabbi Hirsch, "means the realization of the Torah in harmonious unity with all the conditions under which its laws will have to be observed *amidst the developments of changing times.*"[7]

It is the Jew's task to demonstrate that the Torah contains the answer to every social and spiritual question confronting men as individuals and as social beings, to show that "that Judaism, this complete Judaism, תורת ה׳ תמימה, does not belong to an antiquated past but to the vigorous, pulsating life of the present."[8] In his every action, the Jew must bear the stamp of the Torah he received at Sinai and reflect the refining power of the Torah:

> "And the לוחות were written on both their sides, מזה ומזה, on the one side and on the other were they written" (*Shemos* 32:15).
>
> The word from Sinai must not grip us only superficially and one-sidedly. It must penetrate us through and through, it must set its stamp indelibly on every part of our being, and whichever way we are turned, the writing of G-d must everywhere be visi-

> ble on us clearly and legibly. See the Divine tables of testimony! On them there was no above and below, no front and back. The writing pierced right through them, and yet they could be read on both sides. This must be a model for you. Be a Jew through and through. Whichever way you are turned, be a Jew. . . .
>
> In relation to G-d there is no reverse side and no opposite side; everything is turned to G-d and must be taken equally seriously, on every side the stamp of the Divine will is to be placed with the same force and care and directness. Let yourself be penetrated through and through from all sides with the Divine word![9]

Now, if man is meant through his endeavors to mold this world according to the will and teachings of G-d, he can, and should, make full use of all the world offers to accomplish that goal.[10] The Torah, Rabbi Hirsch asserted, not only does not demand the withdrawal of the Jew from the world, it does not view such a withdrawal as an ideal. Clearly, until the coming of the Mashiach no society fully represents the Torah ideal, but this does not mean that the Jew must withdraw from an inherently imperfect society. Rather, he has a crucial role to play as a participant in the world in bringing it ever closer to the realization of the Divine plan, *letakein olam beMalchus Shadai* — to perfect the world under the Kingship of Hashem.[a]

If this is the essence of *Torah Im Derech Eretz,* then in what way was Rabbi Hirsch's idea original? No one would dispute the fact that "Judaism is not a mere adjunct to life: it comprises all of life," and that "to be a Jew is not a mere part, it is the sum total of our task in life."[11] Certainly, one genuine Jewish approach to life has always been that of Rabbi Shimon bar Yochai — that of *miut Derech Eretz,* of keeping one's involvement in worldly pursuits to a minimum. However, the other path has always been that of Rabbi Yishmael who taught that the Jew's mission in life is to ensure the Torah's direction and governance of every dimension of life.[12] The question, then, is clear-cut: What was novel about Rabbi Hirsch's ideas?

Dr. Isaac Breuer has, with his customary acuity, summed up that which

a. Rabbi Hirsch hoped, a misplaced optimism as it turned out, that certain contemporary trends — including a more liberal attitude towards Jews — betokened the dawn of a new era characterized by a purer sense of justice. "It is precisely with and through the social, cultural, and political changes of our era," he wrote, "that the Jews are meant to reach the one supreme objective which will someday no longer be the goal of the Jews alone but will . . . become the goal of the entire family of man."[10*]

was new and startling in Rabbi Hirsch's philosophy. It has always been realized, he wrote, that as the Torah constitutes חוקי חיים, "laws of life," it is intimately connected with the practical realities of life. But while the Torah is eternal and immutable, *derech eretz* is constantly changing. Rabbi Hirsch's bold and pioneering contribution was to free himself from the deep-rooted perception, born of centuries of historical experience, that Torah was inextricably linked to a particular system of *derech eretz.*

In the late 18th century, that age-old system of *derech eretz* which had been the norm in Western Europe for a thousand years suddenly disintegrated, and was replaced with a fluid new one. At that critical juncture, Rabbi Hirsch recognized that the new circumstances, which were facts of life which could not be ignored, had to be controlled, dominated and directed by the Torah, that this new *derech eretz* must be "led to the flaming fire of the Torah, so that it might find in it purification, and, if need be, destruction." Precisely *because* he was so firmly convinced of the total supremacy of Torah over any knowledge or earthly circumstance, he expected it to direct and govern even in the social and intellectual milieu of his time.[b,13]

One Truth

TORAH IM DERECH ERETZ DOES NOT MEAN THAT THERE ARE TWO independent sources of truth, Divine and human, that may conflict with each other and have to be reconciled. Torah cannot be compared to, or equated with, any other branch of knowledge or set of values. To no human knowledge did Rabbi Hirsch grant intrinsic value. The Torah is the only source of truth, and the yardstick by which any knowledge or idea must be measured. Such merit as any given idea, philosophy or approach might possess lies only in the fact that the Torah puts its imprimatur on that idea.[14] "All pure human values," he wrote, "are only fruits of the Jewish spirit."[15] Failure to understand this has led many to improperly cite the ideals of *Torah Im Derech Eretz* in justification of intellectual views, educational practices and lifestyles diametrically opposed to what Rabbi Hirsch taught and practiced.

Derech eretz, that is to say the material, social and economic world, is generally speaking, in itself, neither good nor bad. However, the Torah rejects certain forms and aspects of *derech eretz* as incompatible with its teachings and they are, as a result, unacceptable to the Torah-observant

b. There is a well-known adage that *Austritt* and *Torah Im Derech Eretz* are really two sides of the same coin. Both are corollaries of the underlying conviction of the Torah's rulership over everything, and the conviction that no detail of life or nature, however minute, stands outside the realm of Torah.

Jew. The same holds true for human knowledge. We may allow other types of knowledge "only so much entrance into our intellectual and emotional life as is exactly in accordance with these Divine Truths."[16] Isaac Breuer put it best: "It is incorrect to speak of "Torah *with* ... anything else. There is no synthesis, there is no tension, there is no reconciliation, there is no balance; there is only domination."[c,17]

> *Sieh! Aus der Natur spricht dir der Herr! Und aus der Geschichte wieder*! — Behold! G-d speaks to you through nature, and again through history![18]

Secular Studies

THESE SENTENCES FROM RABBI HIRSCH'S FIRST ADDRESS AS RABBI of Oldenburg (Rosh Hashanah 5591-1830) constitute the essential reason for the study of secular disciplines, specifically science and history. The study of science reveals G-d as Creator.[19] The sacred writings of Judaism, Rabbi Hirsch asserted, are filled with summons "to keep our eyes and senses open to the revelation of G-d in the phenomena and laws of nature."[20] The study of history will show G-d as Director and Guide of the affairs of nations and men, educating men to do His Will through the exercise of their own free will. "An insight into the nature of things and the history of man can only be most welcome to that kind of study which sees as its purpose the practical implementation of the Will of Him Who created the nature of things, Who guides the history of mankind and Who tells us what we should be in relation to nature and history."[21]

Thus the Jew studies science for one primary reason: to reveal Hashem as Creator of the Universe. Nevertheless the Jewish student of science must be aware that notwithstanding man's abilities in uncovering the marvels of the physical world, his approach to scientific research is different than that of the gentile.

> Israel's approach to acquiring knowledge, what men called "science," is at total variance with that of the nations. The other nations try to find solutions to their problems by way of a freely,

c. This is the critical difference between *Torah Im Derech Eretz* and the *Torah u'Madda* approach. Rabbi Norman Lamm describes the *Torah u'Madda* philosophy in the following terms: "Torah, faith, religious learning on the side and *madda*, science, worldly knowledge on the other, together offer us a more over-arching and truer vision than either one set alone. Each set gives one view of the Creator as well as his Creation, and the other a different perspective that may not agree at all with the first. . . . Each alone is true, but only partially true; both together present the possibility of a larger truth."[17*]

creative *search* through the contemplation of nature and history. Israel, on the other hand, endeavors to penetrate into the significance and development of all interrelationships of the world and humanity, in the light of *revealed* truths, the truth from Sinai.[d,22]

Rabbi Hirsch's positive view of the study of secular subjects was not limited to science and history. To fulfill his role in shaping the reality of his times to the Divine Will, a Jew requires, Rabbi Hirsch felt, some knowledge of so-called secular subjects. The prerequisite for the true fulfillment of the Torah's teachings is knowledge, as thorough as possible, of all the realities of human affairs on earth. All knowledge that broadens our understanding of the social and physical realities of the world gives us no little help in understanding the Torah's view of man and creation.[23]

One of the Hirschian educational ideals was also to give students the ability to evaluate from a Torah standpoint the secular learning to which they would in any event be exposed. Rabbi Hirsch recognized that the ghetto walls had fallen and the cultural life of the European nations was now open to the Jew as never before: "The Jew like everyone else is now caught up in the intellectual life of the European nations."[24] That being the case, he felt it preferable that the inevitable exposure to ideas directly or potentially at odds with the Torah should take place under the guidance of those well versed in Torah, who could point out how and why the Torah rejects those ideas. Rabbi Hirsch maintained a buoyant confidence in the ability of the Torah to vanquish all antagonistic ideals:

> Only if one knows the essence of what is antagonistic to Torah can one resist and overcome these influences. That which looms as a fear-inspiring giant specter in the twilight zone of ignorance will shrink into a pygmy before the shining light of thought.[25]

Rabbi Hirsch also advanced practical reasons for some secular studies, having nothing to do with their usefulness for a deeper understanding of the Torah. Some such studies could be justified to facilitate earning a living that met the Torah's standards of an אומנות נקיה וקלה — a clean and easy profession. The fulfillment of the unique vocation of the Jew "neces-

d. Rabbi Hirsch's approach to philosophy was similar. The difference between philosophy and Judaism, he wrote, is that whereas philosophy attempts to view G-d from the perspective of man and the world, Judaism sees man's task as the viewing of man and the world from the perspective of G-d, i.e. through the study of Torah. It is for this same reason that Rabbi Hirsch declared over and over that Judaism was not a religion. Whereas religion is comprised of man's ideas of G-d, Torah and Judaism are the thoughts of G-d on man and on his obligations, a Divine anthropology, as it were.[22*]

sitates the establishment of a home of one's own, an independent household supported by a respectable occupation, morally untarnished and capable of making a contribution to the public welfare."[26] Some secular knowledge will also allow a Torah Jew to function effectively in an alien cultural milieu, and will prepare young Jews to combat the ideological challenge of non-Jewish culture.[27]

Priorities

OUR ATTEMPTS TO UNDERSTAND THE CREATED WORLD THROUGH science, or to understand Hashem's conduct of the world through history, are merely *means* to broaden our understanding of the Torah's teachings concerning our duties in the world. Recognition of this fact dictates the importance and time we assign to the study of Torah versus secular disciplines. In terms of intrinsic value and importance, and in terms of the time we allot to their study, the latter must be clearly subordinate to the former. Any attempt to equate the two, to give secular disciplines equal standing to Torah, Rabbi Hirsch wrote, is equivalent to denying the supremacy of His Torah:

> ודברת בם: עשה אותם עיקר ואל תעשם טפילה שלא יהא משאך ומתנך אלא בהם שלא תערב בהם דברים אחרים שלא תאמר למדתי חכמת ישראל אלך ואלמוד חכמת הכנענים (ספרי) — The teachings of the Torah are to form the real subjects of our mental occupation. We are not to cultivate them as a side issue, nor from the standpoint or for the standpoint of other scientific study, and equally, indeed, take care not to introduce into the sphere of our Torah-studies foreign matter and ideas which have grown on the soil of other scientific hypotheses. We are altogether always to bear in mind the specific higher level of our knowledge which differs from all other scientific knowledge through its Divine origin, and not place it on the same level as the other sciences, as if it, too, rested on the basis of human knowledge.[28]

At a practical level, Torah study must always command the greater portion of the time available for learning. When the Torah commands us: "ללכת בהם — *to walk in them,*" it means that we may never disengage ourselves from them. How then, in practice, is one to reconcile secular learning with the obligation to learn Torah constantly, day and night? Rabbi Hirsch specified the principle to be applied here in his commentary on the following passage in *Toras Kohanim* (*Vayikra* 18:4): *To walk in them — make them [the words of Torah] your primary interest and do not make them subordinate.*

> The Sages said, "make [Torah studies] your primary interest and do not make them subordinate," implying that we may consider other branches of knowledge but must nonetheless give Torah the primary status. However, only as accessory knowledge and in as far as they serve to truly help the study of the Torah and are subordinated as the טפל to the עיקר are they to be studied. . . . Thus, even when we explore other areas we will not abandon the foundation of Torah and its goals and all our spiritual effort will be devoted to Torah, "from which we may never disengage ourselves."[29]

Limitations on Societal Participation and Secular Studies

RABBI HIRSCH BELIEVED THAT THE JEW HAS A VITAL ROLE TO PLAY IN bringing society closer to its ultimate ideal by "integrat[ing] the full splendor of Torah Judaism's enlightening and redeeming spirit into all aspects of the unfolding life of men and nations."[30] At the same time, he gave nothing like carte blanche approval for full participation in that society. The degree of a Jew's participation in society must always be limited by the threat that participation poses to his performance of the Torah's commands. Even as he takes part "in the world-wide interaction of nations, in all endeavors of the arts and sciences, business and commerce, education and politics," the Jew has to be ever ready to give up "any participation that would involve a transgression of [his] Jewish duties" and "never allow [himself] to be swayed by un-Jewish thoughts and actions."[31]

With respect to the choice of career, for instance, he wrote:

> Your only purpose in trying to acquire property . . . should be to . . . work for the advancement of your people and humanity to found a home into every room of which G-d may enter, where His word will be observed. . . . Therefore take up an occupation which will give you this independence uprightly and honorably. . . . *In the choice of an occupation the guiding consideration should be which one involves the least danger to your loyalty to G-d's law.*[32]

Similarly, Rabbi Hirsch's approval of the study of secular disciplines was a qualified one. Though, as we have seen, Rabbi Hirsch believed that the study of secular disciplines could aid in the understanding of the Torah and the performance of its *mitzvos*, he was well aware of the potential dangers inherent in those studies. He was acutely conscious of the Sages' dictum "Heresy has a great power to attract;" indeed the basis for his fight for the *Austritt* principle was an unbending commitment to absolute separation from any identification with heresy.[33] He refused to restate heretical views even for the purpose of refuting them, preferring to do so through more veiled arguments.

Even with respect to the study of science, Rabbi Hirsch warned of the dangers involved. At its best, the knowledge of G-d as Creator of the universe will not by itself provide adequate answers to the ultimate existential questions of "our vocation, our mission, and the Law that is to govern our inner and outer lives, nor can they show us how to shape every aspect of our existence in accordance with the Will of G-d." The answers to these lie only in the Torah.[34] And, at worst, the study of science could lead to an increase in human hubris, not a feeling of one's insignificance in comparison to G-d:

> Research into the marvels of nature tends to lead a person further on the road to self-worship. He kneels before the grandeur of his own spirit which observes the stars in the heavens and the microbes in the depths of the ocean, charting their movement and development. The brilliance of his own spirit blinds him so that he does not see the overpowering radiant glory of that Spirit Whose thoughts are revealed in these very wonders, and Whose greatness, omnipotence, wisdom, magnificence, control and dominion radiate from these marvels.[35]

In addition, the intellectual excitement of science or other secular disciplines could cause a student to lose sight of the fact that such studies have their place only as adjuncts to the study of Torah, not as ends in themselves:

> A situation may arise in which love and esteem for Torah do not completely fill our breast. When this happens, we begin to love and respect other types of knowledge and other possessions not only out of love for the Torah, and not only because they foster knowledge of the Torah and make possible the fulfillment of it. We begin to place upon possessions and forms of knowledge a value that is independent of the Torah. Once such a situation has developed, everything will thereby already have been done which will very quickly bring us to the point of disregarding the Torah. . . .[36]

And when that happens, warned Rabbi Hirsch, "the only possible result will be a discordant soul no longer belonging to G-d in an undivided fashion."[37]

Chapter Eighteen

IN THE MODERN ERA

Traditional Attitudes

THE ISSUE OF WHETHER, AND TO WHAT EXTENT, A JEW should engage in pursuits outside of Torah learning is a very ancient one. It forms the subject of the well-known dispute between Rabbi Shimon bar Yochai and Rabbi Yishmael over the proper understanding of the verse, *"This sefer Torah shall not depart from your mouth"* (*Joshua* 1:8). The latter held that the time available for Torah study is necessarily limited by the requirements of normal life — sowing at the proper time, reaping at the proper time, and harvesting at the proper time. The former, however, asserted that if every Jew acted accordingly, the knowledge of Torah would disappear from the world. The *Gemara* (*Berachos* 35b) concludes, "Many did as Rabbi Yishmael and were successful; many did as Rabbi Shimon bar Yochai and were not successful."

Yet even if the issue of how much time a Jew may spend in pursuit of a livelihood has been settled for the majority of Jews, in most periods of our history, in favor of Rabbi Yishmael, the issue of whether, and under what circumstances, it is permissible to attain forms of knowledge apart from the classic Torah texts has not been so clearly resolved. The requirement of pursuing a livelihood was never considered to provide a blanket warrant for a broad curriculum of secular studies.

As a general rule, the majority of Torah authorities until Rabbi Hirsch's day approved only those studies most directly related to the pursuit of a livelihood — practical mathematics and the language of one's host country. Rabbi Akiva Eiger expressed the typical attitude when he wrote in a letter to Rabbi Shlomo Plessner: "Torah study is good together with *Derech Eretz,* and [students] should be taught the skills of writing and arithmetic for an hour or two a day."[1] Rabbi Shmuel Landau, the son of the *Noda B'Yehudah* and his successor as Rabbi of Prague, also expressed his approbation for studies directly related to earning a living:

> [One should] learn German thoroughly, as well as other required subjects, because without a knowledge of German, including written German, it is impossible to survive in these countries. Someone who does not read and write German cannot succeed in any trade, and every father has an obligation to teach his son the language and customs of the country in which he lives. Parents must be sure that their children excel in both Torah and *Derech Eretz,* and the youth must have a firm grasp of both of them. When the lad reaches the age of 12 it will be possible to determine if he is fit to study more. At that time, he will be tested to determine whether he should study other wisdom or Talmud so that he can enter the rabbinate. If it is evident that he will not succeed in his studies, he should be directed to study a trade or business, each according to his path.[2]

The Hamburg *Talmud Torah,* founded by Rabbi Hirsch's grandfather, Rabbi Mendel Frankfurter, listed as its goals: teach[ing] the student "Torah, morals and wisdom, and good behavior and customs and *Derech Eretz,* impart[ing] the knowledge requisite for earning a livelihood, and train[ing] them in the skills of reading, writing and arithmetic."[3]

Studies, however, that could not be obviously justified on the pragmatic grounds of earning a living and getting along in the world were generally frowned upon. That the study of theoretical science or history could aid a Jew in understanding Hashem's role in the world or the nature of a Jew's obligations was not contemplated. Individual Torah luminaries might have acquired a broad knowledge of secular disciplines, but only in private and after having mastered the traditional branches of Torah study.

Among the reasons for this extreme skepticism about the value of general secular studies was the fear of exposing young minds to heretical ideas. The central reason for the opposition, however, was the conviction that the only proper intellectual endeavor for a Jew is the study of Torah.[4] As Rabbi Hirsch himself put it, the earning of a livelihood was traditionally never viewed as more than an ancillary component of a life devoted to one's "true vocation" of being a Jew: At most, supporting oneself and one's family was viewed as one *mitzvah* among many. One who viewed his vocational activities, however, as the sole purpose of life was viewed as an *am ha'aretz* no matter what proficiency he might attain in any other field of endeavor.[5]

Nevertheless, argued Rabbi Hirsch, the Jewish attitude towards general studies had historically not been so entirely hostile as was commonly assumed. The age of burnings at the stake and the ghetto had been preceded by centuries in which the greatest sages of Jewish scholarship were also "pillars of the general sciences of heaven and earth," producing works whose every page attested to their "deep insights into the nature of man and his social development."[6] In his view, historical circumstance, rather than Torah *hashkafah,* explained much of the hostility to general learning. The physical environment of the ghetto discouraged, for instance, theoretical scientific inquiry: "The narrow slits of open sky that were visible from the tall, somber tenements of the ghettos were hardly conducive to a thoughtful observation of the heavens and their wonders. The high walls that imprisoned the Jewish youths in the alleys of the ghettos also barred them from field and forest, from nature and its beauties. Often the frail bean sprout that a Jewish lad might plant and nurture in front of the dark, narrow window of the dwelling in which he lived was all he ever knew of springtime." Nor was it any wonder that Jews had little inclination to study history:

> All that world history had to offer the Jews were chains and *autos-da-fé*. During an age when the rest of mankind filled history's annals with such a poor reflection of itself in the form of Jewish blood, Jewish tears and Jewish ruins, Israel could hardly be blamed for having little desire or inclination to read the pages of history.[7]

Nor did the effect of general learning on their Christian neighbors do much to commend such learning to the Jewish ghetto dweller, who "did not miss engaging in the science or culture [that had proven] incapable of rescuing its disciples from the shackles of shameful delusion and deplorable error."[8]

AS FAR AS THE GREAT LEADERS OF EASTERN EUROPEAN JEWRY WERE concerned, the reasons militating against general secular studies had not abated in the modern era. If anything, they had grown even stronger. The same intellectual currents that had resulted in the dismantling of the ghetto walls were fiercely antagonistic to religion. Many former ghetto dwellers found themselves dazzled by the bright light of secular learning to which they were exposed for the first time, and rushed in droves to abandon traditional Judaism. It was an era of buoyant confidence in the powers of unaided human reason. In the sciences, the frontiers of human knowledge were expanding, and this progress, it was assumed, was being duplicated in the other realms of human endeavor as well. The history of mankind was viewed as one of unbroken ascent from a primitive, dark past towards an age of enlightenment, a view hardly reconcilable with the traditional Jewish view of increasing darkness as the distance from the Revelation at Sinai grows.

Eastern European Opposition

For his part, Rabbi Hirsch had no difficulty understanding the opposition to secular learning on the part of the Torah leaders of his generation:

> Should we be surprised that the older generation, particularly the acknowledged guardians of our ancestral religious heritage, reacted with consternation to this onslaught of the new era? The younger generation of Jews were declaring war upon everything that, for thousands of years, had given their people the knowledge, the inspiration and the moral stamina that enabled them to survive, even in the face of oppression and degradation, and to triumph over the ordeals that marked their path through history. Should we blame that older generation for rejecting a new era which, by deliberately encouraging the neglect of Jewish studies, raised Jewish youth to despise the heritage of its ancestral religion, so that eventually this youth went so far as to denounce the literature of the Jewish religion to the governmental authorities as "inimical to culture"? Precisely this is what happened in our own city of Frankfurt. . . .
>
> Should it surprise us, therefore, that the older generation perceived the spirit of the new culture, which had been used as a

vehicle to attack their ancient heritage, as the cause of all their troubles?[9]

In the Western World

CIRCUMSTANCES IN THE GERMANY OF RABBI HIRSCH'S DAY DIFFERED markedly from those in Eastern Europe. In Germany, as in the rest of Western Europe, non-Jewish society was increasingly open to Jews. Not only were opportunities heretofore denied to Jews available for the first time, but there was no way for the Jew to cut himself off from the broader society around him in the way the ghetto had once cut him off.[10] Had it still been possible for German Jews to seal themselves off hermetically from the rest of society, wrote the well-known German Jewish historian Dr. Moshe Auerbach, they could not have ignored the warnings of Torah luminaries over the generations concerning the danger of general studies. The issue in Rabbi Hirsch's day, however, was not the avoidance of this threat of alien ideas, for German Jews were exposed to gentile society, like it or not. Divine Providence having thrust German Jews into a situation of confrontation with Western culture, the challenge was to accept the confrontation "not with a sense of pain but with one of happy responsibility."[11]

There can be no doubt that Rabbi Hirsch viewed *Torah Im Derech Eretz* as the one possible antidote to the challenge posed to Jewish belief by exposure to secular society. In a lengthy epistle in 1845, written in response to the Reform conference in Braunschweig, he argued that the only remedy for the ills of the age was the establishment of schools combining Torah and secular studies. While still in Nikolsburg, he advised a young rabbinic colleague that the abandonment of the principle of *Torah Im Derech Eretz* was the cause of all the troubles of the times confronting Jewry, and only its renewed application would effect a cure.[12]

Rabbi Hirsch stressed that his approach of *Torah Im Derech Eretz* was designed, in part, to inoculate Jewish youth against the enticements of the outside world:

> Precisely because our children will be able to move about even more freely in the world outside, and precisely because our children — certainly more so than their forefathers and perhaps even more so than we ourselves — will come into close contact with, and frequently have to meet challenges posed by, the studies, creations, viewpoints, principles and concepts developed by non-

> Jewish minds, will they be all the more in need of a thorough Jewish education so that they will learn to know and appreciate their Judaism and feel the light and the truth that radiate from it. . . . Above all, our children should be trained to apply the Divine truths of Judaism as a test and a standard by which to evaluate all the creations, views, principles and axioms developed by non-Jewish minds, so that they should not be dazzled and led astray by these creations, no matter how great and splendid.[13]

It is beyond cavil that Rabbi Hirsch's vision of *Torah Im Derech Eretz* was the essential factor in the survival of German Orthodoxy. Without that vision, it is doubtful that authentic Judaism could have survived at all in Germany. When Rabbi Hirsch came to Frankfurt there were only 100 Orthodox families left in that once proud community, and Orthodoxy was in rout all over Germany. At his death, however, there were thousands of observant Jews in Germany leading lives marked by rigorous *mitzvah* observance and regular Torah study. Many merchants, industrialists, doctors, lawyers and academicians possessed a broad knowledge of European culture and yet were deeply pious.[14]

Even the great Torah leaders of Eastern Europe, who strongly opposed the introduction of a *Torah Im Derech Eretz* curriculum in their own countries, nevertheless admitted that *Torah Im Derech Eretz* was responsible for the preservation of authentic Judaism in Germany. Rabbi Yitzchak Elchanan Spektor of Kovno lavished praise on Rabbi Hirsch as a *tzaddik* and spoke glowingly of the communities that had formed under his influence in Frankfurt and elsewhere in Germany.[15] Rabbi Chaim Ozer Grodzenski of Vilna similarly praised the German communities fashioned under Rabbi Hirsch's banner and described him as one whose "name will be a blessing for generations [and] who turned the multitudes to righteousness."[16] The highest accolade, however, was left to Rabbi Chaim Halberstam, the revered Sanzer Rav. He concluded his lengthy praise of Rabbi Hirsch and his accomplishments with this pithy summary: "What I am to Galicia, Rabbi Hirsch is to Germany."[17]

Secular subjects today form an integral part of the curriculum of yeshiva day schools and yeshiva high schools throughout the Western world. Thus, with the exception of the yeshiva education of boys in Israel and in Chassidic schools in other countries, *Torah Im Derech Eretz* is the *de facto* principle guiding most Torah education around the world today.[a] Though various aspects of the Hirschian *Weltanschauung* are no longer emphasized — e.g., the Jew's role in bringing all mankind to a recognition of the Almighty — wherever Jews are forced into close contact with the dominant culture, as they were in the Germany of Rabbi Hirsch's day and as they are in the Western world today, the *Torah Im Derech Eretz* curriculum prevails. Jewish yeshiva day schools and high schools in Western countries today teach secular subjects as a serious part of their curriculum, an idea which in pre-World War II Eastern Europe was *muktzah machmas mius* (an abomination). The reason for this is simple: Life in Western countries, in terms of the Jew's contact with the non-Jewish world, is, for the most part, similar to the conditions that prevailed in Rabbi Hirsch's Germany. And so, although many will not accept *Torah Im Derech Eretz* as being the *de jure* guiding principle of Jewish education today, the facts show it to be a reality which is part and parcel of authentic Jewish life in Western countries.

Conclusions

FROM THE FOREGOING DISCUSSION OF THE DIFFERING HISTORICAL circumstances between Germany and Eastern Europe, it might be thought that Rabbi Hirsch's philosophy of *Torah Im Derech Eretz* was restricted to the Germany of his day, and indeed it has been argued on more than one occasion that Rabbi Hirsch developed his philosophy as a *hora'as sha'ah* (a response to an emergency situation).

It is clear, however, that *Torah Im Derech Eretz* was not for Rabbi Hirsch a temporary response to an emergency situation. It was not a "troubled, time-bound notion." Anyone with the most cursory familiarity with his voluminous corpus can not fail to see the central place of *Torah Im Derech Eretz* in his philosophy. Already in *The Nineteen Letters*, he referred to the *Torah Im Deretz Eretz* ideal of realizing "the eternal ideal within the setting of our particular age, and through the use of the specific circumstances that it provides,"[18] and he reiterated that ideal throughout his entire life. *Torah Im Derech Eretz*, Rabbi Hirsch wrote in 1876, "represents the ancient, traditional wisdom of our Sages that has stood the test everywhere and at all times."[19]

However, the specific curriculum and the ratio of *limudei kodesh* to secular subjects which obtained in the Frankfurt *Realschule* were most defi-

a. Of course, a far greater percentage of the day is devoted to Torah studies than was the case in the *Realschule* in Frankfurt. As we shall see in the next chapter, Rabbi Hirsch and his successors in Frankfurt were greatly constrained by the government in the introduction of Torah studies into the curriculum of the *Realschule*.

nitely temporary accommodations dictated by local conditions. The Prussian authorities exercised strict control over the number of hours devoted to general and Torah studies, allowing no flexibility whatsoever.[b]

While Rabbi Hirsch did not view *Torah Im Derech Eretz* as a time-bound concept, he nevertheless did not insist that it had to govern in every place at every time.[20] That determination, he felt, is best left to the local rabbinic authorities. A case in point is the controversy surrounding Rabbi Ezriel Hildesheimer's efforts to establish an orphanage in Jerusalem in which secular subjects would be taught.

In 1872, Rabbi Hildesheimer learned that the desperate situation of Jewish orphans in Jerusalem was being exploited by local missionaries to ensnare Jewish children. In response, he decided to establish a Jewish orphanage there which would emphasize traditional Jewish studies but would include secular subjects necessary to earn a livelihood.

The local rabbis in Jerusalem vehemently opposed the introduction of secular studies into the curriculum, and some local zealots published a pamphlet defaming Rabbi Hildesheimer in the most vile terms. While appalled by the vituperation poured on Rabbi Hildesheimer, the other leading German rabbis — Rabbi Hirsch, Rabbi Bamberger and Rabbi Lehmann — were also opposed to the project. Rabbi Hirsch's opposition stemmed not from any disagreement over the value of secular subjects in the curriculum, but from the fact that the proposal had originated with the historian Heinrich Graetz of Breslau, who made his recommendations following a visit to Palestine. He refused to credit the opinions of Graetz over those of the rabbinic authorities of Jerusalem.

Perhaps even more important to Rabbi Hirsch than Graetz's role in the project was the opposition of the Torah authorities of Jerusalem. "Just as only in Berlin is it possible to determine what is the best and most advantageous course of action for Berlin, and only in Frankfurt can it be known what is best for Frankfurt, so also *only* our brothers in the Holy Land and their rabbis can know what is beneficial and a source of blessing for them," he wrote.[21] His position in this matter was consistent with his oft-stated principle against intervention in the affairs of any other community with competent rabbinic authorities."[22]

Similarly, when Rabbi Zalman Spitzer of Vienna asked in 1879 whether he should support the establishment of a school in Jerusalem where Arabic would be taught — a step opposed by the rabbis of Jerusalem — Rabbi Hirsch replied in the negative. He did, however,

b. See following chapter.

counsel Rabbi Spitzer to suggest to the Torah leaders of Jerusalem that Arabic, which was then the language of commerce in Palestine, be taught in their own school to afford the students the ability to engage in commerce.[23]

On the other hand, in 1878 he wrote to the Hungarian Minister of Education, supporting the establishment of a school in Papa in which secular subjects would be studied, this mostly likely at the request of his son-in-law Rabbi Salomon Breuer, who served as rabbi there.[24]

In summation: Rabbi Hirsch did not consider *Torah Im Derech Eretz* to be limited only to the time and setting in which he lived. The question of whether (and to what extent) it *is* applicable in a particular place and historical setting, he left to the discretion of the rabbinic leadership of that time and place. The specific modality by which it was applied in Frankfurt was dictated by the existing conditions there, and cannot be used as a paradigm for other eras and settings.

Chapter Nineteen
EDUCATOR

WORRY DAY AND NIGHT ABOUT THE STUDIES of the children, the boys and girls of your congregation. Do not rest until you have arranged for them to be led to the sweet waters of Torah's salvation, to draw their hearts along the straight and broad paths that will win them favor and good understanding in the eyes of G-d and man.

This should be the goal of all your thoughts, for does not all our strength and our hope for the future rest in the mouths of our young ones? May it never be beneath your dignity to teach them the path in which they are to go, the mitzvos they are to do. Pay no heed to the voices that whisper in your ear, "It does not become the honor of a Rav to teach Torah to the young." Did not the Sages teach that where Hashem's Name is being profaned we do not honor the Rav? All the more so must we be willing to forgo personal honor when the time comes to implant Hashem's love and fear in their young souls, to train them to go in His ways so that they will not abandon them when they grow older. How else can we save our future from destruction except by strengthening our children and directing their hearts firmly in Hashem's ways before they are led astray by the vain and deceitful ways of the world?

If you devote yourself to this great mitzvah with all your strength, and consecrate all your words, all your thoughts and all your deeds to performing it for the sake of Heaven, then honor will surely come in the end, and the members of your congregation will esteem you as a father to their children, for you will have given them the World to Come and saved their precious offspring from bitter destruction.[1]

Rabbi Hirsch's greatest impact was as an educator. He taught his family, his congregation, the generation in which he lived, and future generations as well. He taught young and old, beginners and scholars; he taught in personal conversation, in daily lectures in his home, in addresses in the synagogue, and as headmaster and teacher in the school. He taught through his books and hundreds of articles. And his impact as an educator remains undiminished today, as new editions of his writings continue to appear more than a century after his passing.

The Realschule

AT THE TIME OF RABBI HIRSCH'S ARRIVAL IN FRANKFURT IN 1851, there was no formal Jewish education in the spirit of Torah. Nor had their been for decades. Every attempt to found a school combining Torah and general studies in Frankfurt was met with determined opposition from the Reformers, who used their influence with the magistrate to have the necessary permission denied. Until 1848, the Reformers successfully blocked all attempts to open such a school. In addition, they expropriated the old educational funds and charitable trusts, made up of the contributions of generations of pious Jews for the support of Torah study, and channeled them to support the Reform *Philanthropin* school.

Upon his arrival in Frankfurt, Rabbi Hirsch's first priority was the founding of a school. The education of its children, Rabbi Hirsch wrote, is the most important responsibility of any Jewish community, and this obligation extends even to children of wealthy families whose parents have the wherewithal to pay for their private education.[2] "There is no hurry to build a synagogue," he told his congregants. "First we need a school to bring up a new generation of faithful Jews who will embrace Torah and make it their primary mission in life. Only afterwards should a synagogue be built, for what good would there be in a having a magnificent house of prayer if there are no young people to pray in it?"[3]

The directors of the *Philanthropin* did not take favorably to Rabbi Hirsch's attempts to obtain the necessary government permission. And even after the *Realschule* was established, its faculty and students endured considerable abuse at the hands of students of the *Philanthropin*.[4]

In addition to trouble from the Reform, Rabbi Hirsch encountered not a little skepticism among the Orthodox. Following in the footsteps of his grandfather Reb Mendel Frankfurter, he visited the homes of his congregants to recruit students. At first he had to beg parents to send their children to the school. Some parents feared the effects of a modern education, which they associated with heresy; at the other end of the spectrum there were those who were unconvinced that the modern education offered in the *Realschule* was modern enough to save their children from the dangers of "religious fanaticism." Many families, not wishing to send Rabbi Hirsch away empty-handed, compromised and sent only their less gifted children on an experimental basis.[5]

But Rabbi Hirsch's persistent efforts bore fruit, and on April 1, 1853 (23 *Adar*, 5613), a year and a half after his arrival in Frankfurt, the *Realschule* opened its doors to 83 boys and girls. This was the first of the four schools that Rabbi Hirsch would establish in Frankfurt: the *Realschule*, a secondary school, a high school for girls and the *Volksschule* for the children of East European immigrants.[6]

Permission to open a building and students to fill it did not mean that the Reform community had come to terms with the *Realschule's* existence. On his way to the opening ceremony, someone thrust into Rabbi Hirsch's hand a venomous article attacking the new school that had just appeared anonymously in the *Frankfurter Journal*. The article, whose author was none other than Dr. Michael Hess, director of the *Philanthropin*, lashed out at the new school as a danger to Jewish and non-Jewish culture alike.

As usual, Rabbi Hirsch's reply was not long in coming. Only five days later, he published an article in the *Frankfurter Intelligenzblatt*, ridiculing the anonymous author for not having even the courage to identify himself. His article, entitled "Rabbinical Judaism and Social Education" (*Das Rabbinische Judentum und die Soziale Bildung*), is a classic example of his polemic pen, and it paints a colorful picture of the challenges the *Realschule* faced in overcoming the influence of the powerful *Philanthropin*. He began by mocking Hess's shallow concept of enlightenment:

Realschule (erected in 1853), corner Rechneigrabenstrasse and Schützenstrasse. To the right is the synagogue of the IRG

In the opinion of the anonymous writer, the only ones who can be called enlightened are those who violate the Sabbath in public, those who work on the festivals, or at the very least who talk about and engage in their everyday affairs on them.

An enlightened person, in his opinion, must like him be so uninformed about the Torah of Moses that he thinks that the prohibitions against eating leavened bread on Passover, insects, blood, forbidden fats, and *neveilah* or *treifah* originate in the Talmud, without even casting a glance into the Torah to see that all these commandments came directly from Hashem.

In the anonymous writer's opinion, someone who does not eat insects during the summer, or whose soul revolts at the thought of eating *neveilah* or *treifah,* blood or forbidden fats, someone who is so deranged that he habitually washes his hands before meals, and is careful during meals not to touch the parts of his body that are normally covered, such people are not admissible in the assembly of the enlightened, and will not share in their "honor."

. . . The time is past, and will not return, when a Jew can be considered "enlightened" simply by virtue of ignorance of the Torah, by virtue of his scorn and ridicule of all that is holy, of his mockery of the time-honored customs of our ancestors, of the smoke of his cigarette on the Sabbath, of his table laid out with *treifas.* All these were once the banners of the "enlightened" Jew, but that time will not return for these easy tasks can now be accomplished, and with excellent results, even by the ignorant and foolish masses.[7]

Rabbi Hirsch's response left Dr. Hess no choice but to reveal himself as the author of the anonymous article. He published a reply in the *Frankfurter Intelligenzblatt* under the name "Pharisaic Judaism and Social Life." Three days later Rabbi Hirsch responded with another blast, entitled "Rabbinic Judaism and Director Hess" which convinced the *Philanthropin's* headmaster that more exchanges would only result in his further humiliation, and he made no further attempts to continue the scuffle. However the machinations of the *Philanthropin* continued for many decades: Fifty-four years later, the Reform community presented a petition to the city council asking it to withhold recognition from the *Realschule.*

As its motto the *Realschule* chose the statement of the Sages (*Avos* 3:21): *Without wisdom there is no fear of G-d; without fear of G-d there is no wisdom.* In his first response to Hess, Rabbi Hirsch gave this description of the educational goals of the *Realschule:*

> Our task is to implant other thoughts in the hearts of the young, a different kind of spiritual enlightenment, to awaken in their hearts a love and faith in Israel's immortal patrimony, and to mold their hearts to receive Hashem's light and the wisdom of our Sages, to adhere to the Jewish faith without guilt. Our task is to open their eyes, to let them be guided by the light of Torah's pillar of fire, to teach them to be courageous in fulfilling Hashem's will so that, like their ancestors and fathers before them, they can be truly kind and giving, to show the world that generosity is Israel's trademark. With open eyes, with pure love for mankind in our hearts let us look on Hashem, on the world and on humanity, to see in humanity the objective and the mission of their people, and to be self-understanding in their efforts to fulfill joyfully all their duties as human being, Jew and citizen.
>
> Our task is to fill ourselves with Hashem's wisdom and His Torah, and with the knowledge the human spirit requires to recognize his worth as a man. If we fill ourselves with everything of true value and worth and goodness, with matters relevant to humanity and to G-d, and do so willingly, then the world will cherish and honor them; they will be respected as trustworthy

View of Realschule (on left) from Rechneigrabenstrasse

> people, peace-loving people of good deeds, not in spite of the fact that they are Jewish, but rather *because* they are Jewish.[8]

In a letter to Amsterdam, Rabbi Hirsch summarized his plans for the curriculum of the new school. The boys would learn Hebrew grammar and composition, *Sefer HaMitzvos, Chumash* with *Rashi, Nach, Mishnah* and *Gemara.* The *Gemara shiur* was designed to enable the boys to study *Gemara, Rashi, Tosafos* and other *Rishonim* on their own. Those boys incapable of following the *Gemara* lessons were taught instead *Menoras HaMaor.*[9]

Education of Girls

RABBI HIRSCH WAS A TRAILBLAZER IN HIS CONCEPTION OF GIRLS' education, one of his most significant and perhaps least recognized innovations. Ideas that he originated are now universally accepted as fundamental principles of education. The girls in the *Realschule* studied the same subjects — including *Chumash* and Hebrew grammar — as the boys, except for Talmud and mathematics, in place of which they were taught handicrafts. Many years before the *Realschule* opened its doors, Rabbi Hirsch had argued in *Horeb* that Jewish girls must be given a meticulous grounding in the basics of Torah and Jewish thought.[10] As Rabbi Hirsch explained his program:

> People forget that Channah and Devorah most certainly understand Channah's prayer and Devorah's song. They also forget that the rescue of future generations of our men as well as of our

Girls' school of Realschule — Am Tiergarten, view from rear

> women depends on our success in winning the devotion of our future wives' and mothers' hearts to the sanctity of our people. The only way we can hope to sway their hearts is by teaching them to draw spiritual nourishment from the original sources, to prefer on their own Yeshayahu and Amos to Goethe and Shakespeare. And this, with G-d's help, we have been able to do. If you wish to provide for your future, do not forget your daughters![11]

Thus, in addition to the decisive influence Rabbi Hirsch's writings had on the establishment of the Bais Yaakov movement (see Chapter Six), organized institutional instruction of young girls actually originated in Frankfurt.

The results of the Hirschian approach to women's education were dramatic. The Orthodox women of Frankfurt and its satellite communities were renowned for their learning as well as for their deep piety.[12] As a general rule, the observant women of Germany were more learned than their Eastern European counterparts, due to the broad Jewish education they received.[a,13] On Shabbos and festivals the women's section of the big *shul* (its official name was *Bais Tefillath Jeschurun*) in Frankfurt was filled to capacity with women of all ages, from young girls to grandmothers — the result of the thorough Jewish education they had received in the *Realschule.*

---

a. Thus, when Sarah Schenirer sought an assistant to develop the girls' seminary she opened in Krakow, she had to look as far afield as Frankfurt to find a suitable candidate: Judith Rosenbaum (later, Dr. Judith Grunfeld).

Realschule — Am Tiergarten, erected 1885

SECULAR STUDIES IN THE REALSCHULE INCLUDED GERMAN GRAMmar, writing, composition and literature; art and music; algebra, geometry, accounting, natural sciences, physics, chemistry, technology, geography, history, French and English. Rabbi Hirsch preferred honest gentile teachers for secular subjects over non-observant Jews, who, he felt, would have a negative influence.[14]

Secular Curriculum

Frankfurt in Rabbi Hirsch's day was a highly developed business center and most members of the *IRG* were businessmen. There was no university in the city until the 20th century, and with the exception of Rabbi Hirsch's sons Mendel, Marcus and Naftali and a few others, the vast majority of *IRG* youth in Rabbi Hirsch's time did not have advanced academic training, but rather went directly to work after high school.[15] Unlike the "Gymnasium" schools, the secular studies in the *Realschule* had, as its name indicated, a commercial orientation and did not include Latin and Greek in the curriculum. The instruction in French and English was because of their usefulness in the multilingual business environment of Western Europe.[16] Study of the arts and humanities was limited to the minimum required by the government; heretical views, such as those of the historian Graetz and the philosopher Spinoza, received no mention at all, nor was Mendelssohn's thought ever studied.[17]

By 1864, the quarters of the *Realschule* had become inadequate to house its hundreds of students, and the congregation had no choice but to expand the buildings housing the school. There were 470 students in 1877, and another building was dedicated in 1885, by which time the student body exceeded 500.[18]

The *Realschule* was a major educational success, and even East European Torah leaders who did not advocate the *Torah Im Derech Eretz* approach in their own countries nonetheless gave high praise to the achievements of the school. During the 1870s, Rabbi Hirsch received letters from Rabbi Yitzchak Elchanan Spektor of Kovno and Rabbi Elya Chaim Meisel of Lodz effusively praising the work of the *Realschule.*[19]

In 1881, it came to Rabbi Hirsch's attention that children of East European immigrants were attending municipal elementary school in Frankfurt, and of 200 such children, only three refrained from writing on Shabbos. He acted quickly, and on June 1, 1882 the *Volksschule,* the Israelite Elementary School, opened in the former building of the *Realschule* with 36 students. After only half a year, the student body had increased eightfold to 290. The school catered to the children of refugees and other immigrants from Eastern Europe who, because of their different background, found it difficult to integrate into the programs of the *Realschule.* The first director of the new school was Dr. Mendel Hirsch, who took on the added responsibility as an unpaid volunteer, in addition to his position as director of the *Realschule.*[20]

Headmaster

FOR THE FIRST 24 YEARS OF THE REALSCHULE'S EXISTENCE, RABBI Hirsch served as its director with no addition to the salary he received as rabbi. Through those years he bore, without assistance, all the burdens of managing the school, including the tedious task of preparing the endless reports and study plans required by the authorities. Finally, in the winter of 1876-77, when the struggle over secession was taking a heavy toll on his health, he stopped giving classes at the school and turned over the direction of the school to his firstborn son, Dr. Mendel Hirsch, a highly qualified educator.

In addition to serving as director, Rabbi Hirsch also taught in the school. At the outset he taught the *Gemara* classes for the older students. Every Shabbos afternoon at precisely 2:30 p.m., winter and summer, he examined the older students in his home. These examinations were given even on those Sabbaths when he addressed the congregation at length in the morning. Several days a week he also gave classes in *Gemara* in his home.[21]

His students, and young people in general, felt comfortable in his presence and treated him with a rare mixture of friendship and admiration.

The Jubilee edition of the *Israelit* (1908) contains recollections of a number of his former students. Among other things, they related that he never failed to take an interest in every minor wound that they received from students of the Reform *Philanthropin* School. "He spoke to us in our language," one student remembered. "He checked to make sure that the stamps we traded were genuine, and he checked our playing ball. He was our friend. But he never asked us about homework." He was a beloved teacher who never raised his voice, and knew how to impart to his students an all-encompassing love of Judaism.

Dr. Mendel Hirsch

The youngest students felt so comfortable with him that they brought him flowers and stopped in to visit him if they happened to be passing his house. For his part, he would invite them in and give them a few minutes of his time before continuing with his work. To fully appreciate the special warmth of his relationship with his students, it is important to remember the awe, and even fear, in which he was held by most of his adult congregants.[22]

One of Rabbi Hirsch's innovations was the holding of annual public examinations in which students were given a chance to display their academic prowess in both Jewish and general subjects. Each year he wrote a long article on some aspect of education, and included it in the invitation to these examinations. Jacob Rosenheim recalled that as a young boy he was once asked in a public examination to explain the *Mishnah* in *Chullin* (108a) that discusses the case of a droplet of milk falling onto a piece of meat cooking in a pot. "What a triumph it was to recite from memory the *Mishnah* together with *Rashi's* commentary under Rabbi Hirsch's exhilarated gaze," he recalled decades later.[23]

Unrelenting Pressure

FROM THE SECOND DECADE OF ITS EXISTENCE, WHEN FRANKFURT became a part of Prussia, the *Realschule* was subject to unceasing pressure on the part of the Prussian authorities, which affected every facet of the school's operations, especially the details of its curriculum. With the institution of compulsory education for Jewish children in Germany, the various local and regional governments became stricter in the enforcement of the legal requirements, and no educational institution could operate without government permission, in spite of the fact that Jewish schools received no financial support whatsoever from the government. Governmental approval was required for curriculum plans, and even textbooks and teachers required official certification.[24]

This interference made itself felt in every minute detail of school life. Especially after the establishment of the German Reich in 1871, the government's view of educational institutions as organs of the state justified in its eyes any and all meddling in school affairs. The motivation for this policy was simple — the government's desire to promote assimilation of Jews into German society.[25]

Throughout Rabbi Hirsch's tenure as director of the *Realschule,* he fought a constant battle against official attempts to limit the hours in the curriculum devoted to religious subjects. His letters are full of diplomatic delaying tactics and expositions of the purpose of the school and its special significance for the future of German Jewry. Each additional class in Jewish subjects was a battle. His replies to government demands were polite but resolute; every year or two the pressure was renewed and the battle had to be fought over again.

Rabbi Hirsch's tireless attempts to moderate, delay or revoke the demands were not always successful. He had predicated his curriculum on 20 hours weekly of *limudei kodesh*; in practice the *Realschule* was permitted to offer less than half that, and as time went on that amount was decreased by government fiat even further. The Orthodox schools were forced to offer voluntary supplementary classes in Talmud, but by no means did all parents avail themselves of these opportunities.[26]

When attempts to completely eliminate religious studies failed, the government tried another tactic. It announced that since teachers' salaries were so low, their hours must be reduced, and it was the religious subjects that had to suffer. Sometimes the authorities intervened on the pretext of concern for the students' health, claiming that the long school day was unhealthy for children of such tender age and that the only solution was to further curtail the hours devoted to religious subjects.

When Rabbi Hirsch retired from the directorship of the *Realschule,* matters took a turn for the worse. The deference the authorities had shown to the elderly rabbi did not extend to his son, and the tone of the government demands became increasingly peremptory and uncompromising. After a 20-year battle, the number of weekly classes in Hebrew had dwindled to ten, six for Bible and four for *Gemara* in the upper classes.[27]

DUE TO GOVERNMENTAL INTERFERENCE, THE ACTUAL BALANCE between religious and secular studies in the *Realschule* was far from the one Rabbi Hirsch had originally contemplated. While Rabbi Hirsch might have chosen to include the same subjects in the curriculum, the determination of the relative time devoted to the various subjects was largely beyond his control. There were those who failed to understand this point and came to make a virtue out of a daily curriculum that had begun as no more than a reluctant adaptation to necessity.[28]

A Utopian Ideal

It must also be stressed that on the whole the members of the *IRG* did not exactly press Rabbi Hirsch to increase the hours of *limudei kodesh*. The reasons for this attitude were several. In addition to feelings of competition with the *Philanthropin* there was the fact that Frankfurt was a highly developed commercial center, and excellence in secular studies was seen as an entry into that commercial life. More importantly, there was a serious misunderstanding on the part of many of the ideals of *Torah Im Derech Eretz*. In terms of the relative amounts of time spent on each, not a few took the study of *Derech Eretz* with much greater seriousness than the study of Torah.[29]

Thus, as Professor Mordechai Breuer has shown, *Torah Im Derech Eretz*, as far as the *Realschule* was concerned, was a utopian ideal that was far from realized in practice. The hours permitted by the authorities never gave nearly as much weight and breadth to Jewish studies as to secular ones, and the importance assigned by many of the parents to *limud haTorah* was far from what Rabbi Hirsch envisioned. The outcome of this state of affairs was that the stress was on practical observance, and that there was much too much emphasis on culture and *Bildung* (a unique German expression which combines the meaning carried by the English word "education" with notions of character formation and moral education), and not enough on *limud haTorah* for its own sake. In the school's early years, only those students who remained part of the overall *Kehillah* structure remained observant; those who moved elsewhere were generally unsuccessful in retaining the educational ideals of the *Realschule*.[30]

In Breuer's view, the ideal of *Torah Im Derech Eretz* was imparted not so much through the studies themselves as through the personality of some of the educators, who combined deep Jewish knowledge, sincere piety, and great expertise in secular disciplines as well, and whose lives were living embodiments of the ideal.[31] One cannot ignore the drawbacks of *Torah Im Derech Eretz* to German Jewry since the 19th century, with its marked decline in Torah study and a concomitant weakening of a feeling of belonging to the wider Torah world.[32]

Rabbi Salomon Breuer

The original draft of the bylaws of the *IRG*, written by Rabbi Hirsch, contained a provision for the establishment of a yeshiva, and in the statutes of the *IRG*, Rabbi Hirsch wrote that the expansion of the school into a training school for teachers and rabbis was its ultimate goal. But these dreams did not materialize in his lifetime. To the contrary, the *Realschule* came to be considered the pinnacle of Jewish education for the *Kehillah* members and there was no understanding at all of the need for a yeshiva. Jacob Rosenheim writes that had he suggested going to yeshiva to his parents when he graduated the *Realschule* in the mid-1880s, they would have viewed it as an act of insanity. In any event, he recalls, the idea never even occurred to him.[33]

When Rabbi Salomon Breuer succeeded his father-in-law in 1890 and stipulated that he be permitted to open a yeshiva, there were a not insignificant number of loyal followers of Rabbi Hirsch who opposed its establishment, thinking, mistakenly, that the master would have opposed it. In their misplaced devotion, they felt that there should be no departure from Rabbi Hirsch's practice. Even after agreeing to let Rabbi Breuer establish a yeshiva, the *Kehillah* placed an ad in a local newspaper announcing that it was not responsible for any financial obligations incurred by the yeshiva. Only some time later did the yeshiva become an integral part of the *Kehillah* and did its members send their sons to study there.[34]

Why Rabbi Hirsch did not himself establish a yeshiva has been the cause of some speculation. Those who argue, however, that he did not view a yeshiva as the centerpiece of a Jewish community are forced to ignore the bulk of Rabbi Hirsch's teachings, the central place Torah study occupied in his philosophy, and his mainstream approach to Torah instruction as evident throughout his halachic writings.[35]

The Frankfurt yeshiva of Rabbi Salomon Breuer

A Dangerous Edict

IN 1888, THE PRUSSIAN GOVERNMENT ISSUED A DECREE REQUIRING all students to take standardized examinations, which were to be administered also on the Sabbath. No special dispensation was granted to Jewish students to take the exams on a different day. Rabbi Hirsch authored a petition to the Prussian Minister of Education Gossler, signed by 115 rabbis from all of Germany, stating that all writing on the Sabbath was prohibited by Jewish law. The petition was sent on October 23, and on November 15, a month and a half before his passing, Rabbi Hirsch received a reply from the Minister of Education assuring him that school principals would be permitted to "judge sympathetically" requests to defer the examination to a weekday. A month before his passing, Rabbi Hirsch published the minister's reply.[36]

In a similar matter, Rabbi Hirsch once received a request for guidance from parents in another city who were forced to send their children to public school because of the absence of a Jewish school. The principal attempted to force Jewish students to attend school and write on Shabbos and Yom Tov, and he informed the parents that anyone who refused to comply would be subject to imprisonment. Rabbi Hirsch responded that the parents should be prepared to go to prison. He advised them to inform the press that the reason for their incarceration was their refusal to betray their religious beliefs, so that the world could hear that in their city, which prided itself on its religious tolerance, people were imprisoned for their desire to remain faithful to their religious beliefs. In Rabbi Hirsch's

Beis Medrash of the Frankfurt yeshiva

opinion there was no other course of action. None of the parents involved were ultimately imprisoned, but one of the students was as a result of his refusal to write on Shabbos. His jailing caused such a public outcry that the government was compelled to rescind its requirement that Jewish children attend school on Shabbos.[37]

Legacy

RABBI HIRSCH'S REALSCHULE FORGED A PATH FOR MANY SIMILAR schools in Germany, and the combination of religious and secular studies he advocated has since been almost universally adapted in the West, albeit with the curriculum reflecting the increased opportunity for Torah study. In Britain, two articles by Rabbi Hirsch about education inspired Rabbi Avigdor Schonfeld to found an elementary school modeled after the one in Frankfurt, which in turn became the nucleus for a whole network of similar schools in Britain.[38] The standard model for girls' elementary and high schools throughout the West is also based on the blueprint Rabbi Hirsch established in Frankfurt. His educational endeavors continue to have a decisive impact on Torah Jewry's educational systems throughout the Western world.

Part Six

CONFRONTATION WITH "THE SCIENCE OF JUDAISM"

Chapter Twenty
"THE SCIENCE OF JUDAISM"

ONE OF THE GREAT BATTLES OF THE LATTER PART OF Rabbi Hirsch's life was with the proponents of *Wissenschaft des Judentums* (The Science of Judaism). Though the movement never commanded the masses in the same way as the Reform Movement, it was in some ways more insidious. Rather than simply discarding the forms of traditional Judaism willy-nilly as the Reform did, "Science of Judaism" purported to prove that such changes were typical of Judaism throughout the ages. By offering a "scientific" picture of the creative genius of Jewish scholars over the millennia, whose "innovations" had allowed the survival of the Jewish people in every historical milieu, the cultural approach of "Science of Judaism" appealed to many who could never be impressed by Reform's blatant efforts to bring Judaism into ever greater conformity with Christianity.[a]

---

a. Rabbi Hirsch mocked the Reform quest for respect in gentile eyes by minimizing any particularistic aspects of Judaism. Such efforts, he asserted, not only entailed the complete distortion of traditional Judaism, they were also counterproductive:

> [R]espect yourself, respect your past, respect your own sanctuary, and you will see that whatever opinion is held of you, whether you are regarded with favor or disfavor—respect

THE SCIENCE OF JUDAISM MOVEMENT CAME INTO FORMAL EXISTENCE with the founding of the *Verein für Kultur und Wissenschaft des Judentums* (Society for Jewish Culture and Science) in Berlin in 1819 by Leopold Zunz (1794-1886) and Eduard Gans (1798-1839). Having rejected the Torah as a source of binding law, these young academics were confronted with the problem of how to define themselves as Jews. Their hope was that the history and literature of the Jewish people would itself provide that Jewish identity. As Professor Mordechai Breuer has pointed out, the Divinely given Torah was to be replaced as the central focus of Judaism by the self-image of the individual Jew, derived from historical and scientific investigation divorced from any religious considerations.[1]

Kulturverein

Not only did the new movement draw its "critical" methodology from Christian sources, but its founders' personal lives revealed how great the lure of Christian society was for them and how much they needed the approval of that society. Gans converted to Christianity in 1825, and Zunz, the movement's leading ideologue, considered doing so in order to secure a university readership.[2] Heinrich Heine, the famous German Jewish poet and essayist, was appointed secretary of the organization in 1822 and baptized three years later. It is revealing of the attraction of Christian society for its members that the *Kulturverein* felt it necessary to include in its bylaws a requirement that members commit themselves not to convert to Christianity.[3] Not that it helped.

The image of the Jew both in the eyes of the Christian world and in the eyes of Jews themselves was one of the new movement's central concerns. The *Verein* came into being in the wake of the anti-Semitic Hep! Hep! riots, and its existence coincided with a general resurgence of anti-Semitism throughout Germany. One of the concerns of the movement's adherents was to combat this anti-Semitism by demonstrating the universal value of Jewish culture through which means they sought to refute the stereotype of the Jew as culturally backwards. By portraying the Jew throughout history as something other than the perpetually wretched outcast, they sought to show that Jews were deserving of emancipation.[4]

But the movement was not just concerned with Christian perceptions of the Jew. Jewish self-identity was no less important to its founders. Though

will not be denied you. But if you do not respect yourself, if you look contemptuously on the tombs of your ancestors, if you no longer consider your sanctuary worthy of respect, even of recognition—how can you demand that a stranger shall respect you, or respect your fathers? You may find many things in the world, but for respect you will beg in vain.[1*]

they tended to start from the assumption that much, or all, of the Torah is not G-d-given, and thereby undercut the very foundations of traditional religious observance, they were, by and large, not drawn to Reform, whose vague monotheism hardly served to give any positive content to Judaism.[b]

One of the primary attractions of the *Wissenschaft* movement was its claim to scientific rigor. Its hallmark was the willingness to submit all sacred texts to "critical" scrutiny. Previously unchallenged traditions of the origins and authorship of the *Tanach* and Talmud were now questioned and "revised," using what proponents claimed were the tools and techniques of modern scientific and historical research.

The claim to scientific objectivity was not one, however, that the movement's proponents could sustain, and their research could never be separated from its particular ideological and political context. That research was inevitably shaped by the desire to create an image of Jews worthy of all the rights and privileges of full citizenship.[5] To that end, the movement's proponents attempted to rewrite Jewish history in a naturalistic idiom designed to bring the history of the Jewish people into closer conformity with that of other nations.[6] Zunz, the movement's founder, admitted this ideological bias: "Since we do not study men and their actions as an end in itself, but rather for the sake of our anticipated advantage, we remain sunk, no less than our scornful enemies, in unfair prejudice toward many works of the past."[7]

Few, if any, of the initial practitioners of the Science of Judaism were fully observant, and their desire to justify their departures from traditional Jewish practice inevitably affected their approach to the ancient texts.[c] One contemporary writer summed up the entire enterprise succinctly: "The entire venture of *Wissenschaft des Judentums* was premised on

b. Proponents of the Science of Judaism frequently expressed antipathy bordering on outright hostility to Reform. Leopold Zunz, for instance, referred to the Reform Movement as "secret or open Christianity" (Breuer, *Modernity*, p. 85). That aversion to Reform, however, did not prevent certain Reform leaders from seeing how useful the *Wissenschaft des Judentums* "critical methodology" could prove in the service of Reform. Abraham Geiger, in particular, recognized that the claim to "scientific scholarship" could confer on Reform rabbis the same legitimacy that Orthodox rabbis possessed by virtue of their Torah knowledge, and that "proof" of the continual flux in the Jewish tradition would provide an intellectual justification of modern reforms as well. Geiger used the *Wissenschaft* approach to portray Judaism as a continually evolving process in which old forms were condemned to the "rubbish heap of history" never to be revived. Thus the Talmud, in his view, represented a complete recasting of Biblical Judaism.[4*]

c. For all the movement's claims to objectivity, somehow practitioners of *Wissenschaft des Judentums* always seemed to reach conclusions consistent with their initial religious positions. Thus the findings of Orthodox proponents were consistent with traditional belief, and the most radical reformers similarly found sustenance for their position in their historical research.

freeing the critical method from the shackles of belief."[8] Eduard Gans, director of the *Kulturverein,* described the Society's purpose as confining "religion to its boundaries and thereby allow[ing] . . . pure reason to rule in its proper sphere. In this sense, our intention is actually anti-religious." Leopold Zunz, hardly the most extreme of the movement's proponents, wrote that, "until the Talmud is toppled nothing can be done."[9]

Even as they sought to draw sustenance from the past and to use the history of the Jewish people as a source for their own self-identity, the practitioners of the Science of Judaism were paradoxically turning Judaism into a fossilized relic. In their fascination with the past, they failed to entertain the possibility that Judaism was still a living, pulsing entity, whose commands were binding on them. Dr. Isaac Breuer has described this phenomenon with his usual incisiveness:

> They killed the nation and then wrote the history of a dead people; they annulled all the laws and then investigated them as one performs an autopsy on a corpse. They abolished the religion and then studied its existence and development. They abolished the prayer service that the Sages had crafted and then spared no effort to uncover the names of those who had composed it. Without any belief in the Torah and the Prophets, they considered the Holy Writings as clay to be molded in their hands. The relationship between their "Science of Judaism" and the study of a living Jewish nation, that begins with the giving of the Torah to Moses and extends without interruption until the leaders of our generation, is exactly the difference between anatomy, the study of corpses, and physiology, the study of the living body. The laws that govern living organisms are entirely different from those that govern inert tissue.[10]

Though the *Kulturverein* existed for little more than four years, its influence lasted long beyond that. Its methodology provided the theoretical legitimation of both the Reform and Conservative Movements, and it cleared the way, in a seemingly scientific manner, for a conception of Judaism based on culture not religion.[11]

Rabbi Hirsch's Response

IN RABBI HIRSCH'S VIEW THE SCIENCE OF JUDAISM HAD NO LEGITImacy from an authentic Torah viewpoint. Study unrelated to action and knowledge that does not have as its goal the knowledge of G-d was for him inherently un-Jewish. But he did not content himself with pointing out the obvious deviations from traditional Orthodox belief by the practitioners of the Science of Judaism.[d] As we shall see in the next chapter, he also subjected the fruits of their research to a withering critique on their own terms, and proved it to be combined of equal parts of fantasy and fabrication.

"The flower of wisdom should be life," Rabbi Hirsch wrote in *Horeb*,[12] and therefore the goal of all Jewish study must be to provide "instruction on living."[13] He frequently quoted Rava's statement (*Berachos* 17a): "The purpose of wisdom is repentance and good deeds. . ., as it says, '*The beginning of wisdom is the fear of G-d — good understanding to all those who perform them*' (*Tehillim* 111:10). It does not say 'to those who study them,' but rather to those 'who perform them.'"[14] By this criterion, Jewish Studies which were unconnected to personal practice would have been more appropriately titled un-Jewish Studies.

Study that does not begin with the fear of G-d, wrote Rabbi Hirsch, can never result in the proper action that is the goal of all true Jewish study. It inevitably ends, rather, in the distortion and misinterpretation of the Torah:

> Particularly the wisdom of the Torah to which the term חכמה primarily refers here (*Avos* 3:11) can be properly grasped only by one who reads it as the G-d-given source of truth and duty. . . .
>
> But he whose approach to wisdom and knowledge is devoid of the fear of G-d and the fear of sin, to whom the fear of G-d and the fear of sin are only to proceed from his wisdom, he will neither gain true wisdom nor acquire the genuine fear of G-d. He will regard every word of the Torah's wisdom only as a hindrance and impediment to the imagined freedom that he has enjoyed heretofore. He will distort its content for his own purposes, changing and perverting them to suit his own view of life which is estranged from G-d — to what extent is immaterial — and finally he will discard it altogether as useless ballast and ignore it as an inconvenient intruder upon his freedom.[15]

Because the Science of Judaism aimed neither at the strengthening of Jewish life nor its practice, it produced nothing but arid scholarship devoid of consequence. Rabbi Hirsch captured the lifeless quality of the study of antiquities for their own sake in an article in 1855:

---

d. In the case of Dr. Zachariah Frankel and the Breslau Seminary, which he headed, much of Rabbi Hirsch's efforts were devoted to calling attention to these deviations because they were so widely ignored or overlooked by his contemporaries. See Chapter 22.

> We, however, if we have genuinely imbibed the spirit of modern Judaism, certainly do not fast on the day of Zion, we do not say any more סליחות or קינות. We should even be ashamed to catch a surreptitious tear in our eye or a sigh in our breast for the fallen Temple, a yearning in our heart for the home of the "bloody sacrificial cult." We have reduced all this to a myth. Our feelings have been "disinfected" by the cooling waters of real knowledge. . . .
>
> Moses and Hesiod, David and Sappho, Deborah and Tyrtaeus, Isaiah and Homer, Delphi and Jerusalem, Pythian tripod and Cherubim — sanctuary, prophets and oracles, psalms and elegy — we pack them all peacefully together in our minds in the same box, they all rest peacefully in the same grave, they all have one and the same human origin, they all have one and the same significance, human, transitory, and belonging to the past. . . .
>
> We let the old Jews fast on תשעה באב, we let them say סליחות and weep over קינות. But in return we know far better than they do in which century one of these "poets" flourished, and in what metre another composed, and who it was that nursed them when they were infants. We cherish in our hearts such reverence for this Jewish antiquity that we rummage through all the dust of libraries and collections in order to find out the date of an author's birth and death and to record correctly the inscriptions on their tombstones.[16]

'How many of the literati," he asked, "who write scientific studies about the *selichoth*, the *yotzeroth* and the *piyutim* still attend *selichoth* services themselves?"[17]

Rabbi Hirsch rejected the Science of Judaism on other grounds as well. Just as any physical science must begin with the natural world as a given, and any hypothesis that contradicts any detail of the physical world is thereby disproved, so, in his view, any true "Jewish Science" must take as a given the receipt of the Torah at Sinai in the presence of 600,000 Jews and cannot contradict any of the 613 mitzvos or any detail of the Oral Law:

> Those concepts which the Jewish "faith" offers as the basis of Judaism are facts, historical realities founded on the living, lucid experiences of a whole nation. These facts are not presented for "believing," but to serve the most vigorous and vital development of theoretical knowledge and practical action. The true science of Judaism is to perceive the world, mankind and Israel in

these terms, and true Jewish life is to translate these perceptions into living reality.[18]

THE FOUNDING OF THE JÜDISCH-THEOLOGISCHES SEMINAR IN Breslau by Dr. Zachariah Frankel in 1853 marked the beginning of the second generation of *Wissenschaft des Judentums*. The Seminary described its approach as Positive-Historical — i.e. it viewed Judaism with a critical and "historical" approach as an evolving entity but with a "positive" attitude towards tradition.

The Breslau Seminary

Rabbi Hirsch was deeply skeptical of the Seminary from the start. In a courteous public letter addressed to the founders, he asked them to clarify whether their educational principles were based on an acceptance of the Oral and Written Torah as Divinely given and the immutability of rabbinic enactments, even those grounded on *minhag*. No reply was ever forthcoming.[19]

In any event, Rabbi Hirsch's suspicions were soon confirmed. The Seminary's students learned to hold many widespread Jewish customs and *mitzvahs* in contempt. Many of the students in the Seminary ignored such basic prohibitions as those against carrying in a public thoroughfare on Shabbos in situations where the prohibition was of rabbinic origin, shaving with a razor, and drinking the milk and wine of non-Jews. In general, wives of students did not cover their hair. Many graduates of the Seminary went on for "ordination" at the Reform *Hochschule* Seminary in Berlin. In the Breslau Seminary, it was "Jewish scholarship," based on the study of the historical development of the Jewish people, rather than *halachah*, which reigned supreme.[20] Solomon Schechter, the founder of the Jewish Theological Seminary of America, could, with justice, view his institution as the continuation of the Breslau Seminary from which it took its name.[21]

Nevertheless, due to Frankel's status as a Torah scholar and the Breslau Seminary's frequent attacks on the Reform Movement, there were few in Rabbi Hirsch's day who perceived the threat posed by the Seminary as clearly as he did.[22] Thus when he launched his attacks on the two most influential educators in the Breslau Seminary — the historian Heinrich Graetz and Frankel himself — the result was a battle royal that shook the intellectual world of German Jewry.

Chapter Twenty-One

GRAETZ'S "HISTORY OF THE JEWS"

FROM 1853 TO 1876, HEINRICH GRAETZ (1817-1891) PUBLISHED his monumental *History of the Jews* in 11 volumes. The first comprehensive history of the Jewish people up to the modern era, the work has continued to exercise a profound influence on all subsequent Jewish historiography.[a] Graetz remains for secular Jewish historians the great father figure to which their work relates.

Graetz did not publish his work according to the chronological order of the periods covered, but rather began with Volume Four, covering the

a. While subsequent secular scholars have quibbled with many of the details of Graetz's work — from his dismissal of Chassidism as mere folk superstition to his lack of appreciation of the significance of *Kabbalah* in Jewish life — his views on the historical development of the Oral Law have become virtually axiomatic for subsequent secular scholars. It was to these views that Rabbi Hirsch addressed himself.

Prof. Heinrich Graetz

period from the destruction of the Second Temple to the final redaction of the Talmud. It was this volume on which Rabbi Hirsch trained his sights in a series of 12 articles published in his journal *Jeschurun* between 1855 and 1858.

In Graetz's view the great *Tannaim* were innovators — "not the *bearers* of the tradition but its *creators*."[1] Rather than interpreting the Oral Law as an objective legal code given at Sinai, Graetz portrayed it, according to Rabbi Hirsch, as the product of the "temperament, psychological makeup, hierarchic positions, and political aims" of the various *Tannaim*.[2]

Rabbi Hirsch was quick to recognize the threat to traditional observance posed by Graetz's presentation of the Oral Law as being continually adapted to new historical circumstances by successive generations of Talmudic scholars from Hillel to Rabbi Yochanan ben Zakkai to Rabbi Akiva. Graetz was not simply dealing with ancient history, wrote Rabbi Hirsch, but attempting to "explain to the contemporary reader certain historical forces still at work," which forces form "the organic basis for all development of [Jewish] religious life through the ages."[3] The polemical thrust of this portrayal of *halachah* as a body of law in a continual state of flux and development, much like English common law, was clear: If *halachah* had changed continuously over the centuries, why were amendments and adjustments in response to modern conditions any less legitimate in the present day?[b]

Master and Disciple

IT IS ONE OF HISTORY'S NICE LITTLE IRONIES THAT THE PROTAGONISTS in the great debate over the character of the Oral Law had once enjoyed a relationship of the greatest intimacy.

In 1836, Graetz, then a 19-year-old rabbinical student in Wollstein, experienced a spiritual crisis, confessing to atheistic tendencies in his diary. In desperation, he addressed a letter to the young Rabbi of Oldenburg whose *Nineteen Letters* had

b. Graetz's book was part of the general attack on the authenticity of the transmission of the Oral Torah from Sinai. *The History of the Jews* was but one of four major works published in Germany in the 1850s which sought to undermine the authority of rabbinic Judaism; The others were: Nachman Krochmal's *Moreh Nevuchei HaZeman* (1851), Abraham Geiger's *Urschrift und Uebersetzungen der Bibel* (1857) and Zachariah Frankel's *Darchei HaMishnah* (1859).

recently created such a stir in the intellectual life of German Jewry. The troubled young man expressed his desire to come and study with the one he saw as the "Ezra of our spiritual *galuth*," and whose book had enlightened him "as the sun."[4]

Rabbi Hirsch responded immediately inviting Graetz to live in his home and even offering economic assistance if he should need it. More than the calf wants to nurse, the mother wants to feed it, Rabbi Hirsch assured his young admirer, and "if you want to learn *Torah Lishmah* (Torah for its own sake), you are welcome." At the same time, he sought to disabuse him of his impression that he would find the author of *The Nineteen Letters* to be the complete person he imagined.[5] For the next three years, Graetz lived in the Hirsch home as a member of the family.

The picture Graetz paints of himself from the period he lived in the Hirsch household is not a pretty one. He makes no attempt to disguise his unbridled ambition, pettiness, and weakness of character. It is clear, however, that he was adept at concealing his true nature from his teacher and the other members of the household.[6]

The Graetz diaries are a valuable repository of information about Rabbi Hirsch's years in Oldenburg. Graetz describes how he and Rabbi Hirsch began the day at four o'clock in the morning with the study of *Gemara* and *Tehillim*. He also studied Kant with Rabbi Hirsch. On one occasion Rabbi Hirsch heard that Graetz was reading a philosophy book which contained offensive passages. Calling the author a טמא ומטמא (impure and contaminating), he advised him to read only the purely philosophical parts.[7] Together they once read *The Salon* by Heinrich Heine, a book about the history of religion and philosophy in Germany, which contained passages of apostasy and desecration of the Divine Name. Rabbi Hirsch, Graetz records, asked him: "Shouldn't one tear *kriah* when one hears such things?" Rabbi Hirsch remarked that he would like to burn the book and pay the librarian for the cost. In the end he cut out the page which contained desecration of the Divine Name.[8]

At the outset Graetz wrote of his unbounded love and admiration for Rabbi Hirsch,[c] but as time went on, he complained of his lack of progress. He confided to his diary, "I don't know what makes my heart so closed. There is no progress, no ascent on the ladder of learning. But there is advancement in my moral dissolution." By his own admission, he was incapable of deciding even a single halachic question in Rabbi Hirsch's

---

c. In 1837, Graetz suggested to the board of the Jewish community of Posen after Rabbi Akiva Eiger's passing that they choose Rabbi Hirsch as Rabbi Eiger's successor.[8*]

absence: "Not one *din* or even one *halachah* was I able to properly find, even after an intensive search."[9]

He began to express irritation in his diary at Rabbi Hirsch's "fanatical religious convictions and his narrow-minded adherence to the *Shulchan Aruch*." He complained that on his travels Rabbi Hirsch drank only black coffee,[10] that he "had few acquaintances besides his big volumes of *Poskim*," and was "more knowledgeable about the laws regarding a *machat be'ovi bais hakosos*[d] than in history."[11]

When Graetz departed from Oldenburg after three years, however, it was on cordial terms, and he dedicated his first book *Gnosticismus und Judenthum* (1846) to Rabbi Hirsch, "the spirited fighter for historic Judaism, the unforgettable teacher and fatherly friend, with sentiments of love and gratitude." When Rabbi Hirsch was Chief Rabbi of Moravia, Graetz taught in a Talmud Torah in Nikolsburg, and apparently also taught Jewish history to the students of the Nikolsburg yeshiva, which was under Rabbi Hirsch's supervision. In 1849, he was expelled from Nikolsburg by the Austrian government as a suspected revolutionary.[12]

The year after his expulsion Graetz married, and, in what can only be described as a calculated slap at Rabbi Hirsch, chose as his *mesader kiddushin* B.H. Fassel, the author of *Chorav Betzayon*, a virulent attack on Rabbi Hirsch's *Horeb*. What had changed in his feelings for Rabbi Hirsch since the dedication of *Gnosticismus und Judenthum* is not clear. Nevertheless Graetz and his bride did visit Rabbi Hirsch shortly after their marriage. Graetz's wife did not cover her hair, and when both she and her husband adamantly refused to accede to Rabbi Hirsch's demand that she do so, Graetz and Rabbi Hirsch parted company for good.[13]

Already in the early 1840s Graetz had come under the influence of Zachariah Frankel of Dresden, and it was he who initiated a circular letter praising Frankel for the latter's departure in protest from the Reform rabbinical conference in Frankfurt in 1845. In 1852, Graetz moved to Berlin and began to contribute regularly to Frankel's *Monatsschrift für Geschichte und Wissenschaft des Judentums*, of which he was the editor from 1869 to 1888. When Frankel established the *Jüdisch-Theologisches Seminar* in Breslau in 1853, Graetz was appointed as a lecturer in Bible and Jewish History. That same year, Volume Four of Graetz's *History of the Jews* — entitled *From the Destruction of the Jewish State to the Conclusion of the Talmud* — appeared. Rabbi Hirsch did not spare his former disciple in his withering critique of that work.

---

d. A needle in the stomach wall of an animal which may render it non-kosher.

THE ESSENCE OF GRAETZ'S THEORY WAS THAT THE SAGES OF THE Talmud, rather than simply committing to writing a body of law that had been passed down by word of mouth since the time of Moses, had instead created the tradition of an Oral Torah to reinforce their views on political and religious questions of their time. Graetz interpreted the history of that period in purely personal and subjective terms. Rather than examining the Sages' teachings against the background of the Written Torah and the traditions they had received, he explained their work as the product of individual psychological make-up and ulterior political motives.[14]

"The History of the Jews"

Graetz had an agenda. He hoped to demonstrate that the Talmud was shaped by the same historical forces that were active in modern times and to provide a foundation for the "positive-historical" school of thought that was to guide the Breslau Seminary.[e] If the Oral Torah was not an unbroken chain going back to Sinai, but merely a creation designed to fill a historical need that arose at a specific point in time, then it was always open to further "creativity and development" as required by historical circumstances.[15]

Critique

IN HIS CRITIQUE OF GRAETZ, RABBI HIRSCH DID NOT FOCUS ON THE latter's explicit denial of the Divine origin of the Oral Law. Instead he demonstrated how the historical material presented by Graetz to buttress that denial could not withstand critical scrutiny. "Leaving aside the religious philosophy," he wrote, "I have found [Volume Four] to be, even from a purely scientific point of view, a product of the most outrageous, irresponsible superficiality."[16] In order to justify his opinions, Rabbi Hirsch wrote, Graetz was forced "to close his eyes to obvious truths, distort facts, invent motives and, led by delusion, give a cavalier, superficial and untruthful treatment to the documentary sources."[17]

Rabbi Hirsch dissected Graetz's arguments point by point, in the process demonstrating that his conclusions were the result of mangling — sometimes deliberately, sometimes inadvertently — the sources, ignoring evidence inconvenient for his thesis, wild extrapolations from a single piece of evidence, and a host of logical fallacies — in short, "more fiction than fact."[18]

Graetz's volume began with Rabbi Yochanan ben Zakkai, whom he viewed as having created a "new center" for Judaism in the wake of the

e. While sharing with Reform the theory of a "developing" Jewish Law, the Breslau Seminary intended to "develop" the Law in a positive way, in contrast to the work of modern Reform which was viewed as essentially destructive.

loss of its spiritual center with the destruction of the Temple. Thus Graetz wrote, "R. Yochanan thus detached the Synhedrial functions from the site of the Temple and transferred them to Yavneh; it was as if he had removed the soul of the Temple from one body and infused it into another."[19] Rabbi Hirsch's refutation of this picture will serve as a good indication of his method in the 12 lengthy articles he devoted to Volume Four of Graetz's history.

Typically, Graetz began with a personality portrait of Rabbi Yochanan. Rabbi Yochanan, he argued, was blessed with a peaceable disposition, and that is why he had counseled surrender to the Roman army surrounding Jerusalem. Graetz's sole proof for Rabbi Yochanan's peaceable disposition was a statement that iron tools, which are weapons of war, were not used in the building of the altar in the Temple, which is the symbol of peace and atonement.

On a polemical level, Graetz sought, by focusing on the individual personalities of the *Tannaim*, to portray the *halachah* as an outgrowth of their individual predilections. But even ignoring the polemical point, Rabbi Hirsch proved that these personality portraits were untenable on historical grounds. In a letter to a friend written shortly after the publication of Volume Four, he ridiculed Graetz's entirely methodology.

> "Look," he says, "this one was always laughing; that one had an evil temper; this one was forever playing games; that one was always deep in thought." Even worse, he passes off these products of his imagination not only as authentic character sketches of his subjects but as prototypes of all their contemporaries; thus, "during this period, people were laughing all the time; during this other period, they tended to be depressed; this era was one of arrogance; that era was an age of anxiety and timidity. . . ."
>
> Say, further, that this artist clings to his fancies as if they were absolute truth, so much so that wherever he needs a historical reference to authenticate his portrait he feels free to invent a reference to suit the portrait. Consider all these caprices of artistic fancy, and you have the *History of the Jews* by Dr. H. Graetz.[20]

"What does our author know about the 'disposition' of R. Yochanan ben Zakkai? What *can* he know about it?" Rabbi Hirsch wondered. A single statement culled from among hundreds quoted in the Talmud and other rabbinic literature, he noted, is a slim reed indeed upon which to hang an entire personality portrait. Even more telling, the statement itself proves nothing about R. Yochanan's personality, for there has never been a sage in Israel who did not praise the value of peace. Indeed, it was R. Eliezer the Great, whom Graetz characterized as rigid and unyielding, who said, "Great is peace, for all the prophets came only to plant the value of peace in the mouths of His creatures" (*Yalkut Tehillim* 29).[21]

Also typical of Graetz, R. Yochanan ben Zakkai is described as possessing liberal and progressive views, which enabled him to undertake the restructuring of Judaism. Thus he was able to engineer the transfer of authority to Yavneh because he, unlike his despairing disciples, "perceived that the essence of Judaism was not indissolubly bound up with the Temple and the altar, and hence did not have to perish with them."[22] Once again, Rabbi Hirsch proved that Graetz's picture was based on the wildest of extrapolations. The only statement cited to prove that R. Yochanan's disciples were in despair was a statement of R. Yehoshua upon passing the place of the Temple: "Woe unto us for this Temple that lies in ruins, the place where atonement was effected for Israel's sins" *(Avos DeRabbi Nosson)*. And yet it was this same R. Yehoshua who opposed as excessive mourning the practice adopted by many after the destruction of the Temple of not eating meat or drinking wine.

Nor had R. Yehoshua or anyone else, argued Rabbi Hirsch, ever viewed the sacrifices as "the essence of Judaism." In *Pirkei Avos,* which is from the period of the Second Temple, there is scarcely any mention of sacrifices. Indeed in all of the literature dating from the period of the First and Second Temples there is not so much as "one verse or even one word that would accord to the sacrifices a pre-eminent role."[f,23] In sum, the

f. Graetz's whole construct was also beset by logical weaknesses. If Rabbi Yochanan had such a liberal view of the importance of the sacrifices, and therefore was not so distraught over the destruction of the Temple, Rabbi Hirsch asked, why did he have to create a "new center" for Judaism in the wake of the destruction at all? (*Collected Writings* V, p. 13.)

Graetz's main thesis that R. Yochanan ben Zakkai was a radical innovator who had transferred the locus of authority from the Temple to the Sanhedrin in Yavneh, in contravention of the prevailing view that the Sanhedrin would lose its legislative and judicial role outside the Temple, (ibid., p. 14) was, Rabbi Hirsch proved, nonsense. For one thing, there was no such prevailing view. Already 40 years before the destruction of the Temple the Sanhedrin had moved from its seat adjacent to the Temple without the attendant loss of any powers other than the imposition of the death penalty. And the power of judicial execution did not return in Yavneh (ibid., pp. 16-17). It was even quite likely that there was already a Sanhedrin in Yavneh prior to the destruction of the Temple, as indicated by R. Yochanan ben Zakkai's famous request to Titus, the conqueror of Jerusalem: "Give me Yavneh and its Sages"(ibid., p. 16). Graetz professed surprise that R. Yochanan's "radical" step of transferring the powers of the Sanhedrin to Yavneh did not arouse more opposition. If one assumed, however, that there was nothing innovative about this step, Rabbi Hirsch pointed out, then the lack of opposition was easily explained.

whole theory of a Judaism in need of radical reconstruction after the destruction of the Temple was a house of cards.[g,24]

BOTH THE WRITTEN AND THE ORAL TORAH WERE GIVEN AT SINAI. Whereas the Written Law consists of general laws and principles, the Oral

The Hermeneutic Rules

Law contains detailed rules necessary to understand the Written Torah. Rabbi Hirsch described the relationship between the Oral and Written Torah as comparable to that between a lecture and a listener's notes. Those who did not hear the lecture (in this case the Oral Law) will have difficulty understanding the notes (the Written Torah), or comprehending how a short notation is really a succinct summation of a much larger and broader picture.[25]

An integral part of the Oral Torah given at Sinai were the *midos sheHaTorah nidreshes bahem,* the hermeneutic rules which are to be employed in interpreting the Written Torah.[h] Through these rules the Oral Torah can be derived from the Written Torah. If these rules were to be thoroughly applied to the Written Torah, the result would be most of the Oral Torah we possess. The hermeneutic rules serve several purposes: First, they protected the Oral Torah, which was not committed to writing for several thousand years, from being forgotten. Second, they ensured a consistency and unity between the Written and Oral Torahs. Furthermore, these principles provided a means to examine and to restore the full scope of the tradition, when parts of it lost some of their clarity under the pressures of exile.[26]

Torah Judaism as we know it rests on the postulate that the *Tannaim* and *Amoraim* changed nothing of the essence of *Torah miSinai,* which included both the Written and Oral Torah. Rabbi Hirsch quoted the *Ramban* to the effect that a denial of the Divine origin of the hermeneutical rules "would destroy the very roots of the tradition that has come down to us through the 13 rules of interpretation, and the major part of the Talmud of which they form the foundation."[27]

The starting point for all reform in Judaism is the assertion that the hermeneutic rules are a rabbinic invention and are not of Divine origin.[28]

---

g. An examination of the nine ordinances R. Yochanan ben Zakkai instituted after the destruction reveals that they all deal only with secondary aspects of the observance of specific laws, a fact that testifies to the "admirable composure and unshaken mental lucidity of those who lived through that unprecedented catastrophe" and "to the basic stability of Jewish religious life, which remained constant even amidst upheavals that amounted to virtual political annihilation."[24*]

h. In addition there are *halachos* which cannot be derived from the Written Torah, called *halachah leMoshe miSinai,* that were given to Moshe at Sinai.

One of Graetz's most crucial assertions, therefore, was that the hermeneutical rules were not given at Sinai but were a much later invention of Hillel's. These rules, in his view, were formulated by later authorities so that they could make new laws to deal with cases not heretofore anticipated. Thus, he wrote, "The seven rules first laid down by Hillel were opposed by Shammai and his school."[29]

Rabbi Hirsch proceeded to demonstrate that Graetz's evidence for the late introduction of the hermenuetical rules was based on falsification and distortion of the evidence. Graetz's primary piece of evidence for the claim that Hillel had introduced the hermeneutical rules for the first time was the *Gemara* (*Pesachim* 66a) where Hillel and the Elders of Bathrya debated whether the Pesach sacrifice could be brought on Shabbos or not. Hillel brought a series of proofs based on his seven hermeneutical principles, and these proofs were each rejected by the Elders of Bathrya, according to Graetz because they had never before heard of these principles. That conclusion, however, Rabbi Hirsch showed, could only be maintained by deliberately excising from the passage quoted the actual response of the Elders of Bathrya. Far from rejecting Hillel's rules out of hand, they raised the same sort of objection to their application in the case at hand that are raised throughout the *Gemara* to the application of these rules in a particular case. Thus, far from showing their out of hand rejection of rules with which they were unfamiliar, the *Gemara* conclusively demonstrates that the Elders of Bathrya not only were familiar with Hillel's rules but accepted them: Their only objection concerned the specific application of the rules to the case at hand.[30]

Graetz also maintained that the debates between Hillel and Shammai and their followers had revolved around the validity of Hillel's hermeneutical principles, with the conservative, Shammaite faction rejecting the use of this powerful new tool in favor of a more literal reading of the Scriptural verses. Typically, he portrayed the ultimate victory of the opinions of Bais Hillel as a triumph of "intelligence over simple-mindedness, of life over inertia, of the human over the Divine," and of the moderate over the rigid.[31]

Rabbi Hirsch made mincemeat of this theory as well. For if it were true, how could Graetz explain that Hillel and Shammai themselves only disagreed over three matters, and only one of these concerned the interpretation of a Scriptural verse? Moreover, in tractate *Kiddushin,* Shammai himself employed three of Hillel's hermeneutical rules. Showing his awesome command of the entirety of the Talmud, Rabbi Hirsch noted that of the approximately 280 disputes between Bais Hillel and Bais Shammai, only 40, at the most, concern the interpretation of a Scriptural verse, and in only one of these cases (according to one *Rishon)* does Bais Shammai reject the use of one of Hillel's hermeneutical rules.[i]

Graetz never responded to or defended himself from Rabbi Hirsch's withering criticism. His only public reaction of any kind was an oblique reference in the preface to Volume Five of his *History of the Jews* to "a heresy-hunting hermit" who had condemned his historical research.[32] The powerful refutation of his theories on the Oral Law was never answered.

For his part, Rabbi Hirsch viewed the fact that Graetz taught in Breslau as sufficient cause to shun the institution. In a letter to Frankfurt resident Raphael Kircheim, Rabbi Hirsch wrote:

> If Graetz's works are the spirit in which they teach in Breslau, then we grieve for our youth who study there, for the community which will take them as rabbis and teachers, and grieve for the generations which will emerge from there. We would shout from the rooftops, "Parents, don't send your children there. Better they should be tailors or cobblers. Then they could only ruin a suit or a pair of boots and not the communities and souls. They say from there will Torah go out *to* Israel. True, from these the Torah will go out *of* Israel" (emphasis added).[33]

i. Throughout his rebuttal of Graetz, Rabbi Hirsch displayed an encyclopedic command of both the Babylonian and Jerusalem Talmuds, as well as the rest of the rabbinic literature. Thus when Graetz attempted to argue that the formality with which Hillel introduced his rules to the Elders of Bathrya — דרש הלל לפני בני בתירה — suggested that totally new principles were being introduced, Rabbi Hirsch was able to show that the words דרש לפני appear in only one other place in the Talmud, and there too it is in a situation in which someone in a subordinate position is addressing those over whom he is about to be elevated.

Elsewhere, Rabbi Hirsch cited 60 proofs that Rabbi Eliezer ben Horkenos made use of Rabbi Yishmael's 13 hermeneutical principles, a point about which Graetz expressed doubts. He also noted that Rabbi Akiva is mentioned in the Talmud approximately 600 times, in 40 of which he based his interpretations on the Biblical words אך ("but") or רק ("only"), but only once on the word את — his well-known exegesis of the phrase את ה' אלקיך תירא — לרבות תלמידי חכמים. Yet from this one instance Graetz attempted to prove that Rabbi Akiva intended to introduce a new principle of interpretation.[31*]

Chapter Twenty-Two

ZACHARIAH FRANKEL'S "DARCHEI HAMISHNAH"

A YEAR AFTER RABBI HIRSCH FINISHED HIS 12-PART CRITIQUE of Graetz's *History of the Jews,* he felt compelled to respond to another work undermining the Sinaic origins of the Oral Law. The work was *Darchei HaMishnah (The Ways of the Mishnah: A Methodological Approach to the Study of Mishnah),* and the author was the head of the Breslau Seminary, Dr. Zachariah Frankel. In that work, Frankel sought to determine the chronology of the compilation of the various *mishnayoth* and speculated as to the circumstances giving rise to the halachic material in the various *mishnayoth.*

Though in retrospect, Frankel's role as the precursor of the present-day Conservative Movement is indisputable — indeed Conservative spokesmen have consistently portrayed themselves as his spiritual and scholarly heirs[1] — his departure from Orthodoxy was not clear to many in his own time. Rabbi Hirsch stood almost alone in the controversy with Frankel, and the latter drew support from many with seemingly impeccable Orthodox credentials. These facts alone ensured that the controversy over Frankel's *Darchei HaMishnah* would be one of the most bitter of Rabbi Hirsch's life.

Dr. Zachariah Frankel

The Young Frankel

ZACHARIAH FRANKEL WAS BORN IN PRAGUE IN 1801, AND AS A young man studied under Rabbi Bezalel Ranschburg, a close disciple of Rabbi Yechezkel Landau and the author of glosses on the Talmud bearing his name. In 1836, Frankel was appointed Chief Rabbi of Dresden.

Soon after that appointment, he gave the first signs of the deviations from traditional Judaism that would mark his subsequent career. In 1835, Rabbi Moshe Sofer (the *Chasam Sofer*) of Pressburg issued a ruling concurring with the decision of Rabbi Elazar Horovitz of Vienna, prohibiting one Yonasan Alexandersohn from serving as Rabbi of Csaba, Hungary. Alexandersohn subsequently traveled from place to place proclaiming his righteousness, and as a result, the *Chasam Sofer* was inundated with correspondence seeking a rescission of his ruling.[2] Alexandersohn himself wrote a book enumerating his grievances against the *Chasam Sofer,* and the liberal Jewish press took up his cause with a vengeance. At that point, Frankel entered the fray with a sharply worded "open letter" to the *Chasam Sofer,* which the latter received a month before his passing in 1839. Even after the *Chasam Sofer's* death, Frankel went ahead and published his "open letter" in the *Orient* and the *Allgemeine Zeitung des Judentums.* So impudent was Frankel's tone that even the liberal *Allgemeine Zeitung des Judentums* published articles denouncing him. Frankel responded that he had written his letter prior to the *Chasam Sofer's* passing and had felt impelled to stand at the side of the "persecuted."[3]

By this time, Frankel had already begun to work out his theory of the "developmental history of *halachah*,"[4] which would subsequently become the mainstay of the instruction at the Breslau Seminary. Among his theories was that much *halachah* had originated in the folk customs of the people. Thus in his first book, *Preliminary Studies on the Septuagint* (1841), he wrote in the preface: "Many laws may have evolved into a [religious] norm without official sanction from a higher authority, but developed from ordinary, everyday life, from practices which folk piety had elevated to the status of guidelines and once they had taken such roots, they attained binding force." Even many *halachos* for which the Talmud gives a Scriptural basis were in his eyes responses to circumstances long after the giving of the Torah at Sinai: "Many other laws which evolved only in response to contemporary needs were incorporated into Scripture" (p. 180). Similarly, in *On the Influence of the Palestinian Exegesis on Alexandrine Hermeneutics* (1851), Frankel described much of the legal material pertaining to the priesthood and sacrifices as "not so much [the] result of deliberate speculation but as rules evolving from custom and eventually elevated to the status of law, and therefore obviously of great antiquity" (p. 133).[a]

Consonant with his theory that much *halachah* originated in folk custom, Frankel argued that throughout history the Jewish people, the *Volk*, have been the ultimate arbiters of what is holy and that if they no longer view some practice or ritual as sacred, it thereby loses that status. Thus he announced that if Jews ceased to regard the covering of one's head or prayer in Hebrew as "holy," he would abide by that decision.[b]

Nor did Frankel confine himself to the realm of theory. In 1842, when Chacham Bernays reissued the earlier ban against the prayer book of the Reform Temple in Hamburg, Frankel published an article sharply criticizing Chacham Bernays and arguing that the prayer book was halachically valid, though deficient from the standpoint of *Wissenschaft*. He was undeterred by the fact that the earlier ban had been supported by 17 of the leading rabbis of the previous generation, including Rabbi Akiva Eiger and the *Chasam Sofer*.

In Dresden in 1834, he himself began introducing various changes into the prayers. He deleted parts of the *brachah* of *velamalshimin* in *Shemoneh Esrei* because he found them offensive and intolerant of sinners. In their place, he substituted formulations of his own. He also omitted several

---

a. These quotations were included by Rabbi Hirsch in his article "Supplementary Notes to *Darchei HaMishnah*" to demonstrate that Frankel, "unlike Yochanan *Kohen Gadol* who had served for 80 years and only became a Sadducee at the end of his life," had already denied the Divine origin of the Oral Torah for 20 years prior to the publication of *Darchei HaMishnah*.[4*]

b. Such decisions, Frankel argued, could be compared to Rabbi Yehudah Nesiah's lifting of the ban on the consumption of oil of a non-Jew, due to its lack of popular acceptance (*Avodah Zarah* 37a).[5*]

verses of the *Vehu Rachum* that is recited on Mondays and Thursdays that he found objectionable.[5] At one point, he even considered doing away with the second day of *Yom Tov*, if that were demanded by the broader Jewish public.[6]

In an 1844 article, "About Reforms in Judaism," Frankel criticized Orthodoxy for being insufficiently responsive to the popular will, and accused the Orthodox of being unwilling, in their "pious egoism," to sacrifice even part of its traditions in order to transmit Judaism "to our children and grandchildren."[7] Though willing to countenance various reforms, and even to initiate them himself, Frankel nevertheless distinguished his position from that of Reform leaders. He wanted changes in Jewish practice to develop organically from the tradition and without changing the "essence" of Judaism, unlike the Reformers to whom nothing was sacrosanct. Such slow, deliberate changes had, in any event, been taking place throughout Jewish history, Frankel argued. Thus he preferred the term "historical Judaism" to Orthodox or *gesetzestreue* (loyal to religious law).[c,8]

Because of his opposition to wholesale reform, Frankel did not attend the first major Reform conference, organized by Abraham Geiger and Ludwig Philippson, at Braunschweig in 1844. But he was present in Frankfurt the next year for the second such conference hosted by Leopold Stein, the Reform rabbi of Frankfurt, who had usurped the position of the venerable Rabbi Zalman Trier. Eventually Frankel walked out of the conference — to massive approbation in the Orthodox press — over proposals to abandon Hebrew entirely as the language of prayer.[9] It was a sign of how embattled Orthodoxy felt itself that Frankel received such bouquets for his departure, without hard questions being asked about what he was doing at the conference in the first place.[10]

Rabbi Hirsch, for one, was not deceived. It was the view implicit in all Frankel's work that the Oral Law was not given simultaneously with the Written Law at Sinai that prompted Rabbi Hirsch to demand from him a statement of principles on this matter in 1854 shortly after the establishment of the Breslau Seminary.[11]

Darchei HaMishnah

IN 1859, FRANKEL PUBLISHED HIS BOOK ON THE ORIGINS OF THE *Mishnah* entitled *Darchei HaMishnah*. Frankel was far more circumspect about his departures from normative Judaism than his colleague Graetz, who was more or less open about his view that the Oral Law was not of Divine origin. Yet

c. *Gesetzestreue* was a favorite term of Rabbi Hirsch's.

Rabbi Hirsch was convinced, after reading *Darchei HaMishnah*, that Frankel shared with Graetz the view that the Sages did not transmit a received tradition, but rather created the Oral Torah, using the hermeneutic principles which they themselves invented, and that the laws characterized as *halachah leMoshe miSinai* (the *halachoth* that were given to Moses at Sinai) did not actually date back to Sinai but were simply of "great antiquity."[12]

With Graetz, Rabbi Hirsch's principal thrust had been to demonstrate the former's portraits of the *Tannaim* were based on misreadings and distortions of the evidence he cited, refuted by other evidence that he ignored, and based on unsupported conjecture. With Frankel, however, the first task was to demonstrate clearly Frankel's denial of the Sinaic origin of the Oral Law. Rabbi Hirsch subjected Frankel's views to the greatest possible scrutiny in order to make known to the broader public that the Breslau Seminary could in no way be termed an Orthodox rabbinical seminary.

The controversy began with the publication in Rabbi Hirsch's journal *Jeschurun* in December 1860 of the first of a critical three-part review of Frankel's book by Rabbi Yedidya Gottlieb Fischer,[d] together with a piece entitled "Supplementary Notes on *Darchei HaMishnah*" by Rabbi Hirsch himself. Though the principal thrust of the articles in *Jeschurun* was to force Frankel once and for all to state unequivocally his position on the origin of the Divine Law, Rabbi Hirsch did wonder at the profundity of scholarship that sought to prove that the laws contained in the *mishnayoth* of *Seder Zeraim* must date back at least to the time of the First Temple, since they are only applicable in *Eretz Yisrael*, and that the categories of *melachah* (forbidden work) on Shabbos must similarly date at least to the prophet Yirmiyahu, who mentions the prohibition on carrying from a private to a public domain. With respect to the first point, Rabbi Hirsch remarked, "Had [the students of the Breslau Rabbinical Seminary] not found this out [i.e., the ancient derivation of the agricultural laws], they might have assumed that these laws had been instituted only after the exile or perhaps not until the days of their own master in the year 1859."[13] Nor did he refrain from pointing out that Frankel's need to adduce such proofs for the antiquity of various parts of the Oral Law could only be explained by his denial of their Sinaic origin.

---

d. Rabbi Fischer was a native of Stuhlweissenburg, where Rabbi Hirsch's oldest son-in-law, Rabbi Joseph Guggenheimer, was the rabbi. Rabbi Ezriel Hildesheimer described him as a man "respected and revered in all of Hungary, with a personality the likes of which I have rarely seen. He is a businessman who has made many sacrifices both in blood and money for the sake of our Holy Torah. He is of clean hands and pure of heart, loyal to Hashem and His Torah. There are few like him."[12*]

As he had with Graetz, Rabbi Hirsch mocked Frankel's wildly conjectural explanations for seemingly straightforward statements of the Sages of the *Gemara.* Thus, Frankel explained that the Men of the Great Assembly enjoined *batei dinim* to be "circumspect in judgment" to prevent Jews from resorting to the courts of the ruling Persian authorities and thereby risking greater Persian involvement in the internal affairs of the Jewish community. Rabbi Hirsch wondered at the need for such a convoluted explanation when "correct verdicts in accordance with the Law is the first and most essential requirement for the management of personal and communal life according to the standards set by the Law of G-d."[14] Similarly, Frankel admitted that he could not explain how the Sages had derived many of the laws they did from Biblical verses — a problem only on the assumption the Oral Law was not given simultaneously — and was left with no other explanation than that they read the Bible in a spirit of "high exaltation" unknown to modern man.[15]

A Stormy Response

WHILE FRANKEL MAINTAINED A POSITION ABOVE THE FRAY WITH respect to the accusations hurled at his work in *Jeschurun,* his students and friends eagerly took cudgels in hand to set upon Rabbi Hirsch. The periodical press of the day was kept busy for a period of months reporting on the melee into which the learned world of the day was plunged by the publication of Rabbi Fischer's and Rabbi Hirsch's articles. So virulent and personal were the attacks on Rabbi Hirsch that he broke his lifelong habit of never referring to himself in print. "Our whole past has been flung at our feet like a mangled, bloody corpse, dragged through the mud by a vulgar mob. . . . [C]alumnies . . . have been flung out into the world regarding my moral, personal, and public character, and the morality of my domestic and public life," he complained bitterly in "A Provisional Statement of Accounts." He felt compelled by the personal nature of the accusations leveled against him to declare in print "before heaven and earth . . . that all the accusations hurled at me are shameful, impudent lies and fabrications."[16]

Standing almost alone in his opposition to Frankel,[e] Rabbi Hirsch did

---

e. One of the only German rabbis to join Rabbi Hirsch in publicly criticizing Frankel's book was Rabbi Zvi Binyamin Auerbach (1808-1872) of Halberstadt, who had been a fellow student of Rabbi Hirsch's in the yeshiva of Rabbi Yaakov Ettlinger. Also supporting Rabbi Hirsch was Rabbi Shlomo Wolf Klein of France, in his *Mipnei Koshet* (1861).

Rabbi Ezriel Hildesheimer who was still Rabbi of Eisentadt, Hungary at the time, did not participate in the controversy. But he fully shared Rabbi Hirsch's criticisms of the Breslau Seminary. "I know for a fact," he wrote of Frankel, "that he is entirely unconcerned with the religious beliefs of the students of the Seminary. This interests him not at all. . . For some time now

not allow himself to be deterred by the character assassination to which he was subjected. The gutter level of their accusations only served to prove the weakness of their cause, he told his accusers:

> Any cause which does not flinch from utilizing such outrageous, shameless means, and whose defenders feel they can save themselves only by taking refuge in a pool of filth and vulgarity to which no decent man will follow them, is null and void before Almighty G-d. . . . You may be able to kill this particular Hirsch and thousands of other such Hirsches — but if his words are truth, they will win the day no matter what you do. You may be able to destroy the man, but you can never destroy truth.[17]

Some of Frankel's most fervent defenders were drawn from the Jewish community of his native Prague. Chief Rabbi Shlomo Yehudah (*Shir*) Rapoport (1790-1867) and the head of the Jewish community circulated a petition defending Frankel. One of the few who refused to sign was Dayan Shmuel Freund. In his opinion, Frankel's "Methodological Introduction" made clear "that in [Frankel's] view all the Torah [laws] contained in the *Mishnah* . . . were not handed down from Mount Sinai. Rather, many of them originated from the Sages, known as *Sofrim*, who constituted the *Anshei Knesses HaGedolah*, others originated from their direct successors, and still others only from the later *Tannaim*." For good measure, Dayan Freund noted that Frankel's silence in the face of the accusations leveled at him should be interpreted as an admission on his part.

Nevertheless, Dayan Freund saw fit in an "open letter" addressed to Rabbi Hirsch to accuse him of having created a *chilul Hashem* and of having acted irrationally. Rabbi Hirsch's only reply was to note that in light of Dayan Freund's own view of Frankel's conclusions "we . . . will not find it difficult to answer that question of whether, under such circumstances, it is speech or silence that should justly be characterized as *chilul Hashem*."[18]

One who appeared to share none of Dayan Freund's reservations was Chief Rabbi Rapoport. A Talmudic scholar of no small stature, with a particular affinity for and expertise in Jewish history, he was the son-in-law

---

I consider it to my credit that I restrain young men from going to study in Breslau. There they can only become hypocrites and worse. . . . Graetz, yes, Graetz! teaches there a class in *Gemara*. What a mockery under the guise of Judaism. It is an unprecedented disgrace, and whoever sees this must suppress his inner anguish. I see with my own eyes how youth are led there to the slaughter, one after another and are reduced to a level lower than the wicked ones of Israel. They are made into hypocrites, Jesuits, and heretics just like Graetz, who, as I know from a reliable source, sways with his four species on *Succoth* like some Chassidic Rebbe."[16*]

Rabbi Shlomo Yehudah Rapoport

of Rabbi Aryeh Heller, author of the classics *Ketzos HaChoshen* and *Avnei Miluim*.[f] The Galician-born Rapoport had a traditional yeshiva education and looked for all the world like a typical Eastern European *talmid chacham*. He was attracted to *haskalah* by Nachman Krochmal's *Guide to the Perplexed of Our Time*, and became a contributor to Abraham Geiger's journal *Wissenschatfliche Zeitschrift* and Frankel's *Zeitschrift für die Religiösen Interessen des Judentums*. His appointment to the Chief Rabbinate of Prague was intended to be a compromise between the *maskilim* and the traditionalists, and as is usually the case in such appointments he wound up satisfying neither side.[19]

Rabbi Rapoport devoted his entire *Shabbos HaGadol drashah* before Pesach of 1861 to attacking Rabbi Hirsch and defending Frankel. He announced that he was going to destroy Rabbi Hirsch's arguments, and he subsequently published a 35-page pamphlet entitled *Divrei Shalom V'Emes* to defend Frankel from his accusers. He calls Frankel "Rosh Yeshiva!" in Breslau, and asserts that he needed no prompting or request to come to the defense of Frankel, who, he says, is well known in his home town of Prague. Towards the end of his 35-page epistle, Rapoport did ask Frankel to state clearly for the record that he did indeed believe that the entire Oral Torah, *"perushei hamitzvoth"* and *halachoth leMoshe miSinai* were of Divine origin and handed down at Sinai.

Rabbi Hirsch wasted little time responding to Rabbi Rapoport's arguments. In an article in *Jeschurun* that appeared only days after he had received this pamphlet,[20] he demonstrated that Rapoport's exposition related entirely to peripheral points, while totally ignoring his most important charge: that Frankel refused to admit that the Oral Torah and the Thirteen Principles had originated at Mount Sinai. He characterized Rapoport's booklet as containing "97 pieces of foolishness, but not one single argument that would save his friend or refute our criticism." In the

f. Rabbi Rapoport was the publisher of the latter work, and some of his comments are included in the index.

main, Rabbi Rapoport confined himself to faultfinding concerning Rabbi Hirsch's scholarship — noting that he had once confused ר' חייא בר אבא with ר' חייא בן אבא — and speculations about whether ר' אבא בן אחא בר ממל, cited by Rabbi Hirsch, should have been instead ר' אבא ממל. Rabbi Hirsch noted only that he admired, but did not envy, the Olympian detachment of "this genial old gentleman [who] just sits there carving his wooden trinkets" while the Gauls are laying siege to Rome.[21]

Rabbi Hirsch felt the necessity of responding to only one point raised by Rabbi Rapoport — the latter's criticism of him for having aired the dispute in the German vernacular rather than in Hebrew, the traditional language of Jewish scholarship. "In your eyes," Rabbi Hirsch replied, "the most lamentable fact is not that there are rabbis who deny the Divine origin of the Oral Law. . . , [but] that this fact was made public by me."[22] Rabbi Hirsch noted that the *Gemara* itself was written in the Aramaic vernacular of the time and that the giants of the Spanish-Arabic era wrote most of their works in Arabic to give them the widest possible circulation.[23]

"[I]n every matter of public concern, particularly when it is a question of finding the cure for a frailty affecting an entire community," wrote Rabbi Hirsch, "the first and most important step toward a cure is to bring the problem to the attention of the largest audience possible."[24] The issue at hand was not some sterile academic debate but one of crucial importance to all Jews of Germany, laymen and scholars alike. As such, Rabbi Hirsch argued, it was his duty to bring the facts to the widest possible audience:

> We want to make certain that if some day a teacher or rabbi who graduated from that Seminary is considered for appointment as a teacher or rabbi for his community, even the lowliest beggar in Israel will know the sort of Judaism for which this Seminary is training teachers and rabbis. He will then be in a position to decide for himself whether that sort of Judaism is indeed his own Judaism and can then make his decision and act with open eyes in keeping with what G-d and his conscience bid him to do. And if he does not accept that sort of Judaism as his own and as part of Judaism eternal, he should be in possession of evidence which he can cite in behalf of his stand.[25]

Rapoport came to Frankel's defense convinced that the latter did in fact accept the Divine origin of the Oral Law. He clearly expected that Frankel would come forth with an unambiguous declaration to that effect, which would justify the effort and prestige that he, Rapoport, had invested in defending this "favorite son" of Prague. But, to Rapoport's chagrin, Frankel refused to deliver the goods and the dogmatic profession which Rapoport said would be forthcoming never came. Frankel never answered the charges leveled against him, and never unequivocally affirmed the Divine source of *halachah leMoshe miSinai*. He rather let the battle be joined by his friends and students, and deigned only to issue an equivocating statement that it was "far from [his] intention to undermine tradition, to detract from it or to weaken its foundation," and that what he had set out to prove was "the profound scientific content of the Oral Law." It had not been his purpose, he continued, to discuss matters of "dogma," and it sufficed if his research furnished proof that "the *halachah* was of great antiquity."[26] That was exactly the point. Frankel had substituted antiquity for Divinity. Rabbi Ezriel Hildesheimer put it precisely when he wrote that Frankel did not answer because he had no answer.[27]

Rabbi Hirsch rejected in toto Frankel's characterization of his work. Far from showing the profound scholarly content of the *Mishnah*, said Rabbi Hirsch, one can read "his entire work without having made the slightest progress towards gaining even a simple . . . understanding of the content of as much as one *mishnah*." Moreover, demonstrating the antiquity of *mishnayoth*, without conceding their Sinaic origin, Rabbi Hirsch pointed out, was a pointless exercise since in matters of pure speculation the rules of Jewish scholarship provide that the more recent opinion prevails.[28]

Truth and Dogma

MOST IMPORTANTLY, RABBI HIRSCH REJECTED OUT OF HAND Frankel's distinction between "dogma" and "scientific knowledge." There are not two separate realms — scientific truth and religious dogma, each true in its own sphere. To argue that traditional belief could somehow be preserved even while refuted by science was to make a mockery of that belief:

> Frankel makes a distinction between dogma and scholarship and by making this distinction he deals the deathblow to that which he calls dogma. There can be only one truth. That which is true by the standards of dogma must be true also according to the standards of scholarship, and, conversely, that which scholarship has exposed as falsehood and delusion cannot be resurrected by dogma as truth. If the results of scholarly research have convinced me that the *halachah* is the comparatively recent creation of the human mind, then no dogma can make me revere *halachah*

as an ancient Divinely uttered dictate and allow it to rule every aspect of my life.

. . . Jewish thought knows of no such distinction between faith and science which assigns faith to the heavenly spheres and science to the earth. The "dogmatic" element is not held in one's vest pocket ready for presentation to the celestial gatekeeper, if necessary, as a ticket to heaven, while "science," which shapes the intellect of man and is planted on another sort of soil, is nurtured from wellsprings of quite a different source. Jewish "dogma" does not teach mysteries which logic cannot follow, which have no common language with reason and to which reason cannot address itself.

Those concepts which the Jewish "faith" offers as the basis of Judaism are facts, historical realities founded on the living, lucid experiences of a whole nation. These facts are not presented for "believing" but to serve the most vigorous and vital development of theoretical knowledge and practical action. The true science of Judaism is to perceive the world, mankind and Israel in these terms, and true Jewish life is to translate these perceptions into living reality.[29]

When Dr. Landau, Frankel's successor as Rabbi of Dresden, attempted to explain that Frankel had not seen the need to affirm the Divine source of the Oral Law because he was not writing a catechism for children, Rabbi Hirsch asked pointedly, "Does this give him the right to keep silent about the Divine origin of the Oral Tradition, at a time when not only the Divine origin of the tradition but the Divine origin of the Torah itself is questioned?"[30] Indeed the fact that Frankel was writing a text for men who would someday be called upon to be "the upholders [and] champions of traditional Judaism" should have made a clear statement by him on the Divine origin of the Oral Torah a matter of the greatest urgency.[31]

Frankel headed the Breslau Seminary for the first two decades of its existence. By 1879, four years after his death, the Seminary had placed 120 teachers, preachers and rabbis in various communities. It graduated 300 students in the first 40 years of its existence.[32] Although at no time was it a very large school, yet the damage it and its graduates managed to inflict on the observance of authentic Judaism was immense. Rabbi Ezriel Hildesheimer wrote that there was little difference in principle between "these Reformers [of the Jüdisch-Theologisches Seminar] who do their

Jüdisch-Theologisches Seminar, Breslau

work with silk gloves and the Reformer Geiger who strikes with a sledgehammer."[33]

RABBI HIRSCH HARBORED DEEP SUSPICIONS OF THE *WISSENSCHAFT* methodology even in the hands of those of impeccably Orthodox credentials. These apprehensions came to the fore with the founding of the Berlin *Rabbiner-Seminar* by Rabbi Ezriel Hildesheimer in 1873.[g] Rabbi Hirsch privately expressed his fears that the sanction of spurious *Wissenschaft* methods by an Orthodox institution would in the long run have an even more devastating effect than the Breslau Seminary.[34]

Orthodox Wissenschaft

Despite the great respect which Rabbi Hirsch had for Rabbi Hildesheimer, and the latter's unequivocal opposition to the Breslau Seminary, Rabbi Hirsch's son Isaac challenged the *Rabbiner-Seminar*, in an article published in Rabbi Hildesheimer's own *Jüdische Presse*, to provide an explicit clarification of the lines of demarcation between it and Breslau. No such declaration was ever forthcoming, and the irritation of those close to the Berlin Seminary at being called upon to prove their

g. Students in the *Rabbiner-Seminar* pursued university studies in conjunction with their rabbinic studies in the Seminary.

Orthodoxy created a rift between Berlin and Frankfurt that never entirely healed.[h,35]

In 1874, not long after the establishment of the Seminary, one of its leading educators, Rabbi David Zvi Hoffmann,[i] published *Mar Shmuel — A Portrait of the Life of a Talmud Scholar.* In a private letter, Rabbi Hirsch leveled withering criticism at *Mar Shmuel,* which seemed to follow the path of Graetz in interpreting various *halachoth* propounded by its subject as an outgrowth of his great love of mankind. In addition he saw the work as giving credence to "critical history" in Orthodox circles. He was disturbed by references to "new laws" instituted by the Sages of the Talmud, and the fact that Rabbi Hoffmann did not shy away from quoting Graetz and other *Wissenschaft* scholars, whom Rabbi Hirsch considered completely beyond the pale. Taken as a whole, the work constituted a "stumbling block," in Rabbi Hirsch's opinion. The appearance of this work by one of the Seminary's most prominent teachers so soon after its founding only fueled Rabbi Hirsch's misgivings.[36]

Whatever his private misgivings about the *Rabbiner-Seminar,* Rabbi Hirsch never went public with his criticisms. Emanuel Schwarzschild, Chairman of the Board of the *IRG* and one of Rabbi Hirsch's most devoted followers, was a central figure on the board of the *Rabbiner-Seminar,* something he would never have done without tacit approval from Rabbi Hirsch.[37] Rabbi Hirsch's refusal to engage in a public dispute with the Seminary no doubt reflected his own recognition that its teachers and students were unquestionably Orthodox, and that the already weak Orthodox camp could not afford a bitter public split.

It must be said that Rabbi Hirsch's fears concerning the *Rabbiner-Seminar* never materialized. In its first 12 years of existence, only one graduate departed from the tenets of Orthodox Judaism, and Rabbi Hildesheimer revoked his ordination and publicized his revocation in the

h. Rabbi Bamburger was also opposed to the *Rabbiner-Seminar* but for different reasons. He felt that the most important qualification of a rabbi was his Torah scholarship and opposed secular scholarship for its own sake.[35*]

i. Rabbi Hoffmann studied under Rabbi Moshe Schick (*Maharam Schick*) of Chust, Rabbi Hildesheimer and Rabbi S.B. Bamberger. Prior to coming to Berlin, he taught for two years in the *Realschule* in Frankfurt. In addition to his positions in the *Rabbiner-Seminar,* he later served as *Av Beis Din* of the Adas Israel Congregation of Berlin, and was recognized as one of Germany's foremost halachic authorities in his later years. He headed the Seminary from Rabbi Hildesheimer's passing in 1899 until his own passing in 1921. His three-volume collection of responsa, *Melamed LeHoil,* was published posthumously in 1926. He authored several classic works in addition to commentaries on *Vayikra* and *Devarim* which debunked the theories of Wellhausen and other Bible critics. The majority of Orthodox German rabbis at the time of the Nazi takeover were his students.

press. From then on, each ordination contained a proviso that it was retroactively void if the recipient served in a synagogue with an organ or without the traditional prayer book.[38]

Besides Rabbi Hoffmann, other leading scholars who taught in the Berlin Seminary included: Rabbi Avraham Eliyahu Kaplan, the famous Slabodka *ilui*; Rabbi Yechiel Yaakov Weinberg, author of the four-volume *Sridei Eish,* who headed the Seminary from 1924 until its closure by the Nazis; Dr. Abraham Berliner and Dr. Moshe Auerbach. Its list of illustrious graduates included Rabbi Meyer Lerner, Chief Rabbi of Altona; Rabbi Ezra Munk; Dr. Leo Deutschländer, who was dispatched by Jacob Rosenheim to Poland to assist Sarah Schenirer in founding the Bais Yaakov movement; Rabbi Joseph Carlebach of Hamburg and Rabbi Avrohom Wolf, headmaster for many years of the Bais Yaakov High School of Bnei Brak, which bears his name. The *Rabbiner-Seminar* produced three generations of pious, upright and erudite *rabbonim,* who served as the backbone of Orthodox Jewry in Germany until its destruction at the hands of the Nazis.

Part Seven

ISRAEL AND THE NATIONS

Plunder of the Frankfurt Ghetto, 1614

Chapter Twenty-Three
EMANCIPATION

The Threat of Assimilation

WITH EMANCIPATION, THE GATES OF THE GHETTO inched open. The young led the flight from the ghetto, followed hesitantly by their elders. Jewish peddlers became merchants; moneylenders and pawnbrokers became bankers and financiers. Jewish students were slowly accepted into the universities, and Jews began to speak pure German rather than Judeo-German.

The immediate result of this entry into European life was that many Jews threw off the yoke of their traditions and attempted to integrate into gentile society. Following hard on the heels of Emancipation was the call to "reform" Judaism, to bring it in line with European notions of civilization and proper comportment. David Friedlaender, a close disciple of Moses Mendelssohn and son-in-law of Court Jew Daniel Itzig of Berlin, summed up the new view. "Our commandments are so little suited to our present customs and liberties that, in my opinion, a revolution in the domain of religion must come about among the Jews in ten years."[1]

Besides Reform, the alternatives for German Jews also included the *Wissenschaft des Judentums* approach, and assimilation, with or without a trip to the baptismal font. Not surprisingly then, the rabbinic leaders of the time harbored grave misgivings about the entire process of Emancipation, with all the assimilationist trends it set in motion.

The Chasam Sofer reportedly expressed concern that Emancipation was also an indication of the prolonging of the *galus*. He compared the bettering of the Jews' position in exile to the king who built a palace for his exiled son. Instead of rejoicing, the son lamented that his improved living conditions only indicated that the king did not intend to bring him home anytime soon.[2]

In addition, the *Chasam Sofer* asserted in an 1834 address, experience has shown that "it is futile to. . . . attempt to become closer to the nations [through the abandonment of the *mitzvos*], because their animosity only increases daily."[3] Rabbi Hirsch echoed this view two decades later when he described a town in Southern Germany where, in the late 1820s, the local rabbi made *Tishah B'Av* a festive occasion and importuned his congregation to demonstrate by means of the festivities their "repudiation of the out-of-date yearning for Palestine, and to give proof of their patriotic attachment to the Fatherland. . . . from which they hoped to obtain full civic freedom and equality." "Jerusalem," the rabbi declared, "is here, and Palestine is now situated on German soil."

In that state, wrote Rabbi Hirsch, Jews gathered in solemn conclave to decide how much of Sabbath observance and other "burdens" they might offer as concessions to the new age. And, continued Rabbi Hirsch, in no German state did grim Jew-hatred luxuriate, inventing ever new restrictions, forging ever new chains and generating ever new scorn, as in that one. "Where [Jews] declare themselves ready to exchange the Torah for the new freedom and the new justice, they will have to wait the longest and perhaps in vain for the blessings of a better time."[4]

"[E]nmity and oppression continue," Rabbi Hirsch wrote in 1860, "not because we are too Jewish and too committed to Judaism, but because we meet our Jewish obligations deficiently, indifferently and frivolously."[5] European Jewish history in the 20th century has tragically confirmed the awesome truth in the *Chasam Sofer's* and Rabbi Hirsch's warning.

Most emancipatory laws had sections which dealt with the internal life of the Jew and made their "regeneration" a condition of obtaining civic rights. Many contained sections which regulated Jewish education and restricted the judicial and administrative prerogatives of the rabbinate. As a matter of policy, Orthodox rabbis always evinced an attitude of loyalty to the civil authorities, and were also loathe to do anything which would in any way endanger the acquisition of civil rights for their brethren. Yet, they knew that behind the government intervention in internal Jewish affairs was usually a group of "enlightened" Jews, using the stick of government intervention tied to the carrot of Emancipation to advance their own agenda for the reform of Jewish life.[6]

Another point deserves mention. Emancipation, as a rule, aimed at freeing Jews from the shackles of political and economic disability and social segregation as individuals, not as a community or as a national entity. To the contrary, the states tried as much as possible to blur ethnic distinctions, and to bring about the disappearance of the Jewish people as a distinct national entity.[7] In keeping with this trend, the Reformers deliberately downplayed any Jewish national bond, choosing instead to see themselves as "Germans of the Mosaic Faith." This preference was not merely philosophical, it guided their outlook on issues pertaining to the relationship of Jew and gentile. Thus, many liberal or non-observant Jews who were socially close to non-Jewish circles, including Reformer Abraham Geiger, favored selective Emancipation, whereby only "enlightened" Jews were to be granted full civic rights.

THE *CHASAM SOFER* DESCRIBED THE DILEMMA OF EMANCIPATION IN an 1832 address:

The Challenge of Emancipation

> There are two types of exile. If the nations of the world oppress Yisrael, then the hardship of the bondage causes them to abandon Divine worship, and breaks body and soul. Sometimes, however, the misfortune is the reverse. The state extends freedom to the Jews, elevates them and draws them close. . . . This can be a greater misfortune than the first because. . . . then the entire goal of the Jews is to become more friendly with the powers that be, to tread in their ways and to willingly renounce Torah and *mitzvos*.[8]

Rabbi Hirsch, too, recognized the enormous spiritual threat posed by Emancipation. Nonetheless, he viewed Emancipation as both a challenge and an opportunity to demonstrate that the Torah is no less applicable to the new open society than it was in the ghetto. Indeed, the concept for which Rabbi Hirsch is best known — *Torah Im Derech Eretz* — is at root an affirmation that the Jew is required to live in accordance with the Torah in *whatever* conditions society may present, and that the eternal lessons of the Torah are not connected with, nor limited to, any specific form of *galus* life. And just as the Jew must be prepared to serve G-d under adverse conditions, so too must he also seize any material and legal opportunities offered by society to accomplish the mission Hashem has given us in the world.[9]

Thus, Rabbi Hirsch welcomed Emancipation, but only on condition that the Jewish people would still be bound by the Torah's laws. The challenge of our times, he wrote in 1836, remains, as always, to "bring about the revelation of G-d . . . ." This can only be accomplished through "[t]he spirit and fulfillment of the Torah, the only treasure it had rescued [in its Exile, which] supported it and enabled it to live amidst suffering and agony, ruin and the blows of unrestrained, savage fanaticism."[10] If harnessed properly, the new opportunities for Divine worship made possible through the relaxation of hardship and persecution could have enormous consequences:

> If the dispersed of Israel were quietly to flourish as the priests of G-d and of true humanity, . . . if only we lived up to what we are supposed to be, if only our lives were a perfect reflection of the Torah, what a mighty force this would be for reaching the ultimate goal of all human education! . . . During the years of misery and contempt, our ideal could be attained only imperfectly; but when milder times beckon us to our goal — that every Jew and Jewess, through the example they provide in their own lives, should become priests of G-d and of genuine humanity — and this ideal and mission await us, can we still deplore our fate...?[11]

Rabbi Hirsch, thus, gave his qualified "blessing" to Emancipation for the relief it offered from the crushing pressures that had stifled the Jewish spirit for so many centuries and for the promise it offered to resuscitate our quintessential nature. Together with this blessing, however, he issued a warning. "I bless emancipation only if. . . . *Yisrael*. . . . seeks to bring about the fulfillment of our mission quite independently of whether or not we are emancipated, . . . [and] only if *Yisrael* regards it not as the goal of its mission, but merely as a new . . . test, infinitely more difficult than the test posed by oppression." If *Yisrael* worshiped Emancipation as just a means to a comfortable life, Rabbi Hirsch continued, it would show that it had not understood the spirit of its Torah and had learned nothing from the *galus*.[12]

Rabbi Hirsch appeared on the German Jewish scene at a time when it was impossible to oppose the movement toward Emancipation, which was, in any case, unstoppable. Isolation from the non-Jewish world was perhaps still possible in the rural village communities. But in the German cities this option no longer existed. Only by harnessing the new freedom in the service of Judaism could the latter be saved. This is what Rabbi Yisrael Salanter was referring to when he remarked that "Rabbi Hirsch succeeded in building a new structure [for Judaism] in Germany, because everything had already been destroyed there. To do the same in Russia would not be possible, because much of the old structure is still in place and in danger of being torn down without the possibility of replacing it with a new one."[13]

As German Orthodoxy after the 1840s gained some measure of renewed confidence in its ability to stand up against the Reformers, it also felt better equipped to face the challenges of the Emancipation. Indeed, here was an opportunity to show the Reformers that it was possible for a fully observant Jew to coexist with other citizens on an equal basis.[14]

Moravian Emancipation

RABBI HIRSCH'S ACTIONS AS CHIEF RABBI OF MORAVIA WERE CONsistent with his generally positive view of the opportunities presented by Emancipation. For centuries prior to the liberalizing trends in the late 1840s, Moravian Jewry was subjected to many cruel restrictions — chief among them the "Familiant Laws" which made it extremely difficult for any but the first-born son in each family to marry.[15]

In early 1848, a wave of nationalist uprisings spread across Western and Central Europe. In the Austro-Hungarian Empire, with its diversity of ethnic groups, long-subjected peoples clamored for independence, and many Jews joined with other citizens in the struggle for equal rights. The revolutions of 1848 led most of the German states to proclaim Emancipation. The principle that religion must not diminish or affect civic obligations and privileges was included in one form or another in the constitutions of most of those German states.[16]

The Revolution of 1848 and the installation of Franz Josef I as Emperor of the Austrian Empire brought great changes for the Jewish population of Moravia as well. On May 11, 1848 Rabbi Hirsch wrote an open letter to all Moravian Jews requesting that they contribute money to the war effort.[a] In a subsequent letter he reminded Moravian Jews of the importance of acting in accordance with the recommendation of Jeremiah (29:7): ודרשו את שלום העיר אשר הגליתי אתכם שמה — *Promote the welfare of the city to which I have exiled you. . . . for with its welfare you, too, will fare well.*[17]

a. At the same time as the internal insurrection, the Austrian Empire was also faced with the revolt of Hungary, which sought to free itself from Austrian control.

When the democratic movement finally achieved its goal of establishing an elected legislature in Austria, Rabbi Hirsch was chosen to head the committee in the Reichstag in Kremsier which dealt with the question of equal rights for Jews.[b] An anti-Semitic deputy moved that he be evicted, but the motion was rejected by a large majority, which instead voted to censure his antagonist. Rabbi Hirsch presented Jewish claims for equality as part of the general drive for equality for all ethnic minorities, without emphasizing the particular situation of the Jews. During this period, Rabbi Hirsch displayed his talents as a leader and statesman in an effort to gain equal rights for Jews, and in impassioned proclamations in Kremsier, seat of the provisional parliament, he pressed claims for Jewish civic rights. In one of his public orations, he declared, "In a constitutional state there is no such thing as partial liberty; neither slavery nor segregation can be tolerated. Either banish the Jew from your land or set him free!"[18]

Rabbi Hirsch galvanized the 52 Moravian communities to action, and during that period wrote a series of open letters to the Jews of Moravia. He exhorted them to remain firm in their commitment to Torah and not to slacken in their performance of *mitzvos.* Again and again he urged them to be on their guard "so that we may emerge from this struggle as Jews, . . . for what value would there be to all of our achievements if we were to become free Jews who had ceased to be Jews." The prohibitions against partaking of non-Jewish wine, shaving with a razor, and the requirement that married women cover their heads, he insisted, must continue to be meticulously observed. Rabbi Hirsch also stressed the need for calm and for internal unity among the Jews, and the importance of maintaining a strong faith in Hashem in such unpredictable and turbulent times. He warned the Jews that hasty, imprudent and ill-advised behavior could spoil any gains they had made.[19]

Rabbi Hirsch opposed the organization of a separate delegation of Jews to pay homage to the new emperor. He argued that Jews should be as inconspicuous as possible and "should submerge [themselves] in the totality of the state's membership and as such require no special representation."[20]

The democratically elected parliament was unable to make any decisions even after months of endless debate. The emperor dissolved the parliament on March 7, 1849 and issued a constitution dated March 4. The new constitution promised civil equality and religious freedom to all cit-

b. There is no evidence to support the legend that Rabbi Hirsch was an elected member of the Austrian parliament.

izens, removed any barriers to marriage,[c] granted freedom to live in the place of one's choosing, and canceled all special "Jew Taxes." Rabbi Hirsch immediately sent another circular to the Moravian Jewish communities advising against provocative conduct and the flaunting of their newly gained rights. Excessive rejoicing, he wrote, might cause ill will among the non-Jewish population, which still had some ways to go before they got used to treating Jews as equals. On March 28, despite his previous reluctance, he headed a delegation of rabbis and elders to Olmütz for an audience with the emperor.[21]

Emancipation for Moravian Jewry greatly weakened its communities. Until then, they had been supported by the taxes of their Jewish residents. After Emancipation, which recognized Jews as individuals but not as communities, many Jews were remiss in discharging their obligations to their local communities. As a result, the communities hovered on the brink of bankruptcy.

At Rabbi Hirsch's invitation there was a meeting in Nikolsburg of community delegates on April 23, 1849, which elected a committee to draft detailed provisions regarding the Jew and the Jewish communities, to be included in the new constitution of the Austrian Empire. The committee, headed by Rabbi Hirsch, completed its draft on August 30, and submitted it to the communities for ratification, to be adopted at an assembly of delegates called for November 4. On October 8, 1849, Rabbi Hirsch sent a circular letter to Moravian Jews entreating them to continue to support their communities.[22]

The very long draft of the proposed reorganization of Jewish communal life prepared by Rabbi Hirsch attempted to strengthen the power of the community rabbis at the local level and to give the communities the means to sustain themselves in the absence of compulsory membership and taxes. The draft did not arouse much overt opposition, but its pro-rabbinic tendencies seems to have antagonized a number of local leaders, and they boycotted the November 4 conference. Another meeting was called for December 31 to which a sizable number of delegates did show up, but the conference produced no tangible results. According to at least one historian, Rabbi Hirsch's frustration at being unable to effect any serious changes in the structure of the Moravian communities was one of the causes that contributed to his acceptance of the call to Frankfurt 15 months later.[23]

---

c. Following the adoption of the new constitution, Rabbi Hirsch responded to a query as to how all those who were secretly married before the abolishment of the "Familiant Laws" should conduct the "new" marriage ceremony, which was being performed only for civil purposes.[21*]

From the time Rabbi Hirsch went to Frankfurt, he did not engage in any more public advocacy to advance the cause of civil equality for Jews. Although *Jeschurun* reported on the issue at length in the 1860s, from him there was not a word.[24] Maybe it was because he had more pressing matters to attend to in Frankfurt. But perhaps this reticence signaled something deeper. In reevaluating the battle for equal rights 15 years after his intense activity in Moravia, Rabbi Hirsch wondered whether the all-out drive for "emancipation" at any price had not been grounds for the further deepening of the exile, and if it had not engendered renewed persecution and increased restrictions on Jews:

> There will be many to blame when the old shadows of *galuth* enfold us again and oppressors everywhere will stand ready to place the ancient chains on Israel once more. Who knows whether it was not they who, through their exaggerated glorification of civic equality as the ultimate freedom, precipitated the return of the ancient animosity of the nations? Through our sudden awakening from dangerous illusions, G-d drew us back to Him, "G-d will not forsake His people, and will not abandon His inheritance" (*Psalms* 94:14).[25]

Chapter Twenty-Four

EXILE AND REDEMPTION

THE JEWISH PEOPLE AND THE TORAH ARE DIFferent from any other people and any other set of laws. They are the only people in history to have laws before it had a land, and this is the only legal code that was not instituted to enrich the life of a people and to establish their prosperity on their national soil. Just the opposite! The Torah is itself the purpose towards which everything else is directed. Every other nation first became a people because it had a land, and then fashioned laws in order to keep its land. But you became a people by virtue of the Torah, and only when you received it were you given a land for its sake. Other nations' laws reflect their unique national character as shaped by their geography and the ebb and flow of their history; while . . . the man through whose hands you received the Torah never set foot on the soil of your land in his life. . . .

The Torah is absolute and eternal, while you and the land are relative and temporary. Its laws do not fluctuate with your fortunes and those of the land, rather you and the land rise and fall according to your devotion to the Torah.

[Y]ou await eagerly the moment when the gates of the land will be opened before you, the land you are given in order to keep the Torah. You are the people of the Torah — not the people of the land, and the land is the land of the Torah — without the Torah it is not the Land of Israel.[1]

Israel as a nation, Rabbi Hirsch stressed, is poor in all that constitutes greatness and power in other nations. As such, its preservation throughout history is a direct revelation of G-d as Creator, Judge, Master of nature and history.[2] Only its faithfulness to G-d, even in dispersion, can explain the existence of the Jewish people. Everything that the Jewish people received from G-d throughout its history has been only to enable the Jewish people to serve as bearers of His Torah: "[A] land, prosperity and the institutions of statehood were to be put at *Yisrael's* disposal not as goals in themselves, but as means for the fulfillment of the Torah. Accordingly, they were granted to *Yisrael* on one — and only one — condition: that it would indeed fulfill the Torah."[3]

These basic postulates on the historical role of the Jewish people, first expressed in *The Nineteen Letters,* constitute the essence of Rabbi Hirsch's views on exile and redemption. He was to reiterate these fundamental principles frequently in his prolific writings over the next 55 years, and they guided his activities relating to the settlement of *Eretz Yisrael.*

Prosperity and Security

SINCE POSSESSION OF THE LAND IS PREDICATED ON OBSERVING THE Torah, Rabbi Hirsch asserted, G-d purposely gave us a stubborn land that does not blossom and flourish in the normal course of nature. Only when Israel dwells on it and keeps Hashem's word does it yield its abundant fruits. In this manner the land itself serves as a perpetual reminder that success or failure in this world is dependent on adherence to G-d's will.[4]

Not only the fruitfulness of the land, but also its physical security and the independence of its people, are the direct result of the degree to which they observe the Torah:

> His land will be ours only if we keep His Torah in total faith. If we pay this tax, then we will have done everything necessary to keep the land in our hands and we will be kept on the land. Knowledge of the Torah and observance of its commandments are our strength and our shield, our skill and our craft, our political and economic wisdom.[5]

> Defending the land was a task taken over by G-d. The security of Israel's borders depended not on standing armies nor on troop or armament deployment. It depended on the quietly devoted and dedicated fulfillment of the G-d-given Law on Israel's own soil, in its own country. In general, all of the national weal, its wealth, peace, health, security and honor, such as the other nations attempt to attain by means of a display of power, were to be attained by the Jewish people purely by means of fulfilling the Divine Law.[6]

Thus, the national life enjoyed by the Jewish people on the land was nothing less than an open miracle:

> [I]ts fruitfulness depends entirely on Heavenly kindness; its central geographical situation, at the crossroads between Europe, Asia and Africa, leaves it open and exposed to conquerers from all sides, so that every major war that has shaken the world has had a particularly severe effect on it. It is for just this reason that it was chosen. Had Israel built a holy life on this land, no foe would ever have dared approach its borders. Thrice a year the land lay empty and exposed, but no one desired it; kings chased each other across the face of the world but no one set foot on this land (see *Vayikra* 26:6) that was the most fruitful of all of them and the most defenseless. But the nations all saw Hashem was there, the rampart of Zion and its bastion. . . .[7]

Since Jewish existence in the land depends entirely on obedience to Hashem, it could not remain there after sinning. Once *Yisrael* ceased to fulfill its purpose in dwelling there, Hashem removed His special protection and the Jewish people reverted to its natural, weak status.[8] Its exile from the land, however, was not just a punishment and a natural result of the removal of Hashem's protection, but also His way of salvaging the Jewish people's spiritual and moral existence. The Jewish people was driven off the land and lost its identity to prevent it from sinking to the depths of abomination that caused destruction of the Canaanites before us.[9]

Settlement of the Land

SINCE THE CAUSE OF ISRAEL'S EXILE IS HER DEPARTURE FROM THE Torah, it follows, Rabbi Hirsch insisted, that her redemption will only take place with her return to the Torah. Even the physical return to the land will bring no redemption without rectification of the underlying causes of the exile: "Judah was sent into the *galuth* because it prized land and soil as the bulwark of its freedom and belittled the Torah. The *galuth* cannot, therefore, end with the same delusion."[10] The land itself, he emphasized, has value only as a means for the observance of the Torah in its entirety: "Only if the Jewish people repents fully and returns to the Torah will its dispersion be ended; the only purpose for ingathering the exiles and returning them to their land is to enable them to observe the entire Torah."[11]

In Rabbi Hirsch's view, settlement of *Eretz Yisrael*, no matter how massive, could provide no guarantee against future eviction. That guarantee could only follow when the lessons of the Exile were fully absorbed:

> From time to time in the course of the centuries G-d allowed His people ever and anon to touch the earth again. He put it to the test to see whether it had become ripe for the external Torah-state on earth, whether the miracle of its existence through centuries of *galuth* had at length taught it to despise utterly the gods of the earth, whether at last the experience of these wonders had eradicated from it the obstinacy — קשה עורף — which was ingrained in it as in all men and which prevented it from acknowledging completely the power of the Divine word, whether it had at length learnt to devote itself unreservedly and exclusively to the Torah, and whether it could preserve this devotion, which had never become alien to it in the *galuth*, also in freedom and in abundance and in independence and power.
>
> But Israel had up to now always given signs that it has not yet reached this point. True, it has shown that it no longer fears the journey through the desert, and that, while having no footing on the earth, it can commit itself with cheerful confidence to the celestial wings of its Divine Law. But it has also shown that it still has reason to fear the ground, and that as soon as it touches the soil and thinks that it has firm ground under its feet, it runs the danger of abandoning the Divine Law and revering as gods, alongside of the Torah of its G-d, the political independence, the social freedom and the civil rights which this soil provides. It runs the danger of devoting its life to them and finding room for the Torah only in its synagogues, committing afresh all the old sins which brought on it the חורבן, the destruction of its state and temple.
>
> Again and again G-d has straightaway allowed this soil to vanish from under its feet.[12]

Rabbi Hirsch opposed movements which agitated for a return to the land, including those attempts to settle *Eretz Yisrael* for messianic purposes. He expressed this opposition over a lifetime, from his first published work, *The Nineteen Letters,* to his last, the commentary to the *Siddur.* His opposition stemmed from several factors.

It would be impossible for Israel to return to its land, Rabbi Hirsch was convinced, unless it first rectified the problems that had originally caused the exile. "Israel can be redeemed only through repentance," was his basic premise. With that repentance there was no impediment to redemption occurring "even today — if you would but heed His call."[13] Rabbi Hirsch pointed out that the task set out for us by our forefathers was "only to be pious with all our might, to perfect ourselves before G-d through Torah, to remove any hindrances from our midst, and to look forward to our redemption each day." The Jew, he insisted, is not mandated to "prepare for the redemption by improving the Holy Land, but rather by improving [his] heart and deeds."[14] And any political attempt to rally the Jewish people to return to its land was not only wrong, but, like the rebellion of Bar Kochba, fraught with great danger, for it looked to human activity rather than Divine intervention as the cause of redemption.[15]

In addition he was concerned that without a unity of purpose of all settlers of *Eretz Israel,* such efforts would be a further source of fragmentation for an already divided Jewish people.

> To speak of paving the way to our homecoming by means of the acquisition of a tract of land is a grievous error. Let us first become brothers in spirit, let us become united through the one unifying spirit of Judaism, become one, a brotherhood, by jointly, unreservedly rallying around the common, hallowed heritage bequeathed to us by our forebears. Then G-d, Who is the Master of time, will, in His *own* time, bestow on us the land. . . . Only as brothers can we make our return to the land.
>
> In our divided Jewish society. . . . the Torah is no longer considered the one, everlasting criterion for any final decision involving the future of the nation. No longer is the Torah the one, eternally mighty spring from which all of us draw one spirit, one ideal, thereby gaining a common point of view and a common direction. Given such unbrotherly divisiveness, where would be the good, the harmony which would make it pleasurable to dwell together on one soil? Was it so good, so beautiful when those who wanted to be "Israelites" — as opposed to being Jewish — sought

to prosper on this soil, when culture-worship and Divine service, Baal-cult and Torah priests, Jezebel's idolaters and Moriah-Kohanim vied for the realm of the spirit? Was it not as a result of this fragmentation that the land went to its ruin? And today, out of the even deeper rifts within contemporary Judaism, the land should arise to renewed blossoming?[16]

Rabbi Hirsch also considered mass resettlement efforts to be a violation of two of the "Three Oaths" with which Hashem enjoined Israel and the nations of the world: that the Jewish people would not retake the land by force and that they would not rebel against the nations of the world.[17] His opposition to mass settlement did not change over 55 years of public life, even during the last three decades of his life, when considerable efforts were made in this area by the *Chibas Zion* movement.

On the other hand, Rabbi Hirsch supported efforts to improve conditions for those Jews living in *Eretz Yisrael.* As early as his tenure in Emden, he formed a close association with the officers *(Pekidim ve'Amarkalim)* of the *Kollel Hod* ("Holland veDeutschland") organization and collaborated with its director, Rabbi Hirsch Lehren of Amsterdam, to raise funds for the benefit of settlers in *Eretz Yisrael.*[18] He maintained this association until the end of his life, and was frequently consulted by that organization concerning various aspects of its activities.[19] Over the years *Jeschurun* published fundraising appeals for the Jews of *Eretz Yisrael* and information about conditions there. In 1874, Rabbi Hirsch collaborated with Rabbi Bamberger and several other German rabbis in a fundraising drive to found a hospital in Jerusalem, which ultimately culminated in the establishment of Shaare Zedek Hospital by Dr. Moshe Wallach.[20]

Rabbi Kalischer's Efforts

IN 1860, RABBI ZVI HIRSCH KALISCHER (1795-1874)[a] LAUNCHED A MASSIVE effort aimed at promoting mass settlement in *Eretz Yisrael,* which he was convinced would bring the *geulah.* According to his view the *teshuvah* referred to in the statement of the Sages, "*Ein Yisrael nig'alim elah bitshuvah*"[21] (usually interpreted to mean that Israel will only be redeemed through repentance), referred not to repentance, but to the return to the land.

Rabbi Kalischer's book *Drishas Zion* (Lyck, 1862) advanced the view

a. Rabbi Kalischer was a disciple of Rabbi Akiva Eiger and of Rabbi Yaakov Lorberbaum, author of the *Chavas Daas* and *Nesivos HaMishpat*. In 1824, he settled in Thorn where he remained until his death.

that the redemption would result from the colonization of the Holy Land and the reinstitution of the sacrificial order. Only following that would the supernatural *geulah* follow. Rabbi Kalischer opposed philanthropic efforts in *Eretz Yisrael* not specifically directed to the central purpose, as he saw it, of settling and working the land on a massive scale.

Rabbi Kalischer attempted to mobilize support from the rabbinic leaders of Europe, among them Rabbi Hirsch, with whom all of his efforts were in vain.[22] He first contacted Rabbi Hirsch in 1862, after the appearance of *Drishas Zion*. He also asked Rabbi Hirsch to give a copy of his book to Baron Willy Rothschild, in the hope of inducing the latter to provide financial support for his activities. Rabbi Hirsch's reply never reached Rabbi Kalischer, and so the latter sent a second request two years later, this one containing an impassioned statement of his beliefs.

In this letter Rabbi Kalischer responded to what he had been told were Rabbi Hirsch's fears that mass settlement in *Eretz Yisrael* to bring the *geulah* would only serve to deter Jews from repenting. Rabbi Kalischer offered three answers to these concerns: 1) Israel would be redeemed even without repentance; 2) the mere remembrance of the traditional love of Zion would by itself bring Jews to repent; and 3) the essence of repentance is the yearning for *Eretz Yisrael*.

In his reply, Rabbi Hirsch presented a clear and concise statement of his position concerning settlement of *Eretz Yisrael* as a goal in itself in the present era. He pointed out that the Jew's obligation is only to be devout with all the strength he is granted, and to look forward to the *geulah* each day. The Sages never obligated us to clear the way for the redemption by developing the Holy Land, but rather by improving ourselves.

Rabbi Hirsch dismissed out of hand Rabbi Kalischer's contention that the prominence of Jewish statesmen like Disraeli in England and Crémieux in France was a harbinger of *geulah*. It is impossible to imagine, he wrote, that Hashem would choose people who reject the Torah as His agents to advance the redemption. Finally, although Rabbi Hirsch agreed that it was important to support those Jews who currently lived in *Eretz Yisrael*, he expressed concern that mass settlement activity would bring in its wake increased risk of Sabbath desecration and the transgression of the agricultural *mitzvos* unique to *Eretz Yisrael*.[b,23]

b. Around the time of Rabbi Kalischer's importunings to support his activities, Rabbi Hirsch published an article in *Jeschurun* clarifying his attitude on the subject:

> The fact that the future of both Israel and mankind will culminate in the achievement of Israel's mission as a nation of priests of G-d's Torah serves to stress the certainty that the preparation for that future requires a fuller and deeper knowledge and an ever more faithful and fuller observance of the Torah. Only then will we render ourselves worthy of

The attempts of Rabbi Kalischer and others to persuade Rabbi Hirsch did not cease. In June and December 1869, Rabbi Avraham Yaakov Levine also broached the subject with Rabbi Hirsch and attempted, despite previous rebuffs, to win his support for activities to promote settlement in *Eretz Yisrael.* He received the following reply: "Concerning the acquisition of the Holy Land of which you spoke, I will not hide the fact that I am disgusted already by this whole matter. In my lowly opinion, there will not emerge from this any benefit for our Torah and Jewish tradition, and it is not fitting for G-d-fearing people to associate with the *Alliance Universelle Israelite,* whose leaders lack all commitment to Torah and to Hashem's covenant. If I err in this matter, may Hashem forgive me."[24] In August 1872, Rabbi Kalischer again requested Rabbi Hirsch to forget his reservations and prevail upon Baron Rothschild to support settlement activities. This effort, too, went unrewarded.[25] In 1884, Rabbi Hirsch wrote to Rabbi Yaakov Lipschitz, close confidant of Rabbi Yitzchak Elchanan Spektor of Kovno, that Rabbi Kalischer had approached him a number of times and finally accused him of delaying the redemption. "I asked him to leave me alone concerning this matter, since what they consider to be a great *mitzvah* is in my eyes no small sin."[26]

Already in 1855, long before anyone even began to dream of a modern Jewish state, Rabbi Hirsch stressed that neither the achievement of political independence nor the return of the Jews to the Land of Israel would be of significance by themselves:

> The modern view is that the Jewish state, both of the past and of the future, is to be regarded as belonging to the same class as all other political phenomena. It has lost all consciousness of the quite peculiar nature of the Jewish state and its difference from all other states. In that state, too, it sees only an institution in which the development of the political elements mentioned above is the goal to which everything else, including Temple and Torah, is to be subordinated as mere means and instruments. . . .
>
> But this modern view is just — modern. It is not the old Jewish view. It is in fact un-Jewish and untrue. . . .
>
> It is for the "*Galuth HaShechinah,*" the "Exile of the Majesty of G-d," as our ancestors with true insight called it, it is for this

the *geulah.* This fact condemns recent efforts of all so-called Reform endeavors that would like to antiquate the law on the one hand, as well as all endeavors which have recently appeared to further the *geulah* by material means.[23*]

sad disfigurement of the Torah that Jewish tears are shed and Jewish hearts grieve. Not for his own *galuth,* but for the *galuth* of the Torah does the Jew mourn. And must this mourning die away, must this sorrow disappear, must these tears dry up if the nations become more humane and just, if they loosen the chains on the hands and feet of *galuth*-weary Israel, and an emancipated Israel steps into the company of non-Jewish states as a fully privileged member? Will the Torah be any the less in exile for this? Will the "Exile of the Majesty of G-d" be brought to an end by this? Will the Torah have found its own soil again, will it be more at home on earth, will it now strike deeper roots and will it put forth blossoms and bring to ripeness all the fruits of blessing and salvation for which it should serve as the everlasting tree of life? Or has it to endure new and harder trials, is it faced with new *galuth* sufferings, is it threatened with a new and more painful and bitter exile?[27]

IT IS IMPORTANT TO NOTE THAT RABBI HIRSCH WAS NOT IN ANY WAY enamored of *galuth* existence, and he stressed time and again the central role of *Eretz Yisrael* to the Jewish people. "As long as the Jewish national organism is in exile," he once wrote, "it is sick."[28]

Support for Settlement

Nor did he oppose the settlement of *Eretz Yisrael* by private individuals and groups. His objection was only to mass immigration as a national effort or for the messianic purpose of hastening the redemption. Thus, in 1882, he wrote that *Eretz Yisrael* would be a suitable haven for Jewish refugees fleeing the pogroms in Russia, if they would be able to make an independent living, without the need for continual assistance from abroad. It was also only after his repeated calls for assistance to the refugees that the local committee in Frankfurt, of whom members of the *IRG* were only a minority, began to make serious fundraising efforts.[c] He was extremely concerned, however, that the committees extending emigration assistance to those fleeing the pogroms in Russia would induce the refugees to desecrate the Shabbos, and demanded public assurances that they would desist from such practices before he agreed to cooperate. He himself raised substantial sums of money which he sent to Rabbi A.B.

c. He himself was not a member of the committee, as it was composed also of members of the *Gemeinde-Orthodoxie* "with whom I have been fighting for many years for the interests of the *IRG.*" But because of the relatively small size of the *IRG,* he felt that forming their own committee would be counterproductive.

Die בתי דינים in ירושלים fordern zu Spenden auf für die Colonisten שומרי שביעית in א"י, die in diesem שביעית-Jahre ihr Feld nicht bestellen.

Ich bitte um Spenden für diese hilfsbedürftigen יראים ושלמים. Ich werde das Eingehende übersenden und veröffentlichen.

Frankfurt a. M., 2. Tewes 5649.

Rabbiner Hirsch.

Public call for assistance to Shmittah observers

Kluger of Brody, the son of Rabbi Shlomo Kluger, to enable the refugees to emigrate to Palestine.[29]

Rabbi Hirsch issued a public call in 1886 for funds to support the fledgling settlement in Petach Tikva, which, he stressed, was to be based on a fully observant Jewish communal life and which strove for economic independence.[30] But when the *Ezra* Aid Society was founded in 1886, *Jeschurun* responded warily: "If the intention of the organizers is to promote true Judaism, then they are worthy of support. However, their nationalistic fervor seems more like disguised propaganda for the Reform Movement, and we must therefore oppose such 'national Judaism' with full force."[31]

Rabbi Hirsch strongly opposed the proposal, advanced for the first time prior to the *Shmittah* year of 5549 (1888-1889), to allow the "sale" of Jewish-held fields to non-Jews in order to permit working the land.[32] But at the same time he publicized an appeal to support Jewish farmers who observed *Shmittah.* He made the first contribution in this campaign, which was to be his last public activity. His progress report on the campaign, the last public announcement of his life, appeared in *Jeschurun* only four days before his death.[33]

A Light to the Nations

ISRAEL'S NATIONAL MISSION IS TO PROCLAIM G-D'S EXISTENCE AND power to the world, to display His kingship to the nations,[34] by being a nation of priests and a holy people. Israel was scattered throughout the world in order that it accomplish its task there as well.[35] And in Exile, Rabbi Hirsch wrote, "it accomplished its task better than in prosperity."[36] In Exile the task of *Yisrael* was to be *Yizrael,* Divine "seeds," which through its way of life — not through proselytizing — are to advance the conception of G-d and his rulership.[37] "This nation, whether complying with its duty or found wanting, whether in prosperity, or in the misery of exile, is nothing else but a testimony of the all conquering power and glory of G-d's moral Law."[38] Nevertheless, it is not Israel's mission to teach the nations in an active sense — the mere fact of Israel's continued existence "awakens the conscience of the nations [and] is a testimonial to G-d and His invisible guidance of the world."[39]

> The Jewish People, without land, without power, without protection, but precisely through this essential absence of power and protection has become the living testimony for the Divine rule and the Divinity of her own message: הן הן גבורותיו, הן הן נוראותיו. . . . This victory, achieved without external support, will be the most brilliant living testimony for the Divinity of the Torah and for the Divine might of its message on earth.[40]

At the same time, Israel's downtrodden state and continued exile convey another aspect of the Divine Will to the nations: "What has been done to Israel is only an example, demonstrated on one nation, which all nations have to fear if they turn their backs to G-d's laws of universal morality."[41]

A Universal Concern

THUS, IN ADDITION TO BEING A PUNISHMENT, EXILE ALSO SERVES AS an opportunity for the Jewish people to advance the ultimate goal of human history: bringing all mankind to a recognition of the Almighty.[42] As such, the Jew is, of necessity, a universalist.[43] The Jew, Rabbi Hirsch taught, is interested in the welfare of all G-d's creatures, and he will view any manifestations of pure humanity and expression of ideas intended to advance the good, the pure, the noble and the just in man, as a further step in the direction of the world being filled with the knowledge of G-d as the "water covers the sea" (*Isaiah* 11:5). Rabbi Hirsch's universalist view is, of course, of a piece with the tenets of *Torah Im Derech Eretz*, which teaches that every aspect of G-d's world can be employed to magnify His glory. This is a far cry from the attitude prevalent in Eastern Europe in his day, which saw Judaism as concerned only with Jews and uninterested in the "*treifene*, anti-Semitic outside world." Although easily understood in light of centuries of ghetto life and unremitting persecution, this view, he held, is nevertheless a distortion of Judaism.[d]

---

d. A more radical manifestation of this attitude sees Judaism as primarily a devotional religion, where worship and ritual-related details constitute the major part of Jewish life to the diminution of almost all else. In 1835, Rabbi Hirsch pointed out to his cousin Z.H. May, that he "could

It is in the context of Rabbi Hirsch's view that everything in the world is a potential vehicle for the sanctification of the Divine Name, that his conditional acceptance of Emancipation and his qualified approval of aspects of German idealism must be viewed. Thus, in 1859, the *Realschule* participated in the 100th-anniversary celebration of the birth of the German poet Friedrich von Schiller (1759-1805),[e] sponsored by the city of Frankfurt, and Rabbi Hirsch delivered his famous *Schillerrede* on that occasion.[f] Rabbi Hirsch saw in Schiller noble expressions of compassion, justice and human decency, a purity of spirit, a freewilled obedience to the Divine imperative, and an attempt to see the wonders of the Creator in every facet of nature. Rabbi Hirsch viewed the popularity of Schiller's writings as a sign that these ideals were on the ascendant. The joyful affirmation of life, the attempt to reveal the wonders of creation and family, and the equality of all men were Jewish ideals which, hopefully, were slowly being accepted by mankind.[44] Schiller was thus welcomed as betokening a movement, however slight, toward the establishment of the world under the kingship of Hashem.

> The Jew knows that the good and the righteous men among nations are working alongside him to build the Kingdom of G-d on earth. . . . He welcomes each new truth as a valuable contribution to the ever more penetrating revelation of G-d in nature and history. . . . The Jew will not be opposed to any science, any art form, any culture that is truly ethical, truly moral, truly contributing to the welfare and progress of man. He will measure everything by the eternal, inviolable yardstick of the teachings of his G-d. Nothing will exist for him that cannot stand up before the Divine Will. . . . Never at any time will the Jew sacrifice one iota of his Judaism, at no time will he bring his Judaism in conformity with the times. But he will gladly accept all values that his time will have to offer, as long as they conform with the spirit of Judaism. In every age he will regard it as his task to evaluate the time and its conditions from the Jewish viewpoint. . . .[45]

---

write a whole treatise on the damage which has been done and which is still being done by the fact that the *Shulchan Aruch* did not appear from the very beginning in one volume. That is how it came about that many a person has thought and still thinks that he is a perfect Jew if he merely observes the laws of *Orach Chaim*. . . . A good deal in *Yoreh Deah*, and even more in *Choshen Mishpat* and *Even Hoezer*, was neglected."[43*]

e. German poet, playwright and philosopher.

f. Whether or not the school was forced to participate is beside the point.

RABBI HIRSCH, HOWEVER, WAS FAR FROM AN UNQUALIFIED ADMIRER of contemporary German culture, nor did he naively assume that anti-Semitism was a thing of the past. In *1857*, two years before the *Schillerrede* and two decades before the outbreak of a new wave of German anti-Semitism of the late 1870s and early 1880s, he warned, in an essay entitled "Sober Thoughts in a Gathering of Drunkards," of the possibility of a monster like Hitler emerging from within German society.

Anti-Semitism

> Has the Emancipation, with its newly found freedom and opportunity, resulted in more joy, greater satisfaction and a still happier existence than what our forebears experienced?. . .
>
> Do you believe you no longer need to remember the past? Do you really think that such somber times will never recur? . . .
>
> O, you deluded ones! Look at the society which is now freely open to you. Look around on the great marketplace of life. Has the race of the Haman died out completely with his ten sons? Could you not find someone from the Rhine to the Oder, from the Volga to the Danube who is capable of being his successor? Be sober and observe. Indeed, the horizon of the Jew may well become somber; sultry clouds hang in the German sky. Even in our own Jewish circles indications for gloom are apparent. No one is secure.[g,46]

When no one in Germany thought of the growing power of anti-Semitism, Rabbi Hirsch remarked in a conversation: "Just as mischievous children are pulled by the ears, so will they deal with us. The Jews are the schoolbooks of the nations; a disorderly pupil tears them. The condition of the Jews is the measure of the nations' level of civilization."[47]

Rabbi Hirsch stressed repeatedly that rising non-observance, far from being a cure for anti-Semitism, would prove to be its cause. In an impassioned appeal to members of a Moravian community in 1848, he warned that persecution of Jews never spared those who desecrated the Sabbath or ate pork, or even those who had lived non-Jewish lives. The hatred of the Jewish way of life, he wrote, was no more than a disguise for hatred of Jews. On the contrary, the only result of deviance from the Torah would be the suffering and the deepening of the difficult exile guaranteed by the Torah and the Prophets for disobedience to the Divine imperative.[48]

---

g. In 1858, Rabbi Hirsch wrote of the bitter disappointment of those who "were convinced that brilliant eras of enlightenment and knowledge, of well-being and peace were . . . on the horizon of nations..."[46*]

Part Eight

A WAY OF LIFE

Chapter Twenty-Five

HALACHIC ISSUES

RABBI HIRSCH'S CONSIDERABLE STATURE AS A *POSEK* (halachic decisor) has been largely overlooked by historians, in part due to the fact that much of his extensive correspondence was burned by one of his daughters some time after his passing, under the impression that this was her father's will. As a result only a small percentage of his responsa were preserved for posterity.[a]

a. The bulk of the extant responsa and the remainder of Rabbi Hirsch's other correspondence were in the hands of Rabbi Hirsch's son Naftali. His son-in-law Joseph Sänger added to the collection (the responsa constituted only a small portion of it), and meticulously catalogued it. The collection was brought to Israel by the latter's daughter Mrs. Ayala Grossman of Haifa, and was subsequently purchased by Bar-Ilan University, where it has been designated the Sänger Collection. Most of the significant Hebrew letters and a few of the German ones have recently been published in *Shemesh Marpeh* (Mesorah Publications: New York, 1992).

The surviving responsa are bunched together in relatively brief time periods and indicate that there were many halachic queries every month. If the number of letters for the periods in which the correspondence has been preserved were extrapolated over Rabbi Hirsch's lengthy rabbinic career, the result would be an extensive halachic correspondence.

The surviving responsa cover all sections of *Shulchan Aruch*, with the exception of *Choshen Mishpat*, and deal with such sensitive topics as adultery, birth control, divorce and bereavement. The virtual absence of responsa on *Choshen Mishpat* issues reflects the fact that the government had abolished the right of local rabbinical courts to adjudicate monetary disputes in every community in which Rabbi Hirsch served.

The surviving responsa indicate a tendency to stringency.[1] Rabbi Hirsch once remarked to his son-in-law Rabbi Salomon Breuer, "There are many things that might be permitted, but we must not allow them in times like ours."[2] He could be unbending if he felt the situation demanded it even if permitted by the letter of the law. In the 1870s, one of the foremost members of his *Kehillah* and an extremely wealthy, strictly observant German Jewish philanthropist conceived the idea of founding a bank, one seventh of whose shares would be sold to non-Jews so as to enable the bank to conduct business on the Sabbath. This practice was followed even in Eastern Europe by scrupulously observant industrialists, who employed this halachic loophole to operate their plants seven days a week. Rabbi Hirsch forbade it. "The *Shulchan Aruch* permits it," he agreed, "but I forbid it." He warned the prospective founders that were they to carry through their plan he would call for a public fast day. The bank was never established.[3]

At the same time, he eschewed stringency for its own sake. Thus he concluded one *tshuvah* dealing with the permissibility of holding the *chuppah* in *shul*[b] with a summary statement of his approach to any change from accepted practice:

> We should be like an iron pillar. . . . to resist proposed innovations . . . which have even the slightest trace of the impermissible and the destruction of Judaism. But in any matter which has not even a trifle of prohibition let us be soft as a reed and not obstinate, for then they will be willing to listen to our reproach as regards serious transgressions. If we oppose them, however, even on matters that have not the slightest trace of *aveirah*, then when we reprove them for serious transgressions, they will not take it seriously and will declare it only to be another instance of our obstinacy . . . cit[ing] our opposition even to permissible matters as proof.[4]

b. In Nikolsburg Rabbi Hirsch instituted the performance of the *chuppah* ceremony in the *shul*. Not longer afterwards he received a query from the Moravian community of Prerau. The congregants wanted to follow Rabbi Hirsch's example, but the rabbi was opposed. In his response, Rabbi Hirsch demonstrated that not only was *chuppah* in *shul* halachically permissible but an ancient and time-hallowed custom.

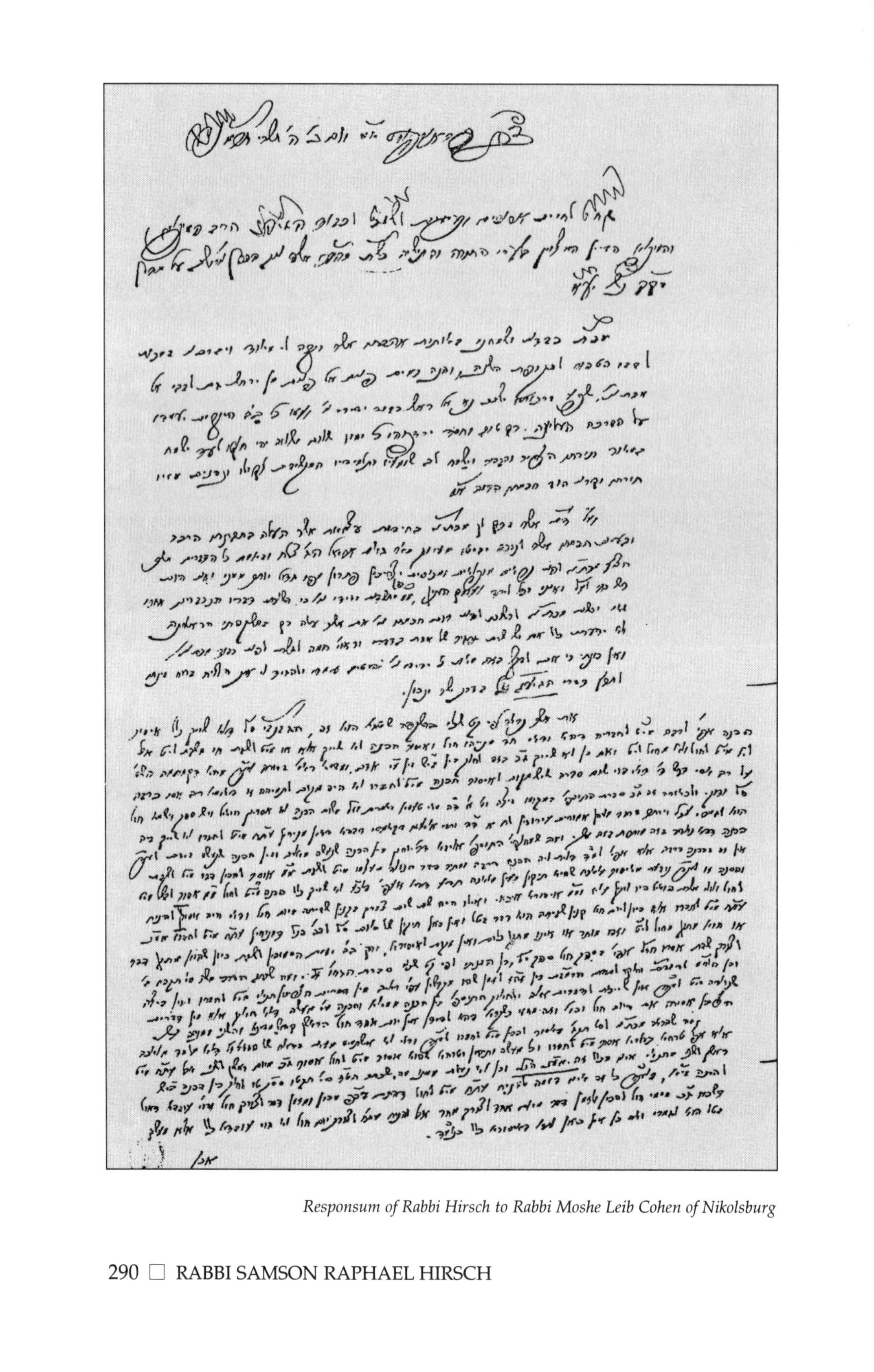

Responsum of Rabbi Hirsch to Rabbi Moshe Leib Cohen of Nikolsburg

Rabbi Moshe Leib Cohen, dayan in Nikolsburg

Rabbi Hirsch steadfastly declined to rule where there were competent local rabbinic authorities, unless requested to by those authorities. Thus when the Hungarian community of Boniyhad asked him in 1850 if they could hold the *chuppah* in *shul*, he replied that they should ask their own rabbi and the rabbinical authorities of Hungary. He agreed only to describe his own practice permitting it and the relevant halachic sources supporting that practice. That refusal stood him in good stead when Rabbi A.S.B. Sofer (the *K'sav Sofer*) of Pressburg actively intervened to ensure that Boniyhad did not introduce the *chuppah* into *shul*, on the basis of the as yet unpublished responsum of his father, the *Chasam Sofer*, prohibiting the practice.[5]

This deference to local rabbinic authority obtained even on important issues, which were of more than limited impact. We have already discussed Rabbi Hirsch's refusal to intervene in educational issues in Jerusalem.[6] Similarly, although Rabbi Hirsch felt there was no halachic requirement that local *kehillas* join together in a national umbrella organization, he refused to permit Rabbi Eliyahu Menachem Goitoin of Hungary to publicize his opinion to that effect, because the *Maharam Schick* of Chust, one of the leading halachic authorities of Hungary, had ruled to the contrary.[7]

Circumcision

IN 19TH-CENTURY GERMANY THERE WERE UNREMITTING ATTEMPTS on the part of government and liberal Jewish circles to abolish *metzitzah*, the drawing of the blood from the area of circumcision by the mouth of the *mohel*, on the grounds that contact between the mouth of the *mohel* and the open wound carried with it the potential transmission of infection or disease. Agitation to abolish *metzitzah bepeh* began in the 1820s and each of the Reform rabbinical conferences in the 1840s called for its abolition. As a result of Reform propaganda, some civil authorities were convinced to prohibit *metzitzah bepeh*.[8]

The issue flared again in the 1880s, and Rabbi Hirsch played a decisive role in ensuring that *metzitzah* remained an integral part of *bris milah*. He rejected outright the claim that *metzitzah* could endanger the infant. He pointed out that the Jewish people had far more experience with *milah* than all contemporary doctors combined — hundreds of thousands were circumcised in one year alone when the Jews entered the Holy Land after their stay in the wilderness. Thus, if the Sages determined that *not* performing *metzitzah* constitutes a danger for the infant there can be no doubt as to the truth of that statement.[9] The only way an infant could contract disease through *metzitzah bepeh*, he wrote, was from an immoral *mohel* whose degenerate lifestyle had exposed him to various diseases contracted through promiscuity. The way to avoid any health hazard, he concluded, was to employ scrupulously moral *mohalim*.[10]

If parents insisted that the *mohel* refrain from performing *metzitzah* with his mouth, Rabbi Hirsch advised that the *mohel* refuse to perform the circumcision since the obligation to circumcise was the father's and not the *mohel's*.[11]

When government pressure against *metzitzah bepeh* became unbearable, Rabbi Hirsch cooperated with Rabbi Michael Cahn of Fulda[c] to find a halachically acceptable solution. The result was the development of a specially formed glass tube filled with cotton, which enabled the *mohel* to draw out the infant's blood with his mouth while preventing any direct contact with the infant's body. Rabbi Hirsch sought and received the agreement of Rabbi Yitzchak Elchanan Spektor of Kovna to this procedure, and even today this tube is used by Orthodox *mohalim* when there is any danger of contact with infectious disease.[12]

Threats to Shechitah

IN THE 1880S VARIOUS ANTI-SEMITIC GROUPS REPEATEDLY REQUESTED the Prussian authorities to ban *shechitah* on the grounds that it constituted inhumane cruelty to animals. To placate these groups, Rabbi Ezriel Hildesheimer was prepared to allow stunning — a blow to the head of the animal — immediately after *shechitah*. Rabbi Hirsch vehemently opposed this concession for several reasons. First, according to some authorities such stunning is halachically unacceptable. That alone was sufficient reason to reject the proposal, he argued.[d] In addition, the proposal, he felt, would have two untoward practical consequences. Any compromise, Rabbi Hirsch argued, would lend credence to the claim that *shechitah* is indeed inhumane and would bring in its wake further demands, as experience in other countries had proven. In a letter to Rabbi Hildesheimer, he wrote that pamphlets or position papers about *shechitah* should avoid any characterization of it even as *unavoidable* cruelty to animals. Only pain inflicted without a compelling reason, he insisted, can be considered cruelty.

c. Rabbi Cahn (1847-1920) was a disciple of Rabbi Ezriel Hildesheimer, and the son-in-law of Rabbi Anselm Stern, Chief Rabbi of Hamburg. His indefatigable energy and prodigious ability to get things done made him one of the leading activists of the *Freie Vereinigung*.

d. Rabbi Hirsch also opposed stunning before *shechitah* to mollify the proponents of "humane slaughter," on the grounds that it would invariably render the animal a *treifah*. And in response to a query from New York, he prohibited the practice of the New York slaughterhouses of bloodletting the animals before *shechitah* in order to whiten the meat to make it look more like pork.[12*]

Anyone who argued otherwise would have to demand a ban on the working of farm animals or killing them for human consumption. Surely, he wrote, the performance of a *mitzvah* is not less important than the use of animals for the sake of satisfying human ambition (farm work) or pleasure (riding or traveling). In any event, he declared, the "Society for the Protection of Animals" had neither the right nor the competence to decide what is acceptable under Jewish Law.[13]

Finally, the anti-*shechitah* agitation constituted, in his view, a *gezeiras shmad* (a decree specifically designed to cause Jews to transgress their religion). In such a situation, he asserted in a circular to German rabbis, one is obligated to give up his life rather than submit, even regarding the color of the "shoelace" (*arkesa demesana*). If Jews held firm in their unwillingness to yield, Rabbi Hirsch maintained, the *Reichstag* would not force them to do something to which their religion was unalterably opposed. Given the contemporary anti-Semitic winds it was imperative not to yield an inch on any Jewish *minhag* no matter how peripheral, for any slight opening would encourage anti-Semites to call for the abrogation of all the *mitzvos*. He urged rabbis to stand firm without fear of the consequences.[14]

Burial

BY THE END OF THE 1870S, THE ANCIENT BURIAL GROUND OF THE Hamburg Jewish community was filled to capacity. After several years of intense efforts to procure more land for a cemetery, it became apparent that the authorities were only willing to lease land in nearby Ohlsdorf, but not to sell it outright. The authorities would agree only that the land be put "at the disposal of the Jewish Community," with a stipulation that if it were needed in the future for public works, such as roads or railways, the graves would be transferred elsewhere. The Rabbi of Hamburg, Rabbi Anselm Stern, held these conditions to be halachically unacceptable on the grounds that a Jewish cemetery must be owned outright. He insisted, instead, on the purchase of land in the nearby town of Langenfelde.

The choice of burial sites in the wake of Rabbi Stern's ruling plunged the Hamburg community into prolonged controversy. Inevitably, other authorities were drawn into the fray. Rabbi Hirsch concurred with Rabbi Stern, as did Rabbi Yitzchak Elchanan Spektor of Kovno and Rabbi Zalman Spitzer of Vienna.[15] Rabbi Ezriel Hildesheimer, however, held that a leased cemetery was acceptable.[16] The wisdom of Rabbi Hirsch's view was tragically realized a century later, when the Hamburg authorities permitted the development of the Ohlsdorf cemetery for commercial purposes.

IN A LENGTHY CORRESPONDENCE WITH HIS SON-IN-LAW RABBI Hirsch Plato of Cologne, Rabbi Hirsch opposed the use of telegraph wires for a citywide *eruv.* Even if the *eruv* were properly constructed, he wrote, there was always the possibility that the wires would tear or be moved. And he viewed it as almost impossible to adequately supervise all the components of a citywide *eruv* that relied primarily on telegraph wires.[17]

Other Issues

Rabbi Hirsch severely criticized those who made light of *tevilas Ezra,* the immersion of men in a *mikveh.* But he warned against using the women's *mikveh* for that purpose if, as a result, even one woman would refrain from using the *mikveh* or from immersing carefully. He suggested that a separate *mikveh* be constructed for men, and proposed that until one was built the men use 40 *se'ah* of drawn water, which is acceptable for *tevilas Ezra.* He cautioned, however, that if such use would cause anyone to think that drawn water is also permissible for a woman's immersion, those who practice *tevilas Ezra* should be *matir neder* (seek a release from their vow) until such time as a separate *mikveh* was available for men.[18]

Rabbi Hirsch Plato

In the last year of his life, Rabbi Hirsch carried on a lengthy correspondence with Rabbi Salomon Breuer concerning a suggestion by his son Dr. Marcus Hirsch that it might be possible to feed an ill person on *Yom Kippur* via an enema without transgressing the biblical prohibition of eating on *Yom Kippur.*[19]

In two responsa to Rabbi Hile Wechsler, he asserted that since the *shiurim* (the various sizes and measurements pertaining to *mitzvah* performance) of the Torah are specified in terms of the size of fruits or the size of various limbs, they vary from region to region, depending on the median size of fruits or people of that region. He contended this was the reason that different regions had historically followed different *shiurim.*[20]

To a questioner from The Hague, he wrote that the custom in Frankfurt for generations had always been not to sell the hindquarters of the animal for fear that those veins that need porging would not be properly removed.[21]

Rabbi Hirsch received queries from as far away as the United States.[e] In 1860, he replied to a question from New Orleans asking about the construction of a monument (not a statue) in memoriam of Judah Touro (1774-1854), the first American Jew to leave large bequests in his will for Jewish causes. Rabbi Hirsch replied that such monuments had no precedent in Jewish practice and were contrary to authentic Jewish custom. Although monuments had been built to memorialize events or important places, none were erected in memory of a person, except for the one Absalom, son of King David, built for himself in Jerusalem. Although the Jewish people had countless great men, Rabbi Hirsch pointed out, nowhere do we find monuments being built in their honor or memory. He cited the Jerusalem Talmud *(Shekalim* 5:4*)*, which recounts Rav Chomo's remark upon passing a magnificent synagogue in Lod: "See how much money my forebears sunk into the ground when they built these edifices." Rav Hoshiya replied: "How many lives have your forefathers put into the ground? Were there not any Torah scholars living at the time whom they could have supported with all the money they wasted on these expensive buildings?" In the same spirit, Rabbi Hirsch concluded, the greatest memorial would be the establishment of a fund to support the spiritual growth of promising people.[22]

---

e. He received *shaalos* from Rabbi Moshe Aharonson of New York, Rev. Isaac Leeser of Philadelphia and Rabbi Yissochor Dov Illowy (1812-1871), a disciple of the *Chasam Sofer*, in New Orleans. The latter was one of the few Orthodox rabbis of his time in the United States. He was an ardent opponent of Reform and a prolific writer in the Anglo-Jewish press on behalf of Orthodoxy. In 1914, his son published *Milchamos Elokim*, a collection of his letters and halachic responsa.

Chapter Twenty-Six

BEIS HAKNESSES

In Perspective

DIGNITY IN THE PRAYER SERVICES AND SCRUPULOUS adherence to the *minhagim* of the *beis haknesses* were elevated to an art form in Frankfurt. Yet Rabbi Hirsch never tired of emphasizing that the synagogue and its services were but a means of "preparation for the real worship of G-d in practical life," and are superseded in holiness by the "*batei medrash*, the houses of learning, which are devoted to the study and teaching of Torah."[1]

The emphasis in Jewish communities in the past, he stressed, has not been on prayer or acts of kindness and generosity but rather on Torah. And the vitality of Torah is measured not by the beauty of the study halls but rather by the numbers of students who study there. Rabbi Hirsch noted sadly that there is rarely a dearth of funding to build new synagogues or to refurbish existing ones, while efforts to mobilize resources for Torah study always meet with resistance.[2]

In an article in *Jeschurun* in 1860, he attacked the attitude of the Reform that to be a good Jew one need do no more than attend synagogue services. He advanced an audacious proposal to uproot this mistaken idea:

> Perhaps the most radical cure in a time of confusion and the loss of all values would be the—provisional—closing of all synagogues! Let such an idea not frighten the reader. The closing of all synagogues would not affect or alter the precepts of the Divine Law one iota. But even a hypothetical announcement of the removal of the prohibition against eating the *gid hanasheh,* the sinew of weakness, for example, would shatter the very foundation of G-d's Law! The closing of all synagogues through Jewish hands would constitute the loudest protest against the denial of the Divine Law in life and home; it would give the most drastic emphasis to the truth that Divine Judaism embraces and dominates the totality of Jewish life and does not find its fulfillment in the halls of prayer and worship.[3]

Rabbi Hirsch's critique must be understood in the context of the religious conditions of that time, especially the growing power of the Reform Movement, which had cast off most of the *mitzvos,* especially Torah study. To compensate for the lack of any genuine Jewish content in their lives, the Reformers felt a pressing need to build spectacular houses of worship. Their Judaism was gauged, in their own eyes, and in those of the Christians they wanted to impress, by the grandeur and opulence of their synagogues.

Rabbi Hirsch, by contrast, fought against the identification of Judaism with the synagogue. Torah was for him a law for all of life, not a devotional religion, confined to houses of worship. Any narrowing of the realm of Torah was anathema to him:

> If the Jewish law, like the other religions which are confined to the temple or the church, were to be practiced only in a synagogue, as is prescribed by the deceiving disciples of modern apostasy, Judaism would have disappeared long ago. The Jews in the Diaspora were preserved as an isolated entity not because the practice of their "religion" demands a synagogue but because their law demands purity in marriage and at the table. . . .
>
> The Torah encompasses all of life and elevates it into one continuous Divine service. . . . The Torah transforms. . . . the Jew into a priest, his home into a temple, his table into an altar, his life into

Main shul on the Schützenstrasse

an offering. . . . This Torah. . . . is his spiritual passport, which unfailingly accompanies him through his journey through life.[4]

Nevertheless, Rabbi Hirsch did not lose sight of the fact that prayer in *shul* is one of the primary means by which a Jew communicates with his Creator. As such, everything connected with it must have a grandeur and dignity. Nowhere was that dignity found to a greater extent than in Frankfurt.

The Synagogue in Frankfurt

ABOUT TWO YEARS AFTER RABBI HIRSCH'S ARRIVAL IN FRANKFURT, on 26 *Elul* 5613 (September 29, 1853), an impressive, new synagogue building was inaugurated on the *Schützenstrasse.* All of Frankfurt's notables, including the mayor and members of the Senate were in attendance. That

Synagogue on the Friedberger Anlage, erected 1907

building became, in time, the focal point of independent Orthodox Jewry in all of Germany. The synagogue was initially designed to hold 450 seats, 200 of which were in the women's section located on a separate gallery.[5] That ratio of seats between the men's and women's sections reflects the fact that most women in the community, young and old alike, attended services regularly.[a] In 1874, the synagogue was expanded to include seating for a thousand. The *shul* building on the *Schützenstrasse* was the center of the *Kehillah's* activities for the next three decades, until 1907, when the *IRG* inaugurated the new and splendid edifice on the *Friedberger Anlage.* The latter was one of the most magnificent *shuls* in Europe.

The grandeur of the *IRG* synagogue reflected Rabbi Hirsch's feeling that the setting for prayer must be commensurate with its holy purpose. He firmly believed that awareness of the beauty of the physical world had the power to elevate man spiritually and cause him to seek in his own life moral beauty. Both physical and moral beauty are the expressions of harmony, and the observation of harmony in nature should lead the sensitive soul to seek it in his own life.

> A young man understands that G-d's world should be beautiful just as paradise is beautiful. And so he is seized by the longing to rise harmoniously to similar beauty and to avoid any discord in this concert of existence of which he is a part.[6]

---

a. This custom continues today in Frankfurt's successor *Kehillah, K'hal Adath Jeschurun* of Washington Heights.

Synagogue on the Friedberger Anlage, interior

GENUINE SERENITY, RABBI HIRSCH TAUGHT, IS THE SPIRITUAL satisfaction that comes with the knowledge that one has fulfilled one's obligations. The delight one experiences when beholding a beautiful plant or any magnificent creation which has fulfilled its function in the world to its fullest flows from that awareness. The exhilaration we experience in observing Hashem's creations fulfilling their function in the world should inspire us to perform of our own free will that which nature performs instinctively — Hashem's bidding:[7]

Hiddur Mitzvah

> Not for naught did G-d clothe the world with the garment of beauty, form the law of harmony into shapes and sounds, and open the eyes and ears of mankind to grasp these harmonies and to enjoy them intellectually and spiritually. Every perception of the loftiness as demonstrated by a star-studded sky, by the rays of the rising or setting sun, every joy experienced by the grace and beauty of a flower elevates man to the level of lofty concepts and ideals.[8]

Rabbi Hirsch trained his congregants to adorn their performance of each *mitzvah* in the most aesthetic fashion possible. He did so not out of a desire to thereby make Judaism more palatable to those impressed by magnificent churches or the pomp and circumstance of non-Jewish rites, but out of his conviction of the relation of aesthetic beauty and moral harmony. In an 1839 letter to his cousin Simon May, he expressed some of his ideas on the importance of beautifying the performance of *mitzvos*.

> If the day comes that you choose a life's companion for yourself, and you find that you love your new wife only when she is attired in her best jewelry and finest clothing but she loses her appeal to you when she goes about her housework in an everyday housecoat, then woe to that love you hold for her. Nonetheless, when someone truly loves his wife, he wants to give her beautiful jewelry, and the stronger his love the finer the jewels he gives, but for *her* sake and not his, only for her sake.
>
> So it is in this matter, my dear cousin. Someone who does not love Judaism even when she is dressed in her old dusty clothes will not love her in her finery either. Therefore, not for those who are weak in their devotion but for you who are strong, or rather for Judaism itself, do those who truly love her desire to see her adorned with the greatest honor.[9]

Rabbi Hirsch taught by example. When he first came to Frankfurt, the custom was for several families to share one small *succah*. Rabbi Hirsch built himself a large new *succah* despite the fact that the apartment building in which he lived already had one. His disapproving landlord commented that such great expense was "*aveirah gelt*," to which he replied, "No, it is *mitzvah gelt*." The people in Frankfurt followed his example and the custom became that each family built its own beautiful *succah*.[10]

The Services

RABBI HIRSCH PUT GREAT EFFORT INTO ENSURING THAT THE atmosphere and decorum in *shul* were befitting its status as a *mikdash me'at*, a miniature Sanctuary. But he made it clear that the improvements in the decorum and dignity of the services were in no way to be construed as a sop to those who sought change as an end in itself, nor to those who were in any case less than fully committed. "But as far our services are concerned," he wrote in 1839 to his cousin, "your complaints are justified, and even more so since it would be so easy to remedy the situation. But not for the sake of the weak, for it seems to me that not one of them would be one iota more Jewish if our services were more dignified."[11]

As Chief Rabbi of Moravia, he sent a detailed list of regulations to every synagogue in the province, designed to increase the reverence appropriate to such holy places. They included the following requirements:

1. Every synagogue must be kept constantly in a state of cleanliness and order so that even its external appearance proclaims to visitors: "You are about to enter a holy place imbued with fear of Hashem's honor."
2. Similarly each participant in the services must maintain a clean and neat appearance. It is forbidden to enter a synagogue during services with dirty clothes or a torn *tallis*.
3. Every step you take and every movement you make in a synagogue must reflect fear and awe of Hashem's honor.
4. Children must not disturb adults with their presence: Therefore children under the age of five may not be brought to the synagogue.
5. It is forbidden to do anything that will disrupt the concentration in prayer of oneself or others.
6. It is strictly forbidden to engage in conversation in the synagogue. Anyone who does so shows that his thoughts are not filled with fear of G-d and that he does not seek to come close to G-d. This attitude erects a barrier between G-d and him.

As Chief Rabbi of Emden he went so far as to order that a particular synagogue be closed for a period of time because its officers were unable to control disruptive squabbles that regularly erupted during services.[12]

Services in Frankfurt always commenced at precisely the scheduled time, and there were generally few vacant seats when *davening* began, even in the middle of the week.[13] Rabbi Hirsch encouraged his flock to pray together in the main synagogue in accordance with King Solomon's dictum, *The King's glory is in a multitude of people (Mishlei* 14:28), and not to split up into smaller groups.[14]

The *chazan* in Rabbi Hirsch's later years was Mr. Julius Friesländer, a man who combined both a deep piety and the ability to enunciate every word clearly and precisely. Rabbi Hirsch made a point of reviewing with him the liturgy and *piyutim* of the entire year, some of which are composed in a difficult poetic Hebrew, to make sure he understood every word and expressed it properly.[15]

Rabbi Hirsch made several additions to the prayer service in Frankfurt. The most noticeable of these was a choir composed of members of the con-

Rabbi Hirsch's handwritten schedule of Yom Kippur services 5625, 5637, 5639

Friday night blessing

gregation and their children.[b] The choir did not join in the prayers in lieu of the *chazan* or the congregation, but rather served the function of leading the congregation in song.[16] The melodies, composed by the deeply pious I.M. Japhet (1818-1892), became part of the spiritual treasury of many Orthodox German congregations. Japhet's book of musical compositions for the synagogue, *Shiré Jeschurun,* was published in 1856, and republished in 1864 and 1881. His melodies were sung in nearly 200 communities.[17]

At Rabbi Hirsch's request, Japhet composed a special melody for the *Shir HaMaalos (Psalm* 128*)* that is recited at the conclusion of the *Maariv* services on *Motzaei Shabbos*. The *chazan*, the choir and the entire congregation all joined together to sing this *Psalm* verse by verse in a measured, stately tempo to give the Sabbath proper honor at its departure. Thus, there was no rushing to the exit at the end of Shabbos in Frankfurt.[18] Another innovation was the recital of *Kabbolas Shabbos* by the entire congregation rather than just by the *Chevra Mekablei Shabbos*, as had hitherto been the custom in Frankfurt.

The prayer service and customs of the *IRG* in Frankfurt, the specially composed melodies sung by the congregation together with the *chazan*

b. Already in Emden, Rabbi Hirsch's *shul* had a choir.

and the choir, and the beautiful design of the synagogue, all combined to inspire awe in everyone who attended services, including those not given to spontaneous feelings of devotion.[c]

RABBI HIRSCH RESISTED ALL ATTEMPTS TO OMIT ANYTHING FROM the traditional *nusach hatefillah*. There were some in Rabbi Hirsch's time who urged the deletion from the prayer service of the *piyutim*, which in any case are difficult to understand. They felt that by giving in a little, the Reformers would refrain from deleting more essential prayers, and buttressed their claim by citing the Talmudic dictum (based on *Psalms* 119:126), "עת לעשות לה' הפרו תורתך — *When there comes a time to act for G-d, abrogate Your Torah.*" Rabbi Hirsch wrote that a close examination of the places in the Talmud where this rule is employed reveals that it applies only to instances where a prohibition is set aside in order that a *mitzvah* might be performed. What possible *mitzvah*, he asked, is performed by refraining from the recital of *piyutim*? In addition, when Elijah and Shimon *HaTzadik* set aside particular prohibitions they did so on a one-time basis, whereas the intention here was to permanently abolish the *piyutim*.[d,19]

Nusach HaTefillah

There was one instance where Rabbi Hirsch did omit a traditional prayer. In 1839 (ת"ר — 5600), Rabbi Hirsch deleted the recitation of *Kol Nidrei* in Oldenburg. Rabbi Hirsch's family in Hamburg was opposed, as was, according to some reports, his *rebbi* Chacham Bernays.[20]

Jewish historians cite this story as proof that Rabbi Hirsch was not averse to making "reforms" in the prayer service.[21] They generally ignore, however, his consistent refusal over a lifetime to delete any part of the

---

c. It is little known that the famed German pronunciation of the חולם as 'ow' was not the original Frankfurt pronunciation, but was originally confined to North Germany, including Rabbi Hirsch's native Hamburg. In Frankfurt, before Rabbi Hirsch, the חולם was pronounced as in Southern Germany, like the 'o' in "go." Rabbi Hirsch brought the North German (Hamburg, Oldenburg, and Emden) pronunciation, with him. In *The Nineteen Letters* and *Horeb* he transliterated the חולם as au (pronounced ow) — e.g., *Rausch Haschono, Schowuaus, Chaudesch* and *Sukauss*. By contrast, in those books and articles which he authored after his arrival in Frankfurt, he either employed the traditional Frankfurt pronunciation when he transliterated or used the Hebrew word itself. *Horeb* and *The Nineteen Letters*, which were fixtures in Orthodox Jewish homes in Germany, contributed in no small measure to the "new" German pronunciation of the *IRG* as we now know it.[18*]

d. In order to instill belief in G-d, *Chazal* permitted the use of His Name when greeting someone (*Berachos* 54a). Similarly, Elijah the Prophet at Mount Carmel offered sacrifices on a *bamah* (temporary altar) to prove the sham of worship of *Baal* (*Berachos* 63a). Shimon *HaTzadik* donned the vestments of the priesthood when he went to greet Alexander the Great in order to prevent the destruction of the *Beis HaMikdash* (*Yoma* 19a). The reading of the *Haftarah* in public and the reduction of the Oral Law to writing were necessary to ensure its transmission to future generations (*Gittin* 60a). These were all instances where the preservation of Judaism was at stake.[19*]

tefillah, including the *piyutim,* which were omitted in many Eastern European congregations. They also ignore his own statement on the matter.

The halachic reason was likely, as Professor Mordechai Breuer has suggested, that reliance on *Kol Nidrei* had led to a general laxity with respect to vows and oaths. Rabbi Hirsch explained it in writing to the correspondent of the liberal *Allgemeine Zeitung des Judentums*: "Although last year the *Kol Nidrei* was deleted for *halachic reasons* (emphasis added), nevertheless I came to the conclusion that this change, although halachically grounded, would better not be instituted by an individual rabbi. Therefore I requested that the congregation recite it, but only once, not three times." In any event, he reinstated *Kol Nidrei* the following year.[22]

Rabbi Hirsch advised the director of an orphanage to resign his post if forced to introduce changes in the synagogue service, even if only to recite the *Av HaRachamim* prayer weekly, in honor of recently fallen soldiers. (In German Jewish *kehillas Av HaRachamim* is recited on only two Sabbaths a year.) Any insistence by the board of the institution to introduce changes, he asserted, was grounds for resignation.[23]

Rabbi Hirsch strongly condemned the repetition of words by the *chazan* for melodic purposes, describing it as making light of the most serious matters. Any congregation, he wrote, which wishes to call itself Jewish, should not allow such practices.[24]

Kaddish, Rabbi Hirsch wrote in a responsa to Würzburg in 1879, should be recited by only one person at a time, since "two voices can not be clearly distinguished when heard simultaneously" (*Rosh Hashanah* 27a). For some to recite *Kaddish* in a low voice was not an option, because the *Kaddish,* the sanctification of G-d's Name, must be declared loudly and clearly.[25]

Part Nine

THE MAN

Chapter Twenty-Seven

THE PERSONALITY

MUCH HAS BEEN WRITTEN ABOUT RABBI HIRSCH'S impressive achievements, but little about his character. Being neither his contemporary nor his equal, we do not presume to capture the essence of the man, but rather to record some glimpses of his personality as revealed in his writings and the accounts of his contemporaries.

The essence of his personality was a deep and genuine fear of Heaven. Already in his youth Samson Raphael Hirsch grasped the deep seriousness of existence,[1] and the rest of his life was an unbroken continuum of tireless activity and fearless action. His demeanor was serious and introverted. He was not talkative.[2] An almost palpable fear of Hashem's greatness (יראת הרוממות) emanates from all his writings, and he constantly conveyed an awareness that he was no more than a servant ready to serve his master in all areas of human endeavor:

> No drop of blood throbs in our veins, no cord quivers in our nervous system, no fiber twitches in our muscles, no sentiment

> moves our hearts that does not make us belong more fully to Him. No thought illuminates our brain, no ground supports our weight, no breeze wafts past us that does not join us to Him. No ray of sunlight shines on us, no fruit ripens for us, no animal lives for our sake, no child thrives for us, through which we do not belong more thoroughly to Him.[3]

Rabbi Zalman Spitzer described him well: "The thread that runs through all his life, through all the depths of his heart and through all his writings, is that a Jew must sanctify Hashem's Name and must devote all of his abilities, physical, intellectual, material, and all other senses to one purpose — to G-d."[4]

An Intrepid Fighter

THROUGHOUT HIS LIFE, RABBI HIRSCH WAGED AN UNCEASING battle to protect traditional Judaism from its attackers; the circumstances in his time left no other choice. Entirely appropriate is the vivid depiction of Rabbi Nota Wolf, *Rosh Beis Din* of Pressburg, who described Rabbi Hirsch as "the blood avenger of Torah in Germany."[5] He did not seek conflict, but neither would he shy away from it.[6] With the establishment of the monthly *Jeschurun*, he defined the perspective which informed his public activity:

> In the present times, as always, those who build the sanctuary are required to work with a sheathed sword ever on the alert. The sword would prefer to remain in its sheath for as long as the construction is allowed to proceed without disruption, stone by stone. However, when the ground crumbles away beneath it, the right hand is forced to fight the battle of truth, while the left hand continues to fulfill its function of seeking peace.[7]

Until the middle of the century, his battles were directed principally, but not exclusively, to combating the Reform Movement. During his tenure in Nikolsburg, he fought for civil rights for Jews and for the organizational viability of the Jewish communities in Moravia. At the beginning of his service in Frankfurt, he struggled to place the *IRG* on a solid footing, to open the *Realschule* and to build the various institutions his congregation needed, in the face of staunch opposition from the Reform-dominated *Grossgemeinde* every step of the way. He conducted a lengthy and contentious public debate with the purveyors of *Wissenschaft des Judentums,* contesting the theories of the historian Heinrich Graetz and Dr. Zachariah Frankel on the "development" of the Oral Torah, despite the invective and calumny his unyielding position brought down on him. In his later years he fought for secession (*Austritt*) from dominant, non-observant community structures. And in the rabbinic world outside of Russia, he stood almost alone in his efforts on behalf of Russian Jewry from 1882-84.

A Willingness to Stand Alone

A CONSTANTLY RECURRING THEME IN RABBI HIRSCH'S WRITINGS IS that one must be prepared to stand alone in the service of truth. It made no difference to him whether he conducted his battles with allies or alone:

> Let him who is convinced that his views are true and right express them . . . at every opportunity . . . without considering how much support or how much opposition he will encounter. Only falsehood is in need of many supporters in order to win the day; falsehood must have the authority of numbers to make up for what it lacks in justification. Truth, by contrast, will always prevail, even if it takes time. Noble, courageous and pure, expressed with all the fiery zeal of conviction and with all the clarity of sure awareness, stated again and again at every opportunity, truth will ultimately gain respect and admiration even of those who do not accept it. The only truth that can be lost beyond recall is that truth whose adherents no longer have the courage to speak up candidly on its behalf. Truth has never gone down in defeat as the result of opposition, it has done so only when its friends are too weak to defend it.[8]

In an 1858 letter to Isaac Leeser (1806-1868) in the United States,[a] he exhorted him not to despair over the sad state of Judaism in America, which he compared to that in Germany. The problem, he wrote, "is not the treachery of the Reformers, but the apathy of the observant." Our mission, he continued, is to inspire our brethren to rally to the defense of Judaism, and, "if we discharge *our* responsibility, Hashem will surely do His, in the proper time."[9]

Mattisyahu and Eliyahu *HaNavi,* he often recalled, were able to turn back the tide — even though they were totally alone — by virtue of their pure intentions:

---

a. Born in Germany, Leeser moved to the United States in 1824. He served as *chazan* and performed rabbinical functions in Congregation *Mikveh Israel* in Philadelphia from 1829 until 1850, and from 1857 until his passing in 1868, was Rabbi of Cong. *Beth El-Emeth*. Leeser founded *The Occident* (1843-1869), the first Anglo-Jewish monthly in the United States, and the only Jewish newspaper in America of the 1800s to remain Orthodox.

Leeser was active in many areas of American Orthodoxy and fought vigorously against the rising Reform Movement. He printed the first Torah-true English translation of the *Tanach* in America, in addition to *Ashkenaz* and *Sefard siddurim* with English translation.[8*]

Let no one disdain the smallest object formed by clean hands and hearts. All seeds are small, but the strength that live in them is great. If the seeds are the right kind, they will gather around themselves others to join them and merge with them into an ever greater organism. What was insignificant at the start flourishes after a few decades; and what was initially an emergency measure becomes increasingly a haven of rescue for all who need it and seek it.[10]

Uncompromising on Jewish Issues

RABBI HIRSCH EMPHASIZED THE IMPORTANCE OF COMPROMISE AND accommodation in one's personal life, "even at the cost of possessions," when all that was at stake were one's "rights or honor."[11] There could be no compromise, however, when dealing with issues of the Divine imperative.

Where goods that we are entitled to call our own are concerned, which we have the right to dispose of, we may and should come to an agreement even at a sacrifice. But if values which are merely in our custody are concerned, we are not entitled to "negotiate a settlement.". . . We may never make concessions just for the sake of having peace, and never sign a compromise peace settlement. On such a document our signature would be null and void, because we lack the authorization.[12]

His approach echoed that of his master Rabbi Yaakov Ettlinger, who taught that the love of peace cannot overshadow love for truth, and the pursuit of harmony is not sufficient justification to countenance religious infractions. One should not refrain from fighting heresy, Rabbi Ettlinger taught, because of the false argument that "great is peace," for although peace between man and his fellow is important, peace between Israel and their Father in Heaven is more important. "Therefore the one who avenges the vengeance of the Lord to strengthen the Torah is the one who desires peace and seeks it diligently."[b,13]

b. Rabbi Hirsch explained the true meaning of peace in terms of the story of Pinchas, the grandson of Aaron the High Priest who, through the act of killing a prince of Israel, merited to Hashem's "Covenant of Peace": True peace, he wrote, is between heaven and earth. Hashem promised the "covenant of peace" to Pinchas, who was accused of being a disturber of the peace, precisely because he opposed every mocking departure from the law of G-d and because his aim was to assert for that Law the sole rule over the acts and consciences of men. It is only under the sole hegemony of the Law that peace reigns, and he who asserts the role of the Law is a bearer and multiplier of peace.[13*]

Weakness in the guise of moderation, Rabbi Hirsch insisted, only invites further demands for concession:

> [Those who have] been overwhelmed by a human weakness which causes them to temporize by flexibility and moderation and all those other appeasing catchwords of the *juste milieu*, the "golden mean" to salvage the cause of G-d and to keep the nation close to that cause . . . do not realize that to surrender half the truth means to surrender the whole truth. . . . Those who cherish such compromises and hope to save the cause by accepting wide concessions do not realize that their opponents will see in their concessions a negation of the Divine character of the cause. They will declare that if certain parts of the Torah are not G-d-given, wherein lies the Divine origin of the remainder?[14]

In a letter to London in 1888, Rabbi Hirsch wrote, "I have learned from experience that there can be no compromise between observant and non-observant Jews in religious matters. Any compromise only brings renewed trouble all over again."[15]

Truth and Peace

A PHRASE FROM THE PROPHET ZACHARIAH (8:19), WHICH APPEARS over and over again in Rabbi Hirsch's writings, informed his public activity in the defense of traditional Judaism: והאמת והשלום אהבו— *You shall love truth and peace.* This verse even appears inscribed in his handwriting over his signature on the first known portrait of him, taken during his first years in Oldenburg.[16] He explained that the concepts of truth and peace invariably occur in that order in *Tanach,* truth first and only afterwards peace, "For peace is not a father of truth; peace is a *child* of truth. Win the people for truth, inalienable truth that can never be sold, not even for the price of peace, when sacred causes are involved, and then true, everlasting peace will follow of itself."[17]

> Is Truth so important to you that you desire only that peace which is not built upon the demise of truth? Or is peace so important to you that you desire only that Truth which is compatible with everything else in your life? Would you bow only before that Truth which has bowed before *you?* . . .
>
> "The Truth is to be found in the middle course," you say? Falsehood is to be found in the middle course! Truth is something that is precise and unequivocal. Two times two is four, not four-

and-a-half and not five-and-a-half. Today, however, one does not profess his belief in this basic arithmetic if he wants to be among those who are "up-to-date."[18]

Scrupulous Honesty

A COROLLARY TO HIS UNSWERVING ADHERENCE TO TRUTH WAS HIS fierce resistance to any word or deed, whether in public or private life, which did not adhere completely to that ideal. He set the example for meticulous honesty in money matters, a principled integrity, which, until today, is the hallmark of German Jews who follow in his footsteps. One of his famous sayings: "*Glatt Kosher? — Glatt Yosher!*" reflects the conviction that Judaism admits of no dichotomy between *mitzvos* which are between man and G-d and those which are between man and his fellow. The same strict adherence is demanded for the latter as for the former.[19]

When he married at the age of 23, Rabbi Hirsch received a sizable dowry from his father-in-law, a banker in the city of Braunschweig, and deposited the entire sum in his father-in-law's bank. A number of years later, realizing that many Jews were lax in the intricate laws of *ribis* (the prohibition against interest), he withdrew the entire dowry from the bank and donated it all to charity, unwilling to receive even the slightest benefit from questionable money.[20]

As Chief Rabbi of Moravia, he sometimes found it necessary to severely reprimand those who sought to influence, through improper methods, the election of local rabbis. He reacted with outrage when pressured to qualify candidates, who, in his view, did not fulfill the necessary requirements, and was indignant that people expected him to bend the truth to satisfy personal ambitions.[21]

The *IRG* paid his salary at the beginning of each quarter of the civil year. When he felt his end drawing near, he instructed his children that in the event he should depart the world before the end of the pay period, they must be sure to return the unearned portion of his salary. As it was, he died on December 31, the last day of the quarter.[22]

In Rabbi Hirsch's view, one in a public position must at all times be willing to demonstrate his unimpeachable honesty. In 1843, the secular Jewish press published vicious attacks on Rabbi Hirsch Lehren (1784-1853) of Amsterdam, accusing him of mismanagement of funds earmarked for indigent Jews in Palestine. Lehren had founded the *Kollel Hod* organization ("Holland veDeutschland") in 1809 for the purpose of raising funds for the *yishuv* in Palestine. By 1824, he had succeeded in concentrating in the organization's hands all collection of funds in Western

Europe, as well as their distribution in Palestine.

Rabbi Lehren, whose honesty was above reproach, was badly hurt by the public smear campaign, and entreated his friends, Rabbi Hirsch among them, to publicly come to his defense by placing articles in the press defending his integrity and trustworthiness. Rabbi Hirsch replied that his overwhelming workload in Emden did not allow him time for any literary work, and that he hardly had the time to learn Torah. He advised Rabbi Lehren, however, to give a public accounting of the disposition of all the funds. Although, according to the *halachah*, a *gabbai tzedakah* has no such obligation, he wrote, it was nevertheless advisable, considering the nature of the times in which they lived, and would demolish all baseless criticism. He begged Rabbi Lehren not to see this as unbecoming, because *vehiyisem nekiyim*, the imperative to be irreproachable in the eyes of G-d and Israel, is never an embarrassment.[23]

As Chief Rabbi of Moravia, he was requested by the same *Kollel Hod* organization to become a member of its presidium. He declined, citing his already numerous responsibilities, but added that were he to find the time to become involved, he would accept such responsibility only if he could first visit the Holy Land, to obtain a firsthand look at the situation there. Only then could he be fully accountable for all the funds entrusted to him.[24]

A Steadfast Determination

THE TRAIT THAT STANDS OUT MOST PROMINENTLY IN RABBI Hirsch's character was undoubtedly his strong character, a firm persistence and consistency that resisted any and all pressures.[25]

It manifested itself in many ways, particularly in his *mitzvah* performance. In his last years, although under doctor's orders to eat and drink frequently, he never ate or drank so much as a glass of water outside a *succah*, even though it meant descending the two flights of stairs from his apartment to the courtyard below.[26]

In his personal life, too, he was possessed of an iron self-control. It was his practice to use snuff, until once he found himself leaving a snuffbox under his pillow, in case he should want to have it available during the night. When he realized what he was doing, he said to his daughter, Sophie Breuer, "Now the time has come to stop." He never again used any form of snuff.[27]

His strong personality inspired not only respect and admiration in the members of his *Kehillah*, but fear as well. More than once he said to one of the members of the *Kehillah* board, "My good sir, these matters are beyond your understanding."[28] But even in his own *Kehillah* things did not always come easy, and he would sometimes come home from a *Kehillah* board meeting with his clothing drenched in sweat, completely exhausted from the effort he was forced to expend to ensure that his view carried the day.

Mrs. Sophie Hirsch-Breuer

His tenaciousness was manifest not only in his contacts with members of the community, but also in his dealings with government officials. During the 1860s, he requested permission from the local authorities to set up an *eruv* (a system of wires surrounding an area of the city to permit Jews to carry on Shabbos within its boundaries). In spite of his attempts to explain to the city's Senate the implications of an *eruv,* he was unable to persuade them to grant permission. They were convinced that an *eruv* would signify that Frankfurt was enclosed and confined, hardly appropriate to its image as a free city.

To this Rabbi Hirsch replied with a quotation from the prophet Jeremiah (17:21, 27): *Thus says G-d: Take heed for the sake of your souls; do not carry anything on the Sabbath day. . . . If you will not listen to Me, to sanctify the Sabbath day, not to carry anything and thus to enter the gates of Jerusalem on the Sabbath day, I will kindle within its gates and it will consume the palaces of Jerusalem, and will never be extinguished.* These words were not heeded either, and within a year Frankfurt was subjugated in war and ceased to be an independent city.[29]

The very wealthy, too, were shown no favoritism. The Rothschilds were, without doubt, the leading Jewish family in Frankfurt. Mayer Amschel Rothschild (1744-1812), the founding father of the Rothschild dynasty, had five sons each of whom he established in a different European city. The eldest son, Amschel Mayer,[c] remained in Frankfurt and died childless. His place at the head of the Frankfurt branch was taken by two of his nephews, Baron Mayer Karl and Baron Wilhelm Karl Rothschild (1828-1901). In addition to being one of the wealthiest men in Prussia and the most famous Orthodox philanthropist in Western Europe, Baron Willy Rothschild was also the chief financial supporter of the *IRG,* his family having paid for

c. Amschel, son of Mayer; his father was Mayer, son of Amschel.

Baron Wilhelm Karl Rothschild

most of the building costs of the *shul* and the school. A devout and righteous Jew, he was on good terms with Rabbi Hirsch.[30]

But the affluence and influence of Rothschild counted for nothing when Jewish principles were involved. In a well-known episode, the Baron's daughter Minka developed a passionate desire to marry a non-religious cousin of hers, Maximilian Goldschmidt. The Baron consulted Rabbi Hirsch as to what to do. The latter replied that under no circumstances was he to permit the match.

"But she threatens to commit suicide!" protested the distraught father.

"Even so (*Auch dann*)," was the response, and when the marriage took place, Rabbi Hirsch did not attend. Rothschild never again spoke to Rabbi Hirsch, although he sent his carriage to the funeral as a gesture of respect. His anger, though, did not stand in the way of paying for a new building for the *Realschule* not long after this incident. But Rabbi Hirsch's view was prophetic. All the children of that union married non-Jews.[31]

Humility

IN SPITE OF THE STRONG PERSONA RABBI HIRSCH FELT IT NECESSARY to show the world, he was fundamentally a modest and unassuming person, who showered great compassion on the poor and lowly of spirit. In letters and responsa he repeatedly asks his respondents forgiveness if he is in error, and he states his views cautiously. In several letters he requested his correspondents to let him know if they find any mistakes in his commentary on the *Chumash*.[d] He exercised the authority of his office with an iron hand because he felt there was no choice, due to the low esteem in which the rabbinate was held in those times. "If I were left to myself," he once confided to his son-in-law Rabbi Salomon Breuer, "I would have long preferred not to be a rabbi."[32] In Nikolsburg and elsewhere he refused all

d. Yet, when queried about the *Chumash* Commentary, especially the halachic discussions, he replied forcefully to prove his point.

the rabbinic emoluments that were traditionally perquisites of the *Rav*, convinced that the practice only diminished the esteem due the position of rabbi.[33]

His imposing personality concealed a natural humility which revealed itself in odd moments. Not long before he passed away, someone asked him why he did not publish a new edition of *The Nineteen Letters,* for which there was still a great demand half a century after its original publication. He answered that he was uncertain that there would still be interest in it, and for this reason it was unlikely that the sales revenue would cover the publishing expenses.

When the questioner reacted with a smile of incredulity, Rabbi Hirsch said, "Do you really think we could be so bold as to print a new edition without financial risk?" The answer was so strongly affirmative that the author responded, "Well, if that is how it is, then you may print it. And since you are willing to take the risk, you may also keep the profits, if indeed there are any."[34]

He received no income at all from the publication of his books (12 volumes) and articles (over 400), and never requested nor accepted any form of payment for them. He once said that his profit from all of his considerable literary output would not suffice to buy him even a pair of gloves.[35]

He was a self-reliant person who did not like to ask for, or receive help, with his personal needs. His daughter and son-in-law reported that he consistently refused personal assistance even when enfeebled in his last years. Even in the last year of his life, he insisted on attending to his personal needs on his own.[36]

The warm and sensitive heart beneath the uncompromising exterior is nicely captured by an incident involving a letter he received from an eminent German rabbi who, in his opinion, had erred in a matter that posed serious danger to German Jewry. Rabbi Hirsch sent him a strongly worded reply, which many thought was overly strident. Not so well known was the fact that when the other rabbi's letter first came into his hands, Rabbi Hirsch broke down in tears that such an important figure had erred so egregiously. Nonetheless, he wiped his tears away and sat down to write an impassioned reply, which had the desired effect.[37]

Despite his reserved personality there was one group of people to whom he was always friendly and easily approachable: the children of his *Kehillah*. He would greet them and tip his hat to them when he met them on the street, and they felt so comfortable in his company that as they grew older they felt guilt and embarrassment for having behaved with such familiarity as children.[38]

Also welcome were the poor and downtrodden, "One had only to be poor and forlorn," his son Mendel related, "to gain admission to see him." Upon hearing the plight of Russian Jews during the pogroms of the 1880s, he broke into tears.[39]

In the wake of those pogroms, hundreds of Russian and Polish refugees arrived in Frankfurt, some of whom became involved in questionable activities. The board of the *IRG* wanted to have them expelled from the city, for fear that they would arouse antagonism against the Jewish community as a whole. Rabbi Hirsch, however, would not hear of it: "First throw the wealthy criminals out of the city. Only afterwards can you do the same to the poor ones."[40]

> Only he is moral, and thereby also happy, [who will] feel outrage at even the slightest injury done to an innocent person but who, at the same time, will calmly suffer even the most flagrant wrong done to himself, . . . he who can become enthusiastic about anything noble and true but can hate everything base and vulgar with a passion.[41]

His compassion extended to all Hashem's creatures. Rebbetzin Hirsch would put food on her windowsill every morning for the sparrows who gathered there. After her passing, one of his children surprised his father in the act of performing the same kindness. He continued this practice until his last days, and even on his final sickbed, when he no longer had the strength to stand, he told his sons not to forget to take care of the birds.[42]

His writings reveal a poetic soul that never ceased to be delighted by the wonders of creation. Typical of his attitude is the famous remark attributed to him, upon returning from a visit to Switzerland. "Now I can answer properly when Hashem asks me in the world of truth, 'Did you see also My Switzerland?' "[e,43]

Physical Attributes

BY ALL ACCOUNTS HE WAS NOT TALL, AND WAS PROBABLY OF shorter than average height. When he came to Frankfurt in 1851, the historian I.M. Jost, a resident of the city and an adherent of Reform, described him as "a handsome man, very much resembling Charles V."[44] One former student described him: "No picture and no artist could capture the fire that emanated from his eyes, the mixture of wisdom and burning energy,

e."[A]ll you who stay at home [will] one day have to atone for your staying indoors, and when you desire entrance to see the marvels of heaven, they [will] ask you, 'Did you see the marvels of G-d on earth?' Then, ashamed, you would mumble, 'We missed that opportunity.'"[43*]

accompanied by a searching and penetrating spirit."[45] He had *payos* (sidelocks), as was the custom among many German *rabbonim.*

Although born with a healthy constitution, already in Oldenburg he experienced periods of such weakness that he was not even able to hold anything in his hands.[46] During his tenure in Emden, while still in his 30s, he contracted malaria and continued to suffer bouts of the illness for the rest of his life. As a result, he had episodes of fever every four weeks, and this was one of the reasons he showed premature signs of age. The battle over *Austritt* in 1876-77 also took a considerable toll on his health and left him with a chronic condition that intensified in 1884-85. Nonetheless, he bore his ailments stoically.[47] In light of his poor health in his later years, it is instructive that he was intensely active on behalf of Russian Jewry even during the period of his greatest physical infirmity.[48]

About a year before his passing, he was visited by Rabbi Tobias Tal of Amsterdam who described him in the following terms:

> He was weak from illness and old age. . . . As I approached him, the forelocks protruding from under his skullcap were white, as was the full beard which framed his face. The hue of his face spoke of illness and the body was bent with age. But the eyes, the eyes spoke of freshness, in the eyes there was still the light of youth, and from them emanated sparks which transfused his entire face. The eyes, underneath the heavy grey eyebrows, were young, and when we began to speak, powerful sparks of fire with the awesome power of his soul began to shoot forth from his countenance. I saw before me not an old and sick man, but a young man, full of a powerful and burning spirit.[49]

A Son's Description

PERHAPS DR. MENDEL HIRSCH, IN AN ADDRESS DELIVERED AT THE *Shloshim*, summed it up best:

> How shall I describe him and how shall I remember him? Shall I speak about the man, about the greatness and the wonder that revealed themselves in his private interactions with people — the son, brother and the husband he was, how the words of the marriage ceremony "You are consecrated to me" were a living reality in his life? Shall I tell what kind of father he was, the glory and splendor of his personality, his lofty character, his firmness of will and his iron self-control?
>
> Shall I speak of his unwavering diligence in Torah study, his tireless dedication to his work, how he pushed himself incessant-

ly and never delayed the fulfillment of his obligations; how he never relinquished a project from the time he embarked on it until he brought it to completion, regardless of the amount of time it took? Or shall I tell of the depth of his intelligence, his boundless creativity and sharp intellect that expressed themselves in the penetrating look with which he scrutinized everything? Who could see those eyes and not feel that they had penetrated to the depths of his soul? Who is there who requested his advice on any matter and did not find the answer that he received, to be anything other than the precisely correct solution to his problem?

Shall I speak of his warm congeniality, his sense of humor and the sharp witticisms that occasionally shot out from him like a bolt of lightning? Shall I speak of his endless patience, his refreshing personality, his incomparable acts of kindness and charity? One had to be only poor and wretched to be assured of finding by him an open door, an attentive ear and a warm heart ready to listen and to help.

Shall I speak of the deep equanimity and serenity of soul that enabled him to persevere in his Torah studies and to continue his prolific work at all times, even on occasions of sadness or joy, when others would not have succeeded in carrying on? Shall I speak of his sensitivity and the profundity of his fear of G-d, and his faith and trust in Hashem? Anyone who had the privilege of seeing him at prayer could not help but recognize these lofty qualities in him, and feel how inadequate he himself was in these areas.[50]

Chapter Twenty-Eight
THE SPOKEN AND WRITTEN WORD

Orator

RABBI HIRSCH WAS AN ORATOR OF RARE TALENT. HE spoke without a text, occasionally keeping a small *Tanach* in front of him. In his early years he would commit his speeches to writing before he delivered them, and a few of these records still exist. After several years, however, he dropped this practice: As he later explained to Rabbi Salomon Breuer, he felt confined by the text. He spoke only in public settings, never at festive meals and private celebrations *(Tischrede)*.[1]

A number of factors contributed to the profound impression he made on his audience: the carefully chosen expressions, the fast tempo, originality of thought and cogency of argument.[2] Celebrated as we know him to be for his literary talents, his oratorical abilities are said to have been even greater yet.[3] His gifts as a speaker do much to explain the great influence he had on his contemporaries.[4]

During Rabbi Hirsch's first years in Frankfurt, his weekly Shabbos address was the bond which unified the members of the *IRG,* and provided them with the strength to overcome the harassment they faced. His addresses left his listeners inspired to put the ideals of the Torah into practice.[5] A visitor to the synagogue commented, "I did not understand one word that was said, but one had the impression that nothing less than the prophet Isaiah was standing up there." Opponents often came to hear him speak and left as ardent followers.[6]

A vivid eye-witness account of his addresses in Nikolsburg captures his power as a speaker:

> When he spoke Shabbos morning, generally from nine o'clock until ten, both men and women came from all 12 synagogues in the city to hear him. Watching him stand on the pulpit as he spoke to the congregation, one could not help being captivated by his appearance, and in particular, by his striking facial expression. One could almost see the Divine Spirit hovering over his head, the fire burning in his heart and the sparks that sizzled and shot forth from his enormous eyes, revealing to everyone the intensity of feeling that lay cached in the depths of his soul. Every word aroused an insatiable desire in the listener's heart to elevate himself from the base material world and rise higher and higher to the loftiest spiritual planes. He stripped away the world's physical shell to reveal the sweet spiritual fruit concealed within. His words had the power of thunder and lightning, and against this backdrop he stood like a sentry at his post, battling for his faith. . . . Hearing him deride the world's vanity in tones of such animated fire, the listener could only shrink to an abject nonentity in his own eyes. Behold, the mighty hero with his giant axe smashing great boulders into puny pebbles. He showed no mercy to the cruel and heartless, who sought the pleasures of the material world without a thought to the needs of others.
>
> Then, just as the listener's heart could no longer bear the anguish, the tone suddenly changed and he became a soothing poet, gently feeling out a path to the delicate inner recesses of the listener's Jewish soul. His soft words were. . . . full of tender love for every Jew, especially the poor and downtrodden, but more, for the whole of creation. At such moments, a sweet light shined

from his eyes and his body swelled with the grace of his holy words. Totally free of personal vanity, he embodied the Jewish soul at the height of its glory and splendor.

When he touched on the history of the Jewish people, its prophets and poets, its scholars and teachers, on the ones who sacrificed their lives to sanctify Hashem's Name, and on the wars and triumphs of our people, his face shone with a radiant light. Before your eyes generations arose and flourished, and whole epochs of history passed before you. In tones of innocent reverence and awe, he evoked bold visions of the end of days, projecting in comforting terms the future, when humanity will eventually rise from the depths of exile, and prophetic justice and pristine faith in Hashem, which currently lies dormant in the inner recesses of the soul, will emerge glorious to everlasting triumph. Such powerful ideals always aroused profound awe in the hearts of the audience. . . .

His addresses were given without the aid of notes or sources and with no preparation at all. After each one I would go for a walk in the forest, away from the city, and try to retain in my soul as much of the fire I had just experienced as I could keep in my memory.[7]

Rabbi Hirsch's two teachers Chacham Bernays and Rabbi Yaakov Ettlinger were the first Orthodox rabbis of note to preach in the German vernacular. As time went on, the use of German was so common even among religious Jews, that its use in a sermon was no longer regarded as an indication of a tendency toward assimilation or reform.[8]

Rabbi Hirsch was once asked by his uncle Moshe Mendelsohn-Frankfurter, a renowned Hebraist, why he delivered his sermons in the German vernacular and not in Hebrew. Rabbi Hirsch replied that the law in East Friesland required him and all the other communal rabbis to preach in the synagogue every Sabbath in the German vernacular. But, he added, even "this evil had its beneficial side which might even be the stronger dimension." "Look around," he wrote to his uncle, "and see how *Krias HaTorah* and the *Haftarah* are virtually ignored because the masses are not proficient in the Holy Tongue. Would that every Shabbos there would be a person like the *meturgeman* (interpreter) of yore to explain to the assembled the meaning of the Torah reading. If we had that custom today, he wrote, it would be more beneficial than any sermon. Not for naught," he continued, "are the houses of worship known as *'shul'* (school in German). They should indeed be a school, where one learns the lessons of life."[9]

RABBI HIRSCH'S POWERS OF WRITTEN EXPRESSION SET HIM APART. No one since has been able to equal his ability to portray to Jews of the modern era the essence of Judaism with such inspirational verve and conviction. His skill at capturing the sanctity and sublime beauty of Jewish life remains unparalleled. Rabbi Hirsch's writings demonstrate the Torah's eternal relevance in a way that has moved generations seduced by the great scientific and technical advances and the overwhelming opportunities for physical gratification of our era. "The surprising thing," wrote Dr. Joseph Wohlgemuth,"is how he responded to the advances of two generations without apologetics or compromise. Simply by displaying classical Judaism in a clear light, he allowed its beauty and glory to convince anyone who had any sentiment of holiness in him."[10]

The Power of the Pen

Rabbi Hirsch employed his mastery of German prose and modern literary techniques in the cause of classical Judaism. He turned the weapons of the Reformers and assimilationists — contemporary thought and culture — back against them. Today it is no longer unusual to see modern modalities used to advance the cause of Judaism, but in those days, when the opponents of Reform were just beginning to take up arms, Rabbi Hirsch's literary sophistication took everyone by surprise.

His essays and books became classics in Jewish consciousness. The timeliness of his writings is remarkable even today, and it is sometimes difficult to believe that some of them were written over 150 years ago. He was the first great Torah scholar to rise to the challenge of explaining Judaism to the modern world, the first to combine deep piety with such extraordinary powers of expression. His writings had a particular influence on the younger generation, and continued to affect German Jewry in the decades after his passing.[11] The publication of his *Gesammelte Schriften* (Collected Writings) in German, 20 years after his death, sparked a spiritual reawakening among the Jewish intelligentsia in Germany.[12]

His gifted pen, which rarely rested during his 60 years of public life,[13] produced a rich and varied output. All his writings, including his letters and halachic responsa, were stamped with his unique style and characterized by a warmth of feeling and a constant awareness of Hashem's Presence.

RABBI HIRSCH'S SKILLS AS A POLEMICIST WERE UNRIVALED. HIS CRItique of the religious renegades of his time can serve for ours as well.

Polemics

Initially he directed his attacks primarily against the Reform Movement, but over the years he was increasingly forced to publicly oppose those who were observant in deed, but who published works which expounded views of Jewish law and history which posed grave dangers to the traditions of Torah Judaism. In his last years he took public issue with those within Orthodox circles who were willing to cooperate with the Reform Movement in a communal framework, even after such membership was no longer demanded by the state.

Rabbi Hirsch's forceful and lucid reasoning gave his writings great persuasive power. When, as was often the case, his opponents were at a loss to defend themselves against the substance of his arguments, they were wont to resort to *ad hominem* attacks in their attempts to sway the public. Rabbi Hirsch steadfastly refused to respond to any of the countless denunciations his uncompromising defense of traditional Judaism brought down on him, except on one occasion, in the course of his dispute with the supporters of Dr. Zachariah Frankel. The following lines are instructive and revealing, especially in view of the fact that this was the only occasion in his 60 years of literary work that he revealed a glimpse of his innermost feelings on the subject:

> In all the 30 years of our public life, we have never once put down our pen. But we have never written so much as one word of personal attack against an individual. We concerned ourselves solely with ideas. We dealt with writing and writers, with the eternal mission of Judaism and the manner in which each generation sought to fulfill it. We consistently kept away from discussing individuals, their civic and moral lives, or their reputations, deserved or undeserved, literary or otherwise. We have never written against any person; we have never attacked or even intentionally offended anyone. Furthermore, all the time that we have been publishing [*Jeschurun*] we have never allowed it to be misused by others as an organ in which to make charges, deserved or undeserved (which the editor is not even in a position to judge), against any individual. The lies spread for years against our own person by other periodicals have been enough to deter us from giving similar treatment to others. They have taught us to employ in our own public utterances at least that modicum of decency which is considered proper in private con-

versation, and also not to give the printed word any license to indulge in vicious gossip.

By the same token, we have never discussed with our readers anything concerning ourselves. We have never uttered a word in our own support and have never used our journal, or any other journal for that matter, to publicize our own achievements and aspirations, our own endeavors and accomplishments. We have never lent a hand to gather even the most meager laurels of recognition for ourselves. We have even allowed lies and calumnies to go unanswered and unrefuted. It simply went against our innermost feelings to speak to our readers about ourselves. We had quite another perception of our purpose.[14]

One of Rabbi Hirsch's classic polemic pieces was written in 1854, three years after his arrival in Frankfurt and around the time of the establishment of the *Realschule*. Reform circles in the city began to feel anxious about the sudden flourishing of the *IRG*, and Leopold Stein, rabbi of the Reform Community, published a venomous article describing "the religious confusions within the Jewish community of Frankfurt." Stein attacked the Orthodox congregation vehemently, calling its members "opponents of progress and fomenters of discord out of the Middle Ages," in contrast to the Reformers, whom he described as "patient as Hillel." Stein urged that practical measures be taken against the *IRG* and called on the government and political leaders to decide how to "deal with this fanatical group." In short, a declaration of war.

Rabbi Hirsch responded with a pamphlet, called "*Die Religion im Bunde mit dem Fortschritt,* v. einem Schwarzen" ("Religion Allied to Progress, By a Reactionary"),[15] in which he eloquently presented the Orthodox case against the Reform Movement. He began with a vivid description of the conundrum of Reform Judaism: If everything is subject to Reform, what then defines Judaism, what constitutes its essence? All that remains are vague invocations of some ideal, mysteriously described as both unchanging and ever unfolding. In total, Reform Judaism boiled down to monotheism spiced with some vague ethical message.[16]

He challenged Stein's assertion that Judaism had no principles of faith, and showed how his reasoning was based on deception and ignorance: "There is not one principle, or three or thirteen, but rather 613, for someone who denies any one of the commandments of the Torah [is considered as if he] denies the Torah in its entirety.[17] Does our author," he asked, "know the meaning of the statement [of our Sages]: Whoever joins the

Name of Heaven with something else is uprooted from the world? It is religion allied to progress."

He described the dishonesty with which the Reformers portrayed authentic Judaism, and showed that the religious and humanitarian "progress" the Reformers claimed to have introduced were nothing more than disguises for social regression and intolerance. He concluded with a lengthy account of the tyranny of the Reform-dominated Community Board in Frankfurt, and its systematic efforts to stamp out any trace of authentic Jewish life in the city.

Jeschurun

ALREADY IN 1836 IN OLDENBURG, RABBI HIRSCH HAD PLANNED TO establish a journal which would bring together all those capable of presenting authentic Judaism in its true light in order to fight the influence of the Reform. But this dream did not come to fruition.[18] From 1845, a German-language weekly called *Der Treue Zionswächter* was published in Altona under the auspices of Rabbi Yaakov Ettlinger.[a] In autumn of 1854, Rabbi Hirsch began to publish a monthly journal in German, named *Jeschurun,* whose stated purpose was to promote "the spirit of Judaism and Jewish life in the home, the community and the school."

Jeschurun appeared under Rabbi Hirsch's editorship for 16 years. Rabbi Hirsch himself contributed approximately 400 articles, most of great length, distinguished by originality and depth of thought, as well as by their literary quality. *Jeschurun* played a crucial role in shaping Jewish public opinion of the time. Its pages reflected the state of Jewish life in Germany and other countries during that era.

The volumes of *Jeschurun* contain treasures from all fields of Jewish thought, including dozens of articles by Rabbi Hirsch on the festivals and months of the Jewish year. The numerous articles on issues of Jewish education profoundly influenced the Orthodox schools of Germany and other countries following the same model.[19] Alongside a vigorous defense of authentic Judaism, and polemics against its detractors, there also appeared valuable series of articles on the Jewish Sabbath,[b] the Jewish Woman, Jewish Symbolism, and essays on the *Psalms* and on the Book of *Isaiah.* From 1862 to 1863 Rabbi Hirsch translated and published in *Jeschurun* selections from the *Sefer Chasidim* by Rabbi Yehuda Hechasid of

a. It is unclear why Rabbi Hirsch never published anything in this journal, which was the mouthpiece of Orthodox Jewry in Germany during its years of publication.

b. The articles on the Sabbath were reprinted years later in pamphlet form and influenced many, including a large business concern in Berlin, to close their businesses on Shabbos.[19*]

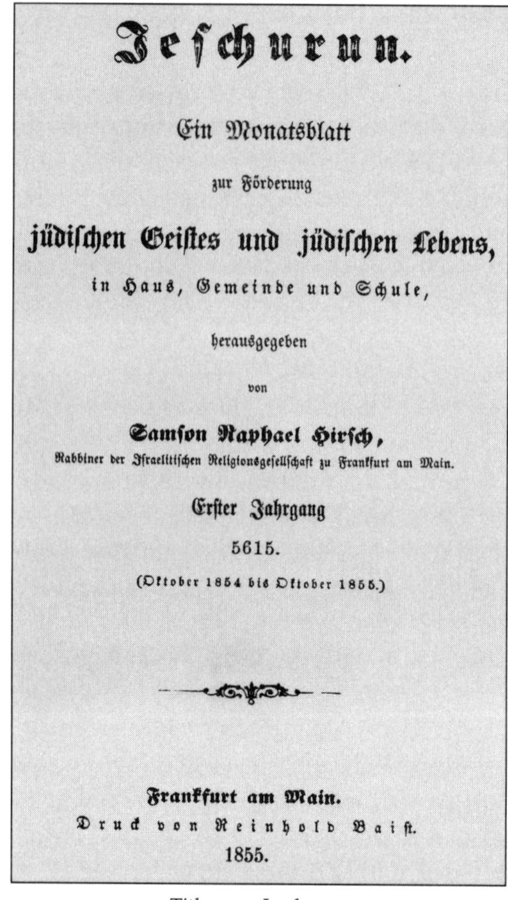
Jeschurun.

Ein Monatsblatt

zur Förderung

jüdischen Geistes und jüdischen Lebens,

in Haus, Gemeinde und Schule,

herausgegeben

von

Samson Raphael Hirsch,

Rabbiner der Israelitischen Religionsgesellschaft zu Frankfurt am Main.

Erster Jahrgang

5615.

(Oktober 1854 bis Oktober 1855.)

Frankfurt am Main.

Druck von Reinhold Baist.

1855.

Title page, Jeschurun

Regensburg (ca. 1148-1217) under the title "Traditional Jewish Piety," for the purpose of obtaining "a better understanding of Judaism as it was lived in the Middle Ages and as it is lived in the present." The selections are fascinating in how they reflect the moral lessons, many of them decidedly "un-modern," which Rabbi Hirsch wished to impart to his audience. *Jeschurun* also served as the vehicle for Rabbi Hirsch's fierce dispute with Graetz and Frankel. For decades after its appearance, the bound volumes of *Jeschurun* were cherished in Jewish homes in Germany, and in many of them, Friday nights or Shabbos afternoons were spent reading from its pages.[c]

Jeschurun was revived as a weekly in 1883 by Rabbi Hirsch's son Isaac in Hannover. It appeared in that form until 1888 when it merged with and was subsequently subsumed by the *Israelit*.[d]

Commentary on the Torah

RABBI HIRSCH'S MAGNUM OPUS, HIS CROWNING LITERARY achievement, was unquestionably his translation and commentary on the Torah, which includes within its pages all the major themes of his long and fruitful life. The first edition was published in Frankfurt, from 1867 to 1878.[20] A new edition was published in 1883 and was reprinted

c. Most of the articles which appeared in *Jeschurun* have been translated into English in the eight-volume *Collected Writings of Rabbi S.R. Hirsch,* New York, 1984-1995. Many have also been translated into Hebrew.

d. The first issue of the merged journal appeared the day after Rabbi Hirsch's funeral.

Shabbos afternoon

many times, as well as translated into Hebrew, English and French.

The preface to the Commentary contains the following explanation of its purpose:

> To explain each verse of Scripture based on the verse itself, drawing the explanation in all its facets from an analysis of the literal text of the Torah, in accordance with the meanings of the words as they are found in the lexicon of *Lashon HaKodesh* (the Holy Tongue); to describe, according to these linguistic explanations and according to the halachic and aggadic traditions that have been passed down to us from the early days of our nation along with the text of *Tanach,* those truths from which the view of the world and of Jewish life have been derived, which comprise the laws by which the life of the Jew is eternally guided.
>
> [The intention of the Commentary is to bring the reader to] a recognition of the total unity of Hashem's word that pulsates throughout the Holy Scriptures, and also to a recognition that this spirit is not merely a relic of a bygone era, but rather an ever vital force that contains in it all future human hopes and aspirations.[21]

A central theme of the Commentary is the demonstration of the harmonious unity of the Written Torah and Oral Torah, including the *Mishnah* and *Tosefta,* the Babylonian and Jerusalem Talmuds, *Midrashim* and halachic rulings. The author explains clearly how the exegetic interpretations of the Sages are actually contained in the words of the Torah themselves, if one understands them in their proper depth.

Another important feature of the Commentary is Rabbi Hirsch's unique etymological system for unveiling the profundity of *Lashon HaKodesh* (the Holy Tongue), with all its subtleties and allusions. Rabbi Hirsch was convinced that the structure of *Lashon HaKodesh,* the original language of Creation,[22] is not merely coincidence, but rather is consciously designed to convey vital teachings about life and the universe, and reflects the Divine Wisdom of its Author. It is therefore essential to examine the linguistic structure of *Lashon HaKodesh,* noting the emphases and connotations of each word, in order to deduce the Torah's teachings about the world and man's role in it.[23]

The Hirschian etymology makes extensive use of the interchangeability of related letters, an approach found in the classic Biblical commentators.[e] Phonetic similarities, Rabbi Hirsch held, were intended to evoke ideational associations in the mind of the listener. For Rabbi Hirsch, as Mordechai Breuer put it, Hebrew etymology is a "serious, sustained and most instructive attempt to listen to the universal ideas hidden in the thought patterns of the Hebrew language, and fulfill them in our lives."[24] Using hundreds of words of *Lashon HaKodesh* as building blocks, he constructed an edifice of Jewish values and the Torah's understanding of the world.[25]

While Rabbi Hirsch made etymological comparisons from within the whole of *Tanach,* he did not engage in comparative philology, even with other Semitic languages. Because *Lashon HaKodesh* is of purely Divine origin, comparative philology, including Semitic philology, was, in his view, totally irrelevant.[26]

Rabbi Hirsch opposed the mention in print of heretical views and Biblical Criticism, even for the purpose of refuting them. He discredited the arguments and theories of the Bible critics by explaining the Torah in a way that demonstrated the fallacy of their theses, and he responded to their arguments without mentioning them by name or stating their arguments.[27]

Although *Kabbalah* is never specifically referred to in the Commentary, a number of scholars of that branch of wisdom have voiced the opinion

---

e. See e.g., *Rashi, Vayikra* 19:16: Letters produced with the same parts of the mouth may be substituted for each other.

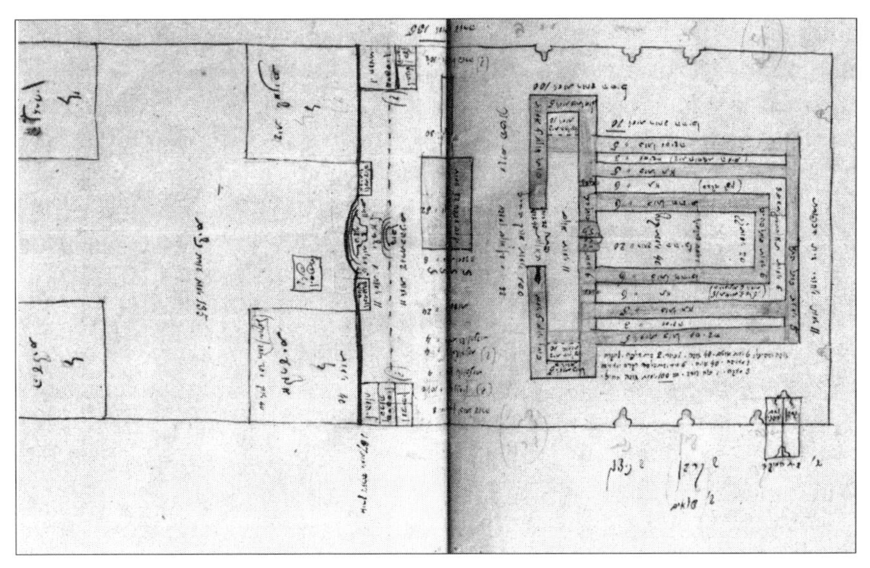

Rabbi Hirsch's own diagram of the Beis HaMikdash

that Rabbi Hirsch's Torah Commentary was deeply influenced by the *Zohar.* The system which the author employed in assigning symbolic meaning to subjects, colors, numbers and materials, and his attention to every detail, greatly resembled the kabbalistic method. To the trained observer his explications of many *mitzvos* have their source in the kabbalistic literature, but are clothed in the terms of rationalism.[f,28]

One of the major objectives of the Commentary was to explain every Divine injunction and to defend it against rationalist attack. For this reason the Commentary explains various facets of each *mitzvah* and their underlying concepts in great detail. Many of the topics which Rabbi Hirsch dealt with at length do not generally receive detailed treatment, because of the breadth of the concepts involved and the intricacy of the details — e.g., the vessels of the Tabernacle, the garments of the High Priest, the Temple sacrifices,[29] the laws of *tumah vetaharah* (ritual purity), the laws of *metzora* (a general term for a number of skin diseases, which also afflicted clothing and houses, and which required special purification procedures, see *Vayikra* 13-15), forbidden foods, and the Sabbath. The laws of *Parshas Mishpatim* are also explained in great detail. Hence the ironic testimony of Jacob Rosenheim: "I knew comprehensively, not from the Talmud and not from *Rashi's* commentary, but rather from having

f. Rabbi Yitzchak Hutner once remarked in a conversation with a disciple that Rabbi Hirsch must have "studied *Maharal* day and night," so influenced was his thought by that of the *Maharal.*

studied Hirsch's Commentary on the Torah, the whole order of the offerings, the laws of *metzora* and ritual purity, and the laws of custodians and damages, with all their manifold details, more clearly and comprehensively than any yeshiva student."[30]

The original basis of the Commentary was a series of lectures Rabbi Hirsch gave evenings in his home on the Book of *Bereishis,* notes of which were kept by several of the regular attendees.[31] The volumes on *Bamidbar* and especially *Devarim* were written during the struggle for secession from the Reform Community, a period so turbulent that Rabbi Hirsch was left considerably weakened physically. Yet the tone is one of such serenity and peace of mind that an uninformed reader would have thought they were written in a time of great tranquility.

The Commentary quickly became *the* definitive commentary on the Torah for German Orthodoxy. There was hardly a religious Jewish home in Germany that did not possess one, and it was not uncommon for entire families to spend Shabbos afternoon reading the Hirsch Commentary on the weekly Torah reading.[32]

Commentary on the Psalms

IN 1882, RABBI HIRSCH PUBLISHED, IN TWO VOLUMES, A TRANSlation and commentary in German to *Tehillim.* This work may be seen as a summary of a fruitful life of scholarship. It was intended to implant in the hearts of his people the same sentiments that inspired King David to write the *Psalms.*[33]

> The *Psalms* sing of G-d's workings both in nature and in the fate of the individual man, of Israel and of the nations. They reveal to us the mental and spiritual life of a man and of a nation basing themselves on the mandates and requirements set forth in the Torah, under the watchful eye of G-d, and guided and trained through his Providence, as they strive upward to an ever more perfect execution of their task and to loyal perseverance for the fulfillment of their destiny.
>
> The *Psalms* give expression to the thoughts and emotions which fill the heart of a man who walks before G-d in this manner in every aspect of his life, both in private and in public. These ideas and sentiments are presented for the personal acquisition of all those who seek to develop their spiritual and emotional lives by arranging them on the same basis and by ennobling and enriching them with the same ends in mind.[34]

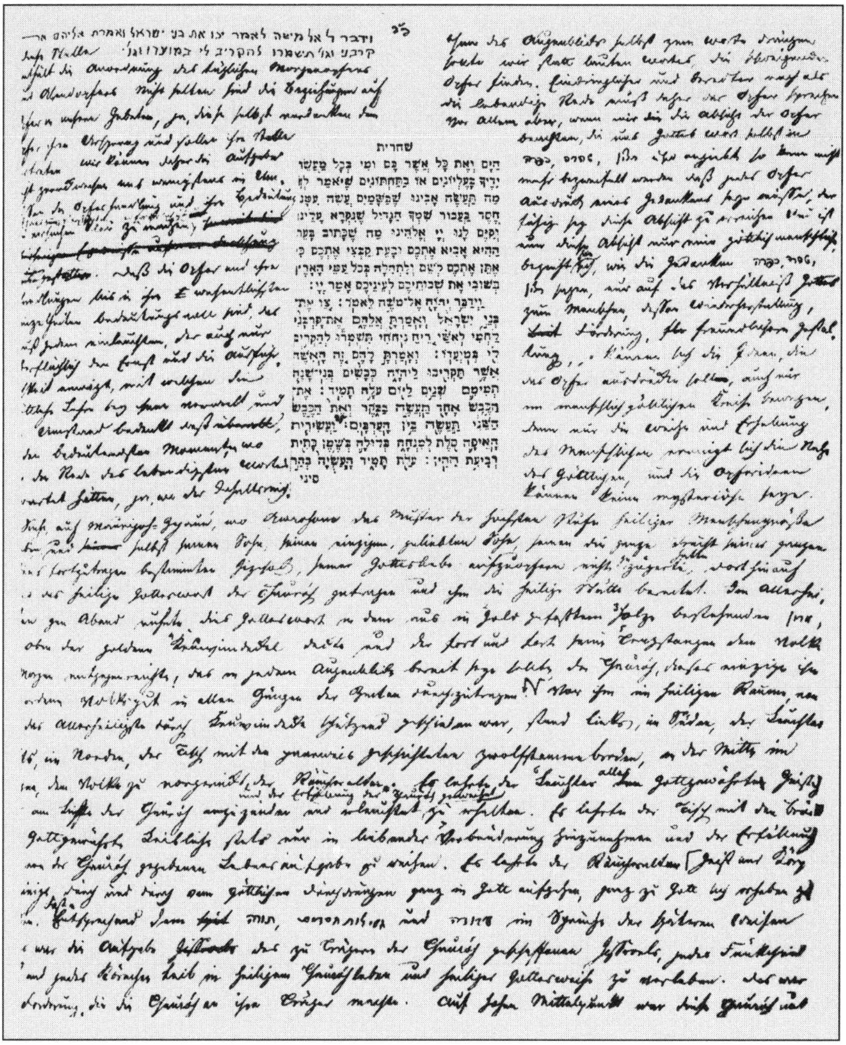

[illegible handwritten German manuscript text]

שחרית

היום ואת כל אשר בם ומי בכל מעשה
ידיך בעליונים או בתחתונים שיאמר לך
מה תעשה אבינו שבשמים עשה עמנו
חסד בעבור שמך הגדול שנקרא עלינו
וקים לנו יי אלהינו מה שכתוב בעת
ההיא אביא אתכם ובעת קבצי אתכם כי
אתן אתכם לשם ולתהלה בכל עמי הארץ
בשובי את שבותיכם לעיניכם אמר יי:
וידבר יהוה אל־משה לאמר: צו את
בני ישראל ואמרת אלהם את־קרבני
לחמי לאשי ריח ניחחי תשמרו להקריב
לי במועדו: ואמרת להם זה האשה
אשר תקריבו ליהוה כבשים בני־שנה
תמימם שנים ליום עלה תמיד: את
הכבש אחד תעשה בבקר ואת הכבש
השני תעשה בין הערבים: ועשירית
האיפה סלת למנחה בלולה בשמן כתית
רביעת ההין: עלת תמיד העשיה בהר
סיני

Rabbi Hirsch's Oldenburg Siddur Manuscript

A characteristic feature of the Commentary is its treatment of each psalm as a separate unit built around a central theme. Rabbi Hirsch tried to identify in each psalm the inspirational force that moved King David at the time he wrote it. Then he tried to examine each word, each thought and each verse in the overall context to show that each word, thought, and verse is not only apt but actually required in order to convey the full meaning King David intended.

Rabbi Hirsch felt a special affinity to the Book of *Psalms,* upon which he had been nurtured.

Truly the happiest hours of my youth were those spent attempting to identify with the mood and train of thought of one of the psalms, to seek out the original thought that first inspired its writing and to find the central idea around which it is built. It was pure delight for me to see the structure of the entire psalm, with all its details, emerging as a living unit with a central theme at its core.

And when at the end of a busy day, I was permitted to come to my father, to whom *Tanach* was a second soul, and who was gifted with a most sensitive perception and clear insight into the beauty and the truths of the Holy Writings, and I would show him the products of my own fledgling efforts, in order to receive his praise or criticism, his guidance and encouragement, there was none happier or more blessed than I.[35]

Commentary on the Siddur

RABBI HIRSCH'S LAST PUBLISHED WORK WAS HIS TRANSLATION AND commentary on the *Siddur*. He began work on it on *Issru Chag Succos* 5644 (1883),[g] but it was published only posthumously in 1896. In his younger years, possibly in Oldenburg, he began a commentary on the *Siddur*, which still exists in manuscript form. Many of the ideas of the later work already appear there. The *Siddur* Commentary contains a synopsis of many of the key ideas and teachings that informed his life. The treatment of the *Psalms* contained in the prayer service was adapted from his Commentary to the *Psalms* and abridged by his son-in-law Rabbi Joseph Guggenheimer to suit the requirements of a prayer book intended for regular use. The Commentary has since been translated into English and Hebrew.

g. The original manuscript is part of the *Sänger Collection*. It was completed in June 1888, several months before his passing.[35*]

Part Ten

LEGACY

Chapter Twenty-Nine
THE SETTING SUN

The Last Drashah

ON THE LAST YOM KIPPUR OF HIS LIFE, THE 81-YEAR-OLD Rabbi Hirsch served as the *chazan* for *Ne'ilah,* something he had not done for several years. When he finished, approximately a quarter of an hour remained until nightfall. He ascended the pulpit to deliver one of the last public addresses of his life. In deeply moving words, he captured the meaning and force of the day, as expressed in the last *Amen* of the last *Kaddish.* Hermann Schwab and others recorded his words for posterity:

> "When times of fear or anxiety come, whenever our good intentions or well-meant promises grow faint during the coming year, then my brothers and sisters, say *Amen,* and Yom Kippur will come back to you with all its blessings!" The breathtaking words emerged with great power from the revered, aged speaker now in his 81st year, and aroused stirrings of indescribable fervor in the hearts of everyone present. Every person there felt that these

Aron HaKodesh and pulpit in the shul on the Schützenstrasse

> words were intended especially for him; no one privileged to experience that will ever forget it to the end of his life.[1]

Another account of this special moment survives in a letter written at the time by Rabbi Gershon Posen, the *dayan* of the *Kehillah*, to Rabbi Hirsch's daughter, Rebbetzin Sophie Breuer, of Papa:

> You have certainly heard by now from our Rabbi himself that he fasted very well on Yom Kippur, thank G-d. His mounting the podium after *Ne'ilah* was a moment I shall never forget, and I imagine the others there will not either. When the Director [Dr. Mendel Hirsch] finished the *Minchah* service, the Rabbi immediately began to say *Ashrei* from his place. I am told that every eye

was filled with tears — I know only of my own — as an awareness of the enormous kindness Hashem has bestowed on our congregation came over all of us. As [the Rabbi's son-in-law] Mr. Roos told me the next day, he and Dr. Marcus [Hirsch] stepped out with the Rabbi for a short time before *Minchah* in order to urge him not to lead the *[Ne'ilah]* services, however the Rabbi declined their advice saying, "You probably feel weak and think that I must also be, but I can still lead the services." And so, indeed, he did.

Every word of the *tefillah* emerged from his mouth with ringing force, and he even sang the last *Kaddish. Ne'ilah* lasted slightly more than an hour and a quarter, leaving a quarter of an hour until nightfall. Rabbi Hirsch mounted the rostrum and spoke for a quarter of an hour with great strength, needing almost no support. It made a very impressive sight. Within a moment the area in front of the pulpit filled with men worried that they would not be able to hear from a distance, but he spoke loudly, as if it were not the fast of Yom Kippur, and his words penetrated every heart. *This* was a Yom Kippur. At the precise moment of nightfall, he descended and said שמות, and would not relinquish the *amud* even for *Maariv*. . . .

The day before yesterday I visited the Rav in connection with a particular question and found him in excellent condition. He had to consult several books and, as you well know of him, he would not allow me to bring them to him but insisted on doing everything for himself. There were no signs of his exertions on Yom Kippur.[2]

About a month before his death, Rabbi Hirsch took ill. On 24 *Teves* (December 28), the Friday of *Parashas VaEira,* Rabbi Hirsch took a turn for the worse. He consented to undergo surgery only after having been assured that it would be completed before Shabbos. His condition, however, did not improve. His last hours in the world, on Monday, 27 *Teves,* were spent reciting *Tehillim.* At 7:30 in the morning, shortly after his daughter Jenny Levy arrived from London, he returned his soul to its Maker.[3]

The Funeral

ALMOST EVERY PROMINENT ORTHODOX RABBI IN GERMANY WAS present at the funeral the next day, including all the rabbis of the Bamberger family. Also attending was the entire student body of the *Realschule,* led by the oldest students, who carried the 16 books he wrote, and over 12,000 residents of

Frankfurt, a rare sight in those days. All accounts of the funeral convey the sense of being orphaned that weighed on his students, the members of the congregation, and the assembled rabbis. For over 50 years he had played the leading role in the restoration of German Orthodoxy and his legacy was a generation of pious Jews, who served as a living and breathing model of his principle of *Torah Im Derech Eretz.*

The funeral lasted from 9:30 in the morning until the mid-winter night fell six hours later, when he was laid to rest along with a *sefer Torah.* Because of the size of the crowd, the fence surrounding the cemetery was taken down to allow the throng to enter. Speaking at graveside, Rabbi Ezriel Hildesheimer of Berlin attempted to give solace to the stricken congregation. He quoted the *Haftarah* of the coming Shabbos, *Parashas Bo* (*Jeremiah* 46:27): *And you, fear not, My servant Jacob, and do not become despondent, Israel, for behold, I shall help you from afar and your seed from the land of their captivity. Jacob will come home; he will dwell at ease, and nothing shall disturb his rest.*

Other eulogies were delivered by Dr. Mendel Hirsch, Rabbi Hirsch's son-in-law Rabbi Joseph Gugenheimer of Kolin, Rabbi Herz Ehrmann of Baden, Rabbi Marcus Lehmann of Mainz, and other rabbis and community leaders. Throughout the *shivah* week, memorial services were held in Frankfurt and other German cities. The Jewish newspapers were filled with accounts of the funeral and the eulogies, as well as descriptions of Rabbi Hirsch and his accomplishments.[4]

Epilogue

PERHAPS THE MOST ACCURATE SUMMARY OF RABBI HIRSCH'S RICH life and fruitful activities are his own words, penned several years before his passing, in his commentary to the verse: למנות ימינו כן הודע ונביא לבב חכמה — *According to the count of our days, so may You teach us; then we shall acquire a heart of wisdom* (*Psalms* 90:12).

> All the happiness man is capable of attaining lies in the blissful certainty that he has lived all his years, days, hours, and minutes on earth in loyalty to G-d, and that he has faithfully done his duty throughout that time. He who knows how to appreciate this kind of bliss, who measures the total worth of his life span accordingly, and who knows how to utilize every moment of his existence for the faithful service of his G-d will find the true purpose of his life in every moment that he spends on earth. And whenever G-d sees fit to call him away, he will heed the summons, serene in the thought that he has happily reached the goal for which he was

The cemetery of the IRG in which Rabbi Hirsch was buried, as well as the adjoining one of the Grossgemeinde, has survived intact until the present day

created. Therefore: "Teach us למנות ימינו, how to number our days, how properly to seek that bliss which we are capable of acquiring during the 24 x 60 x 60 seconds of each day. . . ."

How much we shall be able to gather in from the fields of material acquisitions is, to a great extent, not in our hands to determine. But לבב חכמה, the enrichment of our hearts with the understanding of what is good and true, is one harvest that is entirely within our own power to reap. This is one harvest which we can increase at any moment of our lives, joyous and sad alike. And this, the ennoblement of the heart, is the only harvest which the soul can "bring home" with it as the produce and profit of its stay on earth, when it leaves earthly things behind and returns to its home Above.[5]

APPENDICES

Appendix One

A WORTHY LINEAGE

וחסד ה׳ מעולם ועד עולם על יראיו וצדקתו לבני בנים
(תהילים קג:יז)

THE DAYS OF A MAN. . . [CAN BE] SHORT LIKE THE life span of grass; his bloom is as brief as that of the flower of the field, and once the breath of decay that blows over all things on earth touches him, then he is no more and the site where he has been no longer knows anything of him. He leaves behind nothing that might serve as a memorial of him. But as for those who recognize G-d and walk before Him with awe and respect, His mercy will be upon them for all eternity, and even when they depart from earth, the favor with which G-d had looked upon them will pass on to their children and to their children's children. Children and even children's children will still reap the benefits of זכות אבות, if their parents, and their children, in faithful emulation, will be among those who keep His covenant and preserve the remembrance of His commandments to fulfill them faithfully.[1]

Rabbi Hirsch was blessed with 10 children, each of them an exemplary Jew in his or her own way. Relations between parents and children, as reflected in the family letters, were characterized by unbounded love, mutual respect and devotion.

In his brief will to his family, Rabbi Hirsch noted the unusual privilege of being able to gaze upon all his children and grandchildren before he left the world with pride and satisfaction that they had gone in the Torah way and were all upright and G-d fearing. "You are the greatest accomplishment which we merited in life, you who we took from the iniquitous influences of the age with our sword and our bow," he wrote. Therefore, he continued, it would be improper to exhort them to go in the path of the Torah, for this they would do even without being asked. The only request he and his wife had was that their descendants maintain relations of love and brotherhood between all the siblings. "[R]emain friends to one another," he requested. "If one intentionally or unintentionally hurts another, remember us and do not be insulted or hurt. Ask forgiveness and grant it, and let your hearts bear no grudge and do not go to sleep with a grudge still in your heart."[2]

Rabbi Hirsch's wife and life companion Hannah (Johanna) Jüdel was born in Braunschweig in *Nisan* 5565 (March 1805). Not long after her death, in 1882, he dedicated to her memory the second volume of his *Commentary on the Psalms*. He described her as "the faithful companion of his life, loyal partner in his struggles, trusty support and adviser of his household and his work, teacher, guide and friend of his children and grandchildren. [She is remembered for] the purity and goodness of her heart, her bright spirit and noble mind, her cheerful self-sacrifice and rare wisdom as an educator, untiring joy in her work, her pure and lofty character and the trusting fear of G-d that filled her entire life."

One daughter died in childhood, and all her life the Rebbetzin kept a dress that had belonged to this child as a memento, intending to have it buried with her after her death. When Rabbi Hirsch learned of this intention, in the last year of her life, he told her that it would be far better to give the dress to a girl from a poor family. The Rebbetzin did not hesitate to comply with her husband's bidding, despite the meaning this dress had held for her for so many decades. Dr. Mendel Hirsch described the relationship between his parents as fully exemplifying the words by which a Jewish marriage is performed: *Behold, you are consecrated to me.*[3]

One of Rabbi Hirsch's descendants who has researched the matter reports that by conservative estimate at least 90 percent of his descendants living in Israel today have remained observant Jews.

What was the secret of Rabbi Hirsch's success as a parent? His own observations on the subject of raising children in difficult times are perhaps the best answer:

> People who are only concerned with their own families forget that they may not be able to transmit our heritage even to their own children if their home remains isolated and the spirit that dwells within it is not given access to kindred circles that nurture the Jewish spirit with the same devotion. Indeed, they forget that the danger to the survival of the Jewish spirit and of Jewish life in future generations grows in direct proportion to the inability of that spirit to find a place in the community that surrounds the home. Not everybody has the strength to win his sons and daughters for the spirit in which he seeks to raise them, or to inspire his children so profoundly that they would live and die in this spirit even if the whole world were to laugh at them. Only a man like Abraham might be able to stand alone against all the world, winning "his sons and his house" so completely for the way of G-d that they would continue in this path even אחריו, even after he himself has been gathered to his ancestors. Indeed, it may well be that Abraham succeeded in this respect only, or largely, because he did not confine his attention to his own home but built an altar wherever he pitched his tent, calling upon all the world to worship his G-d and to emulate his own G-d-centered way of life. He was able to influence his sons to preserve his heritage because he had the courage to speak out against the delusions and aberrations of the world around him.[4]

The following is a brief account of his immediate family.[5] Of his many grandchildren, we list here only those who entered the rabbinate or otherwise achieved public prominence.

1. **Dr. Mendel Hirsch** (1833-1900) taught in the *Realschule* in Frankfurt from 1855 on, and assumed the directorship in 1877, when age and other burdens caused his father to relinquish this responsibility. He also served as director without remuneration of the *Volksschule*, from its founding in 1882 until his passing. An educator par excellence, a poet and writer, he authored and published a commentary on the *Haftaros* in the same style as his father's Commentary on the *Chumash*,

which has since been translated into English and Hebrew. He also authored works on Humanism and Judaism, Zionism and Judaism, a commentary on *Trei Asar, Eichah* and other works. The rabbinic ordination he received from his father contains the following sentence: "Although he has delved into other branches of knowledge, his heart and spirit remain true to Hashem, and his steps are firm in the G-dly paths. He has learned to distinguish between the teachings of the living G-d and human wisdom, and delights solely in the love of his religious heritage."

Mendel Hirsch's son-in-law was **Rabbi Dr. Hillel Klein** (1849-1926). A disciple of Rabbi Ezriel Hildesheimer, from whom he received ordination in 1871, he served as rabbi in Kiev (1874-1880), Libau (Liepaja), Latvia (1880-91), and of Cong. *Ohab Zedek* in New York City from 1891-1926. He was president of Agudath Israel of America at the time of his passing.

2. **Sarah** (1834-1909) married **Rabbi Dr. Joseph Gugenheimer** (1833-1896), a *talmid chacham* of stature, who corresponded with his father-in-law on halachic matters,[6] and authored dozens of articles in *Jeschurun*. Rabbi Gugenheimer was appointed Rabbi of Stuhlweissenburg in 1859. There he entered into acrimonious debate with the Reformers, which caused Rabbi Hirsch to publish a pamphlet defending him from their attacks in 1861. In 1862, he became Rabbi of Niederweren, Germany and three years later was appointed Rabbi of Kolin, Bohemia. At the relatively youthful age of 40, he was chosen to eulogize the *K'sav Sofer*, the leader of Hungarian Jewry, at his funeral.[7] A description which Rabbi Hirsch received from a friend before Rabbi Gugenheimer's engagement to Sarah Hirsch praises him for his unswerving dedication to his studies and his sincere and G-d-fearing personality.[8]

   Sarah Gugenheimer was an accomplished authoress who published under the pen name "Friedrich Rott." Her stories, similar in style to those of Rabbi Marcus Lehmann of Mainz, first appeared in installments in the *Israelit* of Rabbi Lehmann and the *Jeschurun* of her brother Isaac Hirsch in Hannover, and were later published in book form. Some of them have been published in Hebrew translation.

   The Gugenheimer's son **Rabbi Dr. Raphael Gugenheimer** succeeded his father as Rabbi of Kolin but died in the prime of life. He authored a commentary on the *Haggadah* and other works.

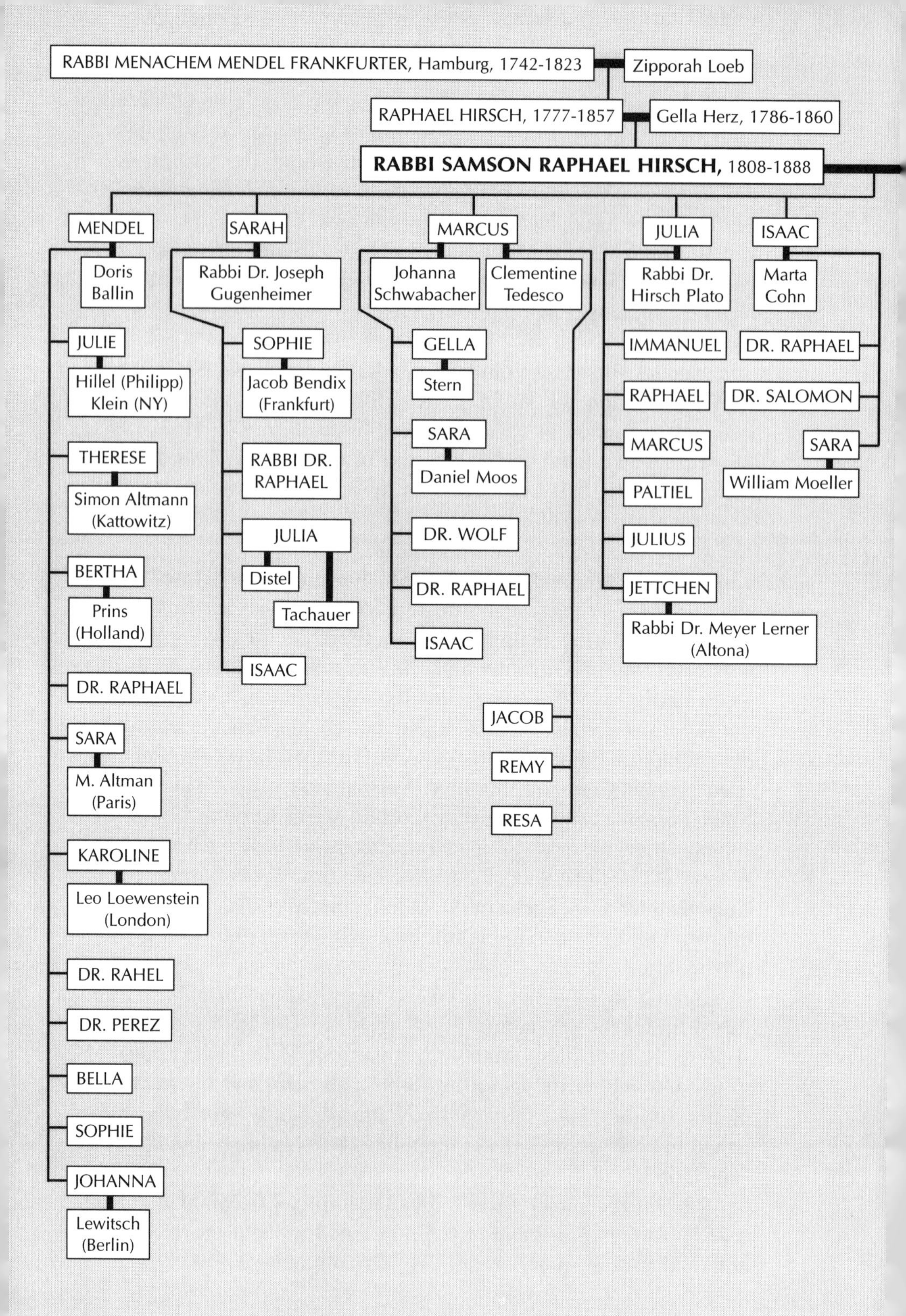
RABBI MENACHEM MENDEL FRANKFURTER, Hamburg, 1742-1823
Zipporah Loeb
RAPHAEL HIRSCH, 1777-1857
Gella Herz, 1786-1860
RABBI SAMSON RAPHAEL HIRSCH, 1808-1888
MENDEL
Doris Ballin
JULIE
Hillel (Philipp) Klein (NY)
THERESE
Simon Altmann (Kattowitz)
BERTHA
Prins (Holland)
DR. RAPHAEL
SARA
M. Altman (Paris)
KAROLINE
Leo Loewenstein (London)
DR. RAHEL
DR. PEREZ
BELLA
SOPHIE
JOHANNA
Lewitsch (Berlin)
SARAH
Rabbi Dr. Joseph Gugenheimer
SOPHIE
Jacob Bendix (Frankfurt)
RABBI DR. RAPHAEL
JULIA
Distel
Tachauer
ISAAC
MARCUS
Johanna Schwabacher
Clementine Tedesco
GELLA
Stern
SARA
Daniel Moos
DR. WOLF
DR. RAPHAEL
ISAAC
JACOB
REMY
RESA
JULIA
Rabbi Dr. Hirsch Plato
IMMANUEL
RAPHAEL
MARCUS
PALTIEL
JULIUS
JETTCHEN
Rabbi Dr. Meyer Lerner (Altona)
ISAAC
Marta Cohn
DR. RAPHAEL
DR. SALOMON
SARA
William Moeller

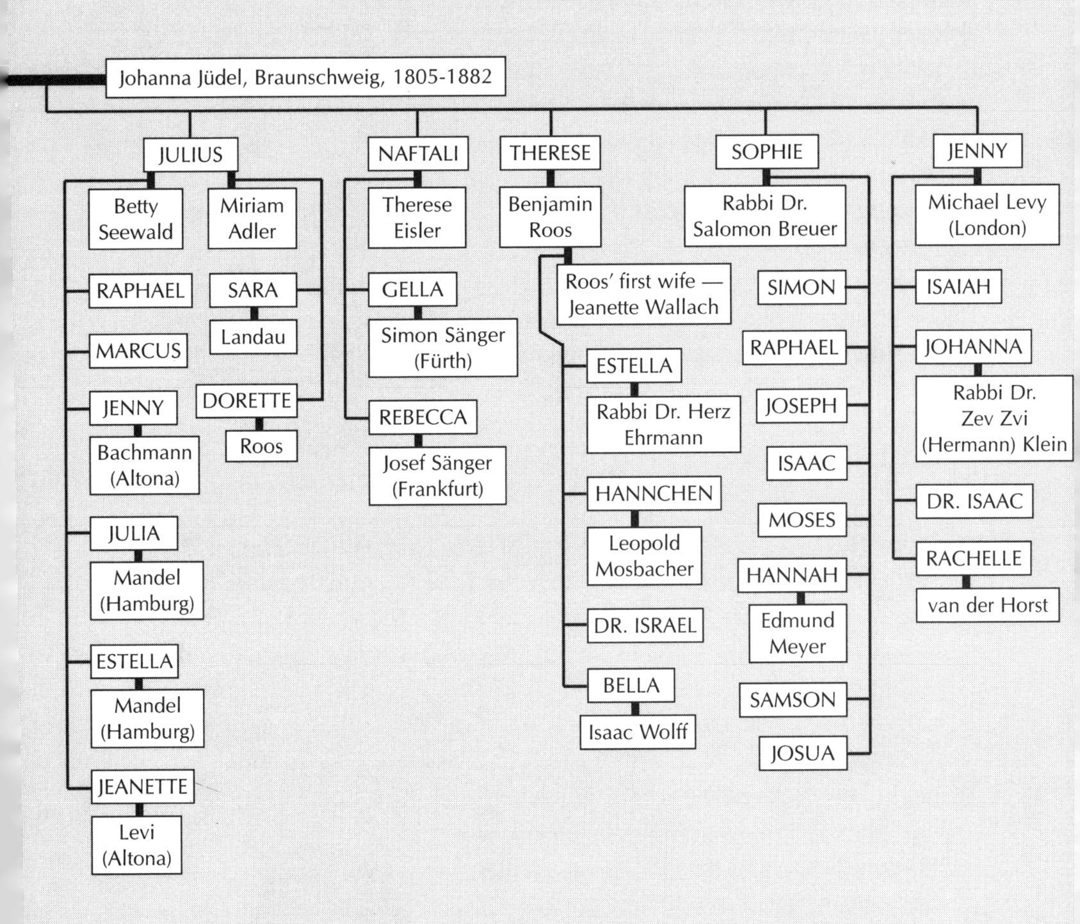

HIRSCH FAMILY TREE

Note: Thick lines indicate marriage, thin lines indicate children

3. **Yitzchak (Isaac) Hirsch** (1836-1899) was a highly talented writer, blessed with powers of expression that his father described as "extraordinary." From 1883 to 1888 he published the second series of *Jeschurun* in Hannover, and penned quite a few polemical pieces reflecting his father's views on issues of the day.

   Isaac Hirsch's grandson **Dr. Raphael Moller** served for many years as president of Congregation *K'hal Adath Jeschurun* of Washington Heights, New York.

Isaac Hirsch

4. **Gella (Julia)** (b. 1838) married **Rabbi Dr. Tzvi Hirsch Plato** (1822-1910). Rabbi Plato was very active in Jewish education, first as a teacher in Frankfurt in the secondary school of the *Realschule* and later as head of the Teachers Seminary in Cologne, where he also served as rabbi of the independent *Kehillah*.[9] A distinguished *talmid chacham*, he authored *Sefer Havlaas HaDam, Kuntras Pasei Bira'os, Kuntras Kundasin v'Tzuras HaPesach,* and other halachic works. He corresponded with Rabbi Hirsch on halachic issues.[10]

   The Platos' son-in-law was **Rabbi Dr. Meyer Lerner** (1857-1930), a *talmid chacham* of note. Born in Czestochowa (Poland), Rabbi Lerner was a descendant of the *Maginei Shlomo*. After studying in Rabbi Ezriel Hildesheimer's *Rabbiner-Seminar*, he served as Rabbi of Winzenheim, Alsace from 1884 to 1890, of the Federation of Synagogues (a group of 23 congregations) in London from 1890 to 1894, and as Chief Rabbi of Altona and the province of Schleswig-Holstein from 1894 to 1930. He authored several works including *Shaalos U'Tshuvos Hadar HaCarmel* (1890).[11]

Rabbi Meyer Lerner

5. **Dr. Mordechai (Marcus) Hirsch** (b. 1838) was a deeply pious medical doctor,[12] who also published an insightful critique of modern anti-Semitism, *Kulturdefizit am Ende des 19 Jahrhunderts* (Frankfurt a.M., 1893).[13]

6. **Yehudah (Julius) Hirsch** (1842-1909) was a businessman who authored a commentary on the Book of *Isaiah* in the style of his father.

7. **Dr. Naftali Hirsch** (1844-1903) had an especially close relationship with his father, and is the only one of the Hirsch children quoted in the *Chumash* Commentary.[14] Naftali was a gifted lawyer and writer, and was active in the *Austritt* struggle, arranging the affidavits for those who seceded from the community and defending them in court against lawsuits seeking payment of the community tax. He was heavily involved in charitable activities in Frankfurt, and he headed the *Freie Vereinigung* (Orthodox Union) founded by his father, after the latter's passing. In 1902, not long before his death, he began publication of his father's Collected Writings (*Gesammelte Schriften),* which were ultimately published in six volumes. His son-in-law, **Joseph Sänger,** assembled much of Rabbi Hirsch's responsa and letters, which form the basis of the Sänger Collection at Bar Ilan University.

8. **Tirtzah (Therese)** (b. 1849) married **Benjamin Roos**, an active member of the Board of Trustees of the *IRG* and a leader in many charitable endeavors.

9. **Tzipporah (Sophie)** (b. 1852) was the elder of twin girls born when her mother was 47 years old. She married **Rabbi Dr. Shlomo Zalman (Salomon) Breuer** (1850-1926).

   Salomon Breuer was born in Szanto, Hungary. His father brought him at the age of four to learn Torah with his grandfather Rabbi Shimon Wiener in Lovasbereny. When he was 12 years old, his father carried him on his shoulders, across snowbound

Rabbi Salomon Breuer

Invitation to Hirsch-Breuer nuptials

Wir beehren uns Sie zu der s. G. w. am

Donnerstag den 7. September

stattfindenden Trauung unserer Kinder

Sophie und **Salomon**

freundlichst einzuladen.

Rabbiner **Hirsch** und Frau,

Marcus Breuer und Frau.

Frankfurt a. M., im August 1876.

Trauung: Schöne Aussicht 5, 2. St. um 1 Uhr.

Diner: Schöne Aussicht 5, 1. St um 5 Uhr.

paths, to study in the Nitra Yeshiva. Later he studied under the *K'sav Sofer* in Pressburg. Rabbi Breuer was first employed as a teacher in the house of Mainz community leader Rabbi Shmuel Bondi. He also attended the University of Heidelberg where he received his doctorate with a thesis on Kant.

Young Shlomo Zalman Breuer first came to the attention of Rabbi Hirsch in 1869, when the latter received a letter from the aged Rabbi Wiener, a close disciple of the *Chasam Sofer*, asking him to take his grandson under his wing. Rabbi Wiener reminded Rabbi Hirsch of a visit he had paid him when he was Rabbi of Nikolsburg.[15]

Rabbi Breuer served as Rabbi of Papa, Hungary from 1876 to 1889, and after the passing of his father-in-law he succeeded him as Rabbi of Frankfurt, where he served until his passing in 1926. During his tenure in Frankfurt, he was the acknowledged leader of Torah Jewry in Germany, one of the prime movers in the founding of the Agudath Israel organization, president of the *Freie Vereinigung*, founder of the Association of Orthodox Rabbis of Germany (which accepted as members only those rabbis who would not cooperate with the Reform Community), and an uncompromising and outspoken champion of authentic Judaism.

Soon after his arrival in Frankfurt he founded a yeshiva (its German name: the *Torah Lehranstalt*), whose entire budget he had to raise on his own. Loosely patterned after the venerable Hungarian

Rabbi Salamon Breuer and family — 1889.
From l. to r. Hannah (Meyer), Mrs. Breuer, Moshe, Raphael, Joseph, Isaac, Rabbi Breuer

yeshivas, it produced many *talmidei chachamim* of note. With the exception of Rabbi Breuer's children and several others, most of its students in the early years were from outside of Frankfurt, especially from Hungary.[16] The yeshiva functioned until closed by the Nazis in 1938.

Divrei Shlomo, a collection of discourses on Talmudic topics (New York, 1948; second ed., Jerusalem, 1990), and *Chochmah U'Mussar* (Frankfurt, 1930-36), discourses on the weekly *sidrah*, were published posthumously.

The Breuer children included:

Rabbi Dr. Raphael Breuer (1881-1932) who studied in his father's yeshiva, and later under Rabbi Sholom Kutna of Eisenstadt and

Rabbi Yeshaya Fürst, rabbi of the Schiffshul of Vienna. He was the author of many articles and several books, including *Unter Seinem Banner* (Frankfurt, 1908), a discussion of many Hirschian concepts, which also contains a section of biographical information on Rabbi Hirsch. He served as Rabbi of Aschaffenburg from 1910 to 1932.

Rabbi Dr. Joseph Breuer (1882-1980) succeeded his father as head of the yeshiva in Frankfurt and later established and served as rabbi of Congregation *K'hal Adath Jeschurun* of Washington Heights, which he led until the day of his passing at the age of 98. It was largely due to his wisdom and leadership that German Orthodoxy took its place at the forefront of Torah life in the United States. He authored various books, including commentaries on *Ezekiel, Jeremiah* and the *Piyutim,* some of which have since been published in English translation. Some of his articles were collected in the three-volume *A Time to Build* (New York, 1975-83). *Divrei Yoseph* (Jerusalem, 1990), a work on Talmudic themes, was published posthumously.

Dr. Yitzchak (Isaac) Breuer (1883-1946), a profound thinker and a prolific writer, was blessed with prodigious persuasive powers in both speech and writing. He authored many books and articles on pressing issues of his time, including *Moriah, Tziyunei Derech* and *Nachliel* in Hebrew, and numerous other works in German. He was one of the founders and leading ideologists of *Agudath Israel* and *Poalei Agudath Israel.*

10. **Gütchen (Jenny)** (1852-1930), twin sister of Sophie, was married to **Michael Levy** (d. 1921), a London native, "a deeply pious man who gave generously to *tzedakah* and raised his children to a life of Torah and *mitzvos.*"[17]

    Of their sons, **Rabbi Isaiah Levy** served as Rabbi of Congregation *Ohab Zedek,* New York. Another son, **Dr. Isaac Levy,** translated into English and published Rabbi Hirsch's *Commentary on the Torah.*

Appendix Two
SECEDERS FROM THE ISRAELITISCHE GEMEINDE FRANKFURT, 1876-1877

Official Document Relating to the Separation from the "Israelitische Gemeinde" of Frankfurt a.M., *pursuant to the Law of July 28, 1876*

To the Royal City Court II, Frankfurt a.M.
Petition by the local citizen and merchant concerning separation from the local Israelitische Gemeinde.

The undersigned, who has continuously been a member of the local Jewish Community known under the name of *"Israelitische Gemeinde,"* intends to separate himself from the former because of religious considerations.

Pursuant to Paragraph 3 of the Law of July 28, 1876, with respect to secession from Jewish Communities, the petitioner herewith requests acceptance of the Declaration of Secession by the Royal City Court and requests that:

The Royal City Court II notify the Board of Directors of the aforementioned *Israelitische Gemeinde* — in care of its present Chairman, Mr. Ignatz Creizenach, Kroegerstrasse 10 — of the above petition.

The list of seceders is a handwritten document which was part of Rabbi Hirsch's papers and is now part of the Sänger Collection. The accepted estimate of the number of secessionists has always been that of Jacob Rosenheim, who put the figure at 80, or a quarter of a total membership of the IRG of 325. His figure was presumably based on a list published on February 2, 1877 in the *Frankfurter Intelligenzblatt.* That list contained 85 names. It was subsequently reprinted in Paul Arnsberg, *Die Geschichte der Frankfurter Juden seit der Französischen Revolution II,* (Darmstadt, 1983), pp. 459-461.

No.	Name	Date Submitted
1.	Adler, Nathan	Oct. 26, 1876
2.	Alexander, J. Seligmann	Oct. 26, 1876
3.	Apelt, Mathias	Oct. 24, 1876
4.	Baer, Hermann	Oct. 26, 1876
5.	Bauer, David	Nov. 28, 1876
6.	Bamberger, Seckel	Nov. 2, 1876
7.	Benjamin, Michael	Oct. 26, 1876
8.	Beer, Emanuel	Dec. 19, 1876
9.	Bier, Max	Oct. 5, 1876
10.	Billmann, Joseph	Oct. 24, 1876
11.	Bondi, David Jonas	Oct. 24, 1876
12.	Dann, Adolph	Oct. 26, 1876
13.	Duerkheim, Heinrich	Oct. 26, 1876
14.	Eisenmann, Samuel	Oct. 24, 1876
15.	Eldodt, Bendix	Dec. 19, 1876
16.	Elkan, Carl	Oct. 24, 1876
17.	Engelbert, Gottschalk	Oct. 26, 1876
18.	Fraenkel, Peretz	Oct. 24, 1876
19.	Fraenkel, Zodrick	Nov. 14, 1876
20.	Fuerth, Abraham	Oct. 24, 1876
21.	Goldschmidt, David	Oct. 26, 1876
22.	Goldschmidt, Falk	Oct. 2, 1876
23.	Goldschmidt, Jacob	Oct. 26, 1876
24.	Goldschmidt, Selig	Oct. 26, 1876
25.	Goldschmidt-Landauer, Salomon	Oct. 26, 1876
26.	Gruenebaum, Samuel	Nov. 28, 1876
27.	Guggenheim, Carl	Oct. 5, 1876
28.	Hackenbroch, Max	Feb. 8, 1877
29.	Hackenbroch, Wilhelm	Oct. 24, 1876
30.	Hahn, Adolf	Oct. 26, 1876
31.	Hahn, Marcus	Nov. 2, 1876
32.	Halberstadt, Salomon	Nov. 28, 1876
33.	Hamburger, Theodor	Oct. 5, 1876
34.	Hamburger, Semmi	Oct. 5, 1876
35.	Hessdorfer, Isaac	Oct. 24, 1876
36.	Hess, Elise geb. Schloss	Nov. 23, 1876
37.	Hess, Jacob S.	Oct. 26, 1876
38.	Hess, Leopold	Oct. 26, 1876

39.	Hirsch, Julius	Oct. 24, 1876
40.	Hirsch, Marcus	Nov. 28, 1876
41.	Hirsch, Marcus, Dr. med.	Oct. 24, 1876
42.	Hirsch, Mendel, Dr. phil.	Oct. 26, 1876
43.	Hirsch, Naphtali, Dr. jur.	Nov. 28, 1876
44.	Hirsch, Salomon	Oct. 26, 1876
45.	Hirsch, Samson Raphael, Rabb.	Oct. 5, 1876
46.	Hirsch, Simon	March 15, 1877
47.	Jessel, Joseph	Oct. 2, 1876
48.	Isaac, Lazarus	Nov. 28, 1876
49.	Isaac, Simon	Nov. 2, 1876
50.	Kahn, Anselm	Oct. 26, 1876
51.	Kann, Moritz Jacob	Oct. 24, 1876
52.	Katzenstein, Meyer	Oct. 24, 1876
53.	Katzenstein, Nathan	Nov. 23, 1876
54.	Koenigshoefer, Samuel	Oct. 26, 1876
55.	Kohn, Amson	Nov. 14, 1876
56.	Kohn, Samuel	Oct. 5, 1876
57.	Levi, Abraham, Dr. phil.	Oct. 2, 1876
58.	Lewis, Meyer	Oct. 2, 1876
59.	Lieberman, Jacob	Nov. 30, 1876
60.	Lob, Henriette, geb. Kann	Nov. 21, 1876
61.	Lob, Ludwig	Oct. 24, 1876
62.	Loeb, Carl	Oct. 26, 1876
63.	Loeb, Leopold	Oct. 26, 1876
64.	Loewenfeld, Jacob	Oct. 26, 1876
65.	Lyon, Emil	Nov. 28, 1876
66.	Mainz, Michael Loeb	Oct. 24, 1876
67.	Marx jr., Isaac	Nov. 3, 1876
68.	Marxsohn, M.	Nov. 3, 1876
69.	Mayersohn, Abraham	Nov. 3, 1876
70.	Metzler, Heymann	Oct. 27, 1876
71.	Moses, Israel	Oct. 25, 1876
72.	Moses, Moses	Oct. 25, 1876
73.	Muenzesheimer, Gottlieb	Oct. 25, 1876
74.	Niedermayer, Meyer	Oct. 25, 1876
75.	Ochs, David Loeb	Nov. 2, 1876
76.	Offenstadt, Anton	Oct. 25, 1876
77.	Oppenheim, Aron	Nov. 21, 1876
78.	Oppenheimer, Joseph	Nov. 28, 1876

79.	Oppenheimer, Meyer	Nov. 30, 1876
80.	Orschel, Hermann	Oct. 25, 1876
81.	Plaut, Hirsch	Oct. 27, 1876
82.	Plaut, Moses	Feb. 8, 1877
83.	Rapp, Abraham	Dec. 19, 1876
84.	Rapp, Ludwig	April 3, 1877
85.	Roos, Benjamin	Oct. 5, 1876
86.	Rosenbaum, Dr. med.	Feb. 27, 1877
87.	Rosenbaum, Michael	Oct. 27, 1876
88.	Rosenthal, Seligmann	Nov. 3, 1876
89.	Rothschild, Isaac	April 3, 1877
90.	Rothschild, Theodor	Oct. 27, 1876
91.	Ruben, Hertz	Oct. 27, 1876
92.	Schames, Isaac	Oct. 27, 1876
93.	Schueler, Jacob	Nov. 2, 1876
94.	Schwab, Marcus	Oct. 7, 1876
95.	Schwab, Jos. M.	Oct. 7, 1876
96.	Schwab, Mos. Sal.	Oct. 7, 1876
97.	Schwab, Mos. Loeb	Oct. 7, 1876
98.	Schwabacher, Elias	Oct. 5, 1876
99.	Schwabacher, Sr. W.	Oct. 24, 1876
100.	Schwarzschild, Abr. Yosi	Oct. 24, 1876
101.	Schwarzschild, Aron Mos.	Oct. 24, 1876
102.	Schwarzschild, Emanuel	Oct. 5, 1876
103.	Schwarzschild, Fanny S.	Nov. 14, 1876
104.	Seckel, Lazarus	Oct. 26, 1876
105.	Sonnenberger, Benjamin	Oct. 24, 1876
106.	Steindecker, Leopold	Oct. 26, 1876
107.	Stern, David Jacob	Oct. 26, 1876
108.	Stern, Meyer	Oct. 26, 1876
109.	Stern, Michael	Nov. 30, 1876
110.	Sondheimer	Feb. 2, 1877
111.	Wallerstein, Loeb	Oct. 26, 1876
112.	Weiskopf, Lazarus	Oct. 26, 1876
113.	Werthan, David	Nov. 21, 1876
114.	Wetzlar, L.	Oct. 26, 1876
115.	Wohlfarth, Veit	Oct. 26, 1876

NOTES

NOTES

Chapter One

1. Eduard Dukesz, *Chachme Ah'u* (Hamburg, 1908), p. 19; Eduard Dukesz, *Iwoh LeMoshaw* (Krakau, 1903), pp. 88-92.

2. Altona, 1815; Vilna, 1888. *HaRechasim LeBik'ah* is quoted twice by his great-nephew Rabbi Hirsch in his Commentary on *Chumash* (*Bereishis* 4:10; *Vayikra* 11:24) and in his *Commentary on the Psalms* (Chap. 144).

2*. Eduard Dukesz, *Iwoh LeMoshav*, p. 88.

3. The following is a list of the published responsa and Torah novellae of Reb Mendel Frankfurter:

a. Approbation to *Mishnas D'Rabbi Eliezer*, by Rabbi Eliezer Lazi, a member of the Hamburg rabbinate.

b. *"Ein Allgemeinizhliches Luach fün Fargangen 50 und Zukinftigen 80 Jahren"* (1819).

c. Responsa printed in *Sefer Koli Yaakov*, p. 24, regarding the prohibition of *muktzah*.

d. Ibid., p. 47, a solution to a question of *Tosafos, Shabbos 87*.

e. Lengthy introduction to *Sefer Zera Avraham* (Hamburg, 1799). At the end of this work there are Torah novellae of Reb Mendel on Tractate *Chullin*.

f. Précis of a halachic discourse, delivered at the circumcision of his grandson Samson Hirsch in: Raphael Breuer, *Unter Seinem Banner* (Frankfurt, 1908), p. 213.

4. Eduard Dukesz, "Zur Genealogie S.R. Hirschs," *Jahrbuch der Jüdisch-Literarischen Gesellschaft* XVII (Frankfurt a.M., 1925), p. 20.

5. Ibid.

6. His gravestone read: *Tohar rucho, noam milaso, veyosher darko itruhu alei adamos* — His pure spirit, pleasant word and straightforward path crowned him in this world.

7. "Essays on the Psalms," *The Collected Writings of Rabbi S.R. Hirsch* (hereafter *Collected Writings)* IV, p. 259.

8. Dukesz, "Zur Genealogie," pp. 13, 17-23.

8*. B. S. Hamburger, *Nesi HaLeviim* (Bnei Brak, 1992), p. 497, n4; B.S Hamburger, *Shoroshei Minhag Ashkenaz* (Bnei Brak, 1995), pp. 415-455; Hermann Schwab, *A World in Ruins* (London, 1946), p. 163.

9. Dedication to *Horeb* (Altona, 1836). Their correspondence is marked by great warmth and affection.

10. Rabbi Joseph Breuer, "Biographical Notations on the Life of Rabbi S.R. Hirsch." This valuable collection of episodes from the life of Rabbi Hirsch was sent by Rabbi

Breuer to Dayan I. Grunfeld of London for inclusion in a biographical work on Rabbi Hirsch.

11. The first reference to *Ashkenaz* in the Torah is in *Bereishis* 10:3, where *Ashkenaz* is mentioned as a grandson of Shem and a great-grandson of Noah. According to the Jerusalem Talmud (*Megillah* 1:9), *Midrash Rabbah* (*Bereishis* 37:1), and *Targum Yerushalmi* (*Bereishis* 10:3), the *Ashkenaz* referred to in the Torah was in Asia. The prophet Jeremiah (51:27) speaks of *Ashkenaz* together with the kingdom of Ararat, indicating a geographical proximity. This, too, would place *Ashkenaz* in Asia.

12. The origin of the name *Ashkenaz* is the subject of controversy among historians. It would appear that *Ashkenaz* is used to describe present-day Germany because the Germanic tribes originally inhabiting the area in Asia known as *Ashkenaz*, or *Germania* in Latin, migrated to Germany.

13. Poland, on the other hand, did not have any substantial concentration of Jews until the 15th century. Even the *Maharshal* and the *Bach*, who themselves lived in Poland, wrote that the Ashkenazi tradition is the reliable and authentic one, and takes precedence over all others. B.S. Hamburger, *Geonei HaDoros al Mishmar Minhag Ashkenaz* (Bnei Brak, 1994), pp. 61-62.

14. *Tshuvos Chasam Sofer, Orach Chaim*, no. 197.

15. Rashi left his home town of Troyes, France to study in Worms, Germany. His grandsons *Rabbeinu Tam* and *Rashbam* were the first of the *Baalei HaTosafos.*

16. *Tshuvos Chasam Sofer, Even HaEzer*, 1:98.

17. The foremost decisor and codifier of *Minhag Ashkenaz* was Rabbi Yaakov ben Moshe Moellin, known as the *Maharil*, whose decisions are set forth in *Tshuvos Maharil* and *Minhagei Maharil*. The *Rema* quotes him extensively in his glosses on the *Shulchan Aruch.*

18. Hermann Schwab, *A World in Ruins*, p. 22.

19. B.S. Hamburger, "Yesodosav HaHistoriim shel Minhag Ashkenaz," introduction to *Minhagei Vormeiseh* (Jerusalem, 1988), pp. 69-105.

20. Until the end of the 11th century, the Jews of Germany were situated primarily along the banks of the Rhine in towns such as Cologne, Mainz, Speyer, and Worms and other smaller towns. In the East they were found in Prague and Regensburg as well.

21. Cf. *Collected Writings* I, pp. 146, 181.

22. Dr. Moshe Auerbach, "Die Jüdische Geschichte und ihr Sinn," *Jeschurun* XII (1925), pp. 75-76.

23. Cf. *Collected Writings* VIII, pp. 292-293.

Chapter Two

1. Peter Berger, cited by David Ellenson in *Rabbi Esriel Hildesheimer and the Creation of a Modern Jewish Orthodoxy* (University of Alabama Press, 1990), p. 17.

2. Max Wiener, *HaDat HaYehudit BiTkufat HaEmantzipatziah* (Jerusalem, 1974), p. 37.

3. Mordechai Breuer, *Modernity Within Tradition; The Social History of Orthodox Jewry in Imperial Germany* (New York, 1992), p. X.

4. Mordechai Eliav, *HaChinuch HaYehudi beGermaniah* (Jerusalem, 1960), p. 1.

5. The *Pnei Yehoshua*, Rabbi Jacob Joshua Falk, was Rabbi of Berlin from 1731-1734. Rabbi Dovid Fraenkel, author of *Korban HaEidah*, the most important commentary on the Jerusalem Talmud and Moses Mendelssohn's teacher, served as rabbi from 1743-1762.

5*. Alexander Altmann, *Moses Mendelssohn: A Biographical Study* (University of Alabama, 1973), p. 371.

6. Michael Meyer, *Response to Modernity: A History of the Reform Movement in Judaism* (New York, 1988), p. 69.

7. Max Wiener, *Hadat HaYehudit*, p. 78.

8. Breuer, *Moriah*, pp. 130-133.

9. He evinced a profound distaste for the language (Yiddish) and culture of the old-world Eastern European Jew.

10. Meyer, *Response*, p. 13.

11. *The Nineteen Letters*, Letter 18.

12. Isaac Breuer, *Moriah*, loc. cit.; *The Nineteen Letters*, Letter 18. See also I. Grunfeld, Introduction to *Horeb* (London, 1962), pp. xci-xcii.

13. Moses Hess, *Rome and Jerusalem* (New York, 1954), p. 97.

14. Judith Bleich, *Jacob Ettlinger, His Life and Works: The Emergence of Modern Orthodoxy in Germany* (Ph.D. dissertation: N.Y.U., 1974), p. 85.

15. Rabbi Yechiel Yaakov Weinberg, *Shaalos U'Tshuvos S'ridei Eish* VI (Jerusalem, 1977), p. 366.

16. Schwab, *A World*, pp. 42, 53. See, however, Salo Baron, "Freedom and Constraint in the Jewish Community," *Essays and Studies in Memory of Linda R. Miller*, (1938), p. 12, n5. Baron doubts whether there really was wholesale conversion to Christianity in Prussia in the first half of the 19th century.

17. Heinrich Graetz, *The Structure of Jewish History and Other Essays*, translated, edited with introduction, by Ismar Schorsch (New York, 1975), introduction, pp. 13-14.

18. *Collected Writings* VI, p. 109.

19. Marcus Lehmann, *The Lehmann Haggadah* (Jerusalem, 1977), p. 17; Meyer, *Response*, p. 11.

20. Evyatar Friesel, *Atlas of Modern Jewish History* (Oxford University Press, 1990), p. 28.

20*. Author's introduction to *Sefer Notrikon* by the *Pri Megadim*.

21. Meyer, *Response*, p. 16.

22. Ibid., p. 18. This demand for "uplifting, inspiring, edification" was a theme that Rabbi Hirsch had to contend with. Cf. *Collected Writings* VIII, p. 251; II, pp. 11, 327.

23. Breuer, *Modernity*, p. IX.

24. Meyer, *Response*, pp. 32-36.

25. Ibid., p. 46.

26. Hermann Schwab, *The History of Orthodox Jewry in Germany* (London, 1951), p. 24.

Chapter Three

1. The component cities of the tri-partite *kehillah* were always politically unconnected. Hamburg was a city-state, and it constituted one of the 26 states which made up the German Reich when it was formed in 1871.

2. Dukesz, *Iwoh LeMoshaw,* p. 66. The history of the rabbis of the "three *kehillos*" are chronicled in two Hebrew books published near the turn of the century by Rabbi Yechezkel (Eduard) Dukesz, *Klausrabbiner* of Hamburg: *Iwoh LeMoshaw* (Krakau, 1903) and *Chachmei Ah'u* (Hamburg, 1908).

3. Letter of Rabbi Hirsch to Rabbi Loewenstein of Gailingen, Jan. 18, 1838. *Israelit* XLVII (1906), 24:4. Cf. Mordechai Breuer, "Emancipation and the Rabbis," *Niv Hamidrashia* XIII (1978/9), pp. 26-30.

4. Meyer, *Response,* pp. 54-56; Tobias Tal, "Samson Raphael Hirsch," *Der Denkende Jude* (Bibliothek des Jüdischen Volksfreundes: Cöln, 1914), p. 4.

5. *Collected Writings* VI, p. 311.

6. Rabbi Baruch Ozer and the other *dayanim* did not have the title of אב"ד or Rabbi but rather signed themselves שומר משמרת הקודש, which is probably the source of Hirsch's usage of that term to describe his role as Rabbi of Frankfurt (see title page to Rabbi Hirsch's Commentary on *Chumash* and Psalms).

7. For a fuller picture of the extensive involvement of the *Chasam Sofer* in the attempt to combat the threat of Reform see *Tshuvos Chasam Sofer* VI, nos. 84-96.

8. *Tshuvos Rabbi Yaakov M'Lissa* (Bnei Brak, 1969), no. 4.

9. *Tshuvos Chasam Sofer, Orach Chaim,* no. 9; *Choshen Mishpat,* no. 79.

10. Paul Arnsberg, *Die Geschichte der Frankfurter Juden seit der Französischen Revolution* III (Darmstadt, 1983), p. 85.

11. See Chapter Seven for a fuller description of the Braunschweig conference.

12. Cf. Bleich, *Ettlinger,* p. 84.

13. Cf. Wiener, *HaDat HaYehudit,* p. 79.

14. Breuer, *Modernity,* p. IX.

15. Meyer, *Response,* p. 62.

16. Dukesz, "Zur Genealogie," p. 23.

17. Tal, pp. 4-5.

18. His teacher Rabbi Avraham Bing of Würzburg wrote a letter of recommendation to the Hamburg community on his behalf.

19. *Der Treue Zionswächter* (hereafter *TZW*) II (1846), p. 364.

20. Author of *Atzei Arazim* and *Atzei Almogim,* commentaries on the *Shulchan Aruch* and later Chief Rabbi of Hamburg. Eduard Dukesz, "Zur Biographie des Chacham Isaak Bernays," *Jahrbuch der Jüdisch-Literarischen Gesellschaft* V (1907), p. 297.

21. Dukesz, *Chachmei Ah'u,* p. 119.

22. Dukesz, *Iwoh LeMoshaw,* pp. 110-114.

23. Dukesz, "Zur Biographie," p. 298; Stephen Poppel, "The Politics of Religious Leadership — The Rabbinate in Nineteenth-Century Hamburg," *Yearbook of the Leo*

Baeck Institute, XXVIII (1983), pp. 439-470.

24. Robert Liberles, *Religious Conflict in Social Context, The Resurgence of Orthodox Judaism in Frankfurt am Main* (Westport, 1985), p. 18.

24*. Jacob H. Sinasohn, *The Gaon of Posen,* (London, 1989), p. 38; Mordechai Breuer, "Emancipation and the Rabbis," *Niv Hamidrashia* XIII (1978/9), p. 32.

25. Dukesz, "Zur Biographie," p. 303.

26. His contract (*ksav rabbonus*) calls him חכם בקהילת האשכנזים. Dukesz, *Zur Biographie,* p. 302.

27. Dukesz, "Zur Biographie," pp. 298, 306.

27*. Cf. Binyamin Zev Jacobson, *Zichronot* (Jerusalem, 1953), p. 23.

28. *TZW* II (1846), p. 373. He also refused any of the traditional rabbinic emoluments, a practice which Rabbi Hirsch emulated.

29. Paul Johnson, *A History of the Jews* (New York: Harper and Row, 1987), p. 343.

30. Jacobson, *Zichronot,* p. 23.

31. Isaac Heinemann, "HaYachas Shebein S.R. Hirsch leYitzchak Bernays Rabbo," *Zion* XVI (1951), p. 79.

32. Moshe Mendelsohn (Frankfurter), *Pnei Teiveil* (The Face of the Earth) (Amsterdam, 1877), p. 54.

33. Raphael Breuer, *Unter Seinem Banner,* p. 216.

34. Dukesz, "Zur Biographie," p. 306.

35. Ibid., pp. 304-305.

36. *TZW* II (1846), p. 364.

37. Dukesz, "Zur Biographie," pp. 305-307; Tal, p. 5.

38. Dukesz, Ibid., p. 308.

39. Ibid., p. 314.

40. Jacobson, *Zichronot,* p. 23.

41. Ibid., p. 22.

42. Dukesz, "Zur Biographie," pp. 308-313.

43. *Der Orient* III (1842), no. 7.

44. *Iwoh LeMoshaw,* pp. 110-114; Bleich, *Ettlinger,* pp. 181, 184.

45. Dukesz, "Zur Biographie," p. 314.

46. Ibid., p. 319.

47. For the full text of the eulogies, see *TZW V* (1849), pp. 147-149, 158.

48. Rabbi Ellingen remained in Hamburg until the arrival of Chacham Bernays in 1821, when he was appointed *Rosh Beis Din* in Bingen. *Chachme Ah'u,* p. 110; cf. *HaMe'asef* תק"ע (1810), p. 28.

49. See memoirs of Isler's son, Meyer, in *Zeitschrift des Vereins fur Hamburgische Geschichte* XLVII (1961), pp. 48-62, especially pp. 52, 60-61.

50. Tal, p. 6.

51. Rabbi Hirsch quotes the Chacham in his commentary on *Bereishis* 4:26; *Bamidbar*

20:8; and on *Tehillim,* Chap. 16.

52. Biographical notations of Rabbi Joseph Breuer.

53. Letter of the director of the Stadtsarchiv of Hamburg to Mordechai Breuer, 1962.

54. Rabbi Joseph Breuer saw the *semichah* in his youth. The Committee for the Election of the Chief Rabbi of England, (London, 1844), also mentions it in its list of testimonials.

55. Raphael Breuer, *Unter Seinem Banner,* p. 218. Rabbi Hirsch's journal as Chief Rabbi of Oldenburg (Sänger Collection) shows him already at the age of 22 to be a mature and erudite Torah scholar.

Chapter Four

1. Cf. *The Nineteen Letters,* Letter 4; *Horeb,* ch. 5. This was also the theme of his first sermon in Oldenburg, see Meyer Lerner, "Die Erste Predigt," *Jeschurun* (Berlin), I (1914), p. 73 ff.; cf. Isaac Heinemann, "The Formative Years of the Leader of Modern Orthodoxy," *Historia Judaica* XIII (1951), pp. 33-35.

2. Transcript of letter in possession of Prof. Mordechai Breuer, portions of which were published by the same in "Rabbi S.R. Hirsch B'yeshivas Rabbi Yaakov Ettlinger," *Harav Yaakov Ettlinger* (Jerusalem: HaMaayan Publications, 1972), pp. 39-41.

3. Small yeshivas, or more correctly *klausen* (endowed study houses), existed in Germany until middle of the 19th century in Berlin, Breslau, Fulda, Halberstadt, Hamburg, Hannover, Karlsruhe, Mainz, Worms and Zell. Breuer, *Modernity,* p. 10.

4. Cited by Mordechai Eliav: "Gishot Shonot LeTorah Im Derech Eretz; Ideal U'Metziut," *Torah Im Derech Eretz: HaTenuah, Isheha, Raayonoteha* (Bar Ilan, 1987), p. 45.

5. Pressburg, 1852, and recently reprinted as part of *Kisvei Rabbeinu Yitzchok Dov Halevi,* (Bnei Brak, 1992) (introduction to *Zechor LeAvraham,* pp. 7-12).

6. Much of the biographical information on Rabbi Ettlinger is drawn from the excellent work, *Jacob Ettlinger, His Life and Works: The Emergence of Modern Orthodoxy in Germany,* Ph.D. dissertation of Dr. Judith Bleich (NYU, 1974).

6*. *Shemesh Marpeh,* p. 100.

7. For Rabbi Ettlinger's view of secular studies and secular culture see Bleich, *Ettlinger,* pp. 242-261.

8. Bleich, *Ettlinger,* p. 23.

9. Ibid., p. 21.

10. In 1867, the Jewish population numbered 2,350, out of total population of 50,000.

11. *Igros Sofrim,* part 1, p. 80, # 60. Rabbi Meyer Lerner, grandson by marriage to Rabbi Hirsch, served as Chief Rabbi of Altona from 1894-1926, followed by Rabbi Joseph Carlebach, who served from 1927-1937.

12. One of the most famous passages in the *Bikkurei Yaakov,* which, since its publication, has not ceased to be the source of discussion in the halachic world, is an assertion that according to the *Rambam* that Jerusalem is considered to be part of the *Beis Hamikdash,* the obligation to take the *lulav* in the Old City of Jerusalem all seven days of *Succos* is Scripturally mandated even today.

13. He also authored *Aruch LaNer* on several other tractates and two volumes of *Shaalos U'Tshuvos Binyan Zion* (Altona, 1868; Vilna, 1878), and a collection of his sermons on *Chumash*, entitled *Minchas Ani* (Altona, 1873).

14. *Shomer Zion HaNe'eman* was reprinted in New York, 1963.

15. Letter of Rabbi Nosson Adler to the government of Oldenburg, dated March 24, 1830. *Jubiläumsnummer*, p. 17; see also *Naphtulei Naphtali* I, p. 67.

16. Rabbi Joseph Breuer; "Report of the Committee for the Selection of Candidates to the Office of Chief Rabbi," (London, 1844).

17. Rabbi Gershon Josaphat, as quoted by Heinrich Graetz, *Tagebuch* , ed. Reuven Michael (Tübingen, 1977), p. 45.

18. See Yonah Emmanuel, *Parshanim U'Poskim Acharonim*, (Jerusalem, 1962), for Rabbi Hirsch's citations of Rabbi Ettlinger in his *Chumash* commentary. See also *Shemesh Marpeh*, pp. 40. 71-74.

19. He appears in the university registry on October 26, 1829, and in March 1830 was already being considered for the Chief Rabbinate of Oldenburg.

19*. *Israelit* XXX (1899), p. 1893.

20. S.R. Hirsch, "Der Rabbi als Redner in Israel," *Nachlath Zvi* III (1932), pp. 174-187. The original manuscript of his speech is still extant.

21. A. Geiger, *Nachgelassene Schriften* V (Berlin, 1878), p. 18 ff. See also M. Breuer, "Perakim Mitoch Biographiah," *HaMaayan* IV (5724) 2:7-12.

Chapter Five

1. Mordechai Breuer, "Samson Raphael Hirsch," *Guardians of Our Heritage*, Leo Jung ed. (New York, 1958), p. 269.

2. *Jubiläumsnummer*, p. 17; Leo Trepp, *Die Oldenburger Judenschaft* (Oldenburg, 1973), p. 121.

2*. Mordechai Breuer's review of Rosenbloom, *Tradition in an Age of Reform*, *Tradition* XVI (1977), no. 4, p. 141.

3. *Jubiläumsnummer*, p. 9.

4. Trepp, *Die Oldenburger Judenschaft*, pp. 122-124.

5. Journal of the Landrabbiner of Oldenburg, Sänger Collection; Zvi Asariah, *Samson Raphael Hirsch* (Hannover, 1970), p. 30.

6. Breuer, *Modernity*, p. 38.

7. Rabbi Hirsch to Rabbi Loewenstein of Gailingen, 21 *Teves*, 5598 (Jan. 18, 1838). *Israelit* XLVII (1906), 24:4.

8. Graetz, *Tagebuch*, pp. 45, 51.

9. Ibid., p. 80.

9*. Ibid., p. 77.

10. *Shemesh Marpeh*, p. 100.

11. Martin Cohen, "100 Jahre 'Neunzehn Briefe'," *Jahrbuch für die Jüdischen Gemeinden Schleswig-Holstein*, (1936-37), p. 23.

12. Trepp, *Die Oldenburger Judenschaft*, pp. 166-169.

13. Ibid., pp. 121-132.

14. Rabbi S.R. Hirsch, "Hesped anlässlich des Todes seiner Gattin," *Nachlath Zvi* II (1934), p. 71.

15. Graetz, *Tagebuch*, p. 55.

16. *HaZofeh*, 29 Adar, 5707.

17. Isaac Breuer, *Moriah*, pp. 135-136, 151.

18. Breuer, *Moriah*, ibid.

19. *Collected Writings* VI, pp. 52-53.

20. Breuer, *Am V'Eidah*, MS.

21. *Collected Writings* VIII, p. 275; cf. *Collected Writings* I, p. 359.

22. He authored *Shaar Zekeinim* (*drashos* and *mussar*; Part Two has halachic responsa), Sulzbach, 1830; *Simlas Binyamin* (responsa on *Orach Chaim* and *Yoreh Deah*), with Part Two called *Nachlas Binyamin* (*Even HaEzer* and *Choshen Mishpat*), 1840-41.

23. *Shaar Zekeinim* (Sulzbach, 1830).

24. Meyer, *Response*, p. 89; Horovitz, *Frankel*, p. 13.

25. Horovitz, *Rabbanei Frankfurt*, p. 155.

26. A. Geiger, *Nachgelassene Schriften* V, p. 18.

27. Meyer, *Response*, pp. 91, 96; *Encyclopaedia Judaica*, 7:359.

28. *Encyclopaedia Judaica*, Ibid.

29. Grunfeld, Introduction to *Horeb*, p. xxvii.

30. Schwab, *History*, p. 85.

31. Breuer, *Am VeEidah*, MS.

32. Meyer, *Response*, p. 97.

33. Rabbi Ezriel Hildesheimer, *Drei Vorträge* (Vienna, 1867), p. 16.

Chapter Six

1. See Moshe Aharonson, "Biography of Rabbi S.R. Hirsch," p. 11, and the approbation of Rabbi Y.E. Spektor, *The Nineteen Letters* (Hebrew) (Vilna, 5651); Bernard Drachman, *The Nineteen Letters of Ben Uziel, with Introduction* (New York, 1899), p. V; Rabbi Marcus Lehmann, *Israelit* XVII (1876), no. 38; Rabbi Joseph Elias, Introduction to *The World of Rabbi Samson Raphael Hirsch: The Nineteen Letters* (Jerusalem, 1995), p. 2.

2. *Tikkun Shlomo* (Vienna, 5691), reprinted in *Shemesh Marpeh*, p. 370.

3. Vilna, 1890; Netzach (Bnei Brak, 1948); Mossad Harav Kook (Jerusalem, 1949).

4. The first translation, entitled "The Vocation of Judaism," appeared in a London-based Jewish weekly *The Voice of Jacob* II (1842), nos. 28-30. Other English translations are: Bernard Drachman (New York: Funk and Wagnalls, 1899); Jacob Breuer (New York: Feldheim, 1960); Rabbi Joseph Elias (Jerusalem: Feldheim, 1995).

4*. Breuer, *Am VeEidah*, MS.

5. I. Grunfeld, Introduction to *Horeb*, p. xxxiv; I. Grunfeld ed., *Judaism Eternal* (London, 1956), p. xxxiv. See also Rabbi Hirsch's letter to Rabbi Gershon Josaphat

of 18 *Adar* 5596 (1836), reprinted in *Shemesh Marpeh*, p. 219.

5*. *Wissenschaftliche Zeitschrift fur Jüdische Theologie* II (1836), pp. 351-359, 518-548, III (1837), pp. 77, 81-82. Abraham Geiger, *Nachgelassene Schriften* V, pp. 48-50, 77-79.

6. First Letter.

7. Second Letter.

7*. For an excellent exposition of this point see: Elias, *The Nineteen Letters,* Letter 18, especially note 8.

8. Elias, p. 242.

9. Sept. 8, 1835 letter to Simon May. Martin Cohen, "100 Jahre 'Neunzehn Briefe,' " *Jahrbuch für die Jüdischen Gemeinden Schleswig-Holstein,* (1936-37), p. 21.

10. *The Nineteen Letters,* Letter 19.

11. Ibid., Letter 18. This is a recurring theme in Rabbi Hirsch's writings. See also *Collected Writings* I, p. 169; II, pp. 196, 209, 234-5; V, p. 104; *From the Wisdom of Mishlé,* p. 62; *Commentary, Siddur,* p. 153; *Commentary, Psalms,* 30:106.

12. Letter to Gershon Josaphat of 18 *Adar,* 5596 (1836). *Shemesh Marpeh,* p. 219.

13. Ibid.

14. Letter to Simon May, Dec. 15, 1839. *Jubiläumsnummer*, p. 18.

15. Rabbi Joseph Breuer.

16. Martin Cohen, "100 Jahre 'Neunzehn Briefe,' " pp. 19, 22.

17. Cohen, loc. cit., p. 20.

18. Jacob Rosenheim, *Ktavim, Mivchar Maamarim U'Neumim* I (Jerusalem, 1970), p. 33.

19. Breuer, *Modernity,* p. 476.

20. Avraham Abba Friedman, Introduction to *She'asani Keretzono,* Detroit, no publication date.

21. Rabbi Naftali Herz Ehrmann, *Israelit* XXIV (1883), 22:362.

22. Dr. Salomon Ehrmann, in a letter to Mordechai Breuer, 21 *Sivan,* 5716 (1956), quoting his father, Rabbi Naftali Herz Ehrmann, a close confidant of Rabbi Salanter.

22*. Interview with Dr. Judith Grunfeld of London, who was on the original staff of the Beis Yaakov School in Krakau; Isaac Breuer, *Moriah,* p. 148; Leo Deutschländer, *Nachlath Zvi* V (1934-35), pp. 170-71; J. Grunfeld, "Sara Schenirer," *Jewish Leaders* (N.Y., 1953), p. 415.

23. *Horeb,* Foreword, pp. clv-clvi.

23*. See I. Grunfeld, Introduction to *Horeb,* pp. xxx-xl.

24. Ibid., p. xix.

25. Letter to Z.H. May, April 13, 1835, translated in Grunfeld, Introduction to *Horeb,* p. cxliv. A photocopy of the original is in my possession.

26. The notebooks are now in the possession of Prof. Mordechai Breuer, Jerusalem.

27. S.R. Hirsch to Z.H. May, April 13, 1835. Translation is from I. Grunfeld, Introduction to *Horeb,* pp. cxlii-cxliii.

28. *Wissenschaftliche Zeitschrift für Jüdische Theologie* IV (1839), pp. 355-381.

29. Grunfeld, *Three Generations* (London, 1958), p. 44.

30. Cited in Grunfeld, Introduction to *Horeb*, p. xxxviii.

31. See also *Collected Writings* I, p. 357; VII, p. 399.

32. Meyer, *Response*, pp. 81-82.

33. Bleich, *Ettlinger*, p. 107.

34. Grunfeld, Introduction to *Horeb*, p. xxxviii.

35. Trepp, *Die Oldenburger Judenschaft*, p. 143.

36. Rabbi Joseph Breuer.

37. Rabbi Joseph Breuer; Tal, p. 12.

38. [Herz Ehrmann,] "S.R. Hirsch, Ein Lebensbild," *Jubiläumsnummer*, p. 10.

39. Letter from Rabbi Hirsch to the government of Hanover, May 30, 1841. Zvi Asariah, *Samson Raphael Hirsch* (Hannover, 1970), p. 11.

40. Asariah, ibid. p. 20.

41. Lippman subsequently worked under Rabbi Hirsch as *Unterrabbiner* in Aurich.

42. "Nachklänge an Hirsch's Wirksamkeit in Ostfriesland," *Israelit* XXX (1889), p. 116; A. Loeb, "Errinerungen an die Tätigkeit S.R. Hirsch's in Emden," *Israelit* LII (1911), Jan. 12.

43. Loeb, op. cit.; Asariah, p. 10.

Chapter Seven

1. From an 1849 letter from Rabbi Hirsch to Rabbi Moshe Leib Engel. *Shemesh Marpeh*, p. 224.

2. Letter from Rabbi Hirsch to Rabbi Loewenstein of Gailingen, March 17, 1837. *Israelit* XLVII (1906), 24:4.

3. In a letter to Rabbi Hirsch Lehren, head of the *Pekidim ve'Amarkelim* of *Kolel Hod* in Amsterdam, dated 18 *Elul*, 5603, Rabbi Hirsch wrote: "If only I were able to fulfill my desire to help *Eretz Yisrael* through my community. However, the present time is not auspicious, for unfortunately the obligations of the community grow more and more numerous and the state of poverty increases constantly. When Hashem turns His mercies to us and causes us to prosper, then we will hope to enlist the hearts of our followers to this purpose also." Journal of the Chief Rabbi of Emden, MS.

4. *The Voice of Jacob*, July 1843, p. 221, quoting from *Der Orient*; A. Loeb, "Erinnerungen an die Tätigkeit S.R. Hirsch's in Emden," *Israelit* LII (1911), 7:8-9.

5. Mendel Hirsch, *Worte bei der zu Ablauf der Shloshim* (Frankfurt a.M., 1889), p. 11; [Herz Ehrmann], "S.R. Hirsch, Ein Lebensbild," *Jubiläumsnummer*, p. 10; A. Loeb, "Erinnerungen an die Tätigkeit S.R. Hirsch's in Emden," *Israelit* LII (1911), 6:5.

6. *Israelit* XXX (1889), p. 117.

7. A. Loeb, "Erinnerungen etc.," *Israelit* LII (1911), 7:3.

8. Letter to Rabbi Hirsch Lehren, dated *Teves*, 5603 (Winter 1842-3). *Shemesh Marpeh*, p. 238.

9. Journal of the Chief Rabbi of Emden, MS.

10. A. Schischa, ed., *VaYosef Avraham* (London, 1994); see also Rabbi Yaakov Ettlinger, *Shaalos U'Tshuvos Binyan Zion* I, no. 128, III, no. 71.

11. *Der Orient* VIII (1847), 8:4.

12. Isaac Heinemann, "The Formative Years of the Leader of Modern Orthodoxy," *Historia Judaica* XIII (1951), p. 35, n12.

13. *The Voice of Jacob*, July 1843, p. 221, quoting *Der Orient*; Schwarzschild, *Die Gründung*, p. 29; *Collected Writings* II, pp. 225, 248, 250, 259.

14. A. Loeb, "Erinnerungen," *Israelit*, loc. cit., 6:5.

15. S.R. Hirsch, "Hesped anlässlich des Todes seiner Gattin," *Nachlath Zvi* II (1931), p. 72.

16. *Shemesh Marpeh*, pp. 237, 239; Journal of the Chief Rabbi of Emden, MS.

17. Cecil Roth, "Britain's Three Chief Rabbis," *Jewish Leaders*, pp. 479-480; cf. H.D. Schmidt, "Nathan Adler," *Leo Baeck Institute Yearbook* VII (1962), pp. 289-311.

18. Meyer, *Response*, pp. 50-54; See *Tshuvos Chasam Sofer* VI, nos. 84-96.

19. *Eileh Divrei HaBris* (Hamburg, 1819).

20. Meyer, *Response*, p. 121.

21. Dr. Moshe Auerbach, "Die Braunschweiger Rabbinervesammlung in Jahr 1844," *Jahrbuch der Jüdisch-Literarischen Gesellschaft* XXII (1931/32), p. 126; Horovitz, *Frankel*, p. 13.

22. Quoted by Breuer, *Am VeEidah*, MS.

23. Ismar Schorsch, "Ideology & History in an Age of Emancipation," Introduction to Heinrich Graetz, *The Structure of Jewish History and Other Essays* (New York, 1975), pp. 19-22.

24. Horovitz, *Frankel*, p. 22.

25. *Shemesh Marpeh*, pp. 188-196.

26. Ibid.

27. Wiener, p. 47.

28. Ibid., pp. 138-140; Meyer, *Response*, p. 138.

29. Cited in Breuer, "Prakim Mitoch Biographiah," *HaRav Samson Raphael Hirsch, Mishnato VeShitato*, Y. Emmanuel, ed. (Jerusalem, 1962), p. 19.

30. "Nikolsburg oder Frankfurt," *Nachlath Zvi* VI (1936), p. 252. According to *Encyclopaedia Judaica* (12:302), the Jewish population in 1848 was 37,548, considerably lower than the 50,000 or 60,000 usually cited.

31. *Der Orient* VIII (1847), 2:3.

32. *Israelit* LII (1911), 12:5.

33. *Der Treue Zionswächter* III (1847), p. 189.

Chapter Eight

1. Hermann Bing, *Atereth Zvi, Umständliche Schilderung* (Vienna, 1847); *Jubiläumsnummer,* p. 19.

2. The first document still extant which mentions Jews in Nikolsburg dates from 1369. It has been surmised from the family names, customs and language, that most of the Nikolsburg community originally came from Germany. *Encyclopaedia Judaica* 11:1531.

3. Yitzchok Zev Kahane, "Nikolsburg," *Arim V'Imahot BeYisrael* (Jerusalem, 1950), p. 230. An idea of the scope of the local community can be gleaned from the fact that in 1821, the community employed more than 20 people including four *dayanim,* three *shochtim,* two *chazzanim,* one *maggid,* two *shamashim,* a tax collector, a doctor, a midwife, four guards and various other functionaries.

4. See *Shemesh Marpeh,* pp. 220-221, for the limitations of Rabbi Hirsch's authority in this area. Cf. Sänger Collection, Hebrew Letters, File 5, Letters 5, 6, 9, 13.

5. *Collected Writings* II, p. 350.

6. Rabbi Banet authored, among other works, *Magen Avos,* a classic on the laws of Shabbos. For a biographical account see J.A. Banet, *Toldos Mordechai Banet* (1832), and the introduction to his Talmudic novellae published by Machon Yerushalayim.

7. He authored *Sh'lom Yerushalayim,* a commentary on the Jerusalem Talmud, and *Sefer Kovetz* a commentary on the *Rambam.* For biographical information, see the introduction to his responsa, *Shaalos U'Tshuvos Rabbi Nachum Trevitsch* (Machon Yerushalayim).

8. *Allgemeine Zeitung des Judentums* VIII (1844), p. 283, carries a notice of the Moravian committee in charge of the selection of a Chief Rabbi, announcing the decision in favor of Rabbi Hirsch and against B.H. Fassel. In a letter to the government in Aurich, dated March 15, 1846, Rabbi Hirsch noted that he had been offered the position of Chief Rabbi of Moravia two years earlier. Zvi Asariah, *Samson Raphael Hirsch* (Hannover, 1970), pp. 19-20.

8*. *Encyclopaedia Judaica,* 11:890-891.

9. Rabbi Kutna subsequently served as Rabbi of Eisenstadt and was the son-in-law of Rabbi Yedidya Gottlieb Fischer of Stuhlweissenburg (see Chapter 22). See Rabbi Hirsch's responsum to Rabbi Kutna in *Shemesh Marpeh,* p. 50.

10. It should be noted that this anecdote does not accord with the lengthy correspondence between Mannheimer and Rabbi Hirsch concerning the former's efforts on behalf of Emancipation in the capital city, Kremsier. Sänger Collection, German Correspondence.

11. I am grateful to Mr. Abraham Schischa of London for this account, which he heard from Rabbi Yeshaya Fürst, Rabbi of the Schiffshul in Vienna, who heard it from his father-in-law, Rabbi Shalom Kutna.

12. "Rabbi S.R.H. als Landrabbiner von Nikolsburg," *Israelit* XLV (1904), pp. 805-808.

13. The baker's letter was originally written in German with Hebrew script, whereas Rabbi Hirsch's response was written in pure German. *Shemesh Marpeh,* pp. 221-223.

14. *Shaalos U'Tshuvos Imrei Eish* II, no. 25.

15. He authored, among other works, *Tshuvos Mahariya (Yehudah Yaaleh)* I (1873), II (1880), which are considered important halachic responsa to this day.

16. *Shemesh Marpeh,* p. 259.

17. *Shemesh Marpeh,* pp. 83-86; *Shaalos U'Tshuvos Yehudah Yaaleh, Even HaEzer,* nos. 15, 16.

18. Ibid., but see also *Shaalos U'Tshuvos Imrei Eish* II (Ungvar, 1894), no. 25.

19. Jacob Katz, *HaKera Shelo Nitachah (The Unhealed Breach: The Secession of Orthodox Jews from the General Community in Hungary and Germany)* (Jerusalem, 1995), p. 61.

20. Some of the correspondence was published in *Shemesh Marpeh,* pp. 101-107. There are thirteen letters altogether regarding this matter in the Sänger Collection, Hebrew MS, File # 3, nos. 4/1-4/13.

21. Rabbi Pashkus is mentioned in *Likutei Tshuvos Chasam Sofer,* no. 37.

22. Philipp Fischer, *In Seinen Spuren* (Satoraljaujhely, 1922), p. 23, quoting an eyewitness. The last comment is a reference to Rabbi Hirsch's attitude towards secular studies. This story also appears in *Jubiläumsnummer,* p. 45.

23. "S.R.H. als Landrabbiner von Nikolsburg," *Israelit* XLV (1904), p. 807.

24. *Shemesh Marpeh,* responsa nos. 79-80, pp. 95-97; *Israelit* loc. cit. p. 806.

25. Y.Y. Greenwald, *LeToldot HaReformatzion HaDatit BeGermaniah U'VeHungariah* (Columbus, 1948), p. 56, quoting Schnitzer, *Jüdische Kulturbilder* (Vienna, 1904).

26. *Shemesh Marpeh,* p. 35.

27. *Der Treue Zionswachter* IV (1848), pp. 109-110; *Shemesh Marpeh,* p. 221.

28. Frankel-Grün, *Geschichte der Juden in Kremsier* II, p. 14n; Breuer, *Modernity,* p. 243.

28*. *Jubiläumsnummer,* p. 35; *Israelit* XXIV (1883), p. 546; *Jüdische Presse,* 1883, p. 182.

29. *Jubiläumsnummer,* p. 36.

30. *Israelit* XLV (1904), p. 807.

30*. "SRH und das Hamburger Oberrabbinat," *Israelit* LI (1910), 1:3-4.

31. Dr. M.H. Friedlaender, "Zur Geschichte des Mährischen Landesrabbinates," *Laubhütte* IV (1887), 44:446.

32. *Laubhütte* IV (1887), 44:445-9; "Nikolsburg oder Frankfurt," *Nachlath Zvi* VII (1936), p. 255.

33. *Laubhütte,* loc. cit., p. 460.

34. *Israelit* XLV (1904), p. 807; "Nikolsburg oder Frankfurt," *Nachlath Zvi,* loc. cit., pp. 252-253; Y.Y. Greenwald, op. cit., pp. 57-58.

35. Letter to his son Mendel Hirsch, a photocopy of which is in my possession.

35*. Mordechai Breuer, Review of Noah Rosenbloom, *Tradition in An Age of Reform, Tradition* XVI (1977), no. 4, p. 143.

Chapter Nine

1. Rabbi Mordechai Horovitz, *Rabbanei Frankfurt* (Jerusalem, 1972), p. 181. The *Raavan* (Rabbi Eliezer ben Nathan), one of the *Rishonim,* mentions the Frankfurt Jewish community repeatedly.

2. Emanuel Schwarzschild, *Die Gründung der Israelitischen Religionsgesellschaft* (Frankfurt a.M., 1896), p. 5.

3. Horovitz, *Rabbanei Frankfurt*, pp. 10-14.

4. *Hagaos V'Chiddushim al Sefer Minhagei Maharil; Sefer Yosef Ometz* (Frankfurt, 1723); *Noheig KaTzon Yosef* (Hanau, 1718); *Divrei Kehillos* (Frankfurt, 1863).

5. *Tshuvos Chasam Sofer* VII, no. 9.

6. Horovitz, *Rabbanei Frankfurt*, pp. 7-148, 183.

7. *Collected Writings* VI, p. 138.

8. A. Freimann and F. Kracauer, *Frankfort* (Philadelphia, 1929), pp. 180-221.

9. Robert Liberles, *Religious Conflict in Social Context: The Resurgence of Orthodox Judaism in Frankfurt am Main* (Westport, 1985), p. 25.

9*. *Collected Writings* VI, pp. 129-150.

10. Ibid., VI, pp. 129-146.

11. *Collected Writings* II, p. 170.

12. Schwarzschild, *Die Gründung*, p. 7.

13. *Collected Writings* VI, p. 135.

14. *Allgemeine Zeitung des Judentums*, 1841, no. 5; Liberles, *Religious Conflict*, p. 37.

15. Emanuel Schwarzschild, *Eine Offenes Wort* (Frankfurt a.M., 1877), pp. 6-7 (translation as per: Schwab, *History*, p. 39).

16. Schwarzschild, *Die Gründung*, pp. 11, 25.

17. Jacob Katz, *HaKera Shelo Nitachah*, p. 33.

18. Jacob Katz, *Bonim Chofshim ViYehudim* (Jerusalem, 1968), pp. 79-81; *Collected Writings* II, p. 170; VI, p. 132 ff.

18*. Liberles, p. 27.

19. Breuer, *Am V'Eidah*, MS.

20. Tobias Tal, "Samson Raphael Hirsch," *Der Denkende Jude* (Bibliothek des Jüdischen Volksfreundes: Cöln, 1914), p. 17.

21. Schwarzschild, *Die Gründung*, p. 15.

22. This Creizenach apple had not fallen far from the paternal tree. His father, Michael Creizenach (1789-1842), a teacher in the *Philanthropin* from 1825, published *Shulchan Aruch oder Enzyklopaedishe Darstellung des Mosaischen Gesetzes. . . .* (4 vols. 1833-40), in which he attempted to prove, through pseudo-Talmudic logic no less, that Talmudic Judaism was in essence a reform of biblical Judaism, and thus, that Reform was a legitimate approach to Judaism. Talmudic and Rabbinic Judaism were, in his view, nothing more than an elaborate system designed to serve as a portable homeland to Jews, a kind of national coping mechanism, which, in the heady days of Enlightenment and Emancipation, had become nothing more than an embarrassing anachronism, which should be disposed of as quickly and as efficiently as possible. His son Theodore ultimately converted to Christianity, as did two of his three siblings. See Hermann Schwab, *The History of Orthodox Jewry in Germany* (London, 1951), p. 26; Meyer, *Response*, pp. 119-120; Wiener, *HaDat HaYehudit*, p. 114; Liberles, p. 43.

23. *Allgemeine Zeitung des Judentums*, 1844, No. 8.

24. Horovitz, *Rabbanei Frankfurt*, pp. 238-239.

25. *Shemesh Marpeh*, p. 187.

26. Bleich, *Ettlinger*, pp. 96-99, 108.

27. Liberles, p. 61.

28. Schwab, *History*, p. 39; Arnsberg, p. 504.

29. *Collected Writings* VI, p. 145.

30. Liberles, p. 87.

31. Breuer, *Am V'Eidah*, MS.

Chapter Ten

1. Schwarzschild, *Die Gründung*, p. 9.

2. *Der Treue Zionswächter* VII (1851), p. 4; *Gedächtnisrolle* (foundation scroll of the Schützenstrasse synagogue), 1852.

3. Schwarzschild, *Die Gründung*, p. 18.

3*. Meir Hildesheimer, "L'Toldot Rabbeinu [E. Hildesheimer]," *Shaalos U'Teshuvos Rabbi Ezriel Hildesheimer* (Tel Aviv, 1969), p. 24.

4. Ibid., p. 27.

5. *Nikolsburg oder Frankfurt*, p. 253; Mordechai Breuer, "Samson Raphael Hirsch," *Guardians of our Heritage* (New York, 1958), p. 281.

6. Schwarzschild, op. cit., p. 29; *Collected Writings* II, p. 248.

7. Jacob Rosenheim, *Zichronot* (Bnei Brak, 1979), p. 10.

7*. Rabbi Nachman Bulman heard the story from Rabbi Nisson Telushkin, who heard it from the Lubavitcher Rebbe, Rabbi Sholom Ber Schneerson, who met the woman.

8. *Der Treue Zionswächter* (TZW) VII (1851), p. 4; *Gedächtnisrolle*, 1852.

9. Liberles, p. 140.

10. Cf. *Collected Writings* VI, p. 224.

11. *TZW* IX (1853), p. 15.

12. Isaac Heinemann, "Mechkarim al Harav Samson Raphael Hirsch," *Sinai* XXIV (1949), pp. 249-271.

13. Breuer, *Modernity*, p. 35.

14. *S'ridei Eish* IV p. 369; See also *Collected Writings* VI, p. 199.

15. *Igros Rabbi Ezriel Hildesheimer*, collected and edited by Mordechai Eliav (Jerusalem, 1966), p. 22.

16. Mordechai Breuer, *Eidah U'Dyuknah* (Jerusalem, 1991), p. 46.

17. Schwarzschild, *Die Gründung*, pp. 46-47; *Shemesh Marpeh*, pp. 111-112.

18. *Collected Writings* VI, p. 178; Rosenheim, *Zichronot* (Bnai Brak, 1979), p. 30; Breuer, *Am VeEidah*, MS.

19. Breuer, *Modernity*, p. 217.

20. Breuer, *Eidah U'Dyuknah*, pp. 202-204.

21. I. Grunfeld, *Three Generations* (London, 1958), p. 22.

22. *Collected Writings* VI, p. 79.

23. Breuer, *Am VeEidah,* MS.

Chapter Eleven

1. *Collected Writings* VI, pp. 35, 62, 64, 77; *Commentary, Devarim* 4:5, 6:1-3, 7:6, 27:9, 31:10; *The Nineteen Letters,* Nos. 8, 9, 16.

2. *Collected Writings* VI, p. 18; II, p. 169; *Commentary, Siddur,* pp. 456, 633; *From the Wisdom of Mishlé,* p. 143.

3. *Collected Writings* VI, p. 40.

4. Ibid., VI, p. 83; I, p. 316

5. Ibid., VI, pp. 3, 13; II, pp. 174-176, 323; *Commentary, Siddur,* pp. 104, 436, 476; *Horeb,* ch. 106

6. *Shemesh Marpeh,* pp. 112-118.

7. Salo Baron, "Freedom and Constraint in the Jewish Community," *Essays and Studies in Memory of Linda R. Miller* (1938), p. 10; Katz, *Secession,* p. 15.

8. Cf. *Shemesh Marpeh,* p. 199, regarding this development in Prague in 1850; Katz, *Secession,* p. 17.

9. Breuer, *Am VeEidah,* MS.

10. *Collected Writings* VI, pp. 172, 215.

11. Ibid., pp. 74, 88, 172, 215.

12. Ibid., p. 90.

13. Ibid., pp. 86-99.

13*. This account is a combination of two separate articles of Rabbi Herz Ehrmann, a close confidant and companion of Rabbi Salanter.

14. *Collected Writings* VI, pp. 175, 180, 194-96, 202, 210, 258, 300.

15. Ibid., p. 81.

16. Breuer, *Am VeEidah,* MS.

17. *Statuten der Kehilath Jeschurun in Frankfurt a.M.* (Frankfurt a.M., 1874) p. 8; Schwarzschild, *Die Gründung,* pp. 46-47; *Shemesh Marpeh,* p. 111.

18. Breuer, *Am VeEidah,* MS.

19. *Shemesh Marpeh,* pp. 111-112.

20. Ibid., pp. 187-188.

21. Ibid., pp. 199-200.

22. *Toras HaKanaus,* 5605 (1845); *Shemesh Marpeh,* pp. 195-96.

22*. *Shemesh Marpeh,* p. 8. Jacob Katz in his *Secession* was not aware of these statements of Rabbi Hirsch when he writes that secession was an option for Rabbi Hirsch only in the 1860s and more emphatically in the 1870s. See also *Collected Writings* I, p. 167, for an early expression of the secession imperative.

24. Breuer, *Am VeEidah,* MS.

25. *Shemesh Marpeh,* p. 200.

26. Katz, *Secession*, pp. 121-123.

27. Ibid., p. 170.

28. Ibid., pp. 184-185.

29. Ibid., pp. 186-188.

Chapter Twelve

1. Katz, *Secession*, p. 26.

2. Breuer, *Am VeEidah*, MS.

3. Schwab, *History*, p. 86; Breuer, *Am VeEidah*, MS.

4. Breuer, ibid.

5. *Collected Writings* II, p. 171; *Jeschurun* I (1854-55), pp. 436-448, IV (1857-58), pp. 253-266.

6. *Collected Writings* VIII, p. 82.

7. *Collected Writings* VI, pp. 27, 54-56, 69-75, 89, 161; II, p. 356.

8. *Shemesh Marpeh*, pp. 199-200.

9. Ibid., p. 241.

10. *Jeschurun* I (1854-55), pp. 333-334; IV (1857-58), pp. 62-90.

11. *Collected Writings* VI, pp. 155-169, cf. also p. 74; VIII, pp. 80-81.

12. Katz, *Secession*, p. 250.

12*. *Machzikei HaDas*, (Piotrokow, 1907); "S.R.H. & Rabbi Yisrael Salanter in Berlin," *Israelit* XLVII, March 22, 1906, pp. 2-4.

13. Baron, "Freedom and Constraint," p. 12; Katz, *Secession*, pp. 248-256.

14. Baron, "Freedom etc.," p. 14

15. *Collected Writings* VI, p. 148.

16. Breuer, *Am VeEidah*, MS.

17. Ibid.

Chapter Thirteen

1. Letter from Rabbi Hirsch to Rabbi Aaron D. Deutsch of Yarmut. *Shemesh Marpeh*, p. 200.

2. Breuer, *Am VeEidah*, MS.

3. *Hildesheimer Briefe*, p. 117.

4. The following is the text of a letter Rabbi Hirsch received not long after *Simchas Torah*: הנה שמעתי בש״ת העבר מדרוש יפפיה של אדוני שהוא חוב גמור על כל אנשי עדתו ושאר תושבי פ״פ להפרד נא מחבורת הכת חדשים. It is unclear from the letter if Rabbi Hirsch spoke about it on *Simchas Torah*, or the man heard about it then, or whether the writer even lived in Frankfurt. Sänger Collection, Heb. MS, File 7.

5. [Saemy Japhet,] "The Secession of the Frankfurt Jewish Community Under S.R. Hirsch," *Historia Judaica* X (1948), no. 2, pp. 109-110.

6. *Collected Writings* VI, p. 271.

7. Breuer, *Am VeEidah,* MS.

8. Rabbi Shimon Schwab, whose grandfather's store was boycotted because he seceded.

9. Rosenheim, *Zichronot,* pp. 28-29.

10. Japhet, op. cit., p. 112.

11. *Collected Writings* VI, pp. 170-186.

12. Japhet, op. cit., p. 117.

13. Breuer, *Am VeEidah,* MS.

14. *Collected Writings* VI, pp. 192-197.

15. *Collected Writings* p. 221. See also pp. 251-252, for Rabbi Bamberger's interpretation of *Torah Im Derech Eretz.*

16. Breuer, *Modernity,* pp. 42, 141.

17. Schwab, *History,* pp. 75-76; *Collected Writings* VI, pp. 238-239; Hamburger, *Nesi HaLeviim,* p. 543.

18. See previous note.

19. *Collected Writings* VI, p. 309.

19*. Schwab, *History,* p. 74.

20. Hamburger, *Nesi HaLeviim,* pp. 539-543.

20*. Ibid., p. 542.

21. Breuer, *Am VeEidah,* MS.

22. *Collected Writings* VI, p. 241; Rosenheim, *Zichronot,* p. 29; Japhet, op. cit., p. 115.

23. Schwab, op. cit., p. 73.

24. *Collected Writings* VI, p. 217.

25. Breuer, *Am VeEidah,* MS.

26. *Collected Writings* VI, p. 279.

27. *Hildesheimer Briefe,* p. 117.

28. *Collected Writings* VI, p. 314.

29. Ibid., pp. 254-317; the section of the "Open Response" with halachic issues appears in translation in *Shemesh Marpeh,* responsum no. 52, pp. 64-68.

30. *Shaalos U'Tshuvos Chasam Sofer* VI, no. 89.

31. Breuer, *Am VeEidah,* MS.

32. Hildesheimer, op. cit., pp. 117-119.

33. Ibid., pp. 119-120.

Chapter Fourteen

1. Cf. Isaac Breuer, *Darki* (Jerusalem, 1988), p. 10.

1*. Jacob Katz, *Secession,* p. 334n.

2. Rosenheim, *Zichronot,* pp. 28-31.

3. Although similar in certain ways, Breslau and Hamburg had different community frameworks due to a variety of factors, including the laws regarding compulso-

ry membership in the Jewish community, and the fact that the Tiktin family dynasty controlled the rabbinate in Breslau for several generations. Breuer, *Am VeEidah,* MS.

4. Breuer, *Am VeEidah,* MS; See also Jacobson, *Zichronot,* p. 21, quoting Rabbi Hirsch's observation on the Hamburg Arrangement: "Is Hamburg considered a *Kehillah*?"

5. Y.L. Maimon, *Sarei HaMe'ah* VI (Jerusalem, 1978), p. 302; Rabbi Boruch Horovitz, English Introduction to *Aruch LaNer* (Jerusalem, 1989), (end of vol. 2, no pagination) # 8; Yehuda Horovitz, Hebrew introduction to *Aruch Laner,* p. 37.

6. *TZW* III (1847), Nov., p. 2; V (1849), Nov. 9; Rabbi Yaakov Ettlinger, *Minchas Ani* (Altona, 5633-1873), *Parshas Pinchas,* as cited by Breuer, *Am VeEidah,* MS.

7. Rabbi Joseph Breuer.

8. Schwab, *History,* pp. 82-86; Maimon in *Sarei HaMe'ah* VI, pp. 302-303, writes that Rabbi A.I. Kook on a visit to Kissingen saw the exchange of letters in which Rabbi Bamberger purportedly forbade the establishment of independent communities. Nowhere in all the writings of Rabbi Bamberger does such a prohibition appear. See the reply of David Henshke, *HaMaayan* XIII (5733), 4:41-44; *Nesi HaLeviim,* pp. 543-547, especially p. 544, n10 and p. 547, n31. There are many others, too numerous to mention, who have drawn this fallacious conclusion.

9. *Collected Writings* VI, p. 250.

10. Mordechai Breuer, "Review of Noah Rosenbloom, *Tradition in An Age of Reform,*" *Tradition* XVI (1977) (4), p. 144.

11. *Collected Writings* VI, pp. 238-239; Schwab, *History,* pp. 75-76.

12. Schwab, ibid., p. 87; See also *Zecher Simchah,* nos. 229, 230.

13. See also the letter of Rabbi Chaim Ozer Grodzensky, *Kovetz Igros Rabbi Chaim Ozer, Achiezer* I (Bnei Brak, 1970), Letter no. 150.

14. Cf. Naftali bar Giora Bamberger, "HaYachasim bein Harav Y.D. Bamberger v'Chevrat Kol Yisrael Chaveirim," *Sefer Aviad* (Mosad Harav Kook: Jerusalem, 1986), pp. 151-161.

15. M.L. Bamberger, "Seligmann Bär Bamberger," *Jewish Leaders,* Leo Jung, ed. (New York, 1953), p. 193.

Chapter Fifteen

1. *Collected Writings* VI, pp. 173-75, 180, 194, 196, 202, 210, 258, 300.

2. Ibid., pp. 175, 180, 194-96, 202, 210, 258, 261, 300; see also vol. I, pp. 167-68; *Commentary, Psalms,* 50:5, 106:30; *Commentary, Siddur,* p. 424.

3. *Shemesh Marpeh,* p. 201.

4. *Jeschurun* X (1864), pp. 23-26.

5. *Shemesh Marpeh,* p. 201.

6. Rosenheim, *Zichronot,* p. 144.

7. A photocopy of the letter is in the possession of Mr. Joseph Munk, London.

8. *Collected Writings* VI, pp. 206, 278, 282, 297.

9. *Commentary, Siddur,* p. 424.

10. *Horeb,* Chap. 118.

11. Isaac Breuer, *Moriah,* p. 154.

12. *Collected Writings* VI, pp. 207, 297.

13. *Shemesh Marpeh,* pp. 187-88; *Rabbinische Gutachten über die Beschneidung* (Frankfurt a.M., 1844), pp. 3-4.

14. Indeed, one of Harry Hirsch's descendants today studies in a Jerusalem yeshiva.

15. *Collected Writings* VI, pp. 171, 180, 187.

16. Cited in Breuer, *Am VeEidah,* MS.

17. *Collected Writings* I, pp. 61-64.

18. *Shemesh Marpeh,* pp. 187-188.

19. Ibid., p. 248.

Chapter Sixteen

1. Rabbi Hirsch stressed the importance of the righteous man being *"besoch ha'ir* — in the midst of the city," and concerned for the welfare of all its inhabitants, as Abraham expressed it when he beseeched Hashem to spare Sodom in the merit of 50 righteous men. *Commentary, Breishis* 18:24.

2. *Commentary, Psalms,* 50:5.

3. Breuer, *Modernity,* p. 257.

3*. Rosenheim, *Zichronot,* p. 107; see also Isaac Breuer, *Moriah,* p. 205; Yisrael Wohlman, "HaRav S.R. Hirsch, Zein Leben un Schaffen," Hirsch Beilage, *Orthodoxische Jugend Blätter* (Warsaw, Jan. 1934).

4. Rosenheim, *Ktavim* I, p. 96; Schwab, *History,* p. 115.

4*. See Rosenheim, *Zichronot,* pp. 82, 107ff, especially his accounts of the initial meetings.

5. For a full account of the pogroms, Rabbi Spektor's activities and Rabbi Hirsch's involvement, see Yaakov Lipschitz, *Zichron Yaakov* III (Kovno, 1930), pp. 1-68. Much of this account is based on that of Lipschitz. See also "Samson Raphael Hirsch und das Jüdische Russland," *Jubiläumsnummer,* pp. 32-33.

6. Lipschitz was the author of the three-volume work, *Zichron Yaakov,* a history of Russian and Polish Jewry; *Toldot Yitzchak,* a biography of Rabbi Spektor; *Machzikei HaDas,* and many articles in Jewish periodicals.

7. Sänger Collection, Hebrew MS, File 5/68. *Shemesh Marpeh,* p. 362.

8. Ibid., p. 250.

9. Ibid., p. 252.

10. *Shemesh Marpeh,* p. 251.

11. Ibid.

12. Ibid., p. 252.

13. Rabbi Simcha Zisel Ziv, *Ohr Rashaz, Bereishis* (Jerusalem, 1960), p. 51.

14. *Shemesh Marpeh,* p. 253.

15. Ibid., pp. 254-256.

16. Ibid., p. 257.

17. Afterward they discussed various details of *Shemos Gittin,* and the visitor was amazed at his host's breadth of knowledge in this arcane subject. Prof. Mordechai Breuer.

18. See his letter to son-in-law Michael Levy of London in *Shemesh Marpeh,* pp. 214-215, and the letter from Rabbi A.B. Kluger of Brody, *Shemesh Marpeh,* p. 256.

19. Lipschitz, *Zichron Yaakov* III, pp. 68-69; "Samson Raphael Hirsch und das Jüdische Russland," *Jubiläumsnummer,* pp. 32-33.

20. Letters of Rabbi Spektor and Rabbi Yitzchak Blaser to Rabbi Hirsch. *Shemesh Marpeh,* pp. 267-268. See also Mordechai Breuer, *The Torah Im Derech Eretz of Samson Raphael Hirsch* (Jerusalem, 1970), pp. 47-48.

In 1888, Rabbi Hirsch received a letter from Rabbi Shlomo Halberstam of Vishnitza (not to be confused with Vizhnitz) and later Bobov (grandfather of the present Bobover Rebbe), soliciting his support for his yeshiva in Vishnitza. *Shemesh Marpeh,* pp. 268-269. This was but one of many such requests. See Sänger Collection, Hebrew MS, file 5.

Chapter Seventeen

1. *Collected Writings* VI, pp. 36-37.

2. Detailed and insightful analyses of *Torah Im Derech Eretz* can be found in Rabbi Yechiel Yaakov Weinberg's *Sridei Eish* IV (Jerusalem, 1977), pp. 360-374 and in Professor Mordechai Breuer's book-length essay *The Torah Im Derech Eretz of Samson Raphael Hirsch* (Feldheim Publishers: Jerusalem, 1970). Rabbi Shimon Schwab compared and contrasted the *Torah Im Derech Eretz* approach with that of "Torah Only" in a classic essay entitled "These and Those," republished in his *Selected Essays* (New York, 1994). Most recently, Rabbi Joseph Elias's annotated edition of *The Nineteen Letters* (Feldheim Publishers: Jerusalem, 1995) contains a number of incisive discussions of *Torah Im Derech Eretz,* particularly in the notes to Letters Seventeen and Eighteen.

3. *Commentary, Bereishis* 9:27, citing *Bereishis Rabbah* 19:13. See also *Collected Writings* I, pp. 193-4; IV, p. 380; *Commentary, Psalms,* 65:5, 92:13.

4. *Collected Writings* II, pp. 24, 43; I, p. 82; VII, p. 35; *Commentary, Shemos* 25:8; *Commentary, Psalms,* 30:1-2.

5. *Collected Writings* VII, p. 77.

6. Rabbi Yechiel Yaakov Weinberg, "Torat HaChaim" *Harav S.R. Hirsch: Mishnato VeShitato,* p. 192; Cf. *Collected Writings* IV, p. 371; see also *Commentary, Avos* 6:6. "במיעוט דרך ארץ — All of the earthly life constitutes the subject of the Torah's wisdom, and the Torah seeks to teach us to view and arrange all human affairs on earth in the light of the Teaching of God."

7. *Collected Writings* VII, p. 294.

8. *Collected Writings* V, p. 287.

9. *Collected Writings* I, pp. 281-282; cf. *Collected Writings* II, p. 46; *Commentary, Psalms,* 30:1-2.

10. Cf. Elias, Letter 15, n8.

10*. *Collected Writings* VII, pp. 66, 89, 288.

11. *Collected Writings* VI, p. 122.

12. See *Talmud Brachos* 35b.

13. Isaac Breuer, "Rabbi S. R. Hirsch KeMoreh Derech laHistoriah HaYisraelit," *Tziyunei Derech* (2nd ed., Jerusalem, 1982), p. 138; I. Breuer, "S.R. Hirsch," *Jewish Leaders*, Leo Jung, ed. (New York, 1953), pp. 169-170; cf. *Collected Writings* VII, p. 153.

14. *Commentary, Vayikra*, 18:4; *Collected Writings* VII, pp. 39, 417.

15. *Collected Writings* II, p. 309; VII, p. 76; cf. *Commentary, Bereishis* 3:24, 4:23.

16. *Collected Writings* I, p. 304.

17. Breuer, *Tziyunei Derech*, p. 137; I. Breuer, "S. R. Hirsch," p. 168; *Collected Writings* II, p. 313.

17*. *Torah U'Madda* (Northvale, 1990), p. 236.

18. *Jeschurun* (Berlin), I (1914), p. 81.

19. See Rabbi Naftali Z.Y. Berlin, *Haamek Davar al HaTorah*, author's introduction, where he states that the nations of the world are enjoined to research the universe, as in this way they give honor to Hashem.

20. *Collected Writings* VII, pp. 252, 254, 260, 293.

21. Ibid., p. 12.

22. *Collected Writings* IV, p. 373.

22*. *Collected Writings* I, pp. 184-190; II, p. 66; VII, pp. 64, 154; *Shemesh Marpeh*, p. 230.

23. *Collected Writings* VII, pp. 12, 90; *Judaism Eternal* I, p. 211; *Commentary, Psalms*, 119:99; *Commentary, Siddur, Avos* 4:1.

24. *Collected Writings* VII, p. 291.

25. Ibid., cf. also p. 169.

26. *Collected Writings* VII, pp. 12, 54, 88.

27. Elias, p. 320.

28. *Commentary, Devarim* 6:7.

29. *Commentary, Vayikra* 18:4.

30. *Collected Writings* II, pp. 17-18.

31. Ibid.

32. *Horeb*, p. 393, *Collected Writings* VII, p. 12.

33. Cf. *Collected Writings* VI, pp. 203-207.

34. *Collected Writings* VII, p. 34; *Commentary, Psalms*, 19:1,8.

35. *Collected Writings* I, p. 157.

36. Ibid., p. 304.

37. Ibid.

Chapter Eighteen

1. *Igros Sofrim* (Vienna, 1929), part I, p. 25.

2. *Ahavas Zion* (Warsaw, 1881), p. 19.

3. Cited in Mordechai Breuer, *The Torah Im Derech Eretz of S.R. Hirsch* (Jerusalem, 1970), p. 12.

4. See, for instance, Rabbi Elchanan Wasserman, *Kovetz Maamarim* (Tel Aviv, 1986), pp. 61-67; Rabbi Boruch Ber Leibovitz, *Birchas Shmuel, Kiddushin,* Chap. 27. Both Rabbi Wasserman and Rabbi Leibovitz were responding to inquiries of Frankfurt-born Rabbi Shimon Schwab, later Rabbi of the successor *Kehillah* of the *IRG, K'hal Adath Jeshurun* of New York.

5. *Collected Writings* VII, p. 13.

6. Ibid.

7. Ibid.

8. Ibid.

9. *Collected Writings* VII, p. 84.

10. Cf. ibid., p. 288.

11. Dr. Moshe Auerbach, "Die Bildungsfrage in der Thoratreuen Jüdenheit Deutschlands," *Vom Sinn des Jüdentums,* Ein Sammelbuch zu Ehren Nathan Birnbaum's, (Frankfurt a.M., 1925).

12. *Shemesh Marpeh,* pp. 194, 224; cf. *Collected Writings* VII, p. 4.

13. *Collected Writings* VII, p. 20; VIII, p. 322.

14. Mordechai Breuer, *Torah Im Derech Eretz,* p. 39.

15. Approbation to the first Hebrew edition of Rabbi Hirsch's *Commentary on the Torah* (Kovno, 1891).

16. Approbation to *Sefer Meitav Higayon* by Rabbi Yitzchak Isaac Hershowitz (Vilna, 1913). See also letters from Rabbi Yitzchak Elchanan Spektor and Rabbi Eliyahu Chaim Meisel praising the work of the *Realschule* in Frankfurt. *Shemesh Marpeh,* pp. 264-265.

17. Aharon Surasky, *Shlucha D'Rabanan* (Jerusalem, 1992), p. 34, *n*30.

18. Letter 17. See Elias, note 2.

19. *Collected Writings* VI, p. 221.

20. In his "Open Letter" to Rabbi Seligman Bär Bamberger of Würzburg, Rabbi Hirsch agreed that *Torah Im Derech Eretz* as an educational principle was not without controversy. *Collected Writings* VI, p. 272.

21. *Shemesh Marpeh,* p. 212.

22. *Collected Writings* VI, p. 221.

23. The original letter is in the possession of the family of Rabbi Joseph Breuer, New York.

24. A copy of the letter is in the possession of Prof. Mordechai Breuer.

Chapter Nineteen

1. From an 1849 letter of Rabbi Hirsch to Rabbi Moshe Leib Engel. *Shemesh Marpeh,* p. 225.

2. *Shemesh Marpeh,* pp. 68-69; *Collected Writings* VII, p. 172.

3. *Jubiläumsnummer* , p. 12; Grunfeld, *Judaism Eternal* I, p. xlii; *Collected Writings* VII, p. 173.

4. S. Goldschmidt, "Vor Dreissig Jahren," *Jubiläumsnummer,* p. 23; Mordechai Breuer, "Chazon U'Metziut Bachinuch HaOrthodoxi ShebeGermaniah BaMe'ah Ha19," *Sefer Hashanah Bar Ilan* XVI-XVII, pp. 321-322.

5. *Jubiläumsnummer,* p. 13; Schwab, *History,* p. 42.

6. Letter to Eliezer Liepman Prins, reprinted in *HaMaayan* XXIX (5749), 1:32; Rosenheim, *Zichronot,* p. 13.

7. Rabbi S.R. Hirsch, "Das Rabbinische Judenthum und die Soziale Bildung," *Jeschurun* (Hannover) IV (1886), 41:643.

8. Ibid.

9. Letter to Prins, see note 6 above.

10. See *Horeb,* Chapter 84.

11. See note 6 above.

12. Rosenheim, *Zichronot,* p. 11; Breuer, *Modernity,* pp. 120, 125.

13. The renowned Slabodka *Rosh Yeshiva,* Rabbi Moshe Mordechai Epstein, once admitted as much to Dr. Moshe Auerbach. "In the education of girls, *you* succeeded." Moshe Auerbach, *Zichronot,* p. 47, *n*7.

14. Breuer, *Modernity,* p. 120; 1879 letter of Rabbi Hirsch to Rabbi Zalman Spitzer of Vienna, concerning the instruction of Arabic in Jerusalem schools.

15. Rosenheim, *Zichronot,* p. 15; Liberles, pp. 149, 153.

16. Rosenheim, *Zichronot,* p. 14.

17. Saemy Japhet, "The Secession of the Frankfurt Jewish Community Under S.R. Hirsch," *Historia Judaica* X (1948), no. 2, p. 105.

18. Eliav, *HaChinuch HaYehudi,* pp. 227-232.

19. *Shemesh Marpeh,* pp. 264-265.

20. Breuer, *Modernity,* p. 108.

21. Rabbi J. Breuer, "Rabbiner Hirsch als Schulleiter," *Nachlath Zvi* VII, p. 239; Schwarzschild, *Die Gründung,* p. 34; Mordechai Breuer, "Chazon U'Metziut BaChinuch HaOrthodoxi ShebeGermaniah BaMe'ah ha19," p. 320.

22. S. Goldschmidt, "Vor dreissig Jahren," *Jubiläumsnummer,* pp. 22-23; also Moritz Loeb, *"Schulerinnerungen,"* ibid., pp. 24-26; Schwab, *Memories of Frankfurt (Aus der Schützenstrasse)* (London, 1958), pp. 7-11.

23. Rosenheim, *Zichronot,* p. 16.

24. This has been discussed at length by Professor Mordechai Breuer in "Chazon U'Metziut Bachinuch HaOrthodoxi ShebeGermaniah BaMe'ah Ha19," pp. 317-335; Breuer, *Modernity,* p. 111.

25. Breuer, *Modernity*, p. 113.

26. Ibid., p. 114; Rosenheim, *Zichronot*, pp. 14-15; Joseph Elias, *The World of Rabbi S.R. Hirsch: The Nineteen Letters*, p. 334.

27. Breuer, *Modernity*, p. 111.

28. Breuer, "Chazon U'Metziut etc.," p. 318ff.

29. Ibid., pp. 321-322.

30. Rosenheim, *Zichronot*, pp. 17-18.

31. Breuer, *Modernity*, pp. 113, 118, 123.

32. Dr. Moshe Auerbach, "Die Bildungsfrage in der Thoratreuen Jüdenheit Deutschlands."

33. Rosenheim, *Zichronot*, p. 19.

34. Ibid., p. 18; Mordechai Breuer, *Torah Im Derech Eretz*, p. 41; Breuer, *Modernity*, pp. 115, 128.

35. Cf. *Collected Writings* VII, pp. 157-158.

36. Breuer, *Modernity*, p. 317; *Jeschurun* (Hannover) VI (1888) 49:779 (2 *Teves*, 5649). The original is in the Sänger Collection.

37. *Jubiläumsnummer*, p. 13.

38. I. Grunfeld, *Three Generations* (London, 1958), p. 96; I. Grunfeld, *Judaism Eternal* I, p. 158*n*.

Chapter Twenty

1. Breuer, *Modernity*, p. 176.

1*. *Collected Writings* II, p. 196.

2. Abraham Schischa, "Hermann Adler, Yeshiva Bahur," *Remember the Days: Essays on Anglo-Jewish History Presented to Cecil Roth* (London, 1966), p. 244, *n*15. As he grew older, Zunz's relationship with authentic Judaism warmed somewhat, and, according to one report, he donned *tefillin* until the end of his life.

3. Tobias Tal, "Samson Raphael Hirsch," *Der Denkende Jude* (Bibliothek des Jüdischen Volksfreundes: Cöln, 1914), p. 7.

4. Max Wiener, *HaDat HaYehudit BiTkufat HaEmantzipatziah* (Jerusalem, 1974), p. 48.

4*. Ibid., p. 42; Meyer, *Response*, p. 75.

5. Ismar Schorsch, "Ideology & History in an Age of Emancipation," Introduction to H. Graetz, *The Structure of Jewish History and Other Essays* (New York, 1975), pp. 9-12.

6. Ibid., pp. 4-5.

7. Leopold Zunz, *Zur Geschichte und Literatur* (Berlin, 1845), p. 28.

8. Schorsch, Introduction to H. Graetz, *Structure of Jewish History and other Essays*, p. 4.

9. Breuer, *Modernity*, p. 177.

10. Isaac Breuer, *Moriah* (Jerusalem, 1982), pp. 134-135; cf. *Collected Writings* VII, p. 161.

11. Breuer, *Modernity*, p. 189.

12. Ch. 1.

13. *The Nineteen Letters,* second letter; cf. *From the Wisdom of Mishlé,* p. 52.

14. *Commentary, Vayikra* 18:4; *Commentary, Psalms* 111:10; *Collected Writings* VIII, p. 249; *Judaism Eternal* II, p. 145.

15. *Commentary, Pirkei Avos* 3:11; cf. *The Nineteen Letters,* Letter Eighteen; *Commentary, Psalms* 50:16, 119:1.

16. *Collected Writings* I, p. 342

17. *Collected Writings* VII, p. 45.

18. *Collected Writings* V, p. 312.

19. *Berliner National-Zeitung,* 1854 no. 179; *Israelit* XX (1879), 31:814-815; *Collected Writings* V, p. 274.

20. E. Hildesheimer, "HaRav Hildesheimer al Zachariah Frankel U'Beit HaMedrash LeRabbanim," *Hamaayan* I (5713), 1:73; *Hildesheimer Briefe,* p. 137; Breuer, *Modernity,* p. 14.

21. Rivka Horovitz, Introduction to *Zachariah Frankel VeReishit HaYahadut HaPositivit Historit,* (Jerusalem, 1984), p. 9.

22. Horovitz, Introduction to *Zachariah Frankel* etc., pp. 9, 14.

Chapter Twenty-One

1. *Collected Writings* V, p. 6.

2. Ibid.

3. Ibid., p. 5.

4. Heinrich Graetz, *Tagebuch und Briefe,* p. 23. Various sections of Graetz's diaries, edited by Markus Brann, were published from 1917 to 1920 in *Monatsschrift für Geschichte und Wissenschaft des Judentums.* A more complete edition is Heinrich Graetz, *Tagebuch und Briefe,* Reuven Michael, ed. (Tübingen, 1977).

5. Ibid.

6. Ibid., pp. 26-30.

7. Ibid., p. 54.

8. Graetz, *Tagebuch,* p. 49.

8*. Ibid., p. 57.

9. Ibid., p. 53.

10. Ibid., p. 74.

11. Ibid., p. 80.

12. "Hirsch und Graetz," *Israelit* XLVI (1905), 1:17; *Tagebuch,* p. 191. Y.Y. Greenwald, *LeToldot HaReformatzion HaDatit BeGermaniah UveHungariah* (Columbus, 1948), p. 57.

13. Phillip Bloch, *Heinrich Graetz: A Memoir* (Philadelphia, 1898), p. 43; "Hirsch und Graetz," p. 17; Mordechai Breuer, "Prakim B'Toldot Rabbi S.R. Hirsch," *HaMaayan* III (5716), 1:46.

14. *Collected Writings* V, pp. 6, 20, 35, 266.

15. Ibid., pp. 5, 60, 75, 123, 138-140, 145.

16. Ibid., p. 5.

17. Ibid., p. 75.

18. Ibid.

19. Heinrich Graetz, *Geschichte der Juden vom Untergang des Jüdischen Staats bis zum Abschluss des Talmuds* (1853), p. 14.

20. Ibid., pp. 4-5.

21. Ibid., pp. 8-9.

22. Graetz, ibid.

23. Ibid., pp. 11-12.

24. Ibid., p. 12.

24*. *Collected Writings* V, p. 27.

25. *Commentary, Shemos* 21:2; See also I. Grunfeld, Introduction to Rabbi Hirsch's Commentary on the Torah, p. xvii.

26. *Collected Writings* V, pp. 39-40, 294; see also *Commentary, Shemos* 21:2, and *Siddur*, pp. 38-41.

27. *Sefer HaMitzvos LeHaRambam*, Shoresh 2, no. 3.

28. Meyer, *Response*, p. 5

29. Graetz, ibid., p. 18.

30. Ibid., pp. 46-8.

31. *Collected Writings* V, p. 75.

31*. Ibid., pp. 65-6, 125, 173, 179, 181.

32. Schwab, *History*, p. 64; "Hirsch und Graetz," p. 18.

33. "Hirsch und Graetz," p. 29.

Chapter Twenty-Two

1. Ismar Schorsch, "Zachariah Frankel and the European Origins of Conservative Judaism," *Judaism* XXX (1981), p. 345.

2. *Igros Sofrim*, pp. 34, 49.

3. Y.Y. Greenwald, *Otzar Nechmad* (New York, 1942), p. 87.

4. Schorsch, "Z. Frankel," p. 352; Rivka Horovitz, Introduction to *Zachariah Frankel* etc., pp. 18-21.

4*. *Collected Writings* V, p. 274.

5. Meyer, *Response*, p. 107.

5*. Schorsch, "Z. Frankel," pp. 347-49; Horovitz, Introduction, ibid.

6. Ibid.; Schorsch, "Zachariah Frankel," p. 347.

7. Breuer, *Modernity*, p. 13.

8. See Frankel, "Al Reformot BeYahadut," *Zachariah Frankel VeReishit HaYahadut HaPositivit Historit* (Jerusalem, 1984), pp. 45-67.

9. See Frankel, loc. cit., "Havikuach al HaSafah HaIvrit BeAsifat HaRabanim HaShniyah," pp. 101-110.

10. Horovitz, *Frankel,* pp. 21, 25.

11. *Berliner National-Zeitung,* 1854 no. 179; *Israelit* XX (1879), 31:814-815; *Collected Writings* V, p. 274.

12. *Collected Writings* V, pp. 263, 268, 294, 303, 310, 320.

12*. Hildesheimer, *Briefe,* p. 27; E. Hildesheimer, "Rabbi Ezriel Hildesheimer al Zachariah Frankel etc.," *HaMaayan* I (5713), 1:69.

13. Ibid., p. 264.

14. Ibid., p. 267.

15. Ibid., p. 295.

16. Ibid., pp. 279-80.

16*. Hildesheimer, *Briefe,* pp. 26-27; see also E. Hildesheimer, "Rabbi Ezriel Hildesheimer al Zachariah Frankel," *HaMaayan* I (5713), 1:68.

17. Ibid., pp. 281-282. For a lengthy account of the entire controversy, see Anonymous, *Meor Einayim: Beleuchtung des Frankel'schen Streites* (Wien, 1861); Shaul Pinchas Rabinowich, *Reb Zachariah Frankel* (Warsaw, 1898), pp. 203-218.

18. *Collected Writings* V, p. 307.

19. A. Schischa, "Hermann Adler, Yeshiva Bahur," pp. 245-246.

20. Vol. VII (July 1860).

21. *Collected Writings* V, pp. 321-2.

22. Ibid., p. 327.

23. Ibid., p. 325.

24. Ibid.

25. Ibid., p. 329.

26. Horovitz, *Frankel,* pp. 126-127. Cf. *Collected Writings* V, p. 308.

27. Schwab, *History,* p. 65; *Hildesheimer Briefe,* p. 27.

28. Ibid., p. 311.

29. *Collected Writings* V, p. 312.

30. Ibid., p. 296.

31. Ibid.

32. Schorsch, "Z. Frankel," p. 345.

33. E. Hildesheimer, "Rabbi Ezriel Hildesheimer al Zachariah Frankel etc.," *HaMaayan* I (5713), 1:66.

34. Letter to Rabbi Hile Wechsler, 16 *Tammuz,* 5634 (1874). My thanks to Prof. Mordechai Breuer for making this letter available to me.

35. See, for example, correspondence between Rabbi Ezriel Hildesheimer and his son, Dr. Hirsch Hildesheimer, and Emanuel Schwarzschild, Hildesheimer, *Briefe,* pp. 207-219.

35*. For a fascinating comparison between the *Torah Im Derech Eretz* of Rabbi Hirsch and Rabbi Hildesheimer's views on scientific research, see Breuer, *Modernity,* p. 131ff.

36. Rabbi Hirsch expressed his views in several letters to Rabbi Hile Wechsler, who had written to him seeking his opinion of Rabbi Hoffmann's book, see note 34. The letters are also cited in Alexander Marx, *Essays in Jewish Biography* (Philadelphia, 1947), pp. 204-206.

37. M.A. Schulvass, "Beit HaMidrash LeRabbanim BeBerlin," *Mosdot HaTorah Be-Eiropah BeVinyanam U'VeChurbanam* (New York, 1956), p. 693; Breuer, *Modernity*, p. 134. Cf. *Hildesheimer Briefe*, pp. 207-216.

38. Breuer, *Modernity*, p. 138.

Chapter Twenty-Three

1. Schwab, *A World in Ruins*, p. 50.

2. Rabbi Shlomo Sofer, *Chut HaMeshulash* (Tel Aviv, 1963), pp. 129-132, who quotes, without attribution, Rabbi Hillel Lichtenstein of Kolomei, *Ais Laasos* I, Chap. 9, no. 87.

3. *Drashos Chasam Sofer* I, p. 334; In his *Sefer HaZikaron* (Jerusalem, 1957), p. 42, the *Chasam Sofer* makes a similar point: "To the extent that we wish to mix with [gentiles], become close with them and adopt their mores, Hashem interposes hatred between them and us." Cf. Mordechai Breuer, "Emancipation and the Rabbis," *Niv Hamidrashia* XIII (1978/9), p. 43. See also *Drashos Chasam Sofer* I, pp. 225-230, concerning Rabbi Sofer's views on secular education in his time.

4. *Collected Writings* I, pp. 335-336.

5. *Collected Writings* II, p. 75.

6. Breuer, "Emancipation and the Rabbis," pp. 26-30.

7. Ibid., p. 37.

8. *Drashos Chasam Sofer* II, p. 500.

9. *The Nineteen Letters*, Letter 16.

10. Ibid., Letter 9.

11. Ibid.

12. Ibid., Letter 16.

13. Dr. Salomon Ehrmann, in a letter to Mordechai Breuer, 21 *Sivan*, 5716 quoting his father, Rabbi Herz Ehrmann, a close confidant of Rabbi Yisrael Salanter.

14. Breuer, *Eidah U'Dyuknah*, p. 246.

15. *Encyclopaedia Judaica*, 6:1162-4.

16. Salo W. Baron, "The Impact of the Revolution of 1848 on Jewish Emancipation," *Jewish Social Studies* XI (1949), p. 195.

17. "S.R. Hirsch und die Österreichische Revolution," *Jubiläumsnummer*, p. 26; For lengthy accounts of Rabbi Hirsch's activities during the revolution of 1848-49 see Adolph Frankl-Grün, *Geschichte der Juden in Kremsier* II (Frankfurt, 1898), pp. 11-20, 122-136; Salo W. Baron, "The Revolution of 1848 and Jewish Scholarship," *Proceedings of the American Academy for Jewish Research*, Vol. XX (1951) pp. 34-43; David Feuchtwang, "Samson Raphael Hirsch als Oberlandesrabbiner von Mähren," *Jubiläumsnummer*, pp. 21-25.

18. Frankl-Grün, *Geschichte der Juden in Kremsier* II, pp. 122-136; Salo W. Baron, "The Revolution of 1848," pp. 34-36; I. Grunfeld, Introduction to *Judaism Eternal* (London, 1956), p. xl.

19. Frankl-Grün, ibid; Baron, "The Revolution of 1848," p. 36.

20. Baron, ibid., p. 38.

21. See ibid., p. 41, for Baron's theory as to why Rabbi Hirsch agreed to a separate Jewish delegation.

21*. *Shemesh Marpeh*, p. 95.

22. Frankl-Grün, *Geschichte der Juden in Kremsier* II, p. 13.

23. Salo W. Baron, "Aspects of Jewish Communal Crisis in 1848," *Jewish Social Studies* XIV (1952), pp. 142-143.

24. Breuer, *Modernity*, p. 292.

25. *Collected Writings* II, p. 26.

Chapter Twenty-Four

1. *Commentary, Devarim* 4:5; cf. *Collected Writings* I, p. 114; II, p. 4; VI, p. 64; VII, p. 96; VIII, p. 293; *The Nineteen Letters*, letters 8, 9, 16; *Commentary, Shemos* 25:13; *Commentary, Psalms* 78:54.

2. *Commentary, Devarim*, 32:9; *Commentary, Psalms* 47:4, 66:8, 83:3; 95:2, 106:2, 135:4; *Collected Writings* VIII, p. 291.

3. *The Nineteen Letters*, Letter 8; cf. Letters 9, 16; *Commentary, Shemos* 25:13; *Commentary, Psalms*, 78:54; *Collected Writings* I, p. 114; II, p. 4; VIII, p. 293.

4. *Commentary, Bereishis* 26:1; *Shemos* 3:8, 23:20; *Vayikra* 18:24; *Bamidbar* 13:18; *Devarim* 4:14, 5:28, 8:10, 16:9, 27:2; *Collected Writings* IV, p. 130.

5. *Commentary, Vayikra* 25:18.

6. *Collected Writings* IV, p. 276; cf. *Collected Writings* I, p. 299; *Commentary, Vayikra* 2:12, *Devarim* 17:14, 25:19.

7. *Commentary, Bereishis* 14:1.

8. *Commentary, Pirkei Avos*, 5:11.

9. *Commentary, Devarim* 4:26.

10. *Collected Writings* I, p. 117; cf. *The Nineteen Letters*, Letter 9; *Commentary, Psalms* 95:7; *Collected Writings* I, p. 288.

11. *Commentary, Devarim* 30:8; *Commentary, Siddur*, p. 699.

12. *Collected Writings* I, pp. 285-286.

13. *Commentary, Siddur*, pp. 138, 238, 699; *Commentary, Psalms* 85:10, 95:7,11; 102:15.

14. *Shemesh Marpeh*, p. 211.

15. *Commentary, Siddur*, pp. 138, 266, 703; *Commentary, Devarim* 8:10. *Collected Writings* II, p. 398; *Commentary, Psalms* 111:9.

16. *Collected Writings* IV, p. 403-404.

17. *Kesubos* 111a. *The Nineteen Letters*, Letter 16; *Horeb* para. 237, 608; *Commentary, Devarim* 8:10; *Commentary, Siddur*, pp. 138, 703.

18. Journal of the Chief Rabbi of Emden; *Shemesh Marpeh,* p. 238.

19. Sänger Collection, Hebrew MS, File 6.

20. Mordechai Eliav, *Ahavat Zion VeAnshei Hod* (Tel Aviv, 1971), p. 75 and n. 161-164.

21. Jerusalem Talmud, *Taanis* 1:1.

22. Dr. Meir Hildesheimer has done excellent research concerning this interesting episode, and our account is based largely on his comprehensive study: "HaRav Zvi Hirsch Kalischer VeHarav Samson Raphael Hirsch," *Sefer Aviad* (Jerusalem, 1986), pp. 195-214.

23. *Shemesh Marpeh,* p. 211.

23*. *Collected Writings* IV, p. 228, article dated *Elul* 5623 (August 1863). My thanks to Prof. Mordechai Breuer for pointing out the discrepancy between the English translation and the original German.

24. Hildesheimer, ibid., p. 214.

25. Ibid.

26. *Shemesh Marpeh,* p. 211. The attempts seem to have continued. As late as 1885, Rabbi Shmuel Mohliver wrote to Leo Pinsker, concerning the possibility of Rabbi Hirsch's participation in such efforts: "I have already expressed my opinion that this is a false hope." A. Druyanov, *Ketavim LeToldot Chibat Zion VeYishuv Eretz Yisrael* (Odessa, 1919), p. 173.

27. *Collected Writings* I, pp. 339, 345.

28. *Commentary, Siddur,* p. 139.

29. *Shemesh Marpeh,* pp. 214, 256.

30. *Shemesh Marpeh,* pp. 216-217. These plans (settlement in general; not specifically Petach Tikva) did not develop along the lines he had hoped. In an article in *Jeschurun,* Isaac Hirsch (the editor at the time and undoubtedly expressing his father's viewpoint) warned:

> To our great sorrow, we have become aware that the settlement project has become associated with harmful ideas that propose immigration as a national enterprise to fulfill the Messianic destiny, rather than as a humanitarian undertaking. This is an error and a deception which must be emphatically opposed.

He warned that while the leaders of the movement called themself "nationalists," they actually resisted the observance of Torah and *mitzvos* in keeping with the rulings of the *Shulchan Aruch,* and considered their activities "as a first step toward establishing a new Jewish state." See following note.

31. *Jeschurun* (Hannover) IV (1886), nos. 19, 20, cited in Eliav, *Ahavat Zion VeAnshei Hod,* p. 77.

32. [Herz Ehrmann,] "Ein Lebensbild," *Jubiläumsnummer,* p. 16.

33. *Jeschurun* (Hannover) VI (1888), no. 52 (23 *Teves,* 5649), p. 832; *Shemesh Marpeh,* p. 217.

34. *Maharsha* (*Pesachim* 87b) explains the statement of the Sages: *"Lo higlah HaKadosh Boruch Hu es Yisrael levein ha'umos elah kedei sheyitosfu aleyhem geirim* — Hashem exiled the Jews so that they could gain converts," to mean that if the purpose of the

Exile was only as a punishment Hashem could have employed other means. Rather, He intended that the Jewish people should spread faith in G-d among the nations of the world. See also *Vayikra Rabbah,* 6:5; *Haamek Davar, Bamidbar* 14:21; Rabbeinu Bachya, *Kad HaHemach (Geulah).*

35. *Commentary, Siddur,* pp. 47, 562; *Collected Writings* IV, p. 20; *Commentary, Shemos* 19:6; *Commentary, Psalms,* 47(entire), 89:48, 105:1,6, 111:6, 120:1, 126:5.

36. *The Nineteen Letters,* Letter 9.

37. *Commentary, Devarim* 4:26-27; See also Elias, Letter 9, note 3.

38. *Collected Writings* IV, p. 287.

39. Ibid., p. 289; *Collected Writings* II, p. 35.

40. *Collected Writings* VIII, pp. 285-286; cf. *Collected Writings* I, p. 177; *Commentary, Psalms,* 118:14.

41. *Commentary, Devarim* 28:37.

42. *The Nineteen Letters,* Letters 9 and 16; cf. *Collected Writings* VII, pp. 267, 269.

43. See *Pesachim* 87b and *Maharsha* there, cited in note 34; *Collected Writings* VII, p. 273.

43*. *Horeb,* introduction, p. cxli. See also *Collected Writings* I, p. 235.

44. S.R. Hirsch, *Worte bei der Schulfeier der Unterrichtanstalt der IRG* (Frankfurt a.M., 1859); *Collected Writings* VII, p. 61; cf. Pinchas Rosenblüth, "Bein Shnei Olamot," *Torah Im Derech Eretz: HaTnuah, Isheha, Raayonoteha* (Bar Ilan, 1987), p. 36.

45. *Collected Writings* VIII, pp. 9-10; cf. *Collected Writings* VII, p. 86; II, p. 19.

46. *Collected Writings* VIII, pp. 246-247.

46*. *Collected Writings* I, p. 23; cf. *Collected Writings* II, p. 26.

47. Mordechai Breuer, "Samson Raphael Hirsch," *Guardians of our Heritage* (New York, 1958), p. 297.

48. *Shemesh Marpeh,* pp. 196-198.

Chapter Twenty-Five

1. See *Shemesh Marpeh,* responsa nos. 1, 2, 3, 4, 8, 9, 10, 18, 25, 26, 29, 34, 36, 41, 43, 45, 46, 47, 63, 91, 92. In all of these, Rabbi Hirsch mentions the precarious state of Judaism at the time as a reason to prohibit.

2. Rabbi Salomon Breuer, *Rede zum Gedächtnis. . .* (Raab, 1889), p. 19, cited by Breuer, *Modernity,* p. 250.

3. Letter of Jacob Rosenheim to Dr. Yaakov Feuchtwanger of Feb. 14, 1934, cited in Mordechai Breuer, "Al Shtar Mechirah U'Maavak Miktzo'i bePolin SheLifnei HaShoah," *HaMaayan* XXXIV (5754), 4:8.

4. *Shemesh Marpeh,* p. 96.

5. Cf. *Igros Sofrim,* section III, no. 9. *Tshuvos Chasam Sofer, Even HaEzer* I, no. 98.

6. See Chapter 18.

7. *Shemesh Marpeh,* pp. 112-118.

8. The entire controversy regarding *metzitzah* is dealt with at length in Bleich,

Ettlinger, pp. 116-128.

9. *Shemesh Marpeh,* pp. 70-71.

10. Ibid., pp. 69-70.

11. Ibid.

12. Ibid., pp. 70-72.

12*. *Shemesh Marpeh,* pp. 36, 38.

13. Ibid., pp. 207-209; Ezriel Hildesheimer, "Chiluf Michtavim bein HaRav E. Hidesheimer, VeHaRav S.R. Hirsch," *Sefer Zikaron Yad Shaul* (Tel Aviv, 1953), pp. 246-249.

14. *Shemesh Marpeh,* pp. 43-44, 207-209.

15. An account of the various opinions siding with Rabbi Stern was printed in a booklet entitled *Der Ohlsdorfer Begräbnitzplatz* (Hannover, 1889). See especially pp. 38-39.

16. *Shaalos U'Tshuvos Rabbi Ezriel, Yoreh Deah,* nos. 256 and 257.

17. *Shemesh Marpeh,* pp. 15-17.

18. Ibid., p. 23.

19. Ibid., pp. 24-31.

20. Ibid., pp. 31-34.

21. Ibid., p. 41.

22. *Shemesh Marpeh,* pp. 57-58.

Rabbi Hirsch issued approbations for the following works:

1. *Sefer Shirah LeChaim,* Rabbi Chaim Perlmutter (Vienna, 1847)

2. *Akeidas Yitzchok im Pirush Mekor Chaim,* Rabbi Yoseph Chaim Pollak (Pressburg, 1849)

3. *Sefer Toras Emes, Toras Taamei Mishlei U'Tehillim,* Yitzchak ben Aryeh Yoseph Baer (Rödelheim, 1853)

4. *Shirei Jeschurun,* J.M. Japhet (Frankfurt, 1855)

5. *Amirah LeBais Yaakov,* Rabbi Yitzchok Dov Halevi Bamberger (Fürth, 1858)

6. *Shaalos U'Tshuvos Rabbi Yitzchok Milotash* (Vienna, 1860). The author was a contemporary of Rabbi Yoseph Karo.

7. *Metek Sefasayim, Hebraeische Sprachlehre mit Praktische Aufgaben,* J.M. Japhet (Frankfurt, 1861)

8. *Limud Aruch, al Mesechta Shabbos,* Rabbi Shlomo ben HaRav Yitzchak Dov Bamberger (Fürth, 1868)

9. *Sefer Pi Shenayim,* Rabbi Klonimus Weiss (Pressburg, 1881)

10. *Sefer HaMadrich,* Rabbi Avraham U'Binyamin Singer (Pressburg, 1882)

11. *Zichron Yehudah,* Rabbi Klonimus Weiss (Pressburg, 1883)

12. *Sidrei Taharos, Maseches Keilim,* in: *Maseches Ahalos,* Rabbi Gershon Chanoch Henach Leiner (Piotrokow, 1903)

Chapter Twenty-Six

1. *Collected Writings* I, p. 193; cf. ibid., pp. 267, 312.

2. *Collected Writings* VI, pp. 31-60; II, pp. 338-346.

3. *Collected Writings* I, pp. 390-391; see also *Commentary, Psalms,* 100:2.

4. *Collected Writings* II, p. 388; cf. *Commentary, Psalms,* 100:2.

5. Schwarzschild, *Die Gründung,* pp. 31, 35.

6. *Collected Writings* I, pp. 43-44.

7. *Commentary, Psalms,* 19:9, 29:4, 47:3, 90:17, 97:11; *Pirkei Avos,* 6:2; *Commentary, Bereishis* 2:9, 9:27.

8. *Collected Writings* II, p. 202.

9. *Jubiläumsnummer,* p. 18.

10. *Jüdische Presse* XI (1880), p. 384.

11. Letter to Simon May, *Jubiläumsnummer,* p. 18.

12. *Israelit* XXX (January 1, 1889); "Nachklänge an Hirsch's Wirksamkeit in Ostfriesland" *Israelit* XXX (1889), p. 116.

13. Schwab, *Memories of Frankfurt,* p. 20.

14. Breuer, *Eidah U'Dyuknah,* p. 54.

15. Isaac Heinemann, "Mechkarim al Rabbi Samson Raphael Hirsch," *Sinai* XXIV (5711), p. 261.

16. For a more extensive treatment of the subject of the choir and other German Jewish *minhagim,* see Rabbi Joseph Breuer, *A Time to Build* (Jerusalem, 1995), pp. 18-20, 40-45.

17. Liberles, p. 143.

18. Schwab, op. cit., p. 24; Breuer, *Modernity,* p. 146.

18*. Binyamin S. Hamburger, *Shoroshei Minhag Ashkenz* (Bnei Brak, 1995), pp. 249-256.

19. MS, from the estate of Rabbi Joseph Breuer, New York.

19*. See previous note.

20. Graetz, *Tagebuch,* p. 83.

21. See, for example, Rosenbloom, *Tradition in an Age of Reform* (Philadelphia, 1976), pp. 68-70.

22. *Allgemeine Zeitung des Judentums* VI (1842), p. 170, cited by Mordechai Breuer, "Perakim Mitoch Biographiah: Al Bitul Kol Nidrei BeOldenburg," *HaMaayan* IV (5624), 2:7-12.

23. *Shemesh Marpeh,* p. 243.

24. Ibid., p. 8.

25. Ibid., p. 9. A similar opinion was expressed by Rabbi Yaakov Ettlinger in *Shaalos U'Tshuvos Binyan Zion* I, no. 122.

Chapter Twenty-Seven

1. See, for example, the letter he wrote to a cousin upon his arrival in Mannheim (Chapter 4).

2. "S.R.H. als Landrabbiner von Nikolsburg," *Israelit* XLV (1904), p. 807.

3. *Collected Writings* I, pp. 53-54.

4. *Shemesh Marpeh,* p. 369.

5. "גואל הדם של התורה בגרמניה" Phillip Fischer, *In Seinen Spuren,* p. 59; *Nachalath Zvi* II (1931), p. 57.

6. *Commentary, Psalms,* 119:160.

7. Prospectus announcing the publication of *Jeschurun,* (Frankfurt, 1854).

8. *Collected Writings* VI, p. 104; cf. VIII, p. 62; *From the Wisdom of Mishlé,* p. 62.

8*."Isaac Leeser," *Guardians of the Spirit,* pp. 247-262.

9. *Shemesh Marpeh,* p. 231.

10. *Collected Writings* I, p. 169; cf. *Collected Writings* II, pp. 196, 209, 234-5; VIII, pp. 266-267; *Commentary, Siddur,* p. 153.

11. *From the Wisdom of Mishlé,* p. 196.

12. Ibid., cf. ibid., p. 105; *Collected Writings* VI, p. 176; *Commentary, Siddur,* pp. 157, 427.

13. Rabbi Yaakov Ettlinger, *Minchas Ani,* pp. 104-106, cited by Bleich, pp. 77, 211.

13*. *Commentary, Bamidbar* 25:12; *Collected Writings* VIII, pp. 62-64.

14. *Collected Writings* II, pp. 30-31; cf. VIII, p. 77.

15. A photocopy of the letter is in the possession of Mr. Joseph Munk, London.

16. A copy of this portrait, with the inscription, is in the possession of Dr. Judith Grunfeld of London.

17. *Collected Writings* V, pp. 326-27; VI, pp. 177, 208; I, pp. 322-24; *Shemesh Marpeh,* p. 117; *Commentary, Psalms,* 85:11, 120:5,6; *Commentary, Siddur,* p. 145.

18. *Collected Writings* I, p. 324.

19. Cf. *Collected Writings* II, p. 77; Rabbi Joseph Breuer, *A Time to Build* (Jerusalem, 1995), pp. 47-48.

20. Rabbi Joseph Breuer.

21. *Shemesh Marpeh,* pp. 220-221.

22. *Israelit* XXX (1899), 1:3.

23. *Shemesh Marpeh,* p. 238.

24. Ibid., p. 213.

25. A. Sulzbach, *Die Vier Münzen* (Frankfurt a.M., 1889), p. 9.

26. Prof. Mordechai Breuer.

27. Rabbi Joseph Breuer.

28. See previous note.

29. Prof. Mordechai Breuer. The Talmud (*Shabbos* 119b) cites this verse to prove that "conflagration is to be found only where the Sabbath is desecrated." See also *Commentary, Shemos,* 35:2.

30. In 1861, Rabbi Hirsch received a warm and extremely laudatory letter from the leading rabbis of Vilna region, including Reb Velvele, the world-renowned Vilna maggid, Rabbi Joseph Peimer of Slutzk, Rabbi Eizele Charif of Slonim, Rabbi Elya Schick of Lida and Rabbi Yitzchak Elchanan Spektor of Novaradok, thanking him profusely for a project which he had convinced the Baron to undertake. *Shemesh Marpeh,* p. 261.

31. Rosenheim, *Zichronot,* p. 56; Paul Arnsberg, *Die Geschichte der Frankfurter Juden seit der Französischen Revolution* III (Darmstadt, 1983), pp. 393, 398; Rabbi Joseph Breuer.

32. Rabbi Joseph Breuer.

33. Sänger Collection, Hebrew MS, File 5. See also Journal of the Chief Rabbi of Oldenburg, MS.

34. *Jubiläumsnummer,* p. 15.

35. Ibid.

36. Rabbi Joseph Breuer; letter from Dayan Gerson Posen to Sophie Breuer in Papa, dated "between Yom Kippur and Succos 5649 (1888)," a copy of which is in the possession of Prof. Mordechai Breuer.

37. *Jubiläumsnummer,* p. 16. See also, Ezriel Hildesheimer, "Chiluf Michtavim bein Rabbi Ezriel Hildesheimer VeRabbi S.R. Hirsch," *Sefer Zikaron Yad Shaul* (Tel Aviv, 1953), pp. 246-247.

38. Hermann Schwab, *Memories of Frankfurt,* London, 1958, p. 7; G. Goldschmidt, "Vor Dreissig Jahren," *Jubiläumsnummer,* pp. 22-24.

39. Prof. Mordechai Breuer.

40. See previous note.

41. *Collected Writings* VII, p. 126.

42. Mendel Hirsch, *Worte bei der zu Ablauf der Shloshim* (Frankfurt a.M., 1889), p. 9.

43. Prof. Mordechai Breuer.

43*. *Collected Writings* VIII, p. 259.

44. In a letter to S.M. Ehrenburg, Nov. 21, 1851. Leo Baeck Institute Archives, AR 4294, cited by Meyer, *Response,* p. 412, note 51.

45. Prof. Mordechai Breuer.

46. Graetz, *Tagebuch,* p. 51.

47. Rabbi Joseph Breuer, based on the account of his mother, Rabbi Hirsch's daughter, Sophie; Rabbi Joseph Guggenheimer, eulogy at Rabbi Hirsch's funeral. In 1870, Rabbi Hirsch wrote that he had been ill for two years and that each summer he was unwell for months at a time. *Shemesh Marpeh,* p. 21.

48. *Shemesh Marpeh,* pp. 249-258.

49. T. Tal, "Samson Raphael Hirsch," *Der Denkende Jude,* (Bibliothek des Jüdischen Volksfreundes: Cöln, 1914), p. 29.

50. Mendel Hirsch, *Worte bei der zu Ablauf der Shloshim* (Frankfurt a.M., 1889), pp. 8-10.

Chapter Twenty-Eight

1. Rabbi Joseph Breuer.

2. [Saemy Japhet,] "The Secession of the Frankfurt Jewish Community under S.R. Hirsch," *Historia Judaica* X (1948), 2:106.

3. "All my life I have engaged in thinking more than in speaking, and in speaking more than in writing." *The Nineteen Letters,* Letter 19.

4. Rabbi Zalman Spitzer, *Tikkun Shlomo* (Vienna, 5652-1892), p. 111; *Shemesh Marpeh,* p. 369.

5. Schwarzschild, *Die Gründung,* p. 29.

6. Samuel A. Hirsch, "Jewish Philosophy of Religion and Samson Raphael Hirsch," *Jewish Quarterly Review,* London, 1890, p. 136. An 1883 newspaper item relates that on the first days of *Pesach* Rabbi Hirsch was ill. On the last days he felt better and a large crowd, including many who were not members of the *IRG* came to hear his sermon. The paper reports that, as always, his address made a strong impression on his listeners, and tells how children would push forward and fill the space in front of the pulpit to ensure that they could hear every word. *Jüdische Presse* XIV (1883), p. 217.

7. "S.R.H. als Landrabbiner von Nikolsburg," *Israelit* XLV (1904), p. 807; Armin Schnitzer, *Jüdische Kulturbilder,* (Vienna, 1904), cited in Y.Y. Greenwald, *LeToldot HaReformatzion HaDatit BeGermaniah U'VeHungariah* (Columbus, 1948), pp. 56-58.

8. Bleich, *Ettlinger,* p. 248.

9. *Shemesh Marpeh,* pp. 239-241.

10. Dr. Joseph Wohlgemuth, "S.R. Hirsch und das Gesetzestreue Judentum," *Jeschurun* (Berlin), XIV (1927).

11. Breuer, *Modernity,* p. 163.

12. I. Grunfeld, *Three Generations* , p. 27.

13. *Collected Writings* V, p. 279.

14. Ibid., pp. 279-80.

15. *Collected Writings* VI, pp. 107-150.

16. Ismar Schorsch, Introduction to *Heinrich Graetz; The Structure of Jewish History and Other Essays* (New York, 1975), pp. 13-14.

17. Cf. *Tshuvos Chasam Sofer, Yoreh Deah,* no. 356.

18. Correspondence with Rabbi Loewenstein of Gailingen, Nov. 24, 1836 and March 17, 1837. *Israelit* XLVII (1906), 22:18. Cf. "Karmel und Sinai" *Nachlath Zvi* II, pp. 257-261. Perhaps that article was the prospectus for the proposed journal, referred to in his letter to Rabbi Loewenstein.

19. I. Grunfeld, *Judaism Eternal* II, p. 155 fn.

19*. Rosenheim, *Ktavim* I, p. 97.

20. *Bereishis,* 1867; *Shemos,* 1869; *Vayikra,* 1873; *Bamidbar,* 1876; *Devarim,* 1878.

21. *Commentary on the Torah,* Author's introduction.

22. See *Rashi* on *Bereishis* 2:23; *Commentary, Bereishis* 11:7.

23. *Commentary, Bereishis,* 19:23; *Collected Writings* VII, pp. 70-75.

24. Mordechai Breuer,"The Pentateuch Commentary of Samson Raphael Hirsch," MS.

25. Cf. Preface to the Hebrew edition on the *Commentary on the Torah* (Jerusalem, 1986); See also Rabbi Hirsch's, "Jewish Weltanschauung — An Attempt to Develop the Jewish outlook on the World and Life from the Hebrew Language and Literature of the Jewish People," *Collected Writings* VIII, pp. 21-60. The Sänger Collection contains a list in Rabbi Hirsch's handwriting of hundreds of Hebrew roots in his Commentary.

26. *Collected Writings* VIII, p. 320.

27. Mordechai Breuer, *Eidah U'Dyuknah,* p. 183. See also Rabbi Joseph Guggenheimer, "Die Hypothesen der Bibelkritik und der Commentar zu Genesis von Rabbiner S.R. Hirsch" (The Hypotheses of Bible Criticism and the Commentary to Genesis of Rabbi S. R. Hirsch), *Jeschurun,* Vols. XIII-XV (1867-69).

28. Rabbi Moshe Hirsch Fuchs, Rabbi of Grossvardein, to Rabbi Salomon Breuer, as related by Rabbi Joseph Breuer; Rabbi Elie Munk, "Rabbiner S.R. Hirsch als Rationalist der Kabbalah," *Nachlath Zvi* III (1932/33), pp. 84-92.

29. This includes a description of the significance of the types of animals acceptable for each type of offering, and the arrangment of the different organs that had to be brought for each, with a thorough explanation of the reasons for all of them.

30. Rosenheim, *Zichronot,* p. 15.

31. Dr. Mendel Hirsch, Moses Schwab (grandfather of the late Rabbi Shimon Schwab of *K'hal Adath Jeschurun,* New York), and Heinrich Heinemann. Hermann Schwab, *Memories of Frankfurt* (London, 1958), p. 9; see also Rabbi Hirsch's preface to the Commentary.

32. Breuer, *Modernity,* pp. 153, 432; Rosenheim, *Zichronot,* p. 15.

33. Rabbi Joseph Breuer, "Introduction to the *Commentary on the Psalms*" (New York, 1960).

34. *Commentary on the Psalms,* Author's Introduction.

35. *Collected Writings* IV, pp. 259.

35*. *Israelit* XXIX (1888), p. 899.

Chapter Twenty-Nine

1. *Jeschurun* (Hannover), VI (1888), 14 *Tishri,* p. 613; Hermann Schwab, *Memories of Frankfurt (Aus der Schützenstrasse)* (London, 1958), p. 11; *Jubiläumsnummer,* p. 50.

2. A letter addressed to Rabbi Hirsch's daughter, Rebbetzin Sophie Breuer of Papa, a copy of which is in the possession of Prof. Mordechai Breuer.

3. The details of the funeral and its aftermath are drawn from *Der Israelit, Die Jüdische Presse,* and *The Jewish Standard* of London, all of which contained extensive coverage in the weeks following his death.

4. See previous note.

5. *Commentary, Psalms* 90:12.

Appendix One

1. *Commentary, Psalms* 103:17.

2. *Shemesh Marpeh,* pp. 234-235.

3. Mendel Hirsch, *Worte bei der zu Ablauf der Shloshim* (Frankfurt, 1889), p. 8.

4. *Collected Writings* VI, p. 102.

5. The birth dates of Rabbi Hirsch's children are listed in the official records of the district government of Nikolsburg, 1852.

6. See *Shemesh Marpeh,* responsa nos. 73-77.

7. See also *Shaalos U'Tshuvos Maharam Schick, Even HaEzer-Choshen Mishpat,* nos. 110, 111, 116.

8. Sänger Collection, Hebrew MS, Folder 9/80.

9. Alfred Kober, *History of the Jews of Cologne* (Philadelphia, 1940).

10. *Shemesh Marpeh,* responsa nos. 9-11.

11. See ibid., responsum no. 22.

12. He is mentioned in *Shemesh Marpeh,* pp. 28-31.

13. Breuer, *Modernity,* p. 140.

14. *Bamidbar* 25:4, *Devarim* 24:16.

15. *Shemesh Marpeh,* pp. 262-3.

16. See Isaac Breuer, *Darki,* pp. 27-31.

17. "Memoirs of Prof. Dov Hyman," *Shanah beShanah* (Jerusalem, 5747).

BIBLIOGRAPHY

BIBLIOGRAPHY

Aaronson, Moshe Aaron, "Toldot Harav S.R. Hirsch," *Igros Tzafun*, Vilna, 1891

Altman, Alexander, *Moses Mendelssohn: A Biographical Study*, University of Alabama, 1973

Arnsberg, Paul, *Die Geschichte der Frankfurter Juden seit der Französischen Revolution* III, Darmstadt, 1983

Asariah, Zvi, *Samson Raphael Hirsch*, Hannover, 1970

Ashkenaz: The German Jewish Heritage, New York, 1988

Auerbach, Moses, "Die Braunschweiger Rabbinervesammlung in Jahre 1844," *Jahrbuch der Jüdisch-Literarischen Gesellschaft* XXII (1931/32), pp. 125-145

——, "Die Jüdische Geschichte und ihr Sinn," *Jeschurun* XI (1924), pp. 520-533

——, "Seligman Bär Bamberger," *Jeschurun* XV (1928), pp. 524-538

——, "Zur Geistigen Struktur der Deutschen Orthodoxie der Gegenwart," *Festschrift für Jacob Rosenheim*, Frankfurt a.M., 1931

Bamberger, M.L., "Seligmann Baer Bamberger," *Jewish Leaders* (Leo Jung, ed.), New York, 1953, pp. 181-195

Bamberger, R. Yitzchak Dov, *Shaalos U'Tshuvos Yad HaLevi*, Jerusalem, 1965

Baron, Salo W., "Aspects of Jewish Communal Crisis in 1848," *Jewish Social Studies* XIV (1952), pp. 99-144

——, "Freedom and Constraint in the Jewish Community," *Essays and Studies in Memory of Linda R. Miller*, 1938, pp. 9-22

——, "The Impact of the Revolution of 1848 on Jewish Emancipation," *Jewish Social Studies* XI (1949), pp. 195-248

——, "The Revolution of 1848 and Jewish Scholarship," *Proceedings of the American Academy for Jewish Research*, Vol. XX (1951), pp. 1-100

Berliner, Abraham, *Chayei HaYehudim B'Ashkenaz BiYmei HaBainayim*, Warsaw, 1900

Bing, Hermann, *Umständlische Schilderung*, Wien, 1847

Bleich, Judith, *Jacob Ettlinger, His Life and Works: The Emergence of Modern Orthodoxy in Germany*, Ph.D dissertation, N.Y.U., 1974
Bloch, Philipp, *Heinrich Graetz: A Memoir*, Philadelphia, 1898
Breuer, Isaac, *Darki*, Jerusalem, 1988
——, *Moriah* (2nd ed.), Jerusalem, 1982
——, "Samson Raphael Hirsch," *Jewish Leaders* (Leo Jung, ed.), New York, 1953, pp. 163-177
——, *Tziyunei Derech*, Jerusalem, 1982
Breuer, Jacob, ed., *Fundamentals of Judaism*, New York, 1949
——, ed., *Timeless Torah — An Anthology of the Writings of Rabbi S.R. Hirsch*, New York, 1957
Breuer, Mordechai, "Al Darkei Hapsika shel Rabbanei Germaniah B'Idan HaEmanzipatziah," *Sinai*, Jubilee Volume (1987), pp. 166-186
——, *Am VeEidah*, (Manuscript)
——, "Chazon U'Metziut BaChinuch HaOrthodoxi ShebeGermaniah Ba-Me'ah Ha19," *Sefer Hashanah Bar Ilan* XVI-XVII, pp. 317-335
——, *Eidah U'Dyuknah*, Jerusalem, 1991
——, "Emancipation and the Rabbis," *Niv Hamidrashia* XIII, (1978/9), pp. 26-51
——, "HaDiyun BeShalosh Shevuot BaDorot HaAcharonim," *Galut U'Medinah*, Jerusalem, 1979, pp. 49-57
——, "Hagalut BeMishnatam shel Harav S.R. Hirsch VeDr. I. Breuer," *Galut: LeBirur Mashmaut HaGalut BaMikra U'Besifrut Hadorot*, Jerusalem, 1959
——, *Modernity Within Tradition: The Social History of Orthodox Jewry in Imperial Germany*, New York, 1992
——, "Perakim BeToldot Rabbi S.R. Hirsch (1)," *HaMaayan* III (5716) (1), pp. 39-50
——, "Perakim BeToldot Rabbi S.R. Hirsch (2)," *HaMaayan* IV (5724) (2), pp. 7-12
——, "Perakim Mitoch Biographiah," *Harav S.R. Hirsch Mishnato VeShitato*, Jerusalem, 1962, pp. 11-44
——, "Review of Noah Rosenbloom, *Tradition in An Age of Reform*," *Tradition* XVI (1977) (4), pp. 140-149
——, "Rabbi S.R. Hirsch BeYeshivat R. Yaakov Ettlinger," *HaMaayan* XII (5732) (2), pp. 55-62
——, "Samson Raphael Hirsch," *Guardians of our Heritage*, New York, 1958, pp. 265-299
——, "S.R. Hirsch Today; Conceptions and Misconceptions," *Jewish Action*, Summer 1989, vol. 49 no. 3, pp. 7-10
——, "The Pentateuch Commentary of Rabbi S.R. Hirsch," (Manuscript)

——, *The Torah Im Derech Eretz of Samson Raphael Hirsch,* Jerusalem, 1970
——, ed., *Torah im Derech Eretz: HaTnuah Isheha VeRaayonoteha,* Ramat Gan, 1987
Breuer, R. Joseph, *A Time to Build* I-III, New York, 1975-1983
——, *Divrei Yoseph,* Jerusalem, 1990
——, "Harav Breuer U'Peulato," *Divrei Shlomo,* New York, 1948
Breuer, R. Shlomo, *Divrei Shlomo,* New York, 1948
[Breuer, Raphael,] "SRH und seine Schule," *Nachlath Zvi* II (1931/32), pp. 104-120
——, *Unter Seinem Banner,* Frankfurt a.M., 1908
Breuer, R. Salomon, *Rede zum Gedächtnis. . .S.R. Hirsch,* Raab, 1889
Cohen, Martin, "100 Jahre 'Neunzehn Briefe'," *Jahrbuch für die Jüdischen Gemeinden Schleswig-Holsteins,* 1936-37, pp. 18-23
Drachman, Bernard, "S.R. Hirsch, A Biographical Sketch," *The Nineteen Letters,* Funk and Wagnalls: New York, 1899
Dukesz, Eduard, *Chachme Ah'u,* Hamburg, 1908
——, *Iwoh LeMoshaw,* Krakau, 1903
——, "Zur Biographie des Chacham Isaak Bernays," *Jahrbuch der Jüdisch-Literarischen Gesellschaft* V (1907), pp. 297-332
——, "Zur Genealogie S.R. Hirschs," *Jahrbuch der Jüdisch-Literarischen Gesellschaft* XVII (1925), pp. 103-132
[Ehrmann, Herz,] "S.R. Hirsch — Ein Lebensbild," *Jubiläumsnummer des Israelit,* Frankfurt a.M., 1908, pp. 5-17
——, "S.R. Hirsch, a Biography," *Moreshes Zvi: The Living Hirschian Legacy,* New York, 1988
Ehrmann, Salomon, ed., *Rabbiner Samson Raphael Hirsch,* Zurich, 1960
——, "Isaac Breuer," *Guardians of Our Heritage,* New York, 1958, pp. 617-646
——, "Rabbi S.R. Hirsch as a Pioneer of Judaism," *Rabbi Joseph Breuer Jubilee Volume,* New York, 1962
Eidelberg, Shlomo, "The Origins of Germanic Jewry: Reality and Legend," *Ashkenaz, The German Jewish Heritage,* New York, 1988, pp. 3-10
Eidut Ne'emanah: Shaalot U'Tshuvot al Maavak HaShechitah B'Eiropah, Jerusalem, 1975
Eileh Divrei HaBris, Hamburg, 1819
Eisemann, Heinrich, "S.R. Hirsch und Seine Kandidatur für das Englische Oberrabbinat im Jahre 1844," *Rabbiner S.R. Hirsch,* Zurich, 1960
Elias, Joseph, *The World of Rabbi S.R. Hirsch: The Nineteen Letters,* Jerusalem, 1995
Elias, Markus, "The Educational Work of Rabbi S.R. Hirsch in Western Europe," *Rabbi Joseph Breuer Jubilee Volume,* New York, 1962, pp. 67-94

Eliav, Mordechai, *Ahavat Zion VeAnshei Hod,* Tel Aviv, 1971
——, *Toldot HaChinuch HaYehudi BeGermaniah,* Jerusalem, 1961
Ellenson, David, *Rabbi Esriel Hildesheimer and the Creation of a Modern Jewish Orthodoxy,* University of Alabama Press, 1990
Emmanuel, Yonah, ed., *Harav S.R. Hirsch Mishnato VeShitato,* Jerusalem, 1962
Ettlinger, R. Yaakov, *Shaalos U'Tshuvos Binyan Zion,* 2 vols., Jerusalem, 1989
Feivelson, E.M., "Moses Mendelssohn," *Netzach Yisrael,* Warsaw 1914
Fischer, Philipp, *In Seinen Spuren,* Satoraljaujhely, 1922
Fischer, R. Gottlieb, "Epistle on Zachariah Frankel's Darchei HaMishnah," *Collected Writings of Rabbi S.R. Hirsch* V, New York, 1988, pp. 211-260
Frankel, Zachariah, *Darchei HaMishnah,* Leipzig, 1859
Frankl-Grün, Adolph, *Geschichte der Juden in Kremsier* II, Frankfurt, 1898
Freimann, A. & Kracauer, F., *Frankfort,* Philadelphia, 1929
Gedenkblätter für S.R. Hirsch, Frankfurt, 1889
Gold, H., ed., *Juden und Judengemeinden Mährens,* 1929
Graetz, Heinrich, *Darchei HaHistoriah HaYehudit: Misot, Pirkei Yoman, Igrot,* Jerusalem, 1969
——, *Tagebuch und Briefe,* (ed. Reuven Michael), Tübingen, 1977
——, *The Structure of Jewish History and Other Essays,* New York, 1975
Greenwald, Y.Y., *LeToldot HaReformatzion HaDatit BeGermaniah U'VeHungariah,* Columbus, 1948
Grunfeld, Isidor, ed. *Judaism Eternal — Selected Essays from the Writings of Rabbi S.R. Hirsch with introduction,* 2 vols., London, 1958
——, "Introduction to *Horeb,*" London, 1962
——, "Introduction to Rabbi S.R. Hirsch Commentary on the Torah," London, 1959
——, *Three Generations,* London, 1958
HaMaayan, periodical, Jerusalem, 1953-
Hamburger, Binyamin Shlomo, "Nesi HaLeviim," *Kisvei Rabbeinu Yitzchok Dov Halevi,* Bnei Brak, 1992
——, "Yesodosav HaHistoriim shel Minhag Ashkenaz," *Minhagim deKehillah Kedoshah Wormeizah,* Jerusalem, 1988
Heinemann, Isaac, "HaYachas Shebein S.R. Hirsch LeYitzchak Bernays Rabbo," *Zion* XVI (1951), pp. 44-90
——, "Mechkarim al Rabbi S.R. Hirsch," *Sinai* XXIV (1949), pp. 249-271
——, "Supplementary Remarks on the Secession," *Historia Judaica* X (1948), pp. 123-134

——, "The Formative Years of the Leader of Modern Orthodoxy," *Historia Judaica* XIII (1951), pp. 29-54

Heller, Max, "Samson Raphael Hirsch," *Yearbook of the Central Conference of American Rabbis*, XVIII (1909), pp. 179ff.

Hess, Moses, *Rome and Jerusalem*, New York, 1954

Hildesheimer, R. Ezriel, "Halvayat Baal Haketav Sofer," *Z'funot* II, no. 2 (VI), Bnei Brak, *Teves* 5750, pp. 63-66

——, *Rabbiner Esriel Hildesheimer Briefe* (Mordechai Eliav, ed.), Jerusalem, 1965

——, *Shaalos U'Tshuvos Rabbi Ezriel* I, Tel Aviv, 1969

Hildesheimer, Ezriel, "Chiluf Michtavim Bein Rabbi E. Hidesheimer, VeRabbi S.R. Hirsch," *Sefer Zikaron Yad Shaul*, Tel Aviv, 1953, pp. 233-249

——, "Harav Hildesheimer al Zechariah Frankel U'Beit HaMedrash Le-Rabbanim," *HaMaayan* I (5713) (1), pp. 65-73

——, "Hitkatvut Bein Harav E. Hildesheimer VeHarav S.R. Hirsch, Al Limudei Chol BeBatei Yetomim BeYerushalayim," *HaMaayan* I (5714), (1), pp. 41-52

Hildesheimer, Meir, "Harav Z.H. Kalischer VeHarav Samson Raphael Hirsch," *Sefer Aviad*, Jerusalem, 1986, pp. 195-214

——, "LeToldot Rabbeinu [E. Hildesheimer]," *Shaalos U'Tshuvos Rabbi Ezriel* I, Tel Aviv, 1969

Hirsch, Mendel, *Samson Raphael Hirsch und die Israelitische Religionsgesellschaft*, Mainz, 1897

——, *Worte bei der zu Ablauf der Schloshim*, Frankfurt a.M., 1889

Hirsch, R. Samson Raphael, *BeMaaglei Shanah* I-IV, Bnei Brak, 1965-66

——, *Collected Writings* I-VIII, New York, 1984-1995

——, *Erste Mitteilungen aus Naphtali's Briefwechsel*, Altona, 1838

——, *From the Wisdom of Mishlé*, Jerusalem, 1976

——, "Hesped anlässlich der Todes Seiner Gattin," *Nachlath Zvi* V (1934), pp. 71-74

——, *The Hirsch Siddur*, Jerusalem, 1969

——, *Horeb*, London, 1962

——, *Judaism Eternal*, London, 1956

——, *Jüdische Anmerkungen zu den Bemerkungen eines Protestanten über die Confession der 22 Bremischen Pastoren*, von einem Juden, Oldenburg, 1841

——, "Nikolsburg oder Frankfurt," *Nachlath Zvi* VI (1936), pp. 252-256

——, *The Nineteen Letters of Ben Uziel, with introduction*, translated by Bernard Drachman, New York, 1899

——, *The Nineteen Letters,* edited and annotated by Joseph Elias, Jerusalem, 1995
——, *The Pentateuch: Translated and Explained,* Gateshead, 1976
——, *Postscripta,* Altona, 1840
——, *The Psalms, Translation and Commentary,* Jerusalem, 1978
——, *Shemesh Marpeh: Shaalos U'Tshuvos, Chidushei HaShas, Igros U'Michtavim,* Jerusalem, 1992
——, *Yesodot HaChinuch* I-II, Bnei Brak, 1966
——, *Zweite Mitteilungen aus Einem Briefwechsel über die Neueste Jüdische Literatur, Altona, 1844*
Hirsch, Samuel A., "Jewish Philosophy of Religion and Samson Raphael Hirsch," *Jewish Quarterly Review,* London, 1990, pp. 109-138
Hoffmann, R. David Zvi, *Shaalos U'Tshuvos Melamed Lehoil,* Frankfurt, 1926-27
Horovitz, Mordechai R., *Rabbanei Frankfurt,* Jerusalem, 1972
Horovitz, Rivka, ed., *Zachariah Frankel VeReishit HaYahadut HaPositivit Historit,* Jerusalem, 1984, with introduction
Israelit, weekly, Mainz-Frankfurt, 1860-1938
Jacobson, R. Binyamin Zeev, *Esah Da'i LeMairachok,* Bnei Brak, 1967
——, *Zichronot,* Jerusalem, 1953
Jakobovitz, Immanuel, *S.R. Hirsch — A Reappraisal of His Teaching in the Light of our Time,* London, 1971
[Japhet, Saemy] "The Secession from the Frankfurt Jewish Community Under S.R. Hirsch," *Historia Judaica* X (1948), pp. 99-122
Jeschurun, monthly (Rabbi S.R. Hirsch, ed.), Frankfurt a.M., 1854-1870
Jeschurun, Neue Folge, weekly (Isaac Hirsch, ed.), Hannover, 1883-1888
Jewish Standard, weekly, London, 1888-1891
Johnson, Paul, *A History of the Jews,* New York, 1987
Jubiläumsnummer des Israelit, Frankfurt a.M., 1908
Jüdische Monatshefte, monthly, Frankfurt a.M. 1914-1920
Jüdische Presse, weekly, Berlin, 1870-1923
Jung, Leo, ed., *Guardians of our Heritage,* New York, 1958
——, ed., *Jewish Leaders,* New York, 1953
Kahane, Yitzchak Zev, "Nikolsburg," *Arim VeImahot BeYisrael,* Jerusalem, 1950, pp. 210-313
Katz, Jacob, *Bonim Chofshim VeYehudim,* Jerusalem, 1968
——, *HaKera Shelo Nitachah (The Unhealed Breach: The Secession of Orthodox Jews from the General Community in Hungary and Germany),* Jerusalem, 1995
Klausner, Joseph, *Ketavim Zioniim shel R. Z.H. Kalisher,* Jerusalem, 1947

Kohler, Kaufmann, "Personal Reminiscences of My Early Life," *H.U.C. Monthly,* May 1918, pp. 224-233
Lamm, Norman, *Torah U'Madda,* Northvale, 1990
Lerner, R. Meyer, *Shaalos U'Teshuvos Hadar HaKarmel,* London, 1970
Liberles, Robert, *Religious Conflict in Social Context: The Resurgence of Orthodox Judaism in Frankfurt am Main,* Westport, 1985
Lipschitz, Yaakov, *Machzikei Hadas,* Piotrokow, 1903
——, *Zichron Yaakov* III, Kovno, 1930
Mayer, Eugen, "Yehudei Frankfurt — Parshiyot min Ha'avar," *Choveret Zikaron leKehillat Frankfurt am Main,* Jerusalem, 1965
Mendelsohn-Frankfurter, Moshe, *Pnei Tevel,* Amsterdam, 1877
Meyer, Michael, *Response to Modernity: A History of the Reform Movement in Judaism,* New York, 1988
Moellin, R. Yaakov, *Sefer Maharil: Minhagim,* Jerusalem, 1989
Moreshes Zvi: The Living Hirschian Legacy, New York, 1988
Munk, R. Elie, "Rabbiner Hirsch als Rationalist der Kabbalah," *Nachlath Zvi* III (1932/33), pp. 84-92
Nachlath Zvi, monthly, Frankfurt a.M., 1930-1938
Orient, weekly, Leipzig, 1840-1851
Orlean, Yehudah Leib, "Zmanah U'Mikumah Shel Shitat Rabbi S.R. Hirsch," *BeMaaglei Shanah* IV, Bnei Brak, 1966
Poppel, Stephen, "The Politics of Religious Leadership: The Rabbinate in Nineteenth-Century Hamburg," *Yearbook, Leo Baeck Institute* XXVIII (1983), pp. 439-470
Posner, A. & Freimann, E., "Rabbi Jacob Ettlinger," *Guardians of Our Heritage,* New York, 1958, pp. 231-243
Rabinovich, Shaul Pinchas, *Reb Zachariah Frankel,* Warsaw, 1898
Rapoport, R. Shlomo Yehudah, *Divrei Shalom VeEmes,* Prague 1861
Report of the Committee for the Selection of Candidates to the Office of Chief Rabbi, London, 1844
Rosenbloom, Noah H., *Tradition in an Age of Reform: The Religious Philosophy of Samson Raphael Hirsch,* Philadelphia, 1976
Rosenheim, Jacob, *Ktavim, Mivchar Maamarim U'Neumim,* Jerusalem, 1970
——, *Samson Raphael Hirsch's Cultural Ideal and our Times,* London, 1951
——, "The Historical Significance of the . . . Secession from the Frankfurt Jewish Community," *Historia Judaica* X (1948), pp. 135-146
——, *Zichronot,* Bnei Brak, 1979
Roth, Cecil, "Britain's Three Chief Rabbis," *Jewish Leaders* (Leo Jung, ed.), New York, 1953, pp. 477-490
Schick, R. Moshe, *Shaalos U'Tshuvos Maharam Schick,* New York, 1965

Schischa, Abraham, "Hermann Adler, Yeshiva Bahur," *Remember the Days: Essays on Anglo-Jewish History Presented to Cecil Roth,* London, 1966, pp. 241-277
Schorsch, Ismar, "Ideology and History in an Age of Emancipation," introduction to H. Graetz, *The Structure of Jewish History and other Essays,* New York, 1975
——, "Z. Frankel and the European Origins of Conservative Judaism," *Judaism* XXX (1981), pp. 344-354
Schulvass, Moshe Avigdor, "Bait HaMidrash LeRabbanim BeBerlin," *Mosdot HaTorah BeEiropah BeVinyanam U'Vechurbanam* (Samuel K. Mirsky, ed.), New York, 1956, pp. 689-713
Schwab, Hermann, *A World in Ruins: History, Life and Work of German Jewry,* London, 1946
——, *Chachme Ashkenaz,* London, 1964
——, *Der Leben und Schaffen fun Rabbi S.R. Hirsch* (Yiddish), Warsaw, 1927
——, *Gedenkblätter zur Erinnerung an die S.R. Hirsch-Feier,* Frankfurt a.M., 1908
——, *Memories of Frankfurt (Aus der Schützenstrasse),* London, 1958
——, *The History of Orthodox Jewry in Germany,* London, 1951
Schwab, R. Shimon, *Selected Essays,* New York, 1994
——, *Selected Speeches,* New York, 1991
——, *Selected Writings,* New York, 1988
Schwarzschild, Emanuel, *Die Gründung der Israelitischen Religionsgesellschaft,* Frankfurt a.M., 1896,
——, *Ein Offenes Wort an S.B. Bamberger,* Frankfurt a.M., 1877
Sofer, R. Shimon, *Igros Sofrim,* Vienna, 1929
Spitzer, R. B.S. Zalman, *Tikkun Shlomo,* Vienna, 1892
Strauss, Berthold, *The Rosenbaums of Zell,* London, 1962
Tal, R. Tobias, "Samson Raphael Hirsch," *Der Denkende Jude,* Bibliothek des Jüdischen Volksfreundes, Cöln, 1914
Thieberger, Friedrich, "Samson Raphael Hirsch," *Der Jude,* 1919-1920, pp. 556-566
Toras HaKanaous, Amsterdam, 1845
Trepp, Leo, *Die Landesgemeinde der Juden in Oldenburg,* Oldenburg, 1965
——, *Die Oldenburger Judenschaft,* Oldenburg, 1973
Treue Zionswächter, weekly, 1845-1854
Trier, R. Salomon, *Rabbinische Gutachten über die Beschneidung,* Frankfurt a.M., 1844
Unna, Isaac, "Ezriel Hildesheimer," *Jewish Leaders,* pp. 215-230
Voice of Jacob, weekly, London, 1841-1848

Weinberg, R. Yechiel Yaakov, *Sridei Aish* I-IV, Jerusalem, 1959-61
Wiener, Max, *HaDat HaYehudit BiTkufat HaImantzipatziah,* Jerusalem, 1974
Wolfsberg-Aviad, Yeshaya, "A"HU: Altona, Hamburg, Wandsbeck," *Arim VeImahot BeYisrael,* Jerusalem, 1948, pp. 5-57
——, "David Hoffmann," *Guardians of Our Heritage,* pp. 363-419
——, "Harav S.R. Hirsch," *Sinai* IV (1939), pp. 164-182

INDEX

INDEX

PHOTO CREDITS:

Adath Israel of Cologne, (Northern Ireland, 1964), 295
Agudath Israel of America Archives, 287
Bilder aus einem altJüdischen Familienleben, (Frankfurt, 1865), 1, 305, 331
Mr. Jacob Breuer, Jerusalem, 353
Prof. Mordechai Breuer, Jerusalem, 4, 6, 70, 76, 79, 191, 231, 232, 317, 335, 351
Frankfort, (Philadelphia, 1929), 111
Hinaus aus der Ghetto, (Frankfurt, 1988), 109, 113, 114, 119, 123, 156, 191
Israelit, 3, 5, 23, 89, 92, 94, 124, 127, 155, 230
The Jewish Standard, London, 131
Juden und Judengemeinden Mährens, 94, 102, 106
Die Jüdische Baudenkmahler (Hamburg, 1984), 32, 33
Levy family, London, 126
Machon Moreshet Ashkenaz, Bnei Brak, 41, 43, 48, 82, 112, 121, 164, 233, 337
Sänger Collection, Bar Ilan University, 50, 51, 101, 304
Mr. Abraham Schischa, London, 105, 290, 291
Schwadron Collection, J.N.U.L. Jerusalem, 45, 91, 197

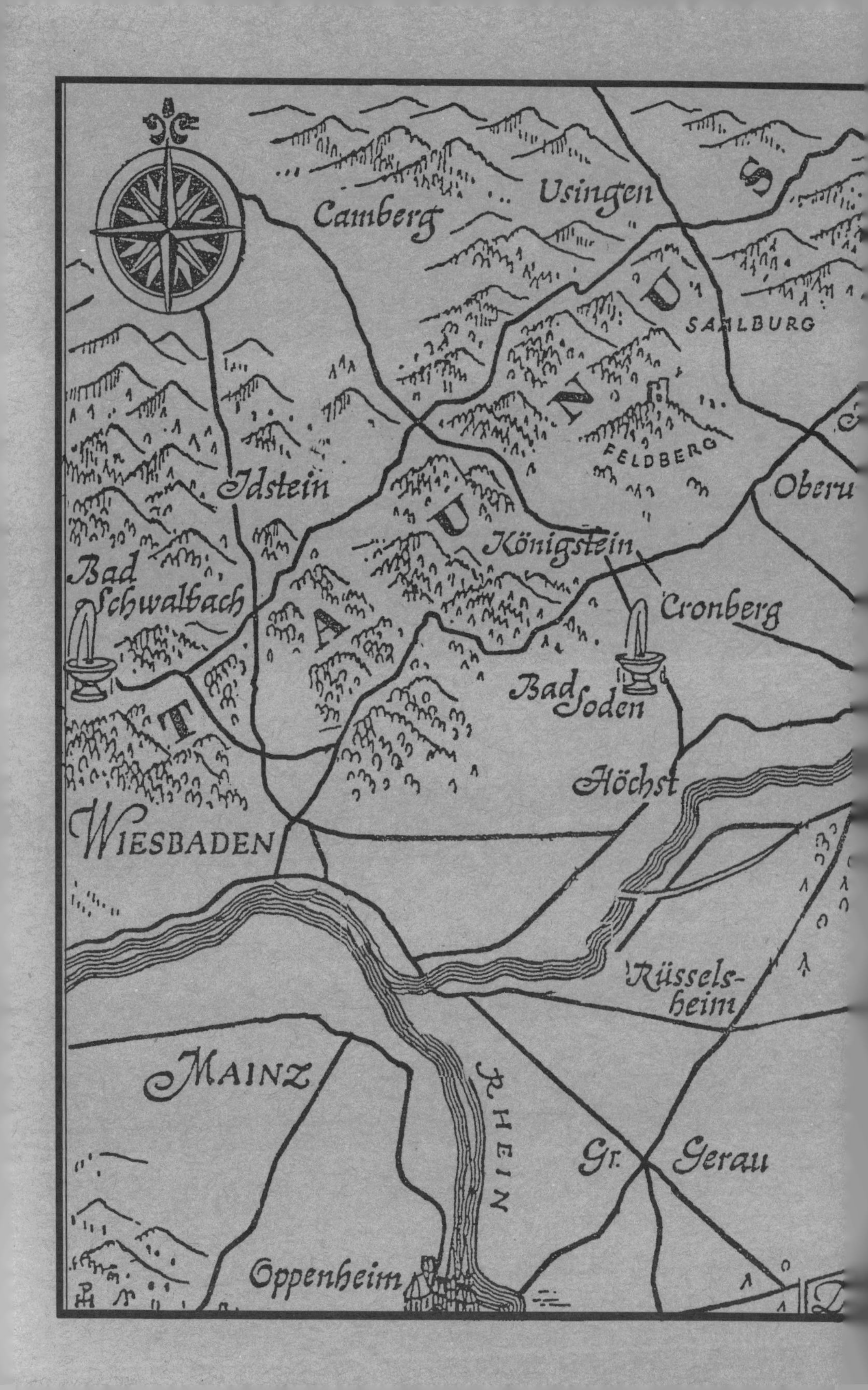
Camberg
Usingen
Idstein
Bad Schwalbach
Königstein
Cronberg
Bad Soden
Höchst
Wiesbaden
Feldberg
Saalburg
Oberu
Rüsselsheim
Mainz
Rhein
Gr. Gerau
Oppenheim
T A U N U S